Rural Migrants in Urban China

After millions of migrants moved from China's countryside into its sprawling cities, a unique kind of 'informal' urban enclave was born – 'villages in the city'. Like the shanties and favelas before them elsewhere, there has been huge pressure to redevelop these blemishes on the urban face of China's economic vision. Unlike most developing countries, however, these are not squatter settlements but owner-occupied settlements developed semi-formally by ex-farmers turned small-developers and landlords who rent shockingly high-density rooms to rural migrants, who can outnumber their landlord villagers. A strong state, matched with well-organised landlords collectively represented through joint-stock companies, has meant that it has been relatively easy to grow the city through demolition of these soft migrant enclaves. The lives of the displaced migrants then enter a transient phase from an informal to a formal urbanity. This book looks at migrants and their enclave 'villages in the city' and reveals the characteristics and changes in migrants' livelihoods and living places.

Using an interdisciplinary approach, the book analyses how living in the city transforms and changes rural migrant households, and explores the social lives and micro-economies of migrant neighbourhoods. It goes on to discuss changing housing and social conditions and spatial changes in the urban villages of major Chinese cities, as well as looking into transient urbanism and examining the consequences of redevelopment and upgrading of the 'villages in the city'; in particular, the planning, regeneration, politics of development, and socio-economic implications of these immense social, economic and physical upheavals.

Fulong Wu is Bartlett Professor of Planning at University College London, UK.

Fangzhu Zhang is Lecturer in China Planning at the Bartlett School of Planning, University College London, UK.

Chris Webster is Dean of the Faculty of Architecture, University of Hong Kong, and Senior Departmental Fellow, Cambridge University Department of Land Economy, UK.

Routledge Contemporary China Series

1 **Nationalism, Democracy and National Integration in China**
Leong Liew and Wang Shaoguang

2 **Hong Kong's Tortuous Democratization**
A comparative analysis
Ming Sing

3 **China's Business Reforms**
Institutional challenges in a globalised economy
Edited by Russell Smyth, On Kit Tam, Malcolm Warner and Cherrie Zhu

4 **Challenges for China's Development**
An enterprise perspective
Edited by David H. Brown and Alasdair MacBean

5 **New Crime in China**
Public order and human rights
Ron Keith and Zhiqiu Lin

6 **Non-Governmental Organizations in Contemporary China**
Paving the way to civil society?
Qiusha Ma

7 **Globalization and the Chinese City**
Fulong Wu

8 **The Politics of China's Accession to the World Trade Organization**
The dragon goes global
Hui Feng

9 **Narrating China**
Jia Pingwa and his fictional world
Yiyan Wang

10 **Sex, Science and Morality in China**
Joanne McMillan

11 **Politics in China Since 1949**
Legitimizing authoritarian rule
Robert Weatherley

12 **International Human Resource Management in Chinese Multinationals**
Jie Shen and Vincent Edwards

13 **Unemployment in China**
Economy, human resources and labour markets
Edited by Grace Lee and Malcolm Warner

14 **China and Africa**
Engagement and compromise
Ian Taylor

15 **Gender and Education in China**
Gender discourses and women's schooling in the early twentieth century
Paul J. Bailey

16 **SARS**
Reception and interpretation in three Chinese cities
Edited by Deborah Davis and Helen Siu

17 **Human Security and the Chinese State**
Historical transformations and the modern quest for sovereignty
Robert E. Bedeski

18 **Gender and Work in Urban China**
Women workers of the unlucky generation
Liu Jieyu

19 **China's State Enterprise Reform**
From Marx to the market
John Hassard, Jackie Sheehan, Meixiang Zhou, Jane Terpstra-Tong and Jonathan Morris

20 **Cultural Heritage Management in China**
Preserving the cities of the Pearl River Delta
Edited by Hilary du Cros and Yok-shiu F. Lee

21 **Paying for Progress**
Public finance, human welfare and inequality in China
Edited by Vivienne Shue and Christine Wong

22 **China's Foreign Trade Policy**
The new constituencies
Edited by Ka Zeng

23 **Hong Kong, China**
Learning to belong to a nation
Gordon Mathews, Tai-lok Lui, and Eric Kit-wai Ma

24 **China Turns to Multilateralism**
Foreign policy and regional security
Edited by Guoguang Wu and Helen Lansdowne

25 **Tourism and Tibetan Culture in Transition**
A place called Shangrila
Åshild Kolås

26 **China's Emerging Cities**
The making of new urbanism
Edited by Fulong Wu

27 **China-US Relations Transformed**
Perceptions and strategic interactions
Edited by Suisheng Zhao

28 **The Chinese Party-State in the 21st Century**
Adaptation and the reinvention of legitimacy
Edited by André Laliberté and Marc Lanteigne

29 **Political Change in Macao**
Sonny Shiu-Hing Lo

30 **China's Energy Geopolitics**
The Shanghai Cooperation Organization and Central Asia
Thrassy N. Marketos

31 **Regime Legitimacy in Contemporary China**
Institutional change and stability
Edited by Thomas Heberer and Gunter Schubert

32 **U.S.–China Relations**
China policy on Capitol Hill
Tao Xie

33 **Chinese Kinship**
Contemporary anthropological perspectives
Edited by Susanne Brandtstädter and Gonçalo D. Santos

34 **Politics and Government in Hong Kong**
Crisis under Chinese sovereignty
Edited by Ming Sing

35 **Rethinking Chinese Popular Culture**
Cannibalizations of the canon
Edited by Carlos Rojas and Eileen Cheng-yin Chow

36 **Institutional Balancing in the Asia Pacific**
Economic interdependence and China's rise
Kai He

37 **Rent Seeking in China**
Edited by Tak-Wing Ngo and Yongping Wu

38 **China, Xinjiang and Central Asia**
History, transition and crossborder interaction into the 21st century
Edited by Colin Mackerras and Michael Clarke

39 **Intellectual Property Rights in China**
Politics of piracy, trade and protection
Gordon Cheung

40 **Developing China**
Land, politics and social conditions
George C.S. Lin

41 **State and Society Responses to Social Welfare Needs in China**
Serving the people
Edited by Jonathan Schwartz and Shawn Shieh

42 **Gay and Lesbian Subculture in Urban China**
Loretta Wing Wah Ho

43 **The Politics of Heritage Tourism in China**
A view from Lijiang
Xiaobo Su and Peggy Teo

44 **Suicide and Justice**
A Chinese perspective
Wu Fei

45 **Management Training and Development in China**
Educating managers in a globalized economy
Edited by Malcolm Warner and Keith Goodall

46 **Patron-Client Politics and Elections in Hong Kong**
Bruce Kam-kwan Kwong

47 **Chinese Family Business and the Equal Inheritance System**
Unravelling the myth
Victor Zheng

48 **Reconciling State, Market and Civil Society in China**
The long march towards prosperity
Paolo Urio

49 **Innovation in China**
The Chinese software industry
Shang-Ling Jui

50 **Mobility, Migration and the Chinese Scientific Research System**
Koen Jonkers

51 **Chinese Film Stars**
Edited by Mary Farquhar and Yingjin Zhang

52 **Chinese Male Homosexualities**
Memba, Tongzhi and Golden Boy
Travis S.K. Kong

53 **Industrialisation and Rural Livelihoods in China**
Agricultural processing in Sichuan
Susanne Lingohr-Wolf

54 **Law, Policy and Practice on China's Periphery**
Selective adaptation and institutional capacity
Pitman B. Potter

55 **China-Africa Development Relations**
Edited by Christopher M. Dent

56 **Neoliberalism and Culture in China and Hong Kong**
The countdown of time
Hai Ren

57 **China's Higher Education Reform and Internationalisation**
Edited by Janette Ryan

58 **Law, Wealth and Power in China**
Commercial law reforms in context
Edited by John Garrick

59 **Religion in Contemporary China**
Revitalization and innovation
Edited by Adam Yuet Chau

60 **Consumer-Citizens of China**
The role of foreign brands in the imagined future china
Kelly Tian and Lily Dong

61 **The Chinese Communist Party and China's Capitalist Revolution**
The political impact of the market
Lance L. P. Gore

62 **China's Homeless Generation**
Voices from the veterans of the Chinese civil war, 1940s–1990s
Joshua Fan

63 **In Search of China's Development Model**
Beyond the Beijing Consensus
Edited by S. Philip Hsu, Suisheng Zhao and Yu-Shan Wu

64 **Xinjiang and China's Rise in Central Asia, 1949–2009**
A history
Michael E. Clarke

65 **Trade Unions in China**
The challenge of labour unrest
Tim Pringle

66 **China's Changing Workplace**
Dynamism, diversity and disparity
Edited by Peter Sheldon,
Sunghoon Kim, Yiqiong Li and
Malcolm Warner

67 **Leisure and Power in Urban China**
Everyday life in a medium-sized
Chinese city
Unn Målfrid H. Rolandsen

68 **China, Oil and Global Politics**
Philip Andrews-Speed and Roland
Dannreuther

69 **Education Reform in China**
Edited by Janette Ryan

70 **Social Policy and Migration in China**
Lida Fan

71 **China's One Child Policy and Multiple Caregiving**
Raising little Suns in Xiamen
Esther C. L. Goh

72 **Politics and Markets in Rural China**
Edited by Björn Alpermann

73 **China's New Underclass**
Paid domestic labour
Xinying Hu

74 **Poverty and Development in China**
Alternative approaches to poverty
assessment
Lu Caizhen

75 **International Governance and Regimes**
A Chinese perspective
Peter Kien-Hong Yu

76 **HIV/AIDS in China – The Economic and Social Determinants**
Dylan Sutherland and
Jennifer Y. J. Hsu

77 **Looking for Work in Post-Socialist China**
Governance, active job
seekers and the new Chinese
labor market
Feng Xu

78 **Sino-Latin American Relations**
Edited by K.C. Fung and Alicia
Garcia-Herrero

79 **Mao's China and the Sino-Soviet Split**
Ideological dilemma
Mingjiang Li

80 **Law and Policy for China's Market Socialism**
Edited by John Garrick

81 **China-Taiwan Relations in a Global Context**
Taiwan's foreign policy and
relations
Edited by C. X. George Wei

82 **The Chinese Transformation of Corporate Culture**
Colin S.C. Hawes

83 **Mapping Media in China**
Region, province, locality
Edited by Wanning Sun and
Jenny Chio

84 **China, the West and the Myth of New Public Management**
Neoliberalism and its discontents
Paolo Urio

85 **The Lahu Minority in Southwest China**
A response to ethnic marginalization on the Frontier
Jianxiong Ma

86 **Social Capital and Institutional Constraints**
A comparative analysis of China, Taiwan and the US
Joonmo Son

87 **Southern China**
Industry, development and industrial policy
Marco R. Di Tommaso, Lauretta Rubini and Elisa Barbieri

88 **State-Market Interactions in China's Reform Era**
Local state competition and global market building in the tobacco industry
Junmin Wang

89 **The Reception and Rendition of Freud in China**
China's Freudian slip
Edited by Tao Jiang and Philip J. Ivanhoe

90 **Sinologism**
An alternative to Orientalism and Postcolonialism
Ming Dong Gu

91 **The Middle Class in Neoliberal China**
Governing risk, life-building, and themed spaces
Hai Ren

92 **The Chinese Corporatist State**
Adaption, survival and resistance
Edited by Jennifer Y.J. Hsu and Reza Hasmath

93 **Law and Fair Work in China**
Sean Cooney, Sarah Biddulph and Ying Zhu

94 **Guangdong and Chinese Diaspora**
The changing landscape of Qiaoxiang
Yow Cheun Hoe

95 **The Shanghai Alleyway House**
A vanishing urban vernacular
Gregory Bracken

96 **Chinese Globalization**
A profile of people-based global connections in China
Jiaming Sun and Scott Lancaster

97 **Disruptive Innovation in Chinese and Indian Businesses**
The strategic implications for local entrepreneurs and global incumbents
Peter Ping Li

98 **Corporate Governance and Banking in China**
Michael Tan

99 **Gender, Modernity and Male Migrant Workers in China**
Becoming a 'modern' man
Xiaodong Lin

100 **Emissions, Pollutants and Environmental Policy in China**
Designing a national emissions trading system
Bo Miao

101 **Sustainable Development in China**
Edited by Curtis Andressen, Mubarak A.R. and Xiaoyi Wang

102 **Islam and China's Hong Kong**
Ethnic identity, Muslim networks and the new Silk Road
Wai-Yip Ho

103 **International Regimes in China**
Domestic implementation of the international fisheries agreements
Gianluca Ferraro

104 **Rural Migrants in Urban China**
Enclaves and transient urbanism
Fulong Wu, Fangzhu Zhang and Chris Webster

Rural Migrants in Urban China

Enclaves and transient urbanism

**Edited by Fulong Wu,
Fangzhu Zhang and Chris Webster**

LONDON AND NEW YORK

First published 2014
by Routledge
2 Park Square, Milton Park, Abingdon, Oxfordshire OX14 4RN

Simultaneously published in the USA and Canada
by Routledge
711 Third Avenue, New York, NY 10017

Routledge is an imprint of the Taylor and Francis Group, an informa business

First issued in paperback 2015

© 2014 selection and editorial material, Fulong Wu, Fangzhu Zhang and
Chris Webster; individual chapters, the contributors

The right of Fulong Wu, Fangzhu Zhang and Chris Webster to be identified
as authors of the editorial material, and of the authors for
their individual chapters, has been asserted in accordance with
sections 77 and 78 of the Copyright, Designs and Patents Act 1988.

All rights reserved. No part of this book may be reprinted or reproduced
or utilised in any form or by any electronic, mechanical, or other means,
now known or hereafter invented, including photocopying and recording, or
in any information storage or retrieval system, without permission in writing
from the publishers.

Trademark notice: Product or corporate names may be trademarks or
registered trademarks, and are used only for identification and explanation
without intent to infringe.

British Library Cataloguing in Publication Data
A catalogue record for this book is available from the British Library

Library of Congress Cataloging in Publication Data
Rural migrants in urban China : enclaves and transient urbanism /
edited by Fulong Wu, Fangzhu Zhang and Chris Webster.
    pages cm. – (Routledge contemporary China series ; 104)
Includes bibliographical references and index.
ISBN 978-0-415-53455-0 (hardback) – ISBN 978-0-203-79659-7 (ebook)
1. Rural-urban migration–China. 2. Internal migrants–China–Social
conditions. 3. Urbanization–China. 4. Sociology, Urban–China. I. Wu,
Fulong. II. Zhang, Fangzhu. III. Webster, Christopher J.
HB2114.A3R874 2013
307.2'40951–dc23   2013004119

ISBN 978-0-415-53455-0 (hbk)
ISBN 978-1-138-64354-3 (pbk)
ISBN 978-0-203-79659-7 (ebk)

Typeset in Times New Roman
by Cenveo Publisher Services

Contents

List of figures	xiii
List of tables	xv
List of contributors	xvii
Preface	xxiii

1	Migrants' transient urbanism in urban China: an introduction FULONG WU AND FANGZHU ZHANG	1

PART 1
Migrants' livelihoods in urban China   **15**

2	The new-generation migrant workers in China C. CINDY FAN AND CHEN CHEN	17
3	Chinese cities and mobile livelihoods: migration, risk and social networks HEATHER XIAOQUAN ZHANG	36
4	Outsiders in the city: migrant housing and settlement patterns WEIPING WU	51

PART 2
Migrants' social lives in urban China   **67**

5	Migrants' job-search in urban China: social networks and the labour market YU CHEN AND GWILYM PRYCE	69
6	Situating translocality in flux landscapes: migrants and urban villages in the city of Guangzhou CECILIE ANDERSSON	84

xii *Contents*

7 Migrant integration in China: evidence from Guangzhou   99
BART WISSINK, ARJAN HAZELZET AND WERNER BREITUNG

8 Migrant integration in China's urban villages: a case study of
Beijing, Shanghai and Guangzhou   121
ZHIGANG LI AND FULONG WU

PART 3
Migrants' habitat in urban China   **145**

9 A tale of Foxconn city: urban village, migrant workers
and alienated urbanism   147
DANIEL YOU-REN YANG

10 Shanghai's urban villages: migrants, temporary
residence and urban redevelopment   164
MINGFENG WANG, XIAOLING LIN AND YUEMIN NING

11 Urban villages as local economic clusters: the case
of the Zhongda cloth market in Guangzhou   182
UWE ALTROCK AND SONIA SCHOON

12 Spatial evolution of urban villages in Shenzhen   202
PU HAO, STAN GEERTMAN, PIETER HOOIMEIJER AND RICHARD SLIUZAS

PART 4
Migrants' transient urbanism: village redevelopment   **221**

13 'Three olds redevelopment': advances in urban
upgrading in Guangzhou   223
SONIA SCHOON AND UWE ALTROCK

14 The symbiotic relationship between urban villages and
the city: implications for redevelopment strategies   240
YANLIU LIN, BRUNO DE MEULDER AND SHIFU WANG

15 Planning for *chengzhongcun* in Guangzhou and Shenzhen:
redevelopment in the Chinese context   256
HIM CHUNG

16 Conclusion   275
CHRIS WEBSTER

Index   293

Figures

1.1	Demolition of urban villages in Guangzhou.	10
2.1	Age structure of rural population, rural labor force, and rural migrant workers	21
2.2	Choice of work among rural labor force of different ages.	22
3.1	Narrator of the story: Mr Ma the business owner	38
3.2	Narrators of the story: the male cousins of the Ma family	38
4.1	Average annual mobility rates over duration of residence	56
4.2	Distribution of local and migrant population in Shanghai, 2000	63
5.1	Ways of finding jobs by residential status for the five job-search processes	77
6.1	Delivery men awaiting new assignments outside Xian Cun, 2008	85
6.2	Xian Cun food market under demolition, September 2010	89
6.3	Xian Cun seen from northeast, September 2010	94
7.1	Research neighbourhoods in Guangzhou, China	105
8.1	The sample villages in (a) Shanghai, (b) Beijing and (c) Guangzhou (2010)	130
10.1	The locations of the sampled urban villages	167
10.2	Hukou status of residents	169
10.3	Comparison of age distribution of urban villages' residents with that of Shanghai's permanent population	169
10.4	Contract situations of householders	170
10.5	Employment situations of the employees	171
10.6	Occupation situations of the employees	171
10.7	Comparison of social insurance of urban villages' residents with that of Shanghai's permanent population	172
10.8	Comparison of urban villages' housing built time with that of Shanghai city	174
10.9	Residential satisfaction of tenants	176
11.1	Older low-rise wholesale center in Wufeng village	186
11.2	Processing factory near Ruikang road	187
11.3	Carrier in front of CJCTC	188
11.4	Main façade of CJCTC	194
12.1	Distribution of urban villages and the city landscape	204

xiv *Figures*

12.2	Gangxia urban village in the city centre of Shenzhen, 2009	206
12.3	LISA cluster maps of urban village development in terms of expansion, densification and intensification, respectively	208
13.1	Urban villages in Guangzhou and important planning projects	225
13.2	Guangzhou 'Three Olds Regeneration' duty allocation on municipal and district levels	232
14.1	Urban development and urban villages	243
14.2	Urban villages and commercial areas/public constructions	245
14.3	Urban villages and external traffic lines	246
14.4	Urban villages and industrial areas	247
14.5	Urban villages and warehouses	248
15.1	The planning framework of Shenzhen's urban villages	265
15.2	The planning framework of Guangzhou's urban villages	267
15.3	A new financial model for Guangzhou's urban villages	269

Tables

2.1	Criteria for the "new-generation" and "second-generation" migrants	18
2.2	Sample studies on the new-generation migrant workers	20
2.3	Average number of years of education among old-generation and new-generation migrants	24
4.1	Migrant spatial mobility between first and current residence by entry cohort, c.2000	57
4.2	Tenure mobility of migrants (by current housing), c.2000	58
4.3	Key sources of assistance in housing search, c.2000	60
5.1	Job-search method and wage per hour for each job in the five years (wage: Yuan, adjusted by CPI)	76
5.2	Results of multinomial logit model and wage model	78
7.1	Migrant characteristics (by neighbourhood type)	107
7.2	Migrants versus locals	108
7.3	Composition, dispersion and dominant source of migrant social networks	109
7.4	Predictors for social network composition, dispersion and dominant source	112
7.5	Composition, dispersion and dominant source for resident groups (%)	114
7.6	Distribution of resident groups over neighbourhoods (%)	115
7.7	Characteristics of the four resident groups: mean values	117
8.1	Migrant integration of the samples	131
8.2	Linear regressions for the determinants of migrant integration for all samples	132
8.3	Linear regressions for the determinants of migrant integration in Beijing	136
8.4	Linear regressions for the determinants of migrant integration in Shanghai	138
8.5	Linear regressions for the determinants of migrant integration in Guangzhou	140
9.1	Living parameter of a day of a Foxconn pugong (ordinary worker)	149

xvi *Tables*

9.2	Statistics of Foxconn employees' wages, expenses, work hours, days-off and wages sent home	153
9.3	Independent sample *T*-test on pugong/non-pugong's expenses on housing	155
9.4	Foxconn employees' choices for working and marriage in Shenzhen for the future	155
10.1	Basic information description of sample	168
10.2	Comparison of migrants' income and expenditures with those of Shanghai's permanent population	172
10.3	Housing facilities of residents	173
11.1	Stages of urbanization and upgrading of ZDCM	183
11.2	Cluster upgrading in comparison	198
12.1	Spatial autocorrelation in terms of expansion, densification and intensification	207
12.2	Main aspects in the evolution from rural village to urban village	213

Contributors

Uwe Altrock, Dr.-Ing., urban planner, is Professor for Urban Regeneration and Planning at the University of Kassel, Germany. He is co-editor of the *German Yearbook of Urban Regeneration* and co-editor of *Spatial Planning and Urban Development* in the new EU Member States (Ashgate 2006). His fields of interest and research are: urban governance, megacities, urban regeneration and planning, planning theory, and planning history.

Cecilie Andersson has a PhD in Urban Design and Planning from the Norwegian University of Science and Technology. She has worked as an architect and has been responsible for several Master's courses and workshops in Architecture and Urban Planning for various Nordic Architecture Schools in collaboration with universities in China. Her research interests include urban transformation, migration, heterogeneity in spatial practice, narrative approaches, participation and implementation as means of interaction. She is currently Vice Dean at Bergen School of Architecture.

Werner Breitung is an urban geographer with degrees from FU Berlin and Universität Basel. He lives in China and has been teaching at the University of Hong Kong, the University of Macau and at Sun Yat-sen University in Guangzhou for 12 years before joining Xi'an Jiaotong-Liverpool University as Professor of Urban Planning in 2013. He has led four major research projects funded by the German DFG and the Chinese NSFC and published widely on urbanization, social geographies and borders in the Pearl River Delta.

Chen Chen is a PhD candidate in the Department of Geography at UCLA. Her research focuses on internal migration in China. She is interested in combining quantitative and qualitative methods to understand how contemporary rural–urban migration changes people's lives, and how it impacts regional development in both rural and urban areas. She has participated in numerous surveys and has conducted extensive fieldwork in China's countryside.

Yu Chen is Lecturer at the School of East Asian Studies, University of Sheffield. She gained a PhD in Urban Studies from the University of Glasgow. Before that, she had obtained a BSc from the Shanghai University of Finance and Economics and MScs from both Fudan University and the University of Oslo.

xviii   *Contributors*

Her research interests are in China's urbanization, rural–urban migration, labour market development and housing market dynamics.

Him Chung is an Associate Professor in the Geography Department at Hong Kong Baptist University. His research areas span across the rural and urban geography of China, including rural transformation, contesting urban space, town planning and state–society relations. His publications include *China's Rural Market Development in the Reform Era* (Ashgate 2004) and papers on China's rural transport development, illegal construction, urban planning and spatial strategy for state governance. He is currently involved in a research project encompassing planning and redevelopment of villages-in-the-city in Guangzhou, China.

C. Cindy Fan is Interim Vice Provost for International Studies and Professor of Geography at UCLA. She formerly served as Associate Dean of Social Sciences and Chair of the Asian American Studies Department. Her research focuses on labour migration, marriage migration, spatial and social inequality, gender and cities in China. She has received grants from the National Science Foundation and the Luce Foundation. She has published numerous articles in flagship journals. Her book, *China on the Move: Migration, the State, and the Household* (Routledge 2008), will soon be translated into Chinese. Her current projects focus on the split households of migrants. A frequent keynote speaker at international conferences, she has been a co-editor of Regional Studies and Eurasian Geography and Economics. She regularly writes commentaries for the New York Times and other media outlets. She recently received the UCLA Distinguished Teaching Award, an Andrew Mellon Foundation grant, and an American Council on Education fellowship.

Stan Geertman is an Associate Professor in Geo-Information Science and Chair of Spatial Planning at Utrecht University. He has published widely in both national and international journals and has published a range of (editorial) books. He is editor of the international peer-reviewed journal *ASAP* (*Applied Spatial Analysis and Policy*) and member of the editorial board of several other scientific journals (e.g. *CEUS*). He has been member of several international conference organizations (EGIS; JECC; AGILE; DDSS) and is chair of the organizing committee of the international CUPUM conference in 2013. His current research interests are: planning and decision support systems (PSS/DSS) in planning practice; sociospatial analysis for sustainable urbanization, notably in Chinese and Western contexts; and methodological issues concerning GI applications.

Pu Hao is a Research Assistant Professor at the David C. Lam Institute for East-West Studies at Hong Kong Baptist University. He received a PhD degree in human geography and urban planning from Utrecht University in 2012. His research interests include global urbanism, urban morphology, urban spatial and social dynamics, and the application of GIS techniques to urban studies and planning.

Contributors xix

Arjan Hazelzet completed a research Master's degree in Human Geography and Urban Planning at Utrecht University, the Netherlands. In 2008, he took up a position as a PhD student at the Faculty of Architecture of the University of Hong Kong. His PhD project focuses on social networks in Chinese cities, and on the influence of gated urban living on community development and solidarity.

Pieter Hooimeijer is Professor of Human Geography and Demography at Utrecht University and Director of the Netherlands Graduate School of Urban and Regional Research. He has published 60 papers in peer reviewed international journals and over 100 publications for a professional audience on demographic change and urban dynamics. He has supervised 25 PhD students who have finalised or are working on their thesis. Current research interests are: urban transformation in China, analysing the effects of economic and population growth on shifts in transportation and land use in Chinese cities (Shenzhen, Nanjing); population and poverty in sub-Saharan Africa, analysing the relation between education, reproductive health and poverty reduction (Rwanda); Youth Geographies in the Netherlands, analysing the role of the geographical context in the personal development and social mobility of adolescents.

Zhigang Li is Professor of Urban Studies and Planning at the School of Geography and Planning, and Deputy Head of the Department of Urban and Regional Planning, Sun Yat-sen University. He is an international editor of the *Journal of Urban Studies*. His research interests include migrants, migrant space and related sociospatial patterns, including housing and segregation. His publications appear in journals such as *Urban Geography*, *Housing Studies*, *Cities* and *Transactions of the Institute of British Geographers*, as well as many journals in China. He is the co-author of *The Transformation of Social Space in Urban China*, published by Southeast University Press in 2011.

Xiaoling Lin is a postgraduate at the Centre for Modern Chinese City Studies at East China Normal University. Her research includes China's urban village (*chengzhongcun*) and urban transition.

Yanliu Lin is a postdoctoral fellow in the Section of Spatial Planning at Utrecht University, the Netherlands. Her research interests centre on urban village, governance in sustainable urbanization, strategic urban project, strategic spatial planning, and planning support system. She is keen to bridge the gap between theory and practice.

Bruno De Meulder is Professor of Urbanism in the Department of Architecture, Urban Design and Regional Planning at K. U. Leuven, Belgium. His research interest is situated at the crossroads of urbanism and urbanization, and of theory and practice.

Yuemin Ning is Professor at East China Normal University and Shanghai Academy of Social Sciences, and Director of the Centre for Modern Chinese City Studies, one of the key research institutes of humanities and social xx *Contributors*

sciences in universities, at East China Normal University. His research mainly focuses on urban geography, urban planning and urban economics. He is the first author of *From Spatial Division of Labour to Spatial Organization in Metropolitan Area* (in Chinese, 2011), *Spatial Organization of Enterprise and Development of City-Region* (in Chinese, 2011), and *History of Chinese Cities* (in Chinese, 1994), and co-author of *Introduction to Urban Geography* (in Chinese, 1983) and *Urban Geography* (in Chinese, 1997).

Gwilym Pryce is Professor of Urban Economics and Social Statistics in the Department of Urban Studies, University of Glasgow. He leads the £1m ESRC Urban Segregation and Inequality Research Project (USIRP), part of the £4m ESRC AQMEN II Research Centre. He is also an appointed member of the Economic Advisor Panel for the UK Department of Environment, Food and Rural Affairs. He was formerly a member of the UK Government's Expert Panel on Housing and Planning, and has previously been an Academic Advisor on a number of UK government initiatives, including the HM Treasury Barker Review of Housing Supply, the National Statisticians Review of Housing Market Statistics, and the Financial Services Authority Mortgage Market Review.

Sonia Schoon, Dr-Phil., sinologist and urban anthropologist, is Research Associate for urban governance in China at the University of Kassel, Germany. She is the author of *Shanghai XXL* (transcript, 2007). Her fields of interest and research are: urban governance, megacities, impacts of mega-urbanization on people's lives, and new phenomenology.

Richard Sliuzas is Associate Professor of Urban Planning at the University of Twente's Faculty of Geographic Information Science and Earth Observation. Much of his research has been focused on monitoring and modelling informal development and urban growth in developing countries, subjects that figure prominently in his peer reviewed papers and other publications. His current major research interests are: urban transformations and planning in China and Vietnam; urban growth and urban village formation; land use and transport planning (studies in Shenzhen, Wuhan and Ha Noi); informal settlement monitoring and upgrading; and studies in Kenya, India and Uganda.

Mingfeng Wang is Associate Professor of regional economics and Deputy Director of the Centre for Modern Chinese City Studies at East China Normal University. His research mainly focuses on globalization, urbanization, and regional development in China. He is the author of *The Production and Consumption of Urban Cyberspace* (Science Press, 2007, in Chinese).

Shifu Wang is Professor and the Head of the Urban Planning Department at South China University of Technology, China. His research interests are in urban design, urban development and planning control.

Chris Webster is Dean of the Faculty of Architecture, University of Hong Kong, and Senior Departmental Fellow, Cambridge University Department of Land

Economy, UK, and a Member of the Advisory Committee of the International Association for China Planning. He is co-editor of the journal *Environment and Planning B: Planning and Design*. His research and writing focuses on spontaneous urban order and much of it addresses the paradoxical question: 'How can we manage spontaneous cities?' He has published over 150 scholarly books and papers. Books include: *China's Urban Poverty* (Edward Elgar 2010); *Private Cities: Local and Global Perspectives* (Routledge 2006); *Public–Private Partnerships in Urban Infrastructure & Service Delivery* (UN ESCAP 2003); and *Property Rights, Planning and Markets: Managing Spontaneous Cities* (Edward Elgar 2003).

Bart Wissink is Assistant Professor in Urban Studies and Urban Policy at the City University of Hong Kong. He received Master's degrees in Urban Planning and Public Administration (both *cum laude*) and a PhD in social and behavioural sciences at the University of Amsterdam, the Netherlands. From 2000 to 2003, he worked as project coordinator at the Netherlands Scientific Council for Government Policy. In 2003, he took up a position as Assistant Professor in urban planning at the Utrecht University, the Netherlands, where he started his comparative research into urban fragmentation, social networks and urban controversies in Asian city regions. He has held visiting scholarships in Tokyo, Bangkok, Mumbai and Hong Kong.

Fulong Wu is Bartlett Professor of Planning at University College London and was previously Professor of East Asian Planning and Development at Cardiff University. His research includes China's urban development and planning and its social and sustainable challenges. He is co-editor of *Restructuring the Chinese City* (Routledge 2005); *Marginalization in China* (Palgrave Macmillan 2010); *International Perspectives on Suburbanization* (Palgrave Macmillan 2011); editor of *Globalization and the Chinese City* (Routledge 2006); *China's Emerging Cities* (Routledge 2007); and co-author of *Urban Development in Post-Reform China: State, Market, and Space* (Routledge 2007) and *China's Urban Poverty* (Edward Elgar 2010).

Weiping Wu is Professor of Urban and Environmental Policy and Planning at Tufts University and senior fellow in the Center for Emerging Market Enterprises at The Fletcher School. Her research is concerned with how migration affects the sociospatial reconfiguration of cities, how planning and policy influence cities' economic vitality and infrastructure building, and how universities transfer knowledge and innovation to industry. She is the co-author of *The Chinese City* (Routledge 2013); author of *Pioneering Economic Reform in China's Special Economic Zones* (Ashgate 1999); co-author of *The Dynamics of Urban Growth in Three Chinese Cities* (Oxford 1997); and co-editor of *Local Dynamics in a Globalizing World* (Oxford 2000) and *Facets of Globalization* (World Bank 2001).

Daniel You-Ren Yang is Associate Professor in the Department of Sociology at Tunghai University, Taiwan. His research includes global electronic production networks, sweatshops and anti-sweatshop movements, China's land institutions and urban–rural transition. He has published articles in many journals, including *Urban Studies, Regional Studies, Environment and Planning A, Advances in Applied Sociology,* and *Growth and Change.*

Fangzhu Zhang is Lecturer in China Planning at Bartlett School of Planning, University College London. Her main research interests include Chinese development, innovation and planning. She has published articles in *Regional Studies, Geography Compass, Progress in Planning* and *European Planning Studies,* and co-edited a special issue on 'Planning the Chinese City' in *Town Planning Review* (2008).

Heather Xiaoquan Zhang is Senior Lecturer in Chinese Studies and Director of Postgraduate Studies at East Asian Studies and the White Rose East Asia Centre, University of Leeds, UK. With a PhD in politics from the University of Strathclyde, UK, she has worked broadly in the field of China's rural and urban development. Her research interests cover livelihoods and rural-urban migration, social policy and citizenship, poverty, inequality and social exclusion, health and well-being, globalization, gender and qualitative research methodology. She has published widely, including journal articles in *Development and Change, The Journal of Peasant Studies, Journal of International Development, Women's Studies International Forum, Geoforum, Public Administration and Development, Modern China,* and *Local Economy.* She is the co-editor of *Marginalisation in China: Perspectives on Transition and Globalisation* (Ashgate 2007).

Preface

This book is about rural migrants and their habitat – urban villages in Chinese cities. In *Urban Poverty in China* (2010, published by Edward Elgar) and *Marginalization in Urban China* (2010, published by Palgrave Macmillan), researchers on urban China examined the poor livelihoods and excluded status of rural migrants. The migrants are studied as a social group together with other groups such as laid-off workers and inner city residents. The focus has been on the rural migrants themselves. However, we feel there is a need to develop a *spatial* understanding of rural migrants and treat neighbourhoods with concentrated rural migrants more seriously. The title of this book may, on the one hand, be read as a quite straightforward descriptive one. On the other hand, there is an underlying meaning which emphasizes how these rural migrants are situated *in* Chinese cities. We strive to discover the *urban* dimension of their lives: their mobility and relations with the city, their social networks and neighbour activities, their habitat known as 'urban villages', and their transient urbanism when their habitat is faced the fate of demolition. Thus, the book extends our understanding from the labour market and the sociological perspective to the scope of urban studies on emerging and transient *urban* forms. To the best of our knowledge, this book is the first systematic book-length treatment of 'urban villages' other than burgeoning journal articles on the subject.

Besides various forms of funding support to the authors in this book, which are acknowledged in their chapters, the book originated from a UK Economic and Social Research Council and UK Department of International Development joint-funded project on 'The Development of Migrant Villages under China's Rapid Urbanization: Implications for Poverty and Slum Policies'. The financial support of these agencies (RES-167-25-0448) is gratefully acknowledged. Following this research, we organized an international conference on China's Urban Transition and City Planning at which the authors of this book presented their papers. They have subsequently revised their papers, focusing on the urban dimension of rural migrants *in* the cities. In addition, this project has led to a collaborative project funded by the Ministry of Education of PRC on the 'Integration of Migrants in Chinese Society' (11JJD840015). We thus thank Professor Yuemin Ning, one of the China partners and the Director of the Centre for

xxiv *Preface*

Modern Chinese City Studies for supporting this output. We would like to thank Peter Sowden, Asian Studies editor at Routledge for his long-term support for our publication projects. We also would like to thank those who helped the organization of the conference and production of this book, in particular, Jie Shen, Yi Li, Zheng Wang and Bruce Hunt.

1 Migrants' transient urbanism in urban China

An introduction

Fulong Wu and Fangzhu Zhang

Introduction

China's rural-to-urban migration and rapid urbanization have produced profound impacts on Chinese cities. The pace of urbanization has accelerated since China joined the WTO in 2001 and became the 'world factory'. In 2011, China reached a remarkable milestone: more than half of its population became an urban population living in cities. Therefore, we need to understand this growing population, especially these new migrants in the cities. Despite earlier studies on rural migrants and discrimination against migrants in cities (e.g. Solinger 1999; Zhang 2001), recent research has paid more attention to rural-to-urban migration (Fan 2008; Murphy 2009) and the division between rural and urban societies (Whyte 2010). Recently, Chan (2010) examined the impact of the global financial crisis on the unemployment situation of migrants. Apparently, attention has been paid to rural migrants, but there has been little systematic research on rural migrants *in* urban China, namely the contextual environment in which migrants stay in Chinese cities, in particular their habitat known as the 'urban village' or 'villages in the city' (*chengzhongcun*).

Earlier studies noted the formation of concentrated migrant enclaves. Ma and Xiang (1998) examined Beijing's 'migrant enclaves' in the 1990s and highlighted the role of these enclaves in migrants' entry into the city. Zhang *et al.* (2003) focused on housing conditions in urban villages in Guangzhou. Xiang (2004) provides a detailed study of Zhejiangcun in Beijing in the 1990s, focusing on the production and living spaces of migrants. More recently, there has been a burgeoning literature on the development of urban villages and their impacts on the cities (Tian 2008; Wang *et al.* 2009; Liu *et al.* 2010; He *et al.* 2010; Lin *et al.* 2011; Hao *et al.* 2011). This book brings together recent studies on rural migrants and focuses particularly on the habitat of migrants in the cities. It aims to provide a synthetic account of Chinese urban villages. The research is timely, as Chinese cities have initiated a movement to redevelop urban villages. In Guangdong, new policies of redevelopment have been formulated and new redevelopment offices were set up; Beijing has listed 50 villages as a priority for redevelopment, and Shanghai has surveyed its residual villages for the next phase of urban regeneration (Wu *et al.* forthcoming).

2 Fulong Wu and Fangzhu Zhang

The remainder of this chapter will introduce the content of this book, while at the same time rearticulating the individual studies to contextualize them in the framework of migrants' 'transient urbanism'. Here we attempt to summarize one sentence from each chapter from this perspective: old migrants have returned to the countryside and new-generation migrants are coming. Migrants' livelihoods have high mobility, high vulnerability and high risk. They drift as tenants, and do not manage to establish a path towards becoming homeowners in the cities. Social networks possessed by migrants help them find jobs, but these jobs are much inferior to the job market. Still, migrants use their spaces adaptively through a trans-local approach. The social space of migrants is not confined within their neighbourhoods. Along with the length of their stay, they are less constrained by *hukou* as they are forging their way *socially* in the city. The development of urban villages represents an effort made by rural migrants themselves to break out of the factory dormitory style of management, although they may not all be successful. Despite insufficient infrastructure, urban villages provide affordable housing as well as jobs to migrants. The habitat of rural migrants grows in a spontaneous way at locations accessible to jobs. Nevertheless, their newly forged urbanism is quite transient, facing aggressive policies of village redevelopment. These redevelopment strategies disregard the urban village as an integral part of the city. The planning of redevelopment is very much aimed at consolidating municipal power. Now, we turn to a more detailed account of these studies.

Migrants' livelihoods in urban China

Not only has the population of rural migrants in urban China increased but their composition has also changed over time. In Chapter 2, Cindy Fan and Chen Chen pay particular attention to 'new-generation' migrant workers, given that second generation migrants now account for more than half of the migrant population. They review both recent Chinese rural-to-urban migration surveys and discuss the definition of this new term of 'new-generation' migrants – commonly referring to those born after 1980. They find that new-generation migrants have some distinctive characteristics; for example, they are better educated, have little experience of farm work and are more likely to start migrant work earlier than their parents. To them, migration and working in the cities are perhaps the norm rather than the exception. If married, they are more likely to bring their families to the city and also are more ready to settle down in the cities, which indicates that they are on a trajectory towards becoming urban residents. However, Fan and Chen point out two constraints besides the institutional hurdles for them to settle down: their social networks continue to rely on native-place ties and the jobs available in the cities require higher educational attainment and skill training. Compared with first generation migrants, new-generation migrants are more likely to work in manufacturing than other sectors, which suggests that their jobs are more formal than being self-employed in markets and low-rank social services. Because of this more formal employment, they have access to the dormitories provided by factories (see Daniel You-ren Yang in Chapter 9, on the dormitory as a way of exerting

Migrants' transient urbanism in urban China 3

discipline and control). The study of new-generation migrants highlights the abrupt road towards becoming urban residents. Despite their improved attainments, new-generation migrants are not better accommodated by the host city compared with their parent generation. It can even be argued that compared with their parents, they are treated more like guest workers for industrial development. Desiring better housing and perhaps more normal family lives, the percentage of migrants in rental housing increases, but they cannot afford to purchase homes in the city (see Weiping Wu in Chapter 4, on migrant housing). The new-generation rural migrants have not been fully integrated in the host city, despite their effort towards adapting to urban lives.

Mobility is essentially the way of life for the migrant population, which brings risks to migrant workers. Heather Zhang in Chapter 3 describes the mobile livelihoods of rural migrants in the cities and argues that because of high mobility, migrants face higher risks. In rural areas, peasants bear the risk through their mutual help in local communities. However, in the cities, while the informal social network is still a source of social support, informality and the lack of social security institutions mean that rural migrants are particularly vulnerable in their pursuit of entrepreneurial activities in the cities. Existing institutional arrangements for migrants are insufficient to mitigate the impact of disastrous accidents. While not necessarily confined within urban villages, Zhang's findings suggest various aspects of informality in coping with difficult situations in the cities. One may argue that relying on informal social networks as social support reflects the human agency in migration and the survival strategies of rural migrants in an unfamiliar and sometimes hostile urban society, while the obstacles towards integrating rural migrants into urban institutions (through collective consumption) reflects the 'transient' and 'informal' nature of urbanism for rural migrants. Their urbanism is not embedded and formalized into urban and social institutions leading to an established and formal urbanism. Zhang's detailed ethnographic account of migrants reveals the insecurity of migrants in urban China and their heroic endeavour to survive in the cities. The history of migration is full of numerous decisions to move from one place to another, following new economic opportunities, developing trans-local social networks, suffering from various difficulties and risks in the city, receiving help from informal social support, and relocating or moving into new places. Such transient and unstable urbanism is perhaps not what migrants want – the question is then how to forge an institutional reform to help migrants eventually settle down in the city and mitigate the impacts of risk on them.

From the perspective of housing, Weiping Wu in Chapter 4 argues that migrants are still treated as the 'outsiders of the city'. Migrant housing is almost exclusively restricted to informal rentals in urban villages, apart from factory dormitory housing. Unlike in other developing countries where squatter settlements are the norm, Chinese rural migrants are not able to build housing themselves. In this sense, there is *no* self-help housing in Chinese cities but only informally built housing for rental purposes. This informal housing, mostly in urban villages, does not necessarily follow a modern building code or city planning. It is developed

4 Fulong Wu and Fangzhu Zhang

through spontaneous construction to pursue the opportunities of rental markets due to rising demand for cheaper housing. Wu finds that migrants continue to change residential locations once they are in the city. She points out that 'few migrants in urban China make the transition from bridgeheaders to consolidators even after years of living in the city', unlike migrants in other developing countries. In essence, rural migrants are 'getting stuck' with informal private rentals, while it has become much easier for migrants to stay for extended time. Wu examined the spatial pattern of migrant housing, and most are found in peri-urban locations. The urban periphery has a particular attraction to rural migrants because of its lower cost of housing and accessible job markets. So, seen from the perspective of the geography of migrant housing, their urbanism is still transient, constantly moving further out when new opportunities for constructing rental housing emerge. In terms of residential mobility, in western market economies changing housing tenure is one of the major reasons for intra-urban residential relocation. But in Chinese cities, rural migrants may change residential location but just move from one urban village to another, without moving into a consolidated 'housing career'. The strength of city planning to prevent squatting is part of the reason for the impossibility of becoming owners of informal housing, while lax rural land management gives opportunities to peri-urban farmers to build rental housing for rural migrants. Formally built housing in the market is unaffordable to rural migrants, because the design of the land leasing system targets the highest bids for land and thus, the higher end of the housing market. So from the housing perspective, migrants experience an urbanism that is 'transient'.

Overall, the first part on migrants and their livelihoods in cities shows a picture of changing composition towards new-generation migrants, self-reliance on themselves and their families to cope with difficulty and risk in the city, and higher mobility in spatial terms although remaining in the rental sector. Their experience of urban lives, or their urbanism, is transient and short-lived – simply disappearing when they return to the countryside.

Migrants' social lives in urban China

Migrants experience hard lives in the city. Their social integration with the host society is becoming a burning issue in China. In the second part, four chapters are devoted specifically to their social lives and networks in the city. In Chapter 5, Yu Chen and Gwilym Pryce aim to identify the role of social networks in migrants' job finding. They distinguish informal ways of job finding through social networks and the formal labour market. Consistently with other studies in the UK, the USA and India, and earlier studies on *guanxi* (relation) in China and the understanding that social networks play a vital role in migrants' initial moves, they find that the social network is very important in migrants' job search. What is interesting in their findings is that the strength of the social network is not the same across migrants of different socioeconomic status. The method of job search is influenced by, for example, educational attainments. More educated migrants are more likely to find jobs through formal job advertisements. They also find the limitations of social networks for job finding, because jobs found through social networks are lower paid. They explain this because migrants tend to make friends with other migrants rather than with established local urban residents. Therefore, because of similar backgrounds among migrants, the information is more constrained to certain jobs, particularly for rural migrants. Many of these jobs are low paid, difficult, dirty and dangerous. The finding is revealing because it indicates the constraints faced by rural migrants. Although migrants develop social networks which are not confined to the local community (see the measure in Chapter 7 by Wissink *et al.*), their social networks bring them fewer economic opportunities and rewards. From the job search perspective, migrants' entry into lower job markets (with lower pay) is not only driven by their lower educational attainment compared with urban households, but also conditioned by their social networks.

While the social network approach seems to suggest that migrants are confined within their social activities, face more restricted social interaction with non-migrants, and hence do not benefit to a greater extent from higher pay jobs, Cecilie Andersson in Chapter 6 investigates the experience of migrants' trans-locality through detailed ethnographic observations. She asks whether urban villages are 'isolated' from the rest of the city (see Chapter 14 by Lin *et al.*, on the 'spatial' relation between urban villages and the city). The question is profound: to what extent can places with migrant concentration be seen as 'migrant enclaves'? By observing everyday practices and interviewing migrants, Andersson argues that rural migrants are 'situated' in the urban context and 'occupy' and use other parts of the city. For example, she observed that the tricycles run by migrants linked the narrow streets of urban villages to the rest of the city. To understand 'urban villages', she argues, we must go beyond urban villages themselves as physically bounded space and look at multi-scalar urban spaces. In the physical landscape, urban villages are crowded and packed, easily distinguishable from the modern high-rises in the rest of the city. But when considering everyday practices, urban villages are part of the city. In contrast to the view that urban villages prevent social integration, Andersson's argument is that they may provide a place to receive rural migrants and later on help them to become integrated into the urban sphere. From this trans-local perspective, migrants' urbanism is under formation.

The notion of trans-locality leads to the need to understand better the social networks of migrants. Bart Wissink, Arjan Hazelzet and Werner Breitung in Chapter 7 examine the social networks of migrants in Guangzhou. In general, in terms of social networks, the role of neighbourhood ties has been decreasing. That is, the neighbourhood is losing its function in organizing social networks. In the city of Guangzhou where they conducted a neighbourhood survey, migrants' social networks diffuse beyond the boundaries of neighbourhoods. They argue that most migrants begin to 'integrate' with the city, although they may have weaker ties with local residents in their neighbourhood. The purpose behind their research on social networks is to ask to what extent migrants are integrated with the city and how they are integrated. They review classical social assimilation theory and its critique, which led to the racially disadvantaged model and segmented assimilation, both emphasizing the institutional barriers to assimilation and viewing assimilation within the same social or racial group. From this perspective, they suggest that new and more established or permanent migrants may have different social networks. They classify migrants according to the characteristics of their social networks, namely composition, dispersion and dominant source of social networks. They find that migrants who predominantly rely on people from the same home town (province) only account for less than 40 per cent of the migrant population. The largest group of migrants do not base their social networks on people from the same province and are more or less integrated into diverse social networks in Guangzhou. It is their view that migrants, including those who came from other cities, are not an isolated social group.

Similar to these findings, Zhigang Li and Fulong Wu in Chapter 8 use a survey from 60 urban villages in Beijing, Shanghai and Guangzhou, and analyse the social integration of migrants. They find significant variation across these three cities, but argue that migrants begin to be integrated *socially* in these urban villages. In many urban villages, migrants outnumber local residents. These villages are largely a dual society where the locals are mainly landlords while migrants are tenants. Rural migrants in these villages are *institutionally* excluded from entitlement to or benefit of land because they do not have any share in collective share companies. They do not even have a formal rental contract. So the question is how institutional exclusion affects social integration, here defined as interaction at the neighbourhood level. They defined the index of social integration based on the scores of a series of questions about interactions between neighbours. In terms of determinants, they find that for more established migrants the level of integration is affected by many factors including income, property rights, and rent, in addition to having children, employment status as rural peasant, and having an employment contract. They argue that along with the length of stay in the city, institutional barriers such as *hukou* are less relevant to the level of rural migrant integration. While all three cities see the declining effect of *hukou* status on the level of integration, there are significant differences between these cities. For more state-led Shanghai, multiple factors affect the level of social integration, including market and institutional forces. For Beijing, housing status such as homeownership is a major factor, while in Guangzhou, arguably more market-oriented, income is one of the determinants for social integration. The study may show that attributes beyond *hukou* have begun to influence social interaction at the neighbourhood level. In urban villages, migrants have begun to be integrated locally in terms of social interaction. However, they still lack power in village management or in the process of village redevelopment.

Overall, the second part on migrants' social lives in urban China finds that migrants' social networks do help them find jobs, but their social networks bring them less economic return. Still, migrants forged their way to develop their networks in the city, and especially in concentrated migrant places such as urban villages migrants are using them 'cleverly' for their life and work. Their space is thus economically and socially related to other parts of the city –these places are thus not ghettoes, and migrants extend their networks beyond their local places. Their social spaces and urban experiences are thus quite pervasive across the city.

Migrants' transient urbanism in urban China 7

Still excluded by the institution of *hukou*, migrants however develop signs of *social* integration; collectively they are not isolated individuals and are experiencing the city as a way of life.

Migrants' habitat in urban China

In Part 3, this book begins to examine the places lived in by rural migrants, in particular urban villages. The main habitat for migrants living in the city is the urban village. However, for younger new-generation migrants, some may first directly enter a factory dormitory when they are employed. Daniel You-ren Yang in Chapter 9 examined the latter in 'Foxconn town' in Shenzhen, widely known for the suicides of young employees. He suggests that the particular system of labour management – the 'factory labour regime' – is responsible for significant experience of alienation. Factory management policy, plus labour market conditions, according to his research, has aggravated the sense of alienation. He describes in detail through ethnographic observations the method of labour control and daily routines of workers. The ordinary and entry-level workers of Foxconn are subject to pressure to increase labour productivity, and time management means that they have little time to develop social activities and thus are not able to settle down in the city. Again, Yang points to social networks for an explanation and suggests that the constraint of their social networks as a result of particular ways of working in the factory significantly prevents migrants' integration into urban society. The cost of living is another hurdle for settling down, because ordinary workers have no chance to match the rent level necessary to bring up a family. From the perspective of migrants' habitat, we see the need to expand social interactions to solve the problem of alienation of migrant workers. In this regard, urban villages provide an alternative form for migrants.

Based on a survey of 23 urban villages in Shanghai, which is part of a larger project funded by ESRC/DFID in the UK (see Preface) in three Chinese cities – Beijing, Shanghai, and Guangzhou – Mingfeng Wang, Xiaoling Lin and Yuemin Ning in Chapter 10 systematically examine the livelihoods of migrants and their living conditions in these villages. Because these villages are sampled through the list of remaining villages in Shanghai, their distribution is uneven. Because Shanghai adopts a relatively stringent control over land, earlier villages within the inner ring road have been largely demolished and have disappeared. Most villages are located outside the inner ring road and concentrated in south-west suburban areas in Xuhui, Minhang and Putuo Districts. Because the sample is randomly drawn for each village, the composition of population can be thus inferred from the sample. As expected, migrants account for the majority of residents, reaching 83 per cent of the total. They found that rural migrants are mainly engaged in informal employment, that is, very few migrants hold a permanent job. A significant proportion of household heads are self-employed, accounting for 22 per cent of total household heads. Compared with urban residents outside the villages, residents inside a village have a lower income. Their space of living is congested, and there is a lack of basic facilities such as kitchens and indoor toilets. The general condition of housing is quite dilapidated. Wang and his colleagues then ask why these residents live in the villages. Original residents who have become landlords live in these villages because they inherited housing from their parents and continue to live there for easier management of their rental units. Although rental income is an important source, the number of spare rooms to let is still limited, partially because Shanghai's control over self-built housing is tighter than in other cities in southern China. That perhaps also explains why the rental sector is quite informal and thus needs landlords to look after the units. Because of this important yet limited rental income, some original residents are not becoming the new rich who can move to commodity housing in other places. For tenants, location is still a very important factor, because urban villages are generally located in convenient places, with good accessibility to schools and markets. Being close to their job location is a very important factor, because the average distance from the place of living to the workplace is only 5.7 kilometres, and many use bicycles. With quite low affordability, when urban villages are demolished, rural migrants are not able to afford the renovated housing. They have to move somewhere else, mostly further out to the suburbs for cheaper rental housing.

Urban villages provide not only cheaper housing to rural migrants but also spaces for industrial development and jobs for migrants. As early as the 1990s in Beijing, private clothing making workshops began to cluster in Zhejiang Village. Uwe Altrock and Sonia Schoon in Chapter 11 describe the recent development of the clothing market in urban villages in Guangzhou. They aim to understand these urban villages as 'economic clusters', which accommodate active business activities. These villages are to be upgraded into new wholesale centres. They describe the development of three major clusters: Guangzhou International Textile City, Chang Jiang (China) Textile City and the Pearl River Textile City. The upgrading aims to build upon the existing strengths of urban villages as densely populated places with easy access to the central area. Some markets are to be modernized into comprehensive business centres, and others aim to evolve into more specialized business areas or mixed-use business centres. Redeveloping the spontaneously built clothing market in urban villages into a modern wholesale market requires infrastructure development and changing governance. The redevelopment process involves complicated compensation issues. They argue that the planned road grid would transform the entire urban fabric, while the strength of these markets is that they are strongly urban-based. Therefore, upgrading these village markets needs to consider the characteristics of complexity of these economic clusters.

The complexity of urban villages as economic clusters is also seen in their spatial pattern of mixed use. Urban villages meet the demand for low-cost housing with greater social and economic diversities. A functional mix of land use is a basic characteristic of urban villages. Pu Hao and his co-authors in Chapter 12 examine the 'spatial evolution' of urban villages in Shenzhen. Through detailed data at the building level, they are able to show that the spatial pattern of urban villages represents a form of organic growth and high adaptability to the surrounding environment. The development of urban villages is clustered in space.

First, villagers try to extend their land holdings as much as possible at a minimal cost and then use the rental income to intensify the buildings and construct multi-floor buildings. They then try to explain the growth pattern of urban villages by examining access to employment location, transport accessibility (such as the distance to the nearby metro station), and constraints on development (such as land slope and the presence of ecological or restricted zones). It is found in their study that the fastest growing urban villages are located near industrial developments as well as the location of the tertiary sector (most likely informal social services to the city) with generally good transport accessibility. In terms of spatial and functional mix, urban villages evolved from more homogenous rural villages to accommodate new economic activities and migrant population. The density increases along with a greater functional mix. However, when urban villages grew, the collectively owned land was appropriated by land acquisition and thus the remaining villages began to become more dependent upon housing rental, and consequently the function has become more residential than a mix of industrial and residential uses. In contrast to the well-planned modern residential district, urban villages grow spontaneously, which gives them greater dynamism and suits the demand of the market. The implication of this spatial and functional complexity is to propose a more incremental way of redevelopment while at the same time maintaining proper building codes to ensure safety, the provision of infrastructure, and the long-term prospect of investment in village development.

Overall, Part 3 describes the function of urban villages as the habitat of rural migrants in urban China. Urban villages provide not only affordable housing to rural migrants, but also a social environment for them to interact with each other, in contrast to the more disciplined dormitories managed by factories. Moreover, urban villages form a space of production, accommodating small workshops and markets. Some of these markets are evolving and have upgraded into larger business centres. Spatially, urban villages show a more functional mix of land uses than state industrial areas. They are built in a bottom-up and incremental way.

Migrants' transient urbanism: village redevelopment

Despite the important functions of urban villages, they are now facing the fate of demolition (Figure 1.1). These features should be carefully considered in the strategy of redevelopment. Part 4 of this book begins to examine the redevelopment of urban villages. Sonia Schoon and Uwe Altrock, in Chapter 13, describe new policies adopted by Guangdong province, which is known as 'three olds redevelopment' (*san jiu gaizao*), namely the redevelopment of old urban areas, old villages and old factories. First, the problem of urban villages can be traced back to lax land management and the unique way of leaving built-up rural villages undeveloped during state land acquisition and urban expansion. Now faced with limited land resources, especially in a province like Guangdong, there is a need to redevelop brownfield land. The organization of mega-events such as the Asian Games in 2010 is an important consideration to speed up city beautification and infrastructure provision. Some urban villages may occupy a central location or

Figure 1.1 Demolition of urban villages in Guangzhou.
Source: Photograph taken by Fulong Wu.

have capable village leaders who are willing to cooperate with the municipal government and are ready to be selected to experiment with a new mode of redevelopment. The other motivation could be using such an opportunity to solve the problem of fragmented land use patterns and ownership complexity. Despite the plausible objective of promoting brownfield redevelopment, the government does not provide a major source of funding but rather allows incentive policies – in essence the 'three olds policies' permit the village to find development partners to share the profit of land development. To avoid unfinished projects and social unrest because of the shortage of compensation, the government also requires the developer to deposit a development fund. The new policy represents a great step forward in stimulating village redevelopment. But such policies do not give adequate consideration to the rural migrants who are dispersed after redevelopment. Village redevelopment is essentially growth-oriented and lacks consideration for the vast number of tenants in urban villages. As the habitat of rural migrants vanishes, such policies are more likely to exacerbate social tensions.

So what should be the proper strategy to redevelop urban villages? To achieve a sustainable way of development, the relation of urban villages with the city should be carefully considered. In Chapter 14, Yanliu Lin, Bruno De Meulder and Shifu Wang argue that urban villages are not isolated spaces but rather are closely linked to the rest of the city (see Cecilie Andersson in Chapter 6 for a similar argument on trans-local social spaces). They examined the land use patterns of urban villages and provide evidence that the land uses of urban villages are in spatial proximity to other urban areas. Some serve important functions, for example, wholesale markets and small workshops. The location of urban villages is generally very accessible, especially through public transport. The local government's investment in road infrastructure in the city indirectly facilitates the formation of these urban villages at good locations. Lin *et al.* argue that this infrastructure development actually 'cross-subsidizes' urban villages and links them into the market system of the city. They studied two well-known urban villages in Guangzhou, Shipai village and Tangxia village, and show how small shops and markets have developed along the main road. For example, IT product shops have been developed in Shipai village, which has become the largest distribution centre of computer and components in Guangzhou. Tangxia village benefited from Tianhe Science Park and developed specialized markets (e.g. electrical equipment). Changes in the economic structure of the city also affect urban villages. For example, the decline of labour-intensive manufacturing industries led to vacant buildings in urban villages, which provided an opportunity for village redevelopment. An understanding of the close linkages between urban villages and the city suggests that the complete demolition of urban villages might not be a proper strategy because this would interrupt the functional linkage between these places. As living places for low-income and flexible workers who serve the rest of the city and as locations for specialized markets and workshops, urban villages should be allowed to co-exist with the city while their built environments are improved and upgraded.

From the perspective of urban planning, Him Chung, in Chapter 15, examines the redevelopment of urban villages. He identifies diverse practices in different cities up to the recent redevelopment policy initiated at the provincial level. He reviews the role of planning in village redevelopment. In the pre-reform period of the centrally planned economy, land use management in cities was under state control. The planning task was essentially evolved around resource allocation and industrial development. In the post-reform era, economic decentralization strengthened the power of local governments. Consequently, planning became a powerful tool to promote economic growth and land development. In rural areas, land management under the dual land management system has been relatively weak. Rapid urban expansion during economic growth led to land conversion in rural areas. The local government strove to capture land revenue and consolidate power in its territory (Hsing 2010). From this perspective, Chung compared urban village redevelopment in Shenzhen and Guangzhou. The redevelopment of urban villages thus provides an opportunity for the local government to capture land resources. However, Guangzhou and Shenzhen adopted a different approach until the recent policies of 'three olds redevelopment'. Shenzhen adopted a comprehensive city-wide strategy and prepared a master plan for village redevelopment, while Guangzhou used a rather flexible policy based on individual villages, known as 'one village, one policy'. More recently, Guangdong province formulated a

12 Fulong Wu and Fangzhu Zhang

policy to redevelop old urban areas, old villages and old factories. Under the special deal with the Ministry of Land and Resources which allows the land from these old areas to be developed without necessarily going through an open auction (which was required by a national policy adopted since 2003, see Wu *et al.* 2007), this new policy of redevelopment opened up new opportunities to absorb investment in urban redevelopment. Policy development at the provincial level has changed the practice of Guangzhou, which previously did not allow private property investment in the redevelopment of urban villages, and has speeded up the process of redevelopment. One important conclusion derived from these case studies is that the motivation for village redevelopment is quite complex, not only targeting the removal of 'dilapidated' villages but also creating land value, extending the power of local government, and capturing development opportunities. Moreover, the practices of land redevelopment vary significantly across different cities, and may change under new circumstances.

Overall, Part 4 reveals a process of rapid village redevelopment in Chinese cities which eventually removes the habitat of rural migrants. New redevelopment policies in Guangdong aim to increase land supply while giving strong incentives for joint development by villages and developers. The wholesale style of demolition and reconstruction has certainly disrupted the function of urban villages. From the perspective of city planning, practices vary across different cities but they all tend to consolidate the control of urban space by the municipality. Rural migrants as tenants in urban villages are marginal in the process of redevelopment.

Conclusion

This collection brings new understandings of rural migrants *in* urban China. Adding to the knowledge of rural to urban migration (Fan 2008), the studies here pay particular attention to migrants' livelihoods, social spaces, village habitats, and the transformation of urban villages. The studies consider the notion of *in* urban China seriously by zooming into the habitat of migrants. This collection focuses on urban villages as migrants' transient habitat in the cities. We find that rural migrants in the cities have unstable and vulnerable livelihoods with various risks, facing relocation due to the demolition of their place of living. Migrants clustered in the urban villages and formed social networks within and beyond the neighbourhoods where they live. They are not an isolated social group, but rather find their own way to live in the cities and form their own social networks. Spatially, the places where they live – urban villages – are close to a variety of urban land uses and hence complement the economic and social activities in the rest of the city. In this sense, the influx of rural migrants into Chinese cities is forging a new kind of urbanism. Without social interaction, rural migrants face deep alienation in factory-managed dormitories. Although the living conditions of urban villages are not desirable, they at least provide cheaper housing and more normal family lives to migrant workers. But urban villages under the current land development regime in China have valuable land resources and bring potential development opportunities for the local government. Under current redevelopment policies, migrants' habitat is quickly disappearing and giving way to new residential areas and towns. Again we see an unstable and transient characteristic of migrants' livelihoods and spaces. With more and more migrants coming to cities and staying longer, it is important to regard them not as 'floating population' or outsiders but rather as new urban residents who are waiting to be integrated into urban society.

What this collection of studies strives to demonstrate is an *urban* dimension of migrants beyond seeing them as temporary workers. Needless to say, migrants still face many institutional hurdles such as *hukou* for them to become permanent urban residents. However, this book emphasizes the need to consider their habitat for them to settle down in the cities, taking into account their ability to stay in urban villages, adapt their livelihoods in the cities and move to other urban areas and live with other urban residents when their needs change. The current policies towards rural migrants are contradictory. On the one hand, the 'social integration of migrants' is raised in the policy agenda, trying to extend some welfare coverage towards rural migrants. On the other hand, the habitats of rural migrants are still regarded as backward places to be modernized. The demolition of urban villages may not only raise the living costs of rural migrants but also have detrimental effects on their process of adaptation and integration in the city. One implication from this volume is perhaps that there is a need to understand better the migrants in urban China and to carefully consider their livelihoods and habitats in the city. Forcing rural migrants to live in a modernized built environment might not be a realistic policy to 'integrate' them with urban society. Instead, such a policy often leads to the *transient* condition of their livelihood and their social space and creates further difficulty for them as they try to settle down in the city.

In sum, rural migrants in urban China show the bizarre course of China's urbanization and the incompleteness of this process. Rural migrants are not granted the entitlement of urban residents and are thus marginalized by this institutional setting (Wu and Webster 2010), and the same is true for farmers at the peri-urban areas who are allowed to keep their land in collective ownership while being deprived of the property right of converting them into an urban asset. These farmers are allowed to enjoy rental income from rural migrants and are even enriched by the redevelopment process (Zhao and Webster 2011). The role of government is missing in the provision of public facilities and infrastructure, while its control over land ownership allows it to capture the benefits of village redevelopment (Wu *et al.* 2007). The transient urbanism of rural migrants reflects the paradoxical incapacities and dominance of the state in Chinese urbanization. The state is simply too powerful – the operational side of the local state is driven by land revenue. For rural migrants in urban China, the state is the source of problem rather than the solution. The transient urbanism of rural migrants is thus a unique angle to illuminate the achievements and limitations of post-reform urban development and governance in China.

References

Chan, K. W. (2010) 'The global financial crisis and migrant workers in China: "there is no future as a labourer; returning to the village has no meaning"', *International Journal of Urban and Regional Research*, 34(3): 659–77.

14 *Fulong Wu and Fangzhu Zhang*

Fan, C. C. (2008) *China on the Move: Migration, the State, and the Household*, London: Routledge.

Hao, P., Sliuzas, R. and Geertman, S. (2011) 'The development and redevelopment of urban villages in Shenzhen', *Habitat International*, 35(2): 214–24.

He, S., Liu, Y., Wu, F. and Webster, C. (2010) "Social groups and housing differentiation in China's urban villages: An institutional interpretation", *Housing Studies*, 25(5): 671–91.

Hsing, Y. T. (2010) *The Great Urban Transformation: Politics of Land and Property in China*, Oxford: Oxford University Press.

Lin, Y. L., De Meulder, B. and Wang, S. F. (2011) 'Understanding the 'village in the city' in Guangzhou: economic integration and development issue and their implications for the urban migrant', *Urban Studies*, 48(16): 3575–90.

Liu, Y., He, S., Wu, F. L. and Webster, C. (2010) 'Urban villages under China's rapid urbanization: unregulated assets and transitional neighbourhoods', *Habitat International*, 34(2): 135–44.

Ma, L. J. C. and Xiang, B. (1998) 'Native place, migration and the emergence of peasant enclaves in Beijing', *The China Quarterly*, 155: 546–81.

Murphy, R. (ed.) (2009) *Labour Migration and Social Development in Contemporary China*, Abingdon: Routledge.

Solinger, D. J. (1999) *Contesting Citizenship in Urban China: Peasant Migrants, the State, and the Logic of the Market*, Berkeley, CA: University of California Press.

Tian, L. (2008) 'The *chengzhongcun* land market in China: boon or bane?: a perspective on property rights', *International Journal of Urban and Regional Research*, 32(2): 282–304.

Wang, Y. P., Wang, Y. and Wu, J. (2009) 'Urbanization and informal development in China: urban villages in Shenzhen', *International Journal of Urban and Regional Research*, 33(4): 957–73.

Whyte, M. K. (ed.) (2010) *One Country, Two Societies: Rural-Urban Inequality in Contemporary China*, Cambridge, MA: Harvard University Press.

Wu, F., Zhang, F. and Webster, C. (forthcoming) 'Informality and the Development and Demolition of Urban Villages in the Chinese Peri-urban Area', *Urban Studies*, in press.

Wu, F. and Webster, C. (eds.) (2010) *Marginalization in Urban China: Comparative Perspectives*, Basingstoke: Palgrave Macmillan.

Wu, F., Xu, J. and Yeh, A.G-O. (2007) *Urban Development in Post-reform China: State, Market and Space*, London: Routledge.

Xiang, B. (2004) *Transcending Boundaries: Zhejiangcun: the Story of a Migrant Village in Beijing* (J. Weldon, translator), Leiden: Brill Academic Publishers.

Zhang, L. (2001) *Strangers in the City: Space, Power, and Identity in China's Floating Population*, Stanford: Stanford University Press.

Zhang, L., Zhao, S. X. B. and Tian, J. P. (2003) 'Self-help in housing and *chengzhongcun* in China's urbanization', *International Journal of Urban and Regional Research*, 27(4): 912–37.

Zhao, Y. and Webster, C. (2011) 'Land dispossession and enrichment in China's suburban villages', *Urban Studies*, 48(3): 529–51.

Part 1

Migrants' livelihoods in urban China

2 The new-generation migrant workers in China

C. Cindy Fan and Chen Chen

Introduction

On 13 June, 2012, a 23-year-old Chinese Foxconn worker jumped to his death in the inland city of Chengdu, renewing public attention on labor suicides in China (Reuters 2012). The blight of China's migrant workers received worldwide scrutiny when 13 young workers attempted or committed suicide at Foxconn plants in Shenzhen between January and May of 2010 (Li and Tian 2010; Chan and Pun 2010). All were between 17 and 25 years old, namely, members of the post-80s generation. In response, Foxconn, along with other manufacturing plants in China that also reported labor suicides around the same time, raised wages and promised to improve working condition. Foxconn also began an aggressive plan to move its production to inland locations in order to access cheaper workers. But the latest suicide in Chengdu suggests that extreme dissatisfaction by young migrant workers is far from over.

Chan and Pun (2010) argue that:

> These better-educated-youths long for a life attuned to the times, and the city is where everything is happening. The higher their aspirations for a better future, the more obvious the contrast to their harsh reality becomes. Through various forms of protest, of which suicide is the most desperate expression, they are trying to reclaim their rights and dignity.

Similarly, Li and Tian (2010) found that the new generation of migrant workers feel more strongly than the older generation about rural – urban inequality and work safety issues. Stresses at work and personal troubles might have been conducive to extreme behaviors, but the series of suicides by young migrants highlight new-generation migrant workers as a group who are more aware of unfairness and more ready to aspire to improving their future than older migrant workers.

There is another reason to pay attention to the new-generation migrant workers – they are now the majority of migrant workers in China according to NPFPC (2008) (see also Demographic Characteristics). Both the number and proportion of new-generation migrants are expected to increase. These young migrants lack

18 *C. Cindy Fan and Chen Chen*

farming experience and aspire to be part of the urban society but they continue to face obstacles similar to those confronting older migrants (Yang 2012). In this chapter, we aim to review, summarize and highlight the characteristics of the new-generation migrant workers in China and how they are different from and similar to the old-generation migrant workers.

Definitions

"Migrant workers" (*nongmingong*), in the Chinese context, refers primarily to individuals who are from rural areas, have a rural registration (*hukou*), and are working outside their village and town (Li and Tian 2010). For the sake of simplicity, in this chapter we use the terms "migrants" and "migrant workers" interchangeably.

The research on migrants in China has increasingly paid attention to "new-generation" (*xinshengdai*) migrants as a group distinct from "old-generation" (*laoyidai*) migrants. The first paper that coined the term "new-generation migrant workers" might be Wang (2001). However, the usage, criteria and definitions of the terms are not consistent. To add to the confusion, other terms such as "first-generation" (*diyidai*) and "second-generation" (*di'erdai*) are also used and sometimes interchangeably with, respectively, the terms "old-generation" and "new-generation." A review of the literature shows that in general, three types of criteria have been used to delineate new-generation and second-generation migrants from old-generation and first-generation migrants, as summarized in Table 2.1.

The most widely accepted criterion is age. The year 1980 is the most commonly used dividing line (migrants born in 1980 and later are commonly referred to as the post-80s[1]); they constitute the new-generation migrants[2] while those born before 1980 are considered old-generation migrants.

Age as a criterion points to four factors that set new-generation migrants apart from the older cohorts: youth, familiarity, farming, and the economic reforms. The youth factor refers to the notion that younger migrants tend to be more concerned with their future and are more resourceful than older migrants. For example,

Table 2.1 Criteria for the "new-generation" and "second-generation" migrants.

	Old-generation or first-generation	*New-generation or second-generation*	*Sample studies*
1. Age	Born before 1980	Post-80s (born in 1980 and later)	Liu *et al.* (2012); NBS (2011); Ye (2011); Yin (2010)
2. Time of first migrant work	1980s	1990s and later	Wang (2001)
3. Migrant generation	First-generation in family	Second-generation or beyond in family	Liang (2011); Xie (2010)

The new-generation migrant workers in China 19

Guan's fieldwork in Tianjin finds that the post-80s depend more heavily on smart phones and the Internet to get information, and they believe more strongly than older cohorts that "mastering knowledge and skills" is "extremely important in life" (Guan 2011). The second factor is the degree of familiarity with migrant work. Unlike the older cohorts, many of whom were pioneer migrants who tended to view migrant work as a short-term solution, the post-80s grew up already knowing and seeing migrant work as an established way of life among rural Chinese. Rather than carving out new paths, the new-generation migrants could follow the footsteps of more experienced migrants in the family and in the village. Third, the post-80s in general lack farming experience, as they typically join the migrant labor force immediately after finishing school, at a younger age than the older cohorts when they started migrant work. The fourth factor refers to China's economic reforms. The post-80s were born and grew up during a period when China pursued a path of development distinctly different from before, when rapid economic growth driven by globalization was the norm as opposed to the Maoist inward-looking development that the older cohorts experienced.

The second type of criteria for defining different generations of migrants is the timing of one's first migrant work. For example, Wang (2001) considers individuals who began migrant work in the 1980s as first-generation (*diyidai*) and those who began in the 1990s as new-generation (*xinshengdai*) migrants. Using this criterion, the old-generation and new-generation may not have a large age difference; in fact, some who began migrant work in the 1990s could be older than those who began in the 1980s. Nevertheless, regardless of one's age, prospective migrants in the 1990s had much more information about migrant work and operated in an economically more vibrant and open environment than those in the 1980s.

The third type of criteria refers to whether an individual belongs to the first generation in the family to do migrant work. That is, children of first-generation migrants who engage in migrant work can be considered second-generation migrants (Liang 2011; Xie 2010). This definition is akin to one used in the literature on international migration, namely, second-generation immigrants are children of first-generation immigrants (Portes *et al.* 2009). But that literature considers individuals born in the destination country to first-generation immigrants as the second-generation, whereas in the Chinese context being born in the destination is usually not part of the definition of the second-generation.

There are certainly overlapping characteristics among new-generation and second-generation migrants defined using the three criteria described above. For example, both the post-80s migrants and the children of first-generation migrants are younger, lack farming experience, and grew up being familiar with migrant work as a concept and practice and with the economic reforms. In addition, children of first-generation migrants have observed and experienced first-hand, from their parents, migrant work as a way of life.[3]

Since age seems to be the most commonly accepted criterion, much of the following discussion focuses on the post-80s as the general definition for the new-generation migrants and does not specifically make a distinction between new-generation and second-generation migrants.

Size

Table 2.2 highlights a sample of studies that report the size of the new-generation migrants defined by age.

Despite the different definitions for migrant workers and the different age criteria used in the above studies, most report that the new-generation migrants are already accounting for more than half of all migrant workers in China. According to a survey issued by the Policy Research Office of the State Council in 2006, of the 120 million migrant workers in China, 61 percent were aged 16–30, 23 percent were 31–40 years old, and 16 percent were 41 years old and above (NPFPC 2008). The 2009 Migrant Worker Monitoring Survey, carried out by the National Bureau of Statistics (NBS 2011) with a sample of 68,000 rural households across all 31 provinces, shows that migrant workers, defined as those who had done migrant work for more than six months in 2009, totaled 145 million (see Figure 2.1). Of those, 58 percent were aged 16–29. These numbers have been cited in many government reports (e.g., NBS 2011; ACWF 2011; ACFTU 2010). In addition, the 2009 NBS report shows that the older the age, the less is the number of migrant workers and the smaller is the proportion of migrant workers relative to

Table 2.2 Sample studies on the new-generation migrant workers.

Age	Size	Proportion (of all migrant workers)	Definition of migrant workers	Sample studies/ sources	Year
16–30 (born between 1976 and 1990)	73 million	61%		Survey by the Policy Research Office of the State Council (NPFPC 2008)	2006
16–29 (born between 1980 and 1993)	85 million	58%	Migrated for more than six months	Migrant Worker Monitoring Survey by NBS (2011)	2009
Post-80s	100 million	60%		Vice Minister Tang Renjian (Zhao 2010)	February 2010
16–30 (born between 1980 and 1994)		47%	Agricultural *hukou*; employment status is "employed," "housework" or "unemployed"	Survey by the National Population and Family Planning Commission (NPFPC) (Duan and Ma 2011)	May 2010

The new-generation migrant workers in China 21

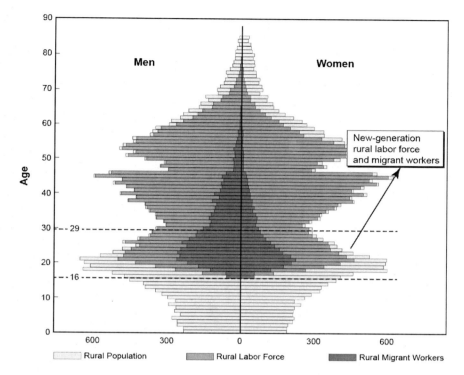

Figure 2.1 Age structure of rural population, rural labor force, and rural migrant workers.
Source: NBS (2009).

total rural labor force, reinforcing the NPFPC report's findings. The decline in number and proportion of migrant workers with increasing age suggests two phenomena. First, the younger the rural Chinese, the more likely he or she participates in migrant work. In other words, a larger proportion of the post-80s than the older cohorts have engaged in migrant work. Second, some of the old-generation migrants have retired or left the migrant labor force, thus disappearing from the category of migrant workers.

In the same vein, the younger the rural Chinese, the less likely they choose to remain in agriculture in their home village and the more likely they choose non-agricultural migrant work. As shown in Figure 2.2, among the 20–29 age group, the percentage of agricultural work locally, non-agricultural work locally, and non-agricultural migrant work is respectively 37.6 percent, 13.2 percent, and 49.3 percent. The respective percentages for the 30–39 age group are 51.8 percent, 20.8 percent, and 27.4 percent.

More recently, in February of 2010, Tang Renjian, the Vice Minister of the Office of the Central Leading Group on Financial and Economic Affairs,

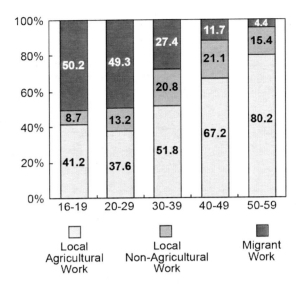

Figure 2.2 Choice of work among rural labor force of different ages.
Source: NBS (2011).

commented in a press conference that the post-80s accounted for 60 percent of the 150 million migrant workers (Zhao 2010). In May 2010, the National Population and Family Planning Commission (NPFPC), which defined migrant workers as individuals who have agricultural *hukou* and whose employment status is "being employed," "housework," or "unemployed," conducted a national-level survey of migrant workers. Among the sample of 102,596 migrant workers in that survey, those aged between 16 and 30 accounted for 47 percent (Duan and Ma 2011); still a large proportion that deserves special attention.

Demographic characteristics

Sex

The findings on gender balance among migrant workers vary considerably because studies tend to focus on certain age groups and certain specific locations. Nonetheless, it is generally agreed that there were more men than women among older migrants. For example, Yue *et al*'s survey in Shenzhen conducted in 2005 shows that 66 percent of the old-generation migrant workers (born before 1975) are male. Also, most studies find that the sex ratio among migrants has declined over time. In other words, female migrants have increased in number at a rate higher than male migrants. In fact, some studies have found that women outnumber men among the new-generation migrants.

The new-generation migrant workers in China 23

According to Wang *et al.* (2011) and drawing from the 2005 One-Percent Population Sample Survey, the proportion of men among the old-generation migrants is 20 percent points higher than that of women. However, in Wang's own survey conducted in 2010 in four major destination cities in Shandong, the percentage of women is 6.8 points higher than men among the new-generation migrant workers (Wang *et al.* 2011). Based on the Special Survey on the New Generation Migrant Workers in 10 Provinces conducted by the National Bureau of Statistics (NBS 2011), respectively 26.9 percent and 40.8 percent of the old-generation migrants and the new-generation migrants are female. According to the All-China Women's Federation's 2011 survey on the new-generation migrant workers, 45.2 percent are male and 54.8 percent are female (ACWF 2011). Drawing from the 2000 census data on the floating population in Guangzhou, the number of women in the 15–24 age group was significantly larger than the number of men, as reflected by a very low sex ratio of 67.17 (Ye *et al.* 2003).

The increased proportion of women among the new-generation migrants underscores changes in migrants' household structure. As migrant work has become a way of life in rural China, it is increasingly acceptable for wives to join their migrant husband, even entailing leaving their children behind to be raised by grandparents. Studies have shown that "sole migration" involving one spouse used to be the dominant model among older migrants but that "couple migration" is increasingly practiced among the younger generation of migrants (Fan 2011; Fan *et al.* 2011).

Educational attainment

As expected, the new-generation migrants are better educated than the old-generation migrants. Table 2.3 summarizes the findings from several recent studies. The new-generation migrants received on average 1–2.2 more years of education than their old-generation counterparts. The average years for the new-generation migrants vary between 8.9 and 10.9, suggesting that most of them have attended senior high (including vocational school) or beyond the officially mandatory nine years of education. This is in contrast to the old-generation migrants whose average years of 7.6–8.8 suggest that junior high rather than senior high was their norm.

Liu and Cheng's (2008) survey in Wuhan provides some specifics about the range of educational attainment. They find that while the average years of schooling of the first-generation migrants is 7.6 years, 31 percent of them are illiterate or semi-illiterate, suggesting a large range of educational attainment. Although the second-generation migrants' average education level is only 1.3 years higher than that of the first-generation migrants, nearly 90 percent of the former have attended junior high or above, 25 percent have attended senior high and 10 percent have finished it. In other words, not only do the second-generation migrants have higher levels of educational attainment, their range is smaller than that of the first-generation migrants, suggesting increased equity of educational opportunities over time.

24 *C. Cindy Fan and Chen Chen*

Table 2.3 Average number of years of education among old-generation and new-generation migrants.

Old-generation	New-generation	Sample studies	Year of study (region)
9.1 (entire floating population in Guangdong)	10.9	Wu and Xie (2006)	2006 (Dongguan)
7.6	8.9	Liu and Cheng (2008)	2008 (Wuhan)
7.8	9.9	Li and Tian (2010)	2009
8.8	9.8	NBS (2011)	2009
7.6 (old-generation: 45+) 8.4 (middle-generation: 31–45)	9.8	Duan and Ma (2011)	2010

National level studies by Li and Tian (2010) and NBS (2011) produce similar findings. Based on the Chinese General Social Survey conducted in 2009 by the Institute of Sociology of the Chinese Academy of Social Sciences, which interviewed 7,100 households from 28 provinces, Li and Tian (2010) report 7.8 years and 9.9 years as the average years of education of, respectively, old-generation and new-generation migrants. Respectively, 8.8 years and 9.8 years of education for the old-generation and new-generational migrants (NBS 2011). Among the new-generation migrants, 9 percent have attended vocational schools and 6.5 percent have attended college; while the respective percentages for old-generation migrants are only 2.1 percent and 1.4 percent.

Dividing migrant workers into three age categories, Duan and Ma (2011) found that the average educational attainment for the old-generation, middle-generation, and new-generation is, respectively, 7.6 years, 8.4 years, and 9.8 years (see Table 2.3). Among the new-generation migrants, illiteracy is basically eradicated, and 5 percent have gone to college.

Yet, despite the improved educational attainment from the old-generation to new-generation migrants, the latter still lag significantly behind urban residents and lack the skills that enable career development in cities (Duan and Ma 2011). Moreover, most urban jobs require educational levels and skills beyond what an average new-generation migrant affords. According to All China Federation of Trade Unions, 60.2 percent of jobs in the urban labor market in 2009 require education levels at or above senior high, but only 30 percent of the new-generation migrants have received equivalent levels of education (ACFTU 2010). In addition, 56.6 percent of urban jobs require vocational and professional skills that only 20 percent of the new-generation migrants have. ACFTU (2010) estimates that only 30 percent of the new-generation migrants will have the capacity to have stable and long-term employment in the city. The mismatch between migrants' skills and urban labor demand is clearly a factor in their (in)ability to settle down.

Marital and household structure

Unlike the old-generation migrants many of whom were married and had older children when they first did migrant work, the new-generation migrants are more likely to be faced with issues of dating, marriage, reproduction, and raising young children than the old-generation migrants (Duan and Ma 2011). By virtue of their younger age, the new-generation migrants are more likely single than the old-generation migrants. According to NBS's 2009 Migrant Worker Monitoring Survey, only about 30 percent of the new-generation migrants are married. Yin (2010) finds that despite the long duration that the new-generation migrants spend in cities, their marriage radius is similar to the rural norm, namely, within the home county.

Among the new-generation migrants who are married and have children, their children tend to be young. The 2010 Floating Population Monitoring Survey conducted by NPFPC reports that among the married new-generation migrants, 85 percent have children younger than 15 years of age. Duan and Ma (2011) illustrate further the differential burdens of supporting children among married migrants of different ages: the new-generation migrants have the youngest children; but the middle-generation migrants (aged 31–45) have more children to support; while migrants older than 45 are less concerned with supporting children than their own need in old age.

Although it is generally assumed that the new-generation migrants are more likely to migrate with their spouse and children than to leave them behind, compared with the old-generation migrants, very few studies produce findings on how the two generations differ in terms of family and household structure. Yue et al.'s (2010) survey of migrants in Shenzhen is an exception, which reports that, respectively, 24 percent and 50 percent of the old-generation migrants leave behind their spouse and children, compared with, respectively, 6 percent and 19 percent of the new-generation migrants. The percentages are small in part because the survey did not distinguish between singles and married.

Two studies focused on the married new-generation migrants highlight their tendency to bring the spouse and children to the city. Based on a special survey on new generation migrant workers, NBS reports that 59.4 percent of the married new generation migrants are engaged in so called couple migration where both husband and wife are migrant workers (NBS 2011). According to the 2011 Migrant Workers Survey conducted by All-China Women's Federation (ACWF 2011), 78.1 percent of the married new-generation migrants work in the same city as the spouse. The same survey shows that 42.7 percent of the children of the married new-generation migrants live with both migrant parents; 15.5 percent live with one of the migrant parents; and 39.5 percent live with the left-behind elders in the home village. The sum of the first two (58.2 percent) suggests that the majority of the married new-generation migrants have brought their children to the city. The high proportions of couple migration and migrant children hint that the new-generation migrants have greater desire and capacity than the old-generation to settle down in cities.

In short, the old-generation and new-generation migrants differ in terms of gender balance, education, and marital and household structure. Most of the old-generation migrants are men, but among the new-generation migrants, women are accounting for increased shares. The old-generation migrants typically have not finished junior high, whereas most of the new-generation migrants have finished junior high. The new-generation migrants are younger and more likely single than the old-generation migrants. Among the married migrants, the new-generation is more likely than the old-generation to bring their spouse and children to the city.

Migration characteristics

Age of first migration

The new-generation migrants tend to start migrant work at a much younger age than the old-generation migrants. According to NBS's 2010 survey, the average age at which the old-generation first started migrant work is 33.7, compared with 20.6 among the new-generation migrants, and 17.2 among the post-90s migrants (NBS 2011). Starting migrant work at such different points in one's life cycle is clearly related to differences in farming experience and migration characteristics.

Farming experience

Studies have found that nearly a quarter of the new-generation migrants have never farmed (Wang 2001; Liu and Cheng 2008; NBS 2011). By virtue of the relatively early age at which the new-generation migrants start migrant work, their farming experience is much more limited and much shorter than that of the old-generation migrants. Typically, the new-generation migrants start migrant work immediately or shortly after they finish school. Unlike the old-generation migrants who typically worked for years as a farmer before doing migrant work, the new-generation migrants practically skip the full-time farming phase of the life cycle. In fact, it is quite common for the old-generation migrants to return to the village for an extended period of time in order to farm before pursuing migrant work again (Fan 2009), a practice less frequently seen among the new-generation migrants.

The new-generation migrants' lack of farming experience has raised some concerns. Wang (2001), for example, points out that they are "farmers without farming experience." Here, the term "farmers" refers to their status as rural Chinese (*nongmin*) without urban *hukou* rather than their occupation. But of greater significance is the sustainability of their livelihood. Given that the new-generation migrants have limited farming experience and skills, and that they have little desire to farm (see Leaving or Staying, below), what will happen to them if migrant jobs dwindle?

Motivation for migrant work

Because agriculture is a poor source of livelihood and because of the lack of non-farm employment opportunities in China's countryside, to both the old-generation and new-generation migrants, the primary goal of migrant work is to increase income. The old-generation migrants count on migrant work to improve their living standard and enable them to "earn some money, build a house, marry a wife, and raise children" (ACFTU 2010). At the same time, research has noted that, in addition to economic gain, the new-generation migrants are also motivated and attracted by the urban lifestyle and potential for development in the city (Wu and Xie 2006).

Industry and occupation

While most migrant workers continue to concentrate in low paid, less prestigious, labor-intensive and manual jobs, the old-generation and new-generation migrants differ in their industries and occupations (Duan and Ma 2011). The old-generation migrants are engaged in a variety of jobs – agriculture, wholesale, retail, catering, construction, and manufacturing – whereas the new-generation migrants are heavily concentrated in manufacturing (Duan and Ma 2011; Liu and Cheng 2008; Cheng and Yao 2005; NBS 2011). In particular, fewer new-generation migrants work in agriculture and construction. Generally, the younger the migrant, the more likely he or she is working in manufacturing versus other sectors (Cheng and Yao 2005).

As discussed earlier, it is not uncommon for the old-generation migrants to continue to farm, through returning home for planting and/or harvesting or even for an extended period of time. According to NBS (2011), in 2009, 29.5 percent of the old-generation migrants participated in farming, versus only 10 percent among the new-generation migrants. While it may be appropriate to refer to some of the old-generation migrants as farmer-cum-migrant, most of the new-generation migrants are far from being a farmer from an occupational point of view.

There is also evidence that the new-generation migrants are more selective about jobs. According to NPFPC's 2008 New Generation Migrant Workers Report (NPFPC 2008), while jobs that are physically demanding, low-paid, socially inferior and lacking career developments were the norm for the old-generation migrants, they are no longer attractive to the post-80s migrants. Instead, the new-generation migrants are asking for equal economic opportunities and equal pay as urban residents, various kinds of insurance, education opportunities for their children, and vacation time, all unimaginable demands only a few years ago. Moreover, the new-generation migrants may organize to quit jobs as a group, resulting in a massive shortage of non-skilled workers (*mingonghuang*) in some industries. According to the Shanghai Labor and Social Security Bureau, labor-intensive enterprises in clothing processing, hotel, and the catering industry, which require low-skilled workers for their labor-intensive jobs, have faced recruitment problems as a result (NPFPC 2008) .

Job search and changes

While social networks through fellow-villagers, relatives and friends continue to be the main sources of information for migrant jobs, the new-generation migrants are also increasingly using formal channels such as advertisements and employment agencies (Liu and Cheng 2008; Cai *et al.* 2009).

What set the old-generation and new-generation migrants apart are job changes – the new-generation migrants change jobs more often than the old-generation migrants. Yue *et al.* (2010) report 1.99 and 1.71 as the average number of jobs held by, respectively, the old-generation migrants and new-generation migrants. Given the difference in age and migration experience between the two groups, those numbers suggest that the new-generation migrants change jobs more readily than the old-generation migrants. It seems that job-hopping reflects the new-generation's strategy to get better jobs, perhaps at the expense of stability, a quality lacking among migrant jobs to begin with (Zhou and Sun 2010).

Wu and Xie (2006) find that the most common reasons for the new-generation migrants to change jobs are, in order of importance, "better pay" (87 percent), "conflict with management" (53 percent), and "closer to spouse and partner" (35 percent). Among those who change jobs, only 31 percent remain in the same line of work; and, "higher income" (98 percent) is a much more powerful motivation than "the same line of work" (55 percent). Yet, frequent job changes across industries and occupations may disrupt skill and human capital accumulation. Fu and Tang (2009) note an inversed-U relationship: the initial job changes result in improvement in social mobility, but such improvement has decreasing marginal returns such that after a certain number of job changes the migrant will experience negative selectivity in destination, occupation, migration reason and job search. They argue that while job changes reflect migrants' agency and capacity in the labor market, a high frequency of job changes adversely affects their economic return.

Destination

The new-generation migrants tend to move over longer distances and be more engaged in inter-provincial (as opposed to intra-provincial) migration than the old-generation migrants (NBS 2011). According to NBS (2011), in 2009, respectively 53.7 percent and 46.8 percent of the new-generation and old-generation migrants participated in interprovincial migration. The new-generation seem to have a stronger preference than the old-generation for large cities: their respective percentages for working in cities at or above the prefecture level are 67.4 percent and 57.5 percent. In terms of geography, Cheng and Yao (2005) report that the new-generation migrants most commonly work in the eastern or coastal region.

Working hours and pay

Despite the differences between the new-generation and old-generation migrants described above, the amount of time they spend on work is similar. NBS (2011) reports 26 days per month and nine hours per day of work for both generations. Based on the "Floating Population Monitoring Survey" conducted by NPFPC in 2010, Duan and Ma (2011) find that both old and new generations work more than

The new-generation migrant workers in China 29

six days a week and more than 10 hours a day. In other words, the new-generation migrants are as hard working as their old-generation counterparts.

Despite the younger age and shorter migrant work span of the new-generation migrants, their wages are not significantly lower than those of the old-generation migrants. According to NBS (2011), the average monthly income of the old-generation and new-generation migrants is, respectively, 1,543 Yuan and 1,328 Yuan. Li and Tian (2010), on the other hand, report 1,088 Yuan and 957 Yuan as the respective average monthly income of the new-generation and old-generation migrants in 2009.

Categorizing migrants into three generations, Duan and Ma (2011) find that the average monthly income for the new-generation, middle-generation and old-generation migrants is, respectively, 1,660 Yuan, 1,800 Yuan and 1,550 Yuan (see also Table 2.3). What is notable from the above studies, is that migrant wages do not necessarily increase with age. Far from it, age may even be an adverse factor, given the labor-intensive and manual nature of most migrant jobs. To better explain wage differentials, education, work experience, industry and occupation must be taken into consideration. For example, the middle-generation migrants in Duan and Ma's (2011) study have the highest income because they have better work experience than the new-generation migrants and are more highly educated than the old-generation migrants. But the wage differentials vary by sector. In the manufacturing and hotel and restaurant sectors, the middle-generation migrants have the higher income. Among wholesale and retail jobs, the old-generation migrants have the highest income. In services, the new-generation migrants receive the highest wages.

Remittances and consumption

Most studies find that the new-generation migrants send back less remittances than the old-generation migrants (Liu and Cheng 2008; NBS 2011). NBS (2011) reports that in 2009 the new-generation migrants send on average 5,564 Yuan annually or 37.2 percent of their income while the old-generation migrants send 8,218 Yuan or 51.5 percent of their income. The large discrepancy is quite consistent across income groups and begs the question if the new-generation migrants have significantly different consumption patterns than the old-generation.

According to NPFPC (2008), the first-generation migrants are thrifty and they save up as much as they could in order to support their children, whereas the new-generation migrants tend to spend as much as they earn – sometimes referred to as "the moonlight group" (*yueguangzu*). NPFPC cites a survey conducted by the Guangdong Youth and Juvenile Research Centre which shows that 68.5 percent of the second-generation migrants spend most of their income on food, clothing, housing and transportation in the city but seldom send remittances home. Another survey conducted by the China Youth and Children Research Centre reports that the post-80s spend a large proportion of their earnings on social expenses (NPFPC 2008).

On the other hand, the new-generation migrants' expenditures do not necessarily suggest that they are irresponsible spenders. Liu and Cheng (2008) argue that those expenditures are driven by the rising cost of living in the city. Also, compared with the old-generation migrants, the new-generation migrants return to the home village less frequently and for shorter durations. Duan and Ma (2011) observe that the new-generation migrants' greater expenses on clothing, grocery, leisure and entertainment as compared to the old-generation migrants reflect not only the former's youth but also their adoption of the urban lifestyle. Nevertheless, the amount that they spend on leisure and entertainment, averaging 116.5 Yuan a month, is still significantly lower than urban residents of a similar age.

In summary, the migration characteristics of the new-generation and old-generation migrants are quite different. The new-generation begin migrant work at a younger age, usually immediately or shortly after finishing junior high, having had little or no farming experience. They pursue migrant work for both economic and self-development reasons. They are more likely than the old-generation to move across provincial borders and work in manufacturing rather than agriculture and construction. They change jobs often and work as hard as the old-generation. Their migrant income is similar to the old-generation but they send back less remittances, taking on to a certain degree an urban lifestyle while still not spending irresponsibly.

Living in the city and the countryside

Housing

Since the new-generation migrants are more likely than the old-generation migrants to be single and work in manufacturing, it is not surprising that a larger proportion of the former live in factory dorms (Yue *et al.* 2010). The old-generation migrants, on the other hand, tend to live in the "community," mixed with urban residents and other migrants, where housing units for couples and families are more readily available. Despite the shorter duration of migrant work among the new-generation migrants, their living conditions are better than the older-generation (Duan and Ma 2011).

Citing NBS, ACFTU (2010) reports that 20.1 percent of migrants in 2006 were living in rented or owned homes, and the percentage increased to 37.7 percent in 2010, suggesting a growing desire for better housing. However, low migrant wages render the vast majority of migrants incapable of owning a home in cities and towns. ACFTU estimates that less than 10 percent of migrants may ultimately be able to afford purchasing a home in the destination city, provided that their income increases at a rate similar to that of housing price.

Social protection

Compared with the old-generation migrants, who are less aware of their rights and are more tolerant of exploitation, the new-generation migrants have a stronger sense of and desire for protecting their rights and labor safety (ACFTU 2010). Duan and Ma (2011) report that the proportion of the new-generation migrants who have a signed contract with the employer is slightly higher than the old-generation migrants but is still lower than 50 percent. Their participation in social security is as low as the old-generation migrants and their participation in retirement plans and health insurance designed for migrants in the city is still less than 10 percent. Their participation rate in rural-based health and retirement insurance is in fact lower than the old-generation and middle-generation migrants, suggesting a weaker rural identity with decreasing age of the migrants.

Assimilation and integration

The new-generation migrants' social identity and integration into the city is one of the burning questions in China. For example, scholars have used various indices to measure the level of integration of the new-generation migrants (Liu and Cheng 2008; Wang *et al.* 2011; ACWF 2011). From a policy-making perspective, attention on young migrants' identity and integration may highlight situations where the lack of community support and the feeling of insecurity and unfairness result in extreme behaviors such as the Foxconn suicides (Wu and Xie 2006; Wang 2001).

Migrants' social network is a useful indicator of their adjustment to city life (Liu *et al.* 2012). Zheng *et al.* (2011) found that after controlling for other factors, the new-generation migrants who are more highly educated can better adapt to the city, whereas the *hukou* status does not significantly impact how well migrants adjust to city life. In general, research has found that the new-generation migrants have a stronger desire than the old-generation migrants to integrate into the city. For example, the new-generation migrants usually master the local dialect – an important step toward integration – better than the old-generation migrants. Wu and Xie's (2006) survey in Dongguan shows that all the new-generation migrants can speak Mandarin without heavy accents and they sometimes even speak to their fellow-villagers (*laoxiang*) in Mandarin, instead of their native dialect. Among the new-generation migrants in that survey, 58 percent can speak Cantonese, 66 percent understand it, and everyone wants to learn it; a sign of their desire to integrate into Dongguan and the Guangdong province where Cantonese is the local dialect. In a study of urban villages in Guangzhou, Liu *et al.* (2012) found that the new-generation migrants are more likely than the old-generation migrants to draw on networks across class, kin, and place of origin, although the native place and the urbanite–migrant dichotomy remain central to defining their social networks.

Leaving or staying?

It is commonly believed that the new-generation migrants have stronger desire than the old-generation migrants to stay permanently in the city. However, evidence to support this notion is scant. Yao's (2010) survey in the Yangtze River Delta area shows that 70 percent of both the new-generation and old-generation migrants want to eventually return to their hometowns. But they differ in the job preference after returning: 63.5 percent of the new-generation migrants want to work in non-agricultural sectors, 13 percent points higher than the old-generation migrants; whereas the proportion of the old-generation migrants who want to work in agriculture is 12 points higher than the new-generation migrants. In a similar vein, Yue *et al.* (2010) find that the younger the migrants, the more likely they intend to return to non-agricultural work (versus agriculture). Given that non-agricultural work is mostly not available in the migrants' home village, it is not surprising that Duan and Ma (2011) find that most of the new-generation migrants who desire to "return" want to return to their region of origin (*jiaxiang*) but not the rural village (*xiangxia*). In the towns near the home village, for example, these returnees can continue working in non-agricultural jobs such as manufacturing.

Summary and conclusion

Since the 1980s, China has transformed itself from a relatively immobile society to one where migrant work has become the way of life for rural families and where migrant workers are part of the urban everyday life. The new-generation migrants, most commonly defined as migrant workers born in 1980 or after, are now accounting for the majority of the migrant population. In this chapter, we have highlighted the ways in which the new-generation migrants are distinct from their older and earlier counterparts.

Due to the increase of the share of women among migrants, the new-generation migrants have a more balanced sex ratio than the old-generation migrants. The new-generation migrants are more highly educated than the old-generation migrants and most have finished junior high. Still, the former are not sufficiently skillful for the urban labor market other than the manual, labor-intensive and less desirable jobs, and their wages remain low. Compared with the older generation, the new-generation migrants are younger and more are single. Among those who are married, the new-generation are more likely than the old-generation to bring the spouse and children to the city.

Growing up observing migrant work as a way of life in the village and for their parents, the new-generation tend to start migrant work at a younger age, typically immediately or shortly after finishing junior high. As a result, they have had little or no farming experience. The new-generation are more likely than the old-generation to work in manufacturing than other sectors, perhaps because the former are younger. The young-generation migrants also have stronger aspirations compared with their previous generation migrants. They move longer distances than the old-generation migrants and are more likely than the old-generation to move across provincial borders. They change jobs frequently in pursuit of better pay, and they work as hard as the old-generation, with long working days and weeks.

The new-generation migrants earn about the same as the old-generation migrants but they send home less remittances. This difference begs the question whether the new-generation are increasingly assuming an urban lifestyle. Several other observations support this notion. Compared with the old-generation, the new-generation tend to pursue migrant work, not only for the purpose of economic return but also for self-improvement and the urban experience. Their expenses are increasingly accounted for by consumption such as food, clothing, housing, transportation, leisure and entertainment, although their spending is still much lower than the average urbanite. The new-generation migrants are also less tolerant of low pay and poor working conditions and are more ready to express their frustration, including resorting to protests and even suicides.

All the above suggests that the new-generation migrants are more ready and have a larger capacity than the old-generation migrants to chart out a more promising future. It is not clear, however, if such a path entails settling down permanently in the city. The skill level and income of the new-generation migrants remain low; the cost of living in big cities is not within reach. The new-generation migrants are more aware of their rights but their participation in health and retirement insurance is low. They have wider social networks in the city than the old-generation migrants but they continue to rely heavily on native-place ties. Compared with the old-generation migrants, many of whom plan to return to farming in the rural village, the new-generation migrants' preference is more likely "returning" to towns near their native place, where they can engage in non-farm work.

Notes

1. In the Chinese language "post-80s" or "after 1980" usually also includes individuals born in the year 1980.
2. Yin (2010) and Ye (2011) refer to them as second-generation migrants.
3. Some studies have focused on the impact of parents' migration experience on how new-generation migrant workers integrate into cities, e.g., Liang (2011).

References

ACFTU (2010) *Guanyu xinshengdai nongmingong de yanjiu baogao* (*A research report on the new generation migrant workers*). Online. Available: http://news.xinhuanet.com/politics/2010-06/21/c_12240721.htm (Accessed June 21, 2010) (in Chinese).
ACWF (2011) *Xinshengdai jincheng wugongzhe hunlian shenghuo zhuangkuang* (*A report on the romantic relationship of the new generation migrant workers*). Online. Available: http://www.chinafc.org.cn/index.php?option=com_flexicontent&view=items&cid=59:2011-12-06-02-52-38&id=1413:2011-12-08-16-13-33&Itemid=58 (Accessed August 16, 2011) (in Chinese).
Cai, H., Liu, L. and Wan, X. (2009) *Chengshihua Jincheng Zhong De Nongmingong: Laizi Zhujiang Sanjiaozhou De Yanjiu (Migrant Workers in the Urbanization Process: A Study from the Pearl Delta Area)*. Beijing: Shehui kexue Wenxian Chubanshe (Social Science Literature Publisher) (in Chinese).
Chan, J. and Pun, N. (2010) "Suicide as protest for the new generation of Chinese migrant workers: Foxconn, global capital, and the state," *The Asia-Pacific Journal*, 37(2): 10.
Cheng, A. and Yao, S. (2005) "Nongmingong de daiji chayi fenxi (An analysis on the generation difference of migrant workers)," *Tongji yu Juece (Statistics and Decision)*, 10: 61–3 (in Chinese).

Duan, C. and Ma, X. (2011) "Dangqian woguo xinshengdai nongmingong de xin zhuang-kuang (A study on the new situation of the younger generation of farmer-turned migrant)," *Renkou yu Jingji (Population & Economics)*, 4: 16–22 (in Chinese).

Fan, C. C. (2009) "Flexible Work, Flexible Household: Labor Migration and Rural Families in China," in Keister L. A. (ed.), *Work and Organizations in China after Thirty Years of Transition*. Durham: Emerald Press, pp. 381–412.

Fan, C. C. (2011) "Settlement intention and split households: Findings from a survey of migrants in Beijing's urban villages," *The China Review*, 11(2): 11–42.

Fan, C. C., Sun, M. and Zheng, S. (2011) "Migration and split households: A comparison of sole, couple, and family migrants in Beijing, China," *Environment and Planning A*, 43(9): 2164–85.

Fu, P. and Tang, Y. (2009) "Dao U xing guiqi yu xinshengdai nongmingong de shehui liudong – Xinshengdai nongningong de liudongshi yanjiu (Inverted U-shaped trajectory and the social mobility of new generation peasant-workers)," *Zhejiang Shehui Kexue (Zhejiang Social Sciences)*, 12: 41–47 (in Chinese).

Guan, Y. (2011) "Xinshengdai nongmingong xiandaixing tezheng guankui - jiyu Tianjing diaocha de bijiao yanjiu (The modernity characteristics of the new generation migrant workers)," *Dangdai Qingnian Yanjiu (Contemporary Youth Research)*, 11: 19–25 (in Chinese).

Li, P. and Tian, F. (2010) "The new generation migrant workers: Social attitudes and behavioral choices," *Chinese Journal of Sociology*, 31(3): 1–23.

Liang, H. (2011) "Shengmin licheng shijiao xia de 'liudong' yu 'liushou' – Dierdai nongmingong tezheng de duibi fenxi (Migrating-out and left-behind in the view of life course: A comparative analysis of the characteristics of the second-generation migrant workers)," *Renkou Yanjiu (Population Research)*, 35(4): 17–27 (in Chinese).

Liu, C. and Cheng, J. (2008) "Di'erdai nongmingong chengshihua: Xianzhuang fenxi yu jincheng cedu (The urbanization of the second generation migrant workers: an analysis on the current progress)," *Renkou Yanjiu (Population Research)*, 32(5): 48–57 (in Chinese).

Liu, Y., Li, Z. and Breitung, W. (2012) "The Social networks of new-generation migrants in China's urbanized villages: A case study of Guangzhou," *Habitat International*, 36(1): 192–200.

NBS (2010) *2009 Nongmingong jiance diaocha baogao* (*2009 migrant worker monitoring report*). March 19. Online. Available: http://www.stats.gov.cn/tjfx/fxbg/t20100319_402628281.htm (Accessed March 19, 2010) (in Chinese).

NBS (2011) *Xinshengdai nongmingong de shuliang, jiegou he tedian* (*The size, structure, and the characteristics of the new generation migrant workers*). March 10. Online. Available: http://www.stats.gov.cn/tjfx/fxbg/t20110310_402710032.htm (Accessed March 10, 2011) (in Chinese).

NPFPC (2008) "A study of the 'post-1980' migrant farming workers," *China Population Today*, 25(4). Online. Available: http://www.cpdrc.org.cn/en-cpdrc/en-cpt/en-CPT-20081231-2.html (Accessed December 31, 2008).

Portes, A., Fernández-Kelly, P. and Haller, W. (2009) "The adaptation of the immigrant second generation in America: A theoretical overview and recent evidence," *Journal of Ethnic and Migration Studies*, 35(7): 1077–104.

Reuters (2012) *Foxconn Says Plant Worker Jumps from Apartment*. June 14. Online. Available: http://www.reuters.com/article/2012/06/14/us-foxconn-idUSBRE85D0S120120614 (Accessed June 14, 2012).

Wang, C. (2001) "Xinshengdai nongcun liudong renkou de shehui rentong yu chengxiang ronghe de guangxi (The relationship between social identities and rural-urban integration among the new generation migrant workers)," *Shehuixue Yanjiu (Sociological Studies)*, 3: 63–76 (in Chinese).

Wang, D., Liu, B. and Lou, S. (2011) "Xinshengdai nongmingong de chengshi rongru – Kuangjia jiangou yu diaoyan fenxi (The integration of new generation of migrant workers into urban society – framework and analysis)," *Zhongguo Xingzheng Guanli (Chinese Public Administration)*, 2: 111–5 (in Chinese).

Wu, H. and Xie, G. (2006) "Xinshengdai nongmingong de tezheng, liyi suqiu ji juese bianqian – jiyu dongguang tangxiazhen de diaocha fenxi (The new generation migrant workers' characteristics, demands and social identities)," *Nanfang Renkou (South China Population)*, 21(2): 21–31 (in Chinese).

Xie, G. (2010) *Xinshengdai Nongmingong Wenti Gaisu (A Review on the New Generation Migrant Workers Issues)*. December 10. Online. Available: http://www.ccyl.org.cn/10hlzc/bzlt/201012/t20101210_436912.htm (Accessed December 10, 2010).

Yang, J. (2012) "Cohort effect or structural effect: Triple disadvantages of young rural migrants in economic integration into the host society in China," in *Population Association of America Annual Meeting*. San Francisco. Online. Available: http://paa2012.princeton.edu/papers/120546.

Yao, J. (2010) 'Lu zai he fang': Xinshengdai nongmingong fazhan quxiang yanjiu ('Where will the future be?': A comparative study on old generation and new generation's future settlement plan)," *Qingnian Yanjiu (Youth Research)*, 6: 31–38 (in Chinese).

Ye, J., Peng, Q., Huang, C., Liu, J. and Zhong, Z. (2003) "Guangdong liudong renkou yanjiu (A study on floating population in Guangdong)," *Nanfang Renkou (South China Population)*, 18(1) (in Chinese).

Ye, P. (2011) "Nongmingong de chengshi dingju yiyuan yanjiu (Residential preferences of migrant workers)," *Shehui (Society)*, 31: 153–169 (in Chinese).

Yin, Z. (2010) "Di'erdai nongmingong hunyin jiating wenti tanxi (The characteristics of marriage and family of the second generation migrant workers)," *Zhongguo Nongcun Guancha (China Rural Survey)*, 3: 13–23 (in Chinese).

Yue, Z., Li, S., Feldman, W. M. and Du, H. (2010) "Floating choices: A generational perspective on intentions of rural-urban migrants in China," *Environment and Planning A*, 42: 545–62.

Zhao, X. (2010) *Xinshengdai Nongmingong Shuliang Yue Yigeyi (The Population of the New Generation Migrant Workers is about 100 Million)*. February 1. Online. Available: http://www.dzwww.com/rollnews/finance/201002/t20100201_5569823.htm (Accessed February 1, 2010).

Zheng, Z., Liu, F. and Ma, K. (2011) "Xinshengdai wailai wugong renyuan chengshi shiyingxing: Geren yinsu yu zhidu yinsu de bijiao – Jiyu zhongshanshi de shizheng yanjiu (The city adaptation of new generation migrant workers: Analysis of individual factors and institutional factors – Based on the empirical research of Zhongshan)," *Renkou Yanjiu (Population Research)*, 35 (3): 76–83 (in Chinese).

Zhou, D. and Sun, X. (2010) "Group Differences among nongmingong: A follow-up ethnographic case study," *International Journal of Business Anthropology*, 1(1): 79–94.

3 Chinese cities and mobile livelihoods
Migration, risk and social networks

Heather Xiaoquan Zhang

Introduction

> History is in part personal history. The two are inseparable – however tiny the individual is in the shape of things.
>
> Peter Townsend (2000: 5)

This chapter tells a story of a migratory family of the Hui Muslim national minority from the Qinghai-Tibet Plateau in north-western China, who ran a Lanzhou-style beef noodle restaurant in the northern coastal city of Tianjin in the late 2000s. It traces the geographical and social mobility of the family at different points of the life course involving three and in particular the older two (grandparent and parent) generations' unremitting efforts to sustain and secure livelihoods through initiating, engaging in and developing a range of entrepreneurial endeavours within the north-western region and later beyond it.[1] It applies a risk concept in 'restorying',[2] examining and interpreting the meanings of the experiences of the migratory family as narrated and understood by its members, and aims to explore themes such as uncertainties, risks and contingencies in the context of China's transition,[3] as well as relationships between livelihoods, social networks, agency and public policy interventions.

The research employs an actor-oriented perspective as developed by Long (2001) and represented by the 'Wageningen School' (Scoones 2009: 173). This perspective directs attention to the crucial importance of carefully recording, delineating, understanding and interpreting the life worlds of individuals, families and communities and the meanings attached to these so as to investigate the ways in which micro-level complex social relationships, interactions and negotiations on the one hand, and larger historical, institutional and structural forces on the other are in constant interplay and mutually influencing, simultaneously enabling and constraining human agency. The emphasis on agency in the actor-oriented perspective requires a microscopic focus on local processes given that social change and transformations (as well as continuities) are understood as emerging 'from the differential responses (that are embedded in various social practices) to changing social, economic, cultural and political conditions' (Ye *et al.* 2009: 175). This has generated spatial and temporal dynamics, and the wider structural forces are considered as not only governing and conditioning, but more importantly, as being reshaped by human actions, as individuals actively and constantly seek and process information and knowledge of diverse sources, reflect on their experiences, build and extend their social networks, engage in social exchanges, interactions, and struggles based on their perceptions of their interests and differing systems of norms and values, and formulate tactics and strategies in their dealings with other actors and institutions (Long 2001).

This theoretical framework guides the study's methodological choice, which combines ethnographic fieldwork with a qualitative, longitudinal, narrative analysis. The longitudinal methodology involves 'restorying', documenting and delineating the livelihood trajectory of the family, and the various entrepreneurial endeavours and business branches attempted by its members across generations through a narrative analysis, which is understood as 'a spoken or written text giving an account of an event/action or series of events/actions, chronologically connected' (Czarniawska 2004: 17). Such a methodological combination allows the voices of the 'grassroots' social actors – members of the migratory family in this case – to be heard, and their lived experiences and life worlds as linked to the themes of the research to be unfolded. The chapter explores the meanings of the narrative about the major events in the livelihood trajectory of the migratory family, situating these in a broader context of rapid and profound societal and institutional change. It intends to provide insights into the complex processes, economic, social, historical and political changes and cultural practices, spatial, temporal and generational dynamics and social trends, and the making of history through the eyes and narratives of the social actors involved. The primary data of the research is drawn from the accounts narrated by members of the 'extended Hui family'– one belongs to the parent generation (father) in his late 40s (Figure 3.1) and two male cousins in their late teens and early twenties (Figure 3.2). The data was collected during my fieldwork in Tianjin between 2008 and 2009 investigating issues in relation to social protection in the informal economy in China and how risks and insecurity were perceived, experienced and dealt with by diverse actors, including in this case the informal workers themselves.[4] The empirical data is supplemented by secondary materials, including for example academic works published in English and Chinese, and relevant information retrieved from the Internet.[5] Such data helps to provide the necessary broader backdrop against which the micro-level social actions and cultural practices constituting the life worlds of the migratory family as social agents are being unfolded.

Given the massive scale of rural–urban migration witnessed in post-reform China and the associated problems with the recognition of their equal citizenship rights in urban settings (*cf.* State Council 2006),[6] this research is of policy relevance. The narrative analysis allows the voice of migrants, who are frequently marginalised, stereotyped and treated as 'the other' in urban China in the dominant discourse and many official or popular representations,[7] to be heard, not only to bring about greater diversity in 'voice' and representation and affirmative image, but also to raise awareness for researchers, relevant policy arenas and the general public of the aspirations, experiences and needs of migrant individuals,

Figure 3.1 Narrator of the story: Mr Ma the business owner.
Source: Photograph taken by author (Sept. 2009).

Figure 3.2 Narrators of the story: the male cousins of the Ma family.
Source: Photograph taken by author (Nov. 2008).

Chinese cities and mobile livelihoods 39

families and communities. This may result in closer public attention and targeted policy interventions to effectively tackle the problems of unequal distribution of risk and insecurity among different social groups, and the unmet needs and unevenly realised rights for the migrant population, if a more equitable and harmonious society is to be constructed, and social solidarity and cohesion are to be fostered.

The analysis, through its methodological approaches, also involves an examination of the larger structural forces that have helped shape personal experiences, and wider economic and social change mirrored in individuals' life histories. By doing so, it intends to extend the existing scholarship on China's rural–urban migration and migrants' social protection via a fresh risk lens, and to contribute to a 'field in the making' (Chase 2005: 651), namely the emerging qualitative, longitudinal and narrative research methods in social sciences in general and in China's migration studies in particular.[8]

This chapter first explores the subtheme of entrepreneurship and risk. It then turns to discuss the changing nature of Chinese society in relation to risk after the inception of market reforms, and how the state and society have responded to this, as well as its implications for livelihood and its security. This is followed by an examination of the ways in which familial ties and social networks serve for migrant individuals and families as a buffer against risk and its materialised form – contingencies. The strategies employed by migrant individuals and families as social actors to deal with risks and insecurity in their daily livelihood struggles are analysed throughout the chapter. Finally, I draw tentative conclusions based on the earlier discussions.

Entrepreneurship and risk

I first met the male cousins of the Ma family in a market area near the entrance of a university in Tianjin in late 2008, where the family were running a restaurant specialising in Lanzhou-style beef noodles (*Lanzhou niurou lamian*) (see Figure 3.1). Lanzhou is the capital city of Gansu Province bordering the Qinghai-Tibet plateau in the north-western part of the country and the Lanzhou-style beef noodle, initiated and developed by people of the Hui national minority in Gansu over 200 years ago, is a famous dish of local tradition and flavour in the region. However, most of the people promoting and selling the product and related services to the seaboard cities are actually from rural Qinghai rather than Gansu, which is sometimes attributed to the greater risk-taking entrepreneurial spirit of the former (Cao 2008).

The Ma family are among the Qinghai Hui minority people. Their native village is in the Qinghai-Tibet plateau's Huzhu Tu Autonomous County, inhabited by a number of nationalities, including Tu, Hui, Tibetan and Han, some 20 kilometres to the Northeast of Xining city, the provincial capital. When I first chatted with the cousins, the older one, Dragon, was 22 and his younger cousin, Tiger, 18.[9] Both started work after finishing the compulsory nine-year schooling, and by the time we met Dragon had worked for some six years and Tiger three years, and the family had run the beef noodle restaurant in Tianjin since mid-2007. Still in his early twenties, Dragon had a lot of work experiences: as a security guard in Xining, an assistant at a local petrol station, and an operator of a loader before starting to work in the family-run business away from his hometown. He is also married at a rather young age of 20 in compliance with local customs, and has a three-month-old daughter. Both cousins, after starting their economic career as migrants, had travelled around the country in search of livelihood opportunities: from the Northwest to the Southeast and then the Northeast to the Northwest and back to Southeast again until settling in the northern city of Tianjin.

Dragon's parents have two children: an older son (Dragon) and a daughter (Pretty) who is five years younger. With only two *mu* of land[10] for the family of four, Dragon's father decided to take up non-agricultural jobs locally well before the family left their native village for the eastern coastal region. He worked as a truck driver and then as a manager of a petrol station. '*He is a wage earner (na gongzi de)*', Dragon stressed – obviously a wage earner was in a much better position than a farmer who only lives off his land in terms of making a living for the family:

He didn't work for state-owned enterprises though, it was a private business. Further back, our family had big vehicles and made a lot of money. Later however, some *minor disaster* (*xiao zai xiao nan*) occurred, and as a consequence we couldn't sustain the business, so the vehicles were sold to fence away such a *minor disaster*, and my father had to start working for others (*dagong*).

(Dragon's narrative, emphasis added)

At this point, Dragon tried to change the subject, but his consciously assumed casual manner in referring to the 'disaster' as *minor* aroused my curiosity. I continued this line of our conversation by asking for an example and in response, Dragon started an account of a calamitous event that took place over 12 years ago, which profoundly affected the nature and direction of the family's livelihood. Dragon's tale was later corroborated and complemented with greater detail from his big uncle, the older brother of his father, 46-year-old Mr Ma (*Ma Laoban*) – a respectable form of address used by local small business owners neighbouring theirs at the market street in Tianjin – when we met a year later in 2009. The story goes as follows.

The older generation of the Ma family, that is, Mr Ma's father and uncle, initiated a small-scale transport business shortly after the inception of the market reforms. Still in their prime, the brothers actively engaged in non-farming activities based on their awareness of the local conditions, and in response to the new central and local government policies to encourage rural economic diversification. Through pooling funds from several members of the extended family, they first gathered enough money to buy a tractor in 1980 as the authorities of their own and neighbouring villages attempted to lease or sell collectively owned assets

Chinese cities and mobile livelihoods 41

such as agricultural machinery at local 'auctions' at the start of agricultural decollectivisation.

The business developed and in a short span of three years, the family accumulated sufficient capital to purchase a second-hand truck. The decision to engage in and expand the transport business was strategic and opportune. Most of Qinghai Province is geographically located on the plateau, remote and difficult to access by train,[11] and thus its economy, communities and people have heavily relied on highways for travel and transport locally and beyond. Major highway networks connecting Qinghai and its neighbouring provinces (Qinghai-Tibet, Qinghai-Xinjiang, Qinghai-Gansu, Qinghai-Yunnan) were constructed during the earlier period of the People's Republic from the 1950s to the1970s. The initiation of market reforms injected new dynamics into the local and regional economy, and therefore helped create a high demand for local transport skills and services. The Ma family took full advantage of the emerging opportunities by starting and developing their business against such a background, and this livelihood strategy soon began to bear fruit: half a year after they bought the truck, they took a bank loan and bought a brand new vehicle. By the mid-1980s, Mr Ma, then in his early twenties, learnt to drive the big vehicle and the family business continued to grow: in 1989, taking a second bank loan they bought a tanker, which allowed them to switch the transport business from carrying construction materials to petrol.

This decision, however, involved considerable commercial and social risk as was borne out by the later development of the event (the *minor disaster* referred to by Dragon above). Yet it was a strategic move based solidly on the actors' knowledge of the local geographical and market conditions, comparative advantages, new government development policies and plans targeting the region, and the livelihood opportunities potentially arising from all this.[12] The native village of the Ma family, though located in a remote and poorer region in the Northwest with low quality of land and low per capita area of land use, is nonetheless endowed with certain advantageous conditions within the region: it is located in relatively low-lying land and in proximity to the provincial capitals of Xining and Lanzhou. The area benefits from extensive transportation networks constructed in the Mao era as a result of state-targeted infrastructural investment, and during the reform period, the networks have continuously been upgraded and extended to meet the increasing need of rapid industrialisation regionally and nationally. The greater mobility of people, flow of goods and information, and the increasing openness of the region to and interactions with other parts of the country since the early 1980s, coupled with a sense of urgent need felt by individuals and families to make a living through diversifying livelihoods and expanding income channels, meant that many local people, particularly those with better education and skills, consciously and persistently sought information on and took advantage of the emerging livelihood opportunities within and beyond the region. Better livelihood chances associated with the market, however, involve risk of various kinds, and the Ma family was typical among the local rural entrepreneurs in respect of playing out their agency and taking risks in their attempt to enhance livelihoods by maximising gains and striving for business success.

42 *Heather Xiaoquan Zhang*

Over the years, the originally familial-tie-based relationships as the sole source of support and resources were gradually extended and reconfigured to entail wider social and business relations, which also included formal institutions, such as banks for loans in the process of business development and expansion. The new generation carefully nurtured personal friendships, established trust, which was often based on their ethnic and religious association with the Hui Muslim identity, and extended social networks through economic and social exchanges and interactions. All this played an important role in obtaining useful information and business contracts, in the development of their economic careers, and particularly in their decision on switching to the new branch of business: in 1989 the Ma family moved their business to Golmud (*Ge'ermu*), a city in central Qinghai 870 kilometres to the west of their native village. They set up a petrol station and engaged in the long distance trade of petrol between Xinjiang, which possesses rich oil and gas reserves, and Qinghai which, strategically located at the centre of the vast Northwest, serves as the gateway to Tibet and the transport hub in the region.

Between the late 1980s and mid-1990s after relocation to Golmud, the Ma family largely focused on running the combined petrol transport and filling station business. They did well; by 1996 the business had grown from a mini-enterprise of transporting construction materials via an old tractor and a few family hands in the early 1980s into a private transport firm having four tankers of the best make of the day, a cross-country jeep and a petrol station employing a number of workers, with a total asset value of over 500,000 Yuan, which represented substantial wealth by the local and national standard of the time.[13] The family, by the account of the third generation Dragon, had become the 'top well-off one locally' (*dangdi shou fu*).

All this and the prospects of the family business were changed overnight when a disastrous fire took place on 15 October 1996. Mr Ma's narrative brought us back to that moment:

> In the early evening of that day, a big fire occurred.... The tankers parked in the courtyard of the residential area caught fire.... We lost everything – four tankers together with petrol, property, the business. Workers and relatives staying in that corner were injured and about 20 households in the neighbourhood were affected: some people suffered from burns and houses were damaged to varying degrees. Six people suffered from serious burns, and we immediately sent them to a local hospital for treatment. We spent some 70,000 Yuan on their hospitalisation in less than a week. In the end we didn't have any money left so once the injured became a bit better they were discharged and brought back to the native village ... my uncle and two tanker drivers were disabled by the burns ... we lost our livelihoods, and the fruit of our 16 years' hard work vanished into thin air overnight.

Risks and formal institutions

This destructive event seemingly specific to the Ma family in effect points to a wider and general issue, namely the real danger of *risk* and *contingency* faced by

Chinese cities and mobile livelihoods 43

people in their daily lives and the threat such risk poses to livelihood. This raises the question of how to deal with such risk in a society witnessing rapid and drastic change in the structure and organisation of production, consumption and other activities. Before the reforms, China could be deemed a 'low risk society' in both economic and societal senses. Tight state control over the economy and society, public and collective ownership of the means of production, and the non-existence of a free market meant that the state and collectives were the main bearers of most risks involved in economic and social activities, and therefore for ordinary citizens there was a sense of certainty and security in most aspects of their lives, including in particular employment and social security. The rapid penetration of market forces into all aspects of everyday life following the initiation of the reforms combined with many structural changes in the economy and society has fundamentally altered such conditions. While reform has brought greater livelihood opportunities and choice, as evidenced in the Ma family's entrepreneurial success, this has gone hand-in-hand with increasing uncertainties, risks and livelihood insecurity also evidenced in the havoc wrought upon the family business and livelihood.

While societal change has happened at an unprecedented pace, the development and establishment of appropriate institutions for managing change and the risks accompanying it have been slow and, in most cases, lagged behind (Allison 2001). This is reflected in Dragon's account of buying insurance against risk and contingencies for the family business:

> We living in the remote area couldn't get much information (*xinxi bise*). Even at the present day people over there are much less informed than people here. Back in 1996 there were even no mobile phone services in our native village.... Due to lack of information, my parents were unclear about insurance. People didn't understand, they didn't have much knowledge about it.... Perhaps they didn't insure, or only insured part of it and the insurance they bought didn't cover accidents like this. The insurance companies may not have come to our area to sell and explain their products. Because of this we had to bear the huge loss ourselves.
>
> (Dragon's narrative)

Commercial insurance, such as property and automobile insurance, as a risk transfer or risk mediating instrument developed slowly in China even in large coastal cities until the late 1990s. This was further compounded by delayed government legislation. For instance, China only promulgated its first Insurance Law in 1995 and the regulation on compulsory automobile insurance was only introduced in July 2006. Implementation, enforcement and compliance with laws and regulations were uneven across the country, with remote regions lagging far behind in this respect. There was also a low sense of risk formed in people who grew up in a relatively secure environment before the market reforms together with a mentality or belief that the state would still ultimately act as an underwriter of risks for private businesses.[14] Furthermore, there was a low awareness and unavailability of insurance information and services in remote and peripheral regions, as indicated

44 *Heather Xiaoquan Zhang*

in Dragon's remarks above. All this rendered the Ma family vulnerable to the damage wrought by the actualised risks, namely the devastating accident.

Social security schemes, especially health insurance, which function as a risk-pooling social safety net covering contingencies such as serious illness-induced healthcare expenses and would help rural people absorb external shocks, alleviate harm caused and protect livelihood through strengthening resilience, collapsed in the wake of agricultural decollectivisation as the provider, the rural commune, was dismantled in the early 1980s. In the years that followed healthcare services at all levels underwent de facto privatisation and functioned much like for-profit entities as the central government considerably reduced its financial commitment to supporting healthcare in a process of fiscal decentralisation and overall commoditisation of post-reform Chinese society (Duckett 2010). While hospitals and medical personnel were motivated to charge increasingly high user fees for medicine and healthcare services in the wider context of the health system reforms, a growing number of people, in particular rural residents, ceased to be covered by any health insurance, generating new health risks and vulnerabilities. This was evidenced in the sharp rise of the proportion of people not covered by health insurance in rural China: from 10 per cent in the late 1970s to 87 per cent in 1993 and 84 per cent in 1998 (Development Research Centre of the State Council 2005), combined with increasing healthcare costs: *per capita* annual expenses on personal health services rocketed from 11 Yuan in 1978 to 442 Yuan in 2002 – an increase of 4,400 per cent (Blumenthal and Hsiao 2005: 1167). Serious attempts to rebuild the rural public health system in the form of a New Cooperative Medical Scheme (NCMS) were not initiated nationally or in the native village of the Ma family until quite recently: the NCMS was piloted in parts of rural China in 2002 followed by gradual nationwide implementation in 2008. As a result there was no formal institutional support available for the Ma family back in 1996 in coping with the calamity as materialised commercial and social risks.

Social networks as an informal social safety net

The huge financial loss and the injuries of family members, employees and neighbours together with the high medical expenses and considerable debt incurred led to the bankruptcy of the Ma family's transport business, causing a serious setback in the entrepreneurial ambitions and economic careers of the middle generation Ma brothers. In the absence of any formal institutional support or protection, the Ma brothers resorted to the reserves of their original social networks for emotional and material support – the familial ties and personal friendships that they had possessed and maintained through their close 'backward linkages': at the end of 1996 the Ma family withdrew from Golmud to their native village. For the Ma brothers the home village played multiple roles in providing basic security and an informal social safety net: as a fall-back base equipped with tangible resources, where their small landholdings, housing, and other personal or familial assets were 'stored' allowing for meeting the immediate subsistence needs of their families and themselves; and as a source of intangible resources providing comfort

Chinese cities and mobile livelihoods 45

and warmth for them, meeting their practical, psychological and emotional needs, and giving them a sense of attachment, relatedness, roots, identity and belonging.

After relocation to Golmud in the late 1980s, the Ma brothers had maintained close links with their native village through regular visits, making significant contributions to the support of their retired parents, and investing substantially in housing, other facilities and personal relationships with members and leaders of the local Hui community, with which they were associated religiously and ethnically. In other words, the contractual relationship and socio-economic exchange, instead of being terminated or lying dormant during their physical absence, were actively and carefully maintained through constant social interactions. This sustained the validity, as well as the associated rights and obligations of their membership of the extended family, and the Hui and village communities at the origin. For example, in return for their financial support, the elderly took care of the school-age children, including Dragon and Tiger, farmed the land, looked after the houses and other familial assets for the Ma brothers, kept them informed of new developments in the village and its vicinity, and helped foster links with the village elite on their behalf. According to the younger generation, Dragon and Tiger, their parents each own a large courtyard comprising seven to eight rooms. Spacious well-built houses are expected for members of the local elite, with which the Ma family became identified alongside their business success, and serve as a status symbol. When they suffered from the accident and the subsequent career setback, the reserve tangible and intangible resources, including the physical, economic, social and symbolic capital, were all mobilised to mediate the devastating impact and alleviate the external shocks. As another example, the Ma family houses, in addition to their practical functions, were used as collateral for loans required for repaying the debts and future risk-taking, migratory entrepreneurial endeavours as demonstrated in the later development of the Ma family enterprise.

The following three years between 1997 and 2000 were a period of great economic uncertainty and a real test for the Ma family in terms of their adaptability, endurance, resilience and will. Initially Mr Ma behaved like a defeated man: he stayed at home doing little but feeling sorry for himself at the broken business and the irrevocable loss. After a year's rest, the sheer need for survival combined with an undying dream of becoming rich or an aspiration for making a better life for his family and himself drove him on to another entrepreneurial endeavour: in 1998 he organised a team of more than a dozen villagers and set off on a gold-digging venture in the Altai (Aertai) Mountains in northern Xinjiang bordering Kazakhstan, Russia and Mongolia, thousands of kilometres to the northwest of his native village. The start capital of some 10,000 Yuan was gathered through pooling borrowed funds, though this time from a larger pool of his expanded locally based networks of relatives and friends. The decision to take the risk was as before firmly rooted in the actors' indigenous knowledge of the rich natural resources reserves in the vast Northwest region: the Altai are known as the 'Mountains of Gold' (meanings in Mongolian and Turkish languages). However, Mr Ma was unlucky this time: while there was gold in the Altai Mountains, his team of migrant workers could not bear the climate in northern Xinjiang, which was very

46 *Heather Xiaoquan Zhang*

different from what they were used to in Qinghai. The strong moral obligations intrinsically entailed in spatially and religiously based close kinship ties and social relations rendered Mr Ma unable to continue.

In 2000, the family moved to Shanghai and started a restaurant business. This move, while apparently driven by sheer survival needs, was in effect carefully thought through and planned based on the key actors' knowledge about available resources, reflections on and learning from the earlier setbacks and lessons, an appraisal of uncertainties and risks involved in inter-regional migration as measured against potential opportunities and gains, and longer-term considerations of security and livelihoods to include the middle generation's old-age support and the coming-of-age younger generation's employment and earning prospects. According to Mr Ma, by 2000, 60–70 per cent of his *laoxiang* friends, or the place-based, religion- and ethnic-associated personal relations and kinship ties, including two of his other younger brothers, had gone outside of the Qinghai-Tibet Plateau to run Lanzhou beef noodle restaurants in different parts of the country, and one of his younger brothers did business in Shanghai. He also reckoned that the risk involved in running a catering business in large cities could be considered 'zero' (*ling fengxian*) compared with that involved in the previous petrol transport and trade business. Balancing all this combined with a close familial linkage serving as an initial stop-over support and point of contact, and again pooling borrowed funds as initial capital, Mr Ma, together with his business partner brother, went to Shanghai to embark on a completely new business – the Lanzhou beef noodle restaurant.

All this happened within a larger context of drastic economic restructuring, particularly in the state-owned enterprise sector, and rapid social change and transformations. By the early 2000s, the Chinese economy had evolved out of the public ownership–dominated structure into a much more diverse one with public, private and mixed ownership contributing about one-third of national GDP each (Lu 2002: 1). The pluralisation of ownership went hand in hand with the continued growth of an informal urban economy, which constituted much of the rapidly expanding private sector, in which most rural–urban migrants found themselves engaged. Systemic reforms of the formal institutional mechanism for controlling population mobility – the household registration system – were piloted, giving rise to easier access to urban markets and facilities by rural–urban migrants. In addition, an urban housing market gradually emerged in the process of the housing reforms, providing the possibility of residential rental housing for people in cities, particularly for non-locals and rural migrants with families. In the meantime, the extant regional development gaps continued to widen, manifested partly in increasing income discrepancies between both urban and rural areas and inland and coastal regions.[15] Information and knowledge of such wider structural change and macro-processes, and the associated new livelihood possibilities and opportunities, were first transferred through the actors' close and extended social networks, and then selected and processed at the receiving end by the Ma brothers as social agents to inform migration decision making: this time it involved inter-provincial, inter-regional, cross-country movement towards the eastern coastal metropolis, where this tenacious Hui family would stage a new phase of the 'play' in respect of their migratory entrepreneurial experiences and endeavours.

Conclusion

This chapter applies an actor-oriented theoretical perspective and a risk concept to the study of rural–urban migration in China through qualitative longitudinal, narrative investigation methods. It analyses a particular case – the Ma family of the Hui ethnic minority from the Qinghai-Tibet Plateau in a remote region of the country. Through closely and carefully documenting, delineating and analysing the narratives of the members of the family across two generations, it details a livelihood trajectory which is full of life's vicissitudes, unravelling a process which involves sustained generational and translocal efforts to seek alternative livelihoods (to farming), to develop, expand and deploy a wide range of social resources in dealing with hardships, difficulties, uncertainties, risks and contingencies, as well as with other actors, social relations and institutions, in an attempt to meet basic material, sociocultural and emotional needs, as well as to create a better life for its members in rural and urban settings. The chapter argues that human agency as manifest in the entrepreneurship, ingenuity, diligence and resilience of the Ma family, despite the differences and variations in individuals' life courses and experiences, echoes, to some extent, the spirit, aspirations and struggles of the wider migrant population. It is this industrious and enterprising group who have individually and collectively helped bring about China's economic and social transformations over the past three decades, and thereby recreated its urban and rural development landscapes. It is in this sense that we can still claim today that '*people are the real drivers in the making of history*' (Mao 1945 [1991: 1031]).

The fresh risk concept employed in the analysis directs attention to the changing nature of risk, vulnerability and insecurity in Chinese society during market transition, revealing patterns and trends of the increasingly unequal exposure to and distribution of risk among different social groups. The chapter argues that while China has increasingly turned from a 'low risk' to a 'high risk' society in all the term's conceivable senses, and its consequences have been experienced and borne by millions of ordinary people, as exemplified in the story of the Ma family, policy interventions and institutional responses to the emerging situation in relation to risk are far from sufficient. While carefully nurtured and expanded informal social networks, together with negotiated and maintained membership rights in local communities, served as intangible social resources for the Ma family to cushion and mitigate the impact of the disastrous accident as actualised commercial and social risks, to strengthen resilience and gradually recover from the external shocks, such individual efforts and strategies work best only in conditions where the state takes effective action in the form of public and social policy making to protect the livelihoods and rights of all its citizens in transcendence of the existing institutional arrangements and barriers based on urban and/or rural differentiations or hukou status. Improving, expanding and enhancing formal social protection mechanisms and their accessibility by socially disadvantaged

48 Heather Xiaoquan Zhang

groups – rural–urban migrants in this case – are therefore vital for mobile liveli-hoods to be sustainable and secure, and ultimately flourishing, which, as demon-strated in this chapter, have affected and will continue to affect both urban and rural families and communities, and for reaching the officially declared goal of constructing a fair and just society of social harmony and common prosperity.

Acknowledgement

I would like to thank the British Academy for providing me with a grant in 2011, which enabled me to trace the migratory family to their home village. My grati-tude also goes to the editors of the volume, in particular Professor Fulong Wu, for carefully editing the original manuscript.

Notes

1. The family's recent migratory history can be divided into two phases. The first phase, between 1980 and 2000, was characterised by intra-regional migration to-gether with various business ventures closely linked to the supply and demand of the local and regional economy. The second and ongoing phase since 2000 has been marked by inter-regional, across country movements in a new line of business tar-geting the catering market of the coastal metropolis. This chapter's focus is on the first phase.
2. Creswell (2007: 56) defines 'restorying' as 'the process of reorganising the stories into some general type of framework ... and then rewriting the stories to place them within a chronological sequence'.
3. Contingency is defined as actualised risk (Taylor-Gooby 2001: 200).
4. It was estimated that nearly 60 per cent of the total urban labour force of 283 million, i.e. 168 million people were employed in the informal economy in 2006, of which rural migrants constituted the main part (Hu and Zhao 2006; Huang 2009).
5. Follow-up fieldworks were conducted in 2010 and 2011. Due to the limit of space, however, the new data are not incorporated in the chapter.
6. It is estimated that there are about 120 million migrants working in China's towns and cities, and if those employed in township and village enterprises (TVEs) are included, there could be as many as 200 million or more migrants (Huang 2009; State Council 2006: 3–4). Behind these 200 million migrants are about 300 million members of their families in urban or rural settings, and together they account for some 40 per cent of China's entire population of 1.3 billion (Zheng and Huang-Li 2007: 18). This suggests that some two-fifths of Chinese people are directly or indirectly affected by migration and its related issues.
7. For example, in the *suzhi* (human quality) discourse, therewith 'low or poor quality' (suzhi di or suzhi cha) is often linked to such background and occupations as rural or blue-collar labour, including migrants, and insofar as gender is concerned, the female sex, particularly women of the 'lower class' (*cf.* Anagnost 2004; Jacka 2004; Murphy 2004).
8. For a brief discussion of the predominance of the quantitative survey methods in social science research in China, see Judd (2009).
9. For confidentiality, pseudonyms are adopted for the interviewees.
10. One *mu* is equivalent to 1/60 of a hectare.
11. The full-range of the Qinghai-Tibet Railway linking Xining and Lhasa through Golmud was constructed in the early 2000s and officially started operation on 1 July 2006.

Chinese cities and mobile livelihoods 49

12. For comprehensive discussions of the historical, economic and social development in Qinghai, including its physical and human geography, see Goodman (2004) and Li *et al.* (2004).
13. Qinghai's rural *per capita* net income in 1997 was only 1,320 Yuan (Anon 1999).
14. This was evidenced during my interviews with Mr Ma, who, while recollecting his experiences in relation to the 1996 disaster, said a few times, 'the government didn't help us'.
15. In 2000, the urban–rural income gap further expanded: with an urban annual *per capita* income of 6,316 Yuan versus its rural counterpart of 2,253 Yuan, the urban–rural ratio (with rural as 1) rose to 2.80:1 as against the mid-1980s' figure of 1.8:1 (Wang 2004). Regional income gaps manifest in the *per capita* income ratios between the western and eastern regions: between 1980 and 2002 this ratio rose from 1:1.92 (with western region as 1) to 1:2.59, respectively (Wang 2004), suggesting that the largest disparities have occurred between the coastal and inland areas, which to a large extent also overlaps with urban–rural inequalities.

References

Allison, T. (2001) 'Risks and rewards in China's insurance market', *Asia Times*, 16 February. Online. Available: http://www.atimes.com/reports/CB16Ai01.html (Accessed 30 April 2010).

Anagnost, A. (2004) 'The corporeal politics of quality (sushi)', *Public Culture*, 16(2): 189–208.

Blumenthal, D. and Hsiao, W. (2005) 'Privatisation and its discontents – The evolving Chinese health care system', *New England Journal of Medicine*, 353(11): 1165–70.

Chase, S. (2005) 'Narrative inquiry: multiple lenses, approaches, voices', in Denzin N. K. and Lincoln Y. S. (eds.) *The Sage Handbook of Qualitative Research*, 3rd edn. Thousand Oaks: Sage, pp. 651–80.

Czarniawska, B. (2004) *Narratives in Social Science Research*, London: Sage.

Cao, M. (2008) *Lanzhou noodles (lanzhou lamian)*. Online. Available: http://www.aibang. com (Accessed 30 April 2010).

Creswell, J. W. (2007) *Qualitative Inquiry and Research Design*, 2nd edn. Thousand Oaks: Sage.

Development Research Centre of the State Council (2005) *An Evaluation of and Recommendations on China's Health System Reform*, Beijing: DRC, State Council.

Duckett, J. (2010) *The Chinese State's Retreat from Health: Policy and the Politics of Retrenchment*, London: Routledge.

Goodman, D. (2004) 'Qinghai and the emergence of the West: nationalities, communal interaction, and national integration', *The China Quarterly,* 178: 379–99.

Hu, A. and Zhao, L. (2006) 'China's informal employment and informal economy in the transition period (1994–2004)' (Woguo zhuanxingqi fei zhenggui jiuye yu fei zhenggui jingji), *Qinghua daxue xuebao (zhexue shehui kexue ban)*, 21(3): 111–9. (in Chinese).

Huang, P. C. C. (2009) 'China's neglected informal economy: reality and theory', *Modern China,* 35(4): 405–38.

Jacka, T. (2004) 'Approaches to Women, "Quality", "Empowerment" and "Development"', paper presented at the international symposium Women's Experience of Policy and Institutional Change in Rural China, Institute of Contemporary Chinese Studies, University of Nottingham, UK, 14–15 April.

Judd, E. R. (2009) 'Starting again in rural west China: stories of rural women across generations', *Gender & Development*, 17(3): 441–51.

50 *Heather Xiaoquan Zhang*

Li, X., Yeung, Y. M. and Qiao, J. (2004) 'Historical legacy and future challenges', in Yeung, Y. M. and Shen, J. (eds), *Developing China's West: A Critical Path to Balanced National Development*, Hong Kong: The Chinese University Press, pp. 27–49.

Long, N. (2001) *Development Sociology: Actor Perspectives*, London: Routledge.

Lu, J. (2002) 'Social development entering into a new phase: Analysis and prospects of China's social development: 2001–2002', in Ru, X., Lu, X., Li, P., Huang, P. and Lu, J. (eds.) *The Blue Book of the Chinese Society 2002*, Beijing: Social Sciences Academic Press, pp. 1–16. (in Chinese).

Mao, Z. (1945 [1991]), 'On Coalition Government' (*Lun lianhe zhengfu*), in *Collected Works of Mao Zedong* (*Mao Zedong xuenji*), Vol. 3, Beijing: Renmin chubanshe. (in Chinese).

Murphy, R. (2004) 'Turning peasants into modern Chinese citizens: "Population quality" discourse, demographic transition and primary education', *The China Quarterly*, 177: 1–20.

Scoones, I. (2009) 'Livelihoods perspectives and rural development', *The Journal of Peasant Studies*, 36(1): 171–96.

State Council (2006) *A Research Report on Migrant Workers in China* (*Zhongguo nongmingong diaoyan baogao*), Beijing: Zhongguo yanshi chubanshe. (in Chinese).

Taylor-Gooby, P. (2001) 'Risk, contingency and the Third Way: evidence from the BHPS and qualitative studies', *Social Policy and Administration*, 35(2): 195–211.

Townsend, P. (2000) 'Post-1945 poverty research and things to come', in Bradshaw, J. and Sainsbury, R. (eds), *Research Poverty*, Aldershot: Ashgate, pp. 5–36.

Wang, M. (2004), 'The two main problems in China's modernisation process – the urban-rural gap and regional discrepancies', Online. Available: www.ccrs.org.cn (Accessed 17 March 2010).

Ye, J., Wang, Y. and Long, N. (2009) 'Farmer initiatives and livelihood diversification: from the collective to a market economy in rural China', *Journal of Agrarian Change*, 9(2): 175–203.

Zheng, G. and Huang-Li, R. (2007) (eds) *Social Protection of Migrant Workers in China* (zhongguo nongmingong wenti yu shehui baohu), Beijing: Renmin chubanshe. (in Chinese).

4 Outsiders in the city
Migrant housing and settlement patterns

Weiping Wu

Introduction

Settlement patterns are an important determinant of the future socioeconomic standing of migrants. Where and how migrants live is likely to affect their general level of satisfaction with urban living and the ease or difficulty to adapt to the new environment. Research on migrant settlement in Latin American cities reveals that new migrants (labeled as "bridgeheaders") initially seek deteriorating rental shelter. Over time, migrants generally occupy better housing – from rented rooms to self-built shanties or houses. Once this transition is made, migrants become consolidators (Klak and Holtzclaw 1993; Turner 1968). To most migrants, proximity to employment ranks high on the list of preferences and needs, as income generation and economic viability are a primary objective for them. Particularly for new arrivals with few acquaintances in the city, an initial residence within walking distance of jobs is essential (Conway 1985; Gilbert and Varley 1990). Others also point out the importance of kinship and friendship ties, acting as social institutions (Abu-Lughod 1961; Banerjee 1983; van Lindert 1991).

These global experiences of residential mobility and migrant settlement will no doubt help our understanding of trends in China. In Chinese cities, however, there are significant barriers for migrants to settle permanently. The urban–rural and local–non-local divides, to a large extent, continue to ensure that their presence is unwanted in the urban society while their labor is desired. These divides also shape their housing choices, mobility patterns, and living arrangements in the cities. Given the institutional context, what are the housing choices migrants make once in the city? What types of housing career do they follow? What are the temporal, spatial and tenure trajectories of migrant settlements? How do these patterns correlate with sociospatial transformation of Chinese cities? This chapter purports to answer these questions, by drawing results from a combination of survey and census data. Before we trace migrant housing and settlement patterns, it is important that we understand how their choices and decisions are affected by China's institutional context.

Migration and socialist institutions

Notwithstanding China's long urban history, the country remained largely an agrarian society until year 2011. But urban superiority has taken hold since the turn of the twentieth century. Despite efforts to reduce the distinction between city and countryside after the Communist Party took power in 1949, an urban–rural divide now forms the basis of the broadest kind of social inequality. Rural areas continue to have the poorest of the poor. Today, income disparity between urban and rural areas has widened – the *per capita* income of the urban resident is more than three times that of the rural resident. Such a disparity, together with a confluence of rising agricultural productivity during the initial phase of market reform and globalizing forces in urban manufactures, opened the floodgate of migration in the early 1980s. Almost 200 million migrants have left the Chinese countryside for cities since 1983. This recent migratory flow is perhaps the largest tide of migration in human history. It has become a prominent feature of China's economic transition and is changing the face of the country (Fan 2008).

But such rising mobility intersects with an institutional structure at urban destinations that separates migrants from local residents. Under state socialism (1949–79), the central government established different systems of property rights, health care, and welfare provision in urban and rural areas. Two types of citizenship have existed in effect (Solinger 1999). Whereas urban citizenship comes with full provision of social welfare, rural citizenship essentially entails self-responsibility in food supply, housing, employment and income, and lacks most of the welfare benefits enjoyed by urban residents. As such, migrants have limited access to local public schools, welfare programs, state sector jobs, and the mainstream housing distribution system. A household registration system (*hukou*), in particular, has long been associated with population management and the provision of social welfare.

Until recently, housing provision exemplified how household registration institutionalized the urban-rural divide. Housing had long been a form of social welfare to urban residents. The dominant route, prior to 1999, was through a system of low-rent public housing. This urban welfare housing system, however, did not apply to local residents with rural hukou or peasants in the countryside, who did not have access to either municipal or work-unit public housing. Traditional family houses and private housing constructed on land allotted by production brigades were the norm for them, even in rural pockets within cities.

Despite repeated calls, reform of the household registration system has been a slow process. Some cities have experimented with less drastic measures to loosen hukou's hold. One such measure introduced in 1992 was the issuance of an interim residence permit, in the name of blue-stamp hukou, that could eventually lead to permanent status. In general, the primary candidates for a blue-stamp household registration were three groups of migrants: investors, property buyers, and professional or skilled workers. The higher the administrative status of a city, the higher the price for a blue-stamp household registration would be (Chan and Zhang 1999). For instance, in Shanghai in the late 1990s, cash purchase of a housing unit

Outsiders in the city 53

worth 100,000 Yuan or more would entitle a non-local resident a blue-stamp household registration that could become permanent after five years. The size and price requirements vary by geographical location within the city. The variations are: 320,000–350,000 Yuan for central areas, 180,000 Yuan in three inner suburban districts, and 100,000–160,000 Yuan in other suburban areas (Wu 2002). The practice of issuing blue-stamp hukou, however, has been discontinued nationwide.

Other recent efforts to expand hukou reform include relaxing limitations on migration to small towns and cities, streamlining hukou registration in some provinces and large cities, and instituting many individual reforms aimed at addressing the abuse of migrants. In 1997, the State Council initiated an experimental program to allow rural migrants who had moved to designated small towns and cities to obtain local hukou. In 2001, the State Council expanded this program to include all small towns and cities. Since 2001, many provinces and large cities also have begun to allow migrants who satisfy certain criteria to obtain local hukou in urban areas. As with the State Council decision on small cities and towns, these measures generally require that applicants possess a "stable place of residence" and a "stable source of income." Many provincial and municipal regulations define these terms stringently, often based on educational or financial criteria (CECC 2005). Defenders of the system contend cities are unable to provide the services migrants demand in the absence of a nationwide and transferable social security network.

Almost all the large cities continue to place significant limits on eligibility for urban registration. Such unwillingness ran true even under the administration of Hu Jintao (President) and Wen Jiabao (Premier), who made fairness and reducing income disparities a hallmark of his administration. In a March 2010 report, Wen did not mention giving migrants equal treatment outside their provinces, or in China's largest cities (Reuter, 11 March 2010). While recent reforms loosen the hukou system for the more privileged migrants, they do not address the primary problem still facing most migrants: the continued linkage of hukou registration to public services. Implementations also vary in scope across cities in response to a 2003 national circular that called for local authorities to abolish discriminatory measures against migrants. The household registration system, as a result, is likely to stay in place for the near future.

Migrant housing and settlement patterns in cities

Housing reforms gradually implemented since the 1980s seem to largely overlook the needs of the migrant population in cities even though they have broadened housing choices for urban residents. A local urban hukou continues to be an important qualification for accessing several types of urban housing, particularly those that are more affordable. For instance, both the Economic and Comfortable Housing and affordable rental units are reserved for local urban residents only. On the secondary housing market where older housing units are traded, migrants can purchase housing after completing a lengthy process of official approval. Commodity housing, the only real property sector open for migrant ownership, is not affordable for most migrants. In addition, a local urban hukou is required to qualify for bank mortgages for new commodity housing. As a result of these restrictions, the urban–rural divide in housing continues even after rural migrants move to cities.

Given this larger context, migrants display different housing behaviors from not only local residents but also migrants in other developing countries. Home ownership is yet to become an attainable goal and, therefore, the security offered by housing tenure is less relevant as a motivation for migrants in making housing decisions. The large majority of them rent old housing units from local residents or stay in dormitories provided by their employers (often seen in factories and on construction sites). Overall, migrant housing conditions are poor – overcrowded, temporary, with limited amenities (e.g., kitchen and bathroom), and located in precarious environments. Very few lucky ones can afford to become home-owners. China's migrants, however, do share some behaviors with their counterparts elsewhere. Low cost and proximity to the workplace are higher priorities than physical quality and space. Accommodations are used mainly as places to sleep and prepare for the next day's labor, given the long hours most work at what are almost inevitably physically exhausting and dirty jobs.

Squatter settlements are not a viable option for China's migrants, unlike in many other developing countries (particularly in Latin America), largely due to municipal authorities' intolerance of migrant congregation and squatting. However, large migrant settlements or communities have existed in some large cities. But unlike most migrant squatter settlements elsewhere, migrants rent from local residents or live in market areas constructed by local governments or private businesses. Often called "urban villages" (*chengzhongcun*), these are neighbor-hoods created as cities expanded outward enveloping villages that were formally on the outskirts of cities. Although located physically within the city, the local peasant residents of *chengzhongcun* have rural hukou status. By virtue of this status, though, the local peasants have stakes in collective land rights. Many local peasants, therefore, expand their homes or build additional structures on their land to rent out to migrants and earn needed supplemental income. Migrants, on the other hand, have affordable housing options that suit their housing needs. In some "urban villages," migrants from the same general area of origin cluster and form a "daughter community" based on place identity.

Migrants' growing demand for housing and their limited access to the main-stream urban housing distribution system contribute to the chaotic situation of the urban rental market. As cities scramble to develop effective rental regulations, an increasing amount of deleterious building and rental activity continues, largely in the form of unauthorized construction and leasing of unsafe dwellings. This prob-lem is particularly serious in urban-rural transitional areas where land is more readily available, the migrant population is more concentrated, and local residents have more incentive to rent out rooms due to the loss of agricultural income. Even when regulations about rental housing take shape in some cities, concerns for adequate housing conditions and rental rights tend to be secondary.

Outsiders in the city 55

It is no exaggeration to say that once in the city, migrants continue to be on the move. The majority has moved at least once, while many have done so multiple times (up to ten moves) within a span of four to six years (see Figure 4.1). Such mobility behavior, however, may not be the result of voluntary or predictive actions as most migrants express little willingness to move again when asked. The frequency of moves in the first year is particularly high, with multiple moves for many. But there is a slow process of settling down for migrants, even though longer-term migrants still experience much higher mobility rates than local residents. The majority of moves are related to work, triggered by such events as job change, change in business location and completion of work projects. For migrants in the construction sector, they live and move with work. The mobility rate of self-employed migrants, such as those operating food stalls and convenience stores, also is primarily determined by their work location and how profitable that location is for business.

Migrants may be moving frequently, but not very far. Most moves are within the same general geographic area within the city (see Table 4.1). They tend to make short-distance residential moves to minimize unfamiliarity with the environment. Worse, few migrants make the transition from renters to owners even after years of living in the city (see Table 4.2). Getting stuck in the private rental sector allows little room for improving their housing conditions. The main explanation would lie with local controls, which force migrants (even those with families in tow) into more of a renter's existence than they may otherwise prefer. Specifically, the system of granting only temporary urban residence permits to migrants discourages them from making substantial investment to alter their residential choices in the city. Many, however, remit most of their income back to the countryside to build better housing for their families.

Few migrants in urban China make the transition from bridgeheaders to consolidators even after years of living in the city, unlike the case in many other developing countries. Therefore, the security offered by housing tenure (ownership) is less relevant as a motivation in making housing decisions.

Getting stuck with private rental also has implications for migrants' housing conditions. Research has shown that such rental, as well as dormitory housing, tends to have worse overall conditions than other housing types. It exposes migrants to a significantly higher level of instability, as the rental market is still immature with a lack of regulatory oversight. When migrants stay with local residents, their housing conditions improve markedly. For those migrants able to afford to buy commodity housing, housing conditions are on par with the locals (Wu 2002; Wu 2008; Wu and Rosenbaum 2008).

Inevitably there are variations among migrants. Some have gained access to limited benefits in the city by signing employment contracts with urban enterprises through official sanctions. Others with capital and skills have resorted to self-employment and prospered. But if the scenario of residential mobility is any indication of socioeconomic mobility, it is clear that most migrants are drifting in the bottom layer of the urban society. Some resort to criminal activities because

56 *Weiping Wu*

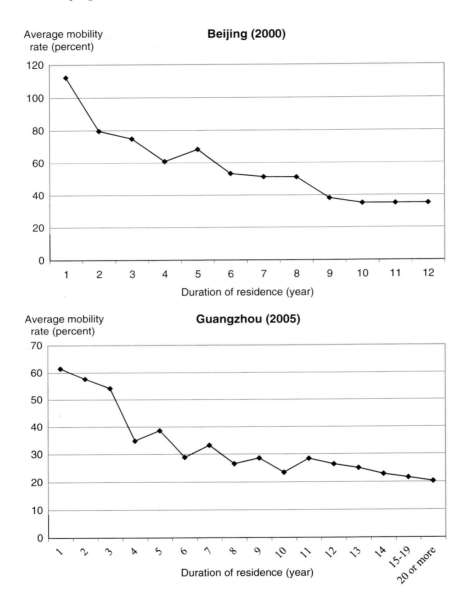

Figure 4.1 Average annual mobility rates over duration of residence.
Source: Wu (2010).

Table 4.1 Migrant spatial mobility between first and current residence by entry cohort, *c*.2000.

Entry cohort	Outward move				Inward move				Within-zone move				Total	
	Central city to inner suburb	Central city to outer suburb	Inner to outer suburb	Subtotal	Inner suburb to central city	Outer to inner suburb	Outer suburb to central city	Subtotal	Within central city	Within inner suburb	Within outer suburb	Subtotal	Number	%
Shanghai														
Before 1980	6.3	0.0	0.0	6.3	6.3	12.5	0.0	18.8	50.0	12.5	12.5	75.0	16	100.0
1980–1984	0.0	0.0	0.0	0.0	19.2	0.0	3.8	23.1	50.0	7.7	19.2	76.9	26	100.0
1985–1989	7.1	3.5	4.3	14.9	10.6	0.7	0.0	11.3	44.7	14.2	14.9	73.8	141	100.0
1990–1994	8.6	1.5	3.3	13.5	9.5	1.5	0.9	11.9	37.8	28.8	8.0	74.6	452	100.0
1995–1999	6.6	0.3	2.1	9.0	8.0	1.9	0.5	10.3	35.3	33.7	11.7	80.6	377	100.0
Total	7.4	1.3	2.9	11.6	9.3	1.7	0.7	11.7	38.3	27.8	10.7	76.8	1012	100.0
Beijing														
Before 1980	7.1	7.1	7.1	21.4	14.3	0.0	0.0	14.3	14.3	50.0	0.0	64.3	14	100.0
1980–1984	17.6	0.0	0.0	17.6	17.6	0.0	0.0	17.6	5.9	52.9	5.9	64.7	17	100.0
1985–1989	6.9	1.7	3.4	12.1	12.1	3.4	0.0	15.5	13.8	53.4	5.2	72.4	58	100.0
1990–1994	6.8	2.1	2.7	11.6	8.9	3.4	0.0	12.3	8.2	58.2	9.6	76.0	146	100.0
1995–2000	7.8	0.8	2.2	10.9	7.8	4.5	0.8	13.1	10.3	56.5	9.2	76.0	359	100.0
Total	7.7	1.3	2.5	11.6	8.9	3.9	0.5	13.3	10.1	56.4	8.6	75.1	594	100.0

Source: Wu (2010).

Table 4.2 Tenure mobility of migrants (by current housing), *c.*2000.

	Renting private housing		Renting public housing		Dorm/workshed		Staying with local residents		Other housing[a]		Total	
	Number	*%*	*Number*	*%*	*Number*	*%*	*Number*	*%*	*Number*	*%*	*Number*	*%*
Shanghai												
Previous housing												
Renting private housing	220	44.1	27	5.4	22	4.4	3	0.6	11	2.2	283	56.7
Renting public housing	20	4.0	22	4.4	2	0.4	2	0.4	1	0.2	47	9.4
Dorm/workshed	25	5.0	2	0.4	98	19.6	1	0.2	3	0.6	129	25.9
Staying w. local residents	2	0.4	7	1.4	4	0.8	7	1.4	3	0.6	23	4.6
Other housing[a]	7	1.4	3	0.6	1	0.2	2	0.4	4	0.8	17	3.4
Total	274	54.9	61	12.2	127	25.5	15	3.0	22	4.4	499	100.0
Initial housing												
Renting private housing	370	36.2	61	6.0	37	3.6	7	0.7	18	1.8	493	48.3
Renting public housing	24	2.4	23	2.3	6	0.6	2	0.2	3	0.3	58	5.7
Dorm/workshed	126	12.3	25	2.4	183	17.9	9	0.9	7	0.7	350	34.3
Staying w. local residents	27	2.6	9	0.9	15	1.5	12	1.2	10	1.0	73	7.1
Other housing[a]	19	1.9	9	0.9	5	0.5	4	0.4	10	1.0	47	4.6
Total	566	55.4	127	12.4	246	24.1	34	3.3	48	4.7	1021	100.0

Beijing

Previous housing												
Renting private housing	89	26.3	40	11.8	11	3.2	0	0.0	5	1.5	145	42.8
Renting public housing	7	2.1	19	5.6	2	0.6	0	0.0	0	0.0	28	8.3
Dorm/workshed	15	4.4	6	1.8	116	34.2	4	1.2	1	0.3	142	41.9
Staying w. local residents	1	0.3	2	0.6	3	0.9	0	0.0	0	0.0	6	1.8
Other housing[a]	7	2.1	4	1.2	0	0.0	1	0.3	6	1.8	18	5.3
Total	119	35.1	71	20.9	132	38.9	5	1.5	12	3.5	339	100.0
Initial housing												
Renting private housing	101	16.4	57	9.3	25	4.1	3	0.5	6	1.0	192	31.2
Renting public housing	15	2.4	19	3.1	3	0.5	0	0.0	1	0.2	38	6.2
Dorm/workshed	70	11.4	33	5.4	192	31.2	7	1.1	9	1.5	311	50.5
Staying w. local residents	5	0.8	3	0.5	12	1.9	4	0.6	2	0.3	26	4.2
Other housing[a]	15	2.4	10	1.6	14	2.3	0	0.0	10	1.6	49	8.0
Total	206	33.4	122	19.8	246	39.9	14	2.3	28	4.5	616	100.0

Note: [a]'Other housing' includes commercial housing, and living in self-built shed, on the street or other temporary space.

60 *Weiping Wu*

they have no social safety nets in cities, face fewer employment opportunities, or use unlawful means to revenge unfair treatment they have experienced.

Given the high mobility rates and limited access to housing opportunities, where do migrants gather information and obtain assistance in their housing career? It appears that the absence of a formal housing market available to migrants leaves them heavily reliant on informal social network for information. Responses from in-depth interviews with migrants in Beijing and Shanghai indicate that more than half of them have found their initial housing through the help of friends, relatives, or co-villagers (Wu 2006; also see Table 4.3). Although this reliance on social network by migrants declines gradually over duration of residence, a substantial proportion of migrants continue to do so for the next couple of residential moves. As migrants stay longer in the city, they begin to make friends locally and rely less on relatives for housing-related information. For a substantial number of migrants, residential move decisions are also facilitated by people at work. Although the proportion remains small for migrants who are fully self-sufficient in housing searches, it increases significantly as migrants proceed in their residential career over time. This is likely suggesting a process of adaptation on their part.

The more positive consideration for migrants is that it has become much easier to stay and work in urban areas for extended time. Most cities now have temporary registration for migrants and allow for much more leeway for their self-employment. Due to their significant presence in small-scale commercial activities and services, migrants are contributing to the development of the private as well as informal sectors in cities. Some such activities yield an adequate livelihood (e.g., small traders and food vendors) while others involve a daily struggle for a subsistence living (e.g., scavengers). For the latter, urban life is marginalized and precarious – with low and uncertain earnings, and worsened living conditions.

Table 4.3 Key sources of assistance in housing search, *c.*2000.

	Initial housing		*Previous housing*		*Current housing*	
	Number	*%*	*Number*	*%*	*Number*	*%*
By self	10	12.3	21	20.6	31	22.8
Through work	49	33.3	36	35.3	41	30.1
With help from people at work	5	1.8	6	5.9	15	11.0
Assigned dorm or housing	44	28.1	30	29.4	26	19.1
Through informal network	70	54.4	40	39.2	52	38.2
Friends and acquaintances	8	7.0	20	19.6	26	19.1
Relatives	38	28.1	12	11.8	13	9.6
Co-villagers	24	19.3	8	7.8	13	9.6
Inconclusive responses	1	0.8	5	4.9	12	8.8
Total valid interviewees	130	100.0	102	100.0	136	100.0

Source: Wu (2006).

Impact on the sociospatial transformation of Chinese cities

Patterns of migrant settlement are a major influence on urban spatial development, as exemplified in many developing cities in Latin America, Africa, and Asia. Much of the prevailing theoretical inquiries on spatial distribution of migrant residence and mobility have evolved in a context in which private land ownership and housing markets are more or less functional. Spatial distribution of migrant residence is often determined by a common set of factors. Proximity to existing or potential employment is a major factor underlying choices of site for the first residence as well as subsequent relocation. It ranks high on the list of preferences and needs of migrants for at least two reasons. First, income generation and economic viability are a primary objective for them. Second, most migrants work long hours at what are almost inevitably physically exhausting jobs. For many, their first place of residence in the city is largely predetermined by the location of kin or friends. New arrivals to the city may stay with members of their social networks, or rely on the information controlled by the networks to find a place to stay. The social networks that sustain migration flows also lead to spatial concentration of migrants, often in the form of satellite or "daughter" communities of migrants from a single village. Any study of migrant settlement patterns also requires some understanding of how existing urban residential areas are distributed geographically by socioeconomic status (Vaughan and Feindt 1973). Accounts of such patterns need to be adequately linked to the changing spatial patterns of the destination city and, in particular, location of employment opportunities. The formation and development of migrant settlements often reflects changes in the economic activity of the surrounding areas (Conway 1985).

Market forces are increasingly the dominant force behind urban processes in China, particularly in housing and land development. There is evidence that the importance of location, which was irrelevant in socialist cities without land markets, has led to the emergence of a land rent gradient similar to that of cities in capitalist systems (Ma 2003). Some cities now show three rings of differentiated urban space: pre-1949 historic areas, a socialist planned work-units ring (1949–85), and the new estates ring (built during the property boom years since 1985) (Wang and Murie 2000).

Rapid expansion of the built-up areas and population suburbanization has transformed once compact Chinese cities into a more dispersed and often polycentric form. Spatial expansion gravitates towards new suburban centers and leapfrog development. With rising income and availability of the private car, no doubt there is demand for suburban living. Jobs have suburbanized too. On the outskirts of the city proper, one can find high-tech development zones, and office and industrial parks. These peripheral areas also house a large number of wholesale markets for agricultural products because of their proximity to suburban farms.

Migration and migrant settlements have been a key driver of spatial expansion. At the turn of the 1980s when the migrant influx first began, the central city was the chosen residential location of most new arrivals. But with urban expansion

62 *Weiping Wu*

and downtown redevelopment, inner suburbs have become a more important receiving area for migrants. Central-city housing is becoming less attractive to migrants due to higher-end real estate development and in turn the rapid rise of costs. The spatial distribution of migrants, as a result, has experienced a gradual shift, mirroring a trend in many cities elsewhere in developing countries undergoing continuing urbanization. This shift also coincides with the deconcentration trend seen in local population. In Shanghai, for example, inner suburban areas immediately flanking the central-city boundary are now residential centers for both migrants and, to some extent, the locals (see Figure 4.2). "Urban villages" have emerged there as well, as urban expansion gradually encroaches on formerly rural areas. Although municipal agencies attempt to impose control over the "urban villages," chaotic land uses, crowding, and irregular rental activities persist there.

One of the most well known "urban villages" is Beijing's Zhejiang Village, located in an area called Dahongmen, just south of the Third Ring Road. The ongoing, intense struggle over housing and the use of urban space by Wenzhou migrants there illustrates how a migrant community has formed on the basis of a shared place identity. Successive waves of migrants from around the Wenzhou region in Zhejiang Province have congregated. Many have been engaged in garment manufacturing (in small workshops) and trading. They first rented from local residents in this urban–rural transitional area. Then a group of migrants with more economic and social capital invested in the development of large, private housing compounds. They gained access to land for housing construction and obtained limited infrastructure resources by buying off local village and township cadres and forming informal economic alliances with them. Built on extended kinship ties, clientelist networks with local cadres, and voluntary gang-like groups, a shadow migrant community and leadership structure emerged (Xiang 2000; Zhang 2001; Zhang 2002). Within the community, allocation of housing, production and marketing space, and policing and social services proceeded through networks centered on the migrant bosses of housing compounds and market sites. This explosive growth outside party-state structures worried authorities and led them to order the demolition of many housing compounds several times. The migrants, desperate to stay in the lucrative urban market at the center of the national transportation network, continued to rebuild their community within months of each raid.

The Zhejiang Village also is a microcosm showing the attraction of the urban periphery to migrants, where both employment opportunities and rental housing are plentiful. Neighborhoods in the urban periphery often are the primary receiving area for newly arrived migrants. Suburban towns there have diversified their economies since 1979, with an increasing number of township industrial enterprises. Many such enterprises prefer to hire migrant workers because of their willingness to work hard for less pay. In the urban periphery, there is more self-constructed private housing by local peasants or former farmers on land allotted by their production brigades. Rental housing, therefore, is more readily available and costs less.

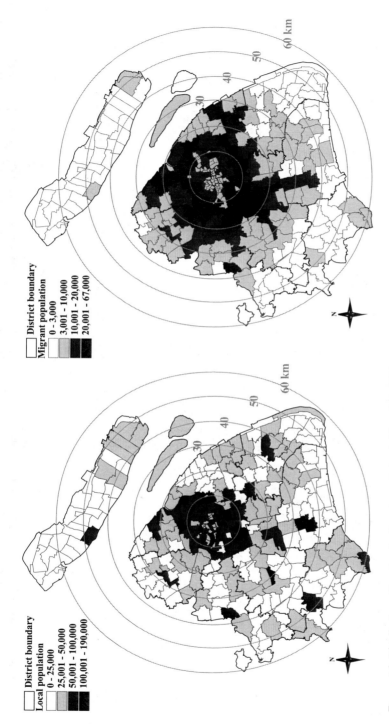

Figure 4.2 Distribution of local and migrant population in Shanghai, 2000.
Source: Wu (2008).

64 *Weiping Wu*

In the urban periphery, migrants are a major force behind small businesses. These areas do not have the same level of established services as the downtown areas. This may actually be an attraction to many migrants as opportunities to open small businesses are more abundant and competition with established local establishments is less fierce. These businesses cater to the everyday need of nearby residents and passing commuters – selling Chinese-style fast food, fruits and snacks, small household tools, and toiletries. Then, there are the proverbial hair salons, massage parlors, and bicycle and motorcycle repair shops. Often, the clientele of migrant businesses are migrants themselves, particularly for street vendors selling regional dishes. The street scene is lively and bustling.

Conclusion

Market transition and growing urban–rural disparities, combined with loosened control of population movement, have contributed to enormous tides of migration. But such rising mobility intersects with an institutional structure at urban destinations that separates migrants from local residents through a household registration system. As such, migrants have limited access to local public schools, welfare programs, state sector jobs, and the mainstream housing distribution system. These and other restrictions inevitably increase the costs and hardship borne by migrants. Despite a lengthy residence in the cities, the majority of migrants are renters and remains so. They experience substantially higher mobility rates than local residents, but such mobility is not necessarily driven by the need for tenure or even amenity. Though resembling the behavior of seasonal migrants elsewhere, the housing career of China's migrants is truncated – without the transition to a consolidator status. This partially stems from the tight reign over public land by municipal authorities and, hence, the lack of opportunities to build self-help housing. Home ownership through the formal commercial market is even less attainable for most migrants.

Compared to cities in other developing countries, the intra-urban mobility trajectories of migrants in China are much more spatially confined. They may be moving just as frequently, but not very far. Most moves are within the same general geographic area. Increasingly, urban peripheries are where both employment opportunities and rental housing are plentiful, and therefore are the primary receiving areas for migrants. Upon first arrival there, many migrants seem to remain more or less stationary geographically in their subsequent moves. On top of this, getting stuck in the private rental sector allows little room for improving their housing conditions. If this scenario of residential mobility is any indication of socioeconomic mobility, it is clear that most migrants are drifting in the bottom layer of the urban society and getting stuck there.

Much like trends elsewhere, China's migrants rely on social networks to find housing. This leads to their concentration in certain areas. For new arrivals in particular, their first residence in the city is often determined by the location of their relatives or friends. Given the long-standing urban-rural divide, there is a large gap in the cultural values and social relations between their areas of origin

Outsiders in the city 65

and destination. Being close to people like themselves provides a more familiar environment to new arrivals. As they gradually acculturate to the urban environment, some become more self-sufficient in their housing searches.

The geography of migrant residence will continue to figure in the matrix of urban sociospatial development, as the large migrant influx remains unabated. Since most migrant housing is in much worse condition than local housing, increasing migrant concentration may aggravate existing residential differentiation. In addition, settlement patterns will be an important determinant of the future socioeconomic standing of migrants, as where and how they live are likely to affect their general level of satisfaction with urban living and the ease or difficulty to adapt to the new environment. Such residential characteristics as tenure and conditions of dwelling, access to facilities and services, and geographic location are essential to migrants' quality of life. Attributes associated with urban living, including the higher density of urban housing and use of community facilities, also will have profound social impacts on the lifestyle of migrants.

Given the magnitude of migration and its potential impact on cities, it is important to explore ways in which migrant access to urban amenities may be broadened. To properly respond to the need of migrants and their quest for citizenship rights entails that the linkage between hukou and the provision of urban services be discontinued. With more tolerant migration policies in China, over time, urban ties will surpass rural ties and many migrants may choose to settle permanently at urban destinations.

References

Abu-Lughod, J. (1961) "Migrant adjustment to city life: The Egyptian case," *The American Journal of Sociology*, 67(1): 22–32.

Banerjee, B. (1983) "Social networks in the migration process: Empirical evidence on chain migration in India", *Journal of Developing Areas*, 17(2): 185–96.

Chan, K. W. and Zhang, L. (1999) "The hukou system and rural-urban migration in China: processes and changes," *China Quarterly*, 160: 818–55.

Congressional Executive Commission on China (CECC) (2005) "Local governments resist reforms to household registration system", CECC Virtual Academy. Online. Available: http://www.cecc.gov/pages/virtualAcad/index.phpd?showsingle=32168 (Accessed March 16, 2008).

Conway, D. (1985) "Changing perspectives on squatter settlements, intraurban mobility, and constraints on housing choice of the third world urban poor," *Urban Geography*, 6(2): 170–92.

Fan, C. C. (2008) *China on the Move: Migration, the State, and the Household*. London: Routledge.

Gilbert, A. and Varley, A. (1990) 'Renting a home in a third world city: Choice or constraint?', *International Journal of Urban and Regional Research*, 14(1): 89–108.

Klak, T. and Holtzclaw, M. (1993) "The housing, geography, and mobility of Latin American urban poor: The prevailing model and the case of Quito, Ecuador," *Growth and Change*, 24(2): 247–76.

66 *Weiping Wu*

Ma, L. J. C. (2003) "Some reflections on China's urbanization and urban spatial restructuring," paper presented at the Urban China Research Network Workshop on Urban Studies and Demography in China, Minneapolis, MN, April 2003.

Solinger, D. J. (1999) "Citizenship issues in China's internal migration: Comparisons with Germany and Japan," *Political Science Quarterly*, 114(3): 455–70.

Turner, J. F. C. (1968) "Housing patterns, settlement patterns, and urban development in modernizing countries," *Journal of the American Planning Association*, 34(6): 354–63.

Van Lindert, P. (1991) "Moving up or staying down? Migrant-native differential mobility in La Paz," *Urban Studies*, 28(3): 433–63.

Vaughan, D. R. and Feindt, W. (1973) "Initial settlement and intracity movement of migrants in Monterrey, Mexico," *AIP Journal*, 39(6): 388–401.

Wang, Y. and Murie, A. (2000) "Social and spatial implications of housing reform in China," *International Journal of Urban and Regional Research*, 24(2): 397–417.

Wu, W. (2002) "Migrant housing in urban China: Choices and constraints," *Urban Affairs Review*, 38(1): 90–119.

Wu, W. (2006) "Migrant intraurban residential mobility in urban China," *Housing Studies*, 21(5): 747–67.

Wu, W. (2008) "Migrant settlement and spatial distribution in metropolitan Shanghai," *Professional Geographer*, 60(1): 101–20.

Wu, W. (2010) "Drifting and getting stuck: Migrants in Chinese cities," *City: Analysis of Urban Trends, Culture, Theory, Policy, Action*, 14(1): 10–20.

Wu, W. and Rosenbaum, E. (2008) "Migration and housing: Comparing China with the United States," in John Logan (ed.) *Urban China in Transition*, Oxford: , Blackwell Publishing, pp. 250–67.

Xiang, B. (2000) *A Community That Crosses Boundaries: The Living History of Beijing's Zhejiang Village* (kuayue bianjie de sheqiu: Beijing zhejiangcun de shenghuo shi). Beijing: Sanlian Publishing House.

Zhang, L. (2001) *Strangers in the City: Space, Power, and Identity in China's Floating Population*. Stanford: Stanford University Press.

Zhang, L. (2002) "Spatiality and urban citizenship in late socialist China," *Public Culture*, 14(2): 311–34.

Part 2

Migrants' social lives in urban China

5 Migrants' job-search in urban China

Social networks and the labour market

Yu Chen and Gwilym Pryce

Introduction

Migration to cities for job opportunities is an important means of pursuing a better life in many developing countries. In China, self-initiated migration was strictly controlled by the government through the household registration (hukou) system during the central planning era (1958–78). Since the initiation of the economic reforms in 1978, over 100 million people have moved to cities in search of higher living standards. Despite the relaxation of migration controls, the overwhelming majority of migrants have been denied access to welfare and services at their destinations, such as unemployment benefits and minimum living allowance (Chan 2009). Jobs are therefore crucial for migrants to survive in cities. However, as newcomers, migrants may find it difficult to secure decent jobs due to lack of knowledge about the local labour market. Previous studies have focused on migrants' working conditions, showing that migrants are concentrated in low-skilled jobs with low levels of pay, and that they have become a significant group of the urban poor (Knight and Song 2005; Xu *et al.* 2006). Yet, very few studies have examined migrants' ways of finding jobs and the extent to which their search methods influence labour market outcomes.

This chapter aims to fill the gap by examining migrants' job-search methods, drawing on data from a retrospective survey in Shanghai which recorded information on migrants' work experience from 2001 to 2005. We identify formal search methods, such as job adverts and employment agencies, and informal ones, namely, social networks, and examine the determinants of these methods. We further investigate the impact of search methods on wages, one of the most important indicators of job desirability. It is important to study job-search methods because effective job-search reduces search time and costs, improves the quality of job-match, and diminishes the likelihood of unemployment and poverty. We use longitudinal data to control for fixed unobserved individual heterogeneity which is likely to be correlated with search effectiveness. We aim to deepen understanding of the determinants of effective job-search and inform policies aimed at reducing urban poverty through improved labour market services towards migrants.

70 *Yu Chen and Gwilym Pryce*

Consistent with most of the literature (e.g. Good and West 2002), migrants, in this chapter, are defined as people who moved to cities while their household registration status remains in their places of origin. Social networks, one of the important means of accessing job information, have been discussed widely in the literature (e.g. Granovetter 1995; Lin 1999, 2000). Our aim here is not to explain the existence or stability of social networks. Rather, we take networks as given and investigate the relative effectiveness of job-search through networks and the open labour market.

The remainder of the chapter proceeds by first situating the study in the broad literature on job-search methods and labour market outcomes. Then we review studies on migration and networks, and migrants' job-search in urban China to provide context. This is followed by a discussion of the data and methods used in the study. Empirical results are then presented, and the chapter concludes by summarizing the main findings.

Job-search methods and wages

The standard economic model of job-search typically assumes imperfect information for job-seekers and explains how individuals collect and use information about jobs to make rational decisions in an uncertain environment (Stigler 1961). Early work focuses on job-seeking behaviour and job-shopping experiences on an individual basis (Johnson 1978; Jovanovic 1979). Following Granovetter's (1973) seminal work on job referrals from friends and relatives, a burgeoning literature has developed in both economics and sociology, discussing the effect of social interaction on job-search process (Loury 2006). As Ioannides and Loury (2004: 1056) indicate, 'access to information is heavily influenced by social structure and that individuals use connections with others, such as friends and social and professional acquaintances, to build and maintain information networks'.

Research reveals that social networks have been used worldwide as an important and effective way of finding jobs, even in advanced economies where market forces dominate (Ioannides and Loury 2004). Drawing on US data in the 1980s, both Holzer (1987) and Blau and Robins (1990) find that utilizing networks of friends or relatives was the most productive, and frequently used, job-search method. Bewley (1999) reviews 24 studies on job-search and concludes that 30–60 per cent of jobs are secured through friends or relatives; and younger and lower-educated people are more likely to use social networks. There are at least three explanations for the wide use of social networks in job-search. First, it is a cheap way of finding jobs. Second, job referrals help lower uncertainty about job-seekers' productivity for employers. Lastly, the method improves quality of job-match as referrals may provide realistic views of the nature of the job. Research consistently shows that people who find jobs through friends or relatives are less likely to quit and have longer tenure (Datcher 1983; Simon and Warner 1992).

However, the findings on job-search methods and wages are mixed. Some studies, for example, show that people who found jobs through social networks earn more than those using formal methods (Rosenbaum *et al.* 1999; Marmaros and Sacerdote 2002). Other studies support this initial wage advantage for jobs

Migrants' job-search in urban China 71

secured through networks, but find that the premium declines over time (Corcoran *et al.* 1980; Simon and Warner 1992). In contrast, Bridges and Villemez (1986) and Marsden and Gorman (2001) reported no correlation between wages and job-search methods. Moreover, Elliott (1999) and Bentolila *et al.* (2010) demonstrate significant wage discounts for jobs found through social networks compared with those secured through formal methods.

One explanation for the mixed findings discussed above concerns the strength and characteristics of social networks. Granovetter (1995) posits that weak ties, i.e. acquaintances, have a more beneficial effect on earnings than strong ties, i.e. relatives, because weak ties tend to offer more diversified job information (Bridges and Villemez 1986; Montgomery 1991) though this may alternatively be explained by the degree of reciprocal obligation. Lin (1999) further indicates that weak ties link people of different hierarchical ranks associated with different access to resources, and contacts with more resourceful people generate more information about jobs of higher status and wages. However, Lin (2000) argues that individuals are likely to socialize with those in the similar social and occupational positions, and networks tend to develop along lines such as race, ethnicity, education and social hierarchy. Studies which examine the effects of social networks on earnings without scrutinizing the characteristics of networks themselves, are likely to yield mixed findings. It is shown empirically that contacts with people who are employed with higher earnings and who are located in extensive networks, are likely to yield information about better-paying jobs (Montgomery 1991; Simon and Warner 1992). For example, Marmaros and Sacerdote (2002) reported positive correlation between social networks and wages for Dartmouth College seniors. In contrast, using contacts of people with low wages or the unemployed, especially female, non-white, individuals in poor neighbourhoods, tend to result in lower-paying occupations (Beggs and Hurlbert 1997; Smith 2000; Korenman and Turner 1996). For example, Elliott (1999) shows that people who found their jobs through non-white contacts earn substantially less than those using other means, in poor urban neighbourhoods in the USA. Green *et al.* (1999) find that earnings of Hispanics who found their jobs through family members or friends are significantly lower than those using other search methods.

There are questions to be asked, however, regarding the applicability to the particular group we seek to investigate in this study of existing theoretical and empirical research on social networks. For example, might social network effects be different for migrant workers who may have qualitatively different job search patterns compared with native workers? And given that the bulk of the literature has been developed in a North American/Western European context, how applicable is it to mainland China with a radically different socioeconomic, historical and cultural context? We now turn to review studies on migrants and networks, together with Chinese migrants' access to job information.

Migrants and social networks

It is possible that social networks could be more important for migrants than for native residents in accessing information of jobs, because migrants are newcomers

72 *Yu Chen and Gwilym Pryce*

and may find it difficult to search for jobs through formal methods, especially when a functioning labour market is missing (Chiswick 1982; Munshi 2003). Using Labour Force Survey Data during 1997 and 2001, Frijters *et al.* (2003) find that immigrants in the UK are more likely to search for jobs through social networks than native residents whose main search methods are job centres and adverts. It is well established in the migration literature that networks facilitate migration by substantially reducing the costs and risks of migration, as prospective migrants draw on social ties with established migrants and gain access to financial assistance and knowledge of destination, jobs and housing (Massey *et al.* 1987; Massey and Espinosa 1997). Networks may provide migrants with useful information on job opportunities, and techniques for interviews and wage negotiation, and thus improve the effectiveness of job-search. Studies on Mexico-US migrants show that social contact with the Mexican community improves wages in the US labour market (Munshi 2003; Aguilera and Massey 2003). Aguilera and Massey (2003) further indicate that such an effect is greater for undocumented than documented migrants, because of the more precarious status of the former.

Despite the widely evidenced positive effects of social networks on migrants' job-search, Mitra (2010) argues that networks reduce the probability of migrants' upward occupational mobility. Drawing on data from a slum survey in four Indian cities during 2006–07, the author finds that social networks are important for migrants' accessing urban jobs as a surviving strategy, but result in excess supply of labour in certain activities which depress migrants' chances of upward job mobility.

Networks and migrants' access to job information in urban China

Guanxi is a Chinese phrase describing a form of social network. It literally means 'relationship'; 'its essence is a set of interpersonal connections that facilitate exchange of favours among people on a daily basis' (Bian 1997: 367). The importance of guanxi in accessing good jobs has been discussed widely (Bian 1994; Knight and Yueh 2002). When jobs were allocated through governments during the central planning period and the early 1980s, guanxi was used by people who approached job-assigning authority, directly or indirectly, to obtain jobs with better working environments or close to home (Bian 1994). In Bian's study of a representative sample of 938 workers in Tianjin in 1988, over half of the respondents used guanxi to get their first allocated jobs, and even more used guanxi to change their jobs (Bian 1994). The labour allocation system was gradually abolished in the 1980s, yet social networks have continued to play a role in finding jobs. Drawing on data on 1,505 first-time job seekers in Zhongshan during 1988 and 2000, Zang (2003) shows that network resources remain important in attaining good jobs, although human capital is also rewarded in the labour market. Based on survey data covering 7,500 urban workers in thirteen cities in 2000, Knight and Yueh (2002) found that numbers of personal contacts have a positive effect on income.

Similar to other countries, migration networks play a vital role in facilitating migration in China. Although self-initiated migration was allowed by the state after 1978, migrants were treated as second-class citizens in cities, and confronted with social, economic and institutional constraints, such as job quotas in state companies, occupational constraints, and limited access to social benefits and services (Chan 2009). They were blamed for increasing urban traffic congestion and crime, and risked being deported if they could not provide valid documents in the 1990s.[1] All these issues, together with insufficient information flows, resulted in huge costs and risks of migration, especially for those originating from isolated rural hinterland. Established migrants have assisted prospective ones from their own villages to gain information about destination and job opportunities. Therefore, the Chinese internal migration has been reported as 'chain migration' on the basis of places of origin (Ma and Xiang 1998; Roberts 2001). For instance, a sample survey of 1,504 peasant workers in Jinan, Shandong Province in 1996, indicated that 75 per cent of rural migrants found their first jobs through information from their relatives or co-villagers (Cai 1997). Moreover, 30 per cent of migrants in this survey obtained jobs before they arrived in the city, and many who had not secured jobs before migration found jobs within a month of arrival (Cai 1997).

Research has been undertaken relating migrants' origins with their occupations at destination. For example, in Beijing in the 1990s, migrants from Wenzhou (Zhejiang Province) were concentrated in the clothing industry; those from Henan were engaged in the garbage recycling sector; and many women migrants from Anhui worked as maids (Ma and Xiang 1998). In Shanghai, the 1993 Fifth Migrant Sampling Survey showed that migrants from Zhejiang tended to be self-employed in retail; those from Sichuan were inclined to work in the construction sector (Roberts 2001). Additionally, studies of migrant women factory workers in South China in the 1990s revealed that many women migrants from the same province clustered in the same production lines; some even shared the same dormitory (Lee 1998: 117–23). Both Ma and Xiang (1998) and Roberts (2001) argue that village-based networks led to clusters of migrants in particular destinations and occupations.

In summary, existing studies on Chinese migrants focus on the significance of social networks on both migration and migrant's job search. Yet, little is known about migrants' alternative methods of securing urban jobs and the relative effectiveness of these methods. This study fills the gap by examining the determinants of migrants' job-search methods and the impact on wages. Moreover, most studies on job-search are based on cross-sectional data. A major methodological problem arises from the endogeneity of job-search methods when examining the impact of search methods on wages, because fixed unobserved individual wage-enhancing characteristics are likely to be correlated with choices of search methods, resulting in biased estimates. We draw on longitudinal data from a retrospective survey of migrants in Shanghai, to better control for unobserved individual characteristics.

Data

Our data come from a questionnaire survey of migrants in Shanghai's manufacturing sector at the end of 2005. The survey, conducted in Minhang and Putuo Districts, adopted a stratified random sampling method. First, companies in each district were classified into three groups by ownership: public, private, and foreign or joint ventures, as different labour market practices may occur in companies with different ownership (Dong and Bowles 2002). Twenty-one companies (75 per cent of those contacted) were proportionately included in the survey. Second, migrants were randomly selected from these companies to fill in questionnaires. With a response rate of over 80 per cent, the survey yielded 525 questionnaires with valid information on job history, including 417 migrants originating from the countryside (rural migrants) and 108 migrants originating from other cities (urban migrants). About 44.57 per cent of the respondents were female, 65.33 per cent were married and 39.58 per cent worked in Shanghai without accompany of family members.

The questionnaire recorded information on migrants' jobs lasting over one month between January 2001 and December 2005. The five-year period was used to reduce recall errors, following Pollock *et al.* (2002) and Schaeffer and Presser (2003). For each job spell, respondents were asked about their starting and ending months, ways of finding jobs, company ownership, nature of the job, wages at the time of entering and leaving the job, and reasons for job change. For migrants who worked in Shanghai before January 2001,[2] information on job-search method, starting time and wage of their first job during 2001 and 2005 was also recorded. The sample includes both complete and incomplete spells of employment. The number of jobs an individual held in the five years ranges from one to five, with 58.86 per cent of respondents experiencing no job change, 33.71 per cent having two jobs and 5.71 per cent having three jobs.

Two limitations about the survey data need to be taken into account. First, the survey was conducted in manufacturing companies. Although respondents had previous work experience in other sectors, most of them were employees in manufacturing and service sectors. Self-employed migrants were largely ignored. Therefore, the results of this study may not be generalized to all migrants. Second, the retrospective survey included migrants who were in Shanghai at the time of the survey. Those who could not find jobs and left the city during 2001 and 2005 were thus excluded.

The survey identifies three major job-search methods: friends and relatives, job adverts and employment agency. Other methods, such as setting up companies or self-employment, were recorded in only two cases, and therefore dropped from the study. Both job adverts and agencies belong to formal labour market methods. Job adverts include those in the newspapers, magazines, labour fairs, TV, the internet and on the walls outside of factories. Employment agency refers to private ones which provided vacancy information and collected fees from job-seekers, as migrants were denied access to services from public employment agencies which targeted established local urban residents. We distinguish between job adverts and agency, because our fieldwork suggested significant difference between their users. For example, migrants with high educational levels tend to search for jobs themselves rather than relying on agency.

Table 5.1 displays the proportions of job-search methods for each job in the five years, together with the average wage per hour when starting the job. Wage per hour has been adjusted for inflation to the 2005 price level.

Table 5.1 shows that friends or relatives are important ways of securing jobs for migrants; 54.27 per cent of their jobs between 2001 and 2005 were secured in this way. According to the survey, 58.70 per cent of respondents found their first jobs in Shanghai through friends or relatives, and 27.67 per cent secured jobs through their urban contacts before arrival in the city. These findings are consistent with both Western and Chinese migration literature, demonstrating the crucial role of social networks in reducing migration costs and assisting job-search for migrants.

Table 5.1 also shows that job adverts are important ways of finding jobs; over 20 per cent of jobs for each job-search were secured through adverts. Job agencies offer an alternative way of finding jobs, especially for those newly-arrived migrants who do not have wide social networks. The survey indicates that 21.10 per cent of migrants secured their first jobs in Shanghai through agency, with an average agent fee half of their monthly salary. The majority of the jobs offered by agencies were low-skilled. Private employment agency was a relatively new institution in China, and lack of proper regulation from the government. They were the subject of complaints by both migrants and employers during our survey, including exploitative fees,[3] unreliable information about jobs, and provision of forged educational certificates or skill qualifications in order for migrants to get the job and pay agent fees.

Significant difference exists between migrants originating from rural and urban areas in terms of their ways of finding jobs, as shown in Figure 5.1. Compared with rural migrants, urban migrants are more likely to secure jobs through adverts in the labour market, than through agencies or social networks. This could be because urban migrants are more familiar with urban environment, and know where to find information about vacancies. Moreover, their educational level is significantly higher than that of rural migrants (12.49 years of schooling versus 9.48 years). Such educational differential reflects the pronounced rural-urban divide in China with its impact on educational opportunities for people who were raised in the countryside and cities (Zhang and Kanbur 2005). Better education helps individuals access various adverts (Holzer 1987). Our data do suggest that respondents who found jobs through adverts had the highest educational levels, an average of 12.10 years of schooling, compared with 10.52 years for those who found jobs through agencies and 9.40 years for migrants using social networks.

Simple t-tests with unequal variances show that average wage per hour is significantly higher for jobs which were found through adverts compared with two other methods.[4] As the wage pattern might be affected by differences in characteristics besides ways of finding jobs, for example, people with more work experience may have higher wages, we now turn to a more structured investigation of

Table 5.1 Job-search method and wage per hour for each job in the five years (wage: Yuan, adjusted by CPI).

Job-search method	1st job		2nd job		3rd job		4th job		5th job		Total	
	%	Wage	%	Wage	%	Wage	%	Wage	%	Wage	%	Wage
Social network	59.85	4.13	45.12	4.75	34.21	6.31	42.86	6.22	0	0	54.27	4.35
Job advert	21.41	6.51	26.51	8.09	36.84	8.39	57.14	13.97	100	13.45	24.07	7.36
Employment agency	18.74	4.11	28.37	4.53	28.95	5.23	0	0	0	0	21.66	4.33
Number	523	511	215	210	38	37	7	7	2	2	785	767

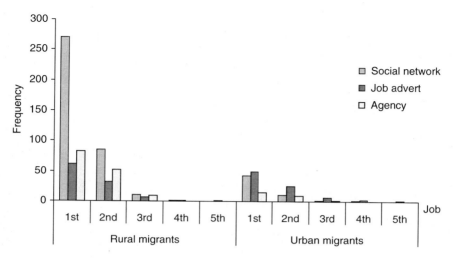

Figure 5.1 Ways of finding jobs by residential status for the five job-search processes.

the choice of job-search methods and its impact on wages, while controlling for individual characteristics.

Methods

There are two significant methodological challenges that our estimation approach attempts to address. First, as data on job-search come from repeated measurements from the same individuals during 2001 and 2005, we need to account for the likely correlations between job search patterns from the same individual. We do this using multilevel modeling techniques, which treat job-search at a lower level and individuals at a higher level.[5] Second, because individuals who search for jobs through social networks or the labour market are not random, an important methodological issue concerns the endogeneity of job-search methods in the wage model. We follow Wooldridge (2002: 623–5) and adopt a two-stage least squares modeling procedure to tackle this problem. At the 1st stage, we estimate the model of job-search methods and predict the probabilities of each method for each job-search. As the dependent variable of search method has three categories with no intrinsic order, a multilevel multinomial logit model with random intercept is used.[6] At the 2nd stage, the predicted probabilities are used as instruments for job-search method dummies, rather than regressors, in the wage model with random effects.[7]

According to literature on labour market outcomes (Mincer 1974), human capital factors, such as years of education and work experience, are crucial wage determinants, which also influence job-search behaviour. These two variables are

Yu Chen and Gwilym Pryce

included in the models, together with the squared term of work experience (years of work) to capture potential non-linear effects between work experience and outcomes. Demographic characteristics, such as gender and marital status, existence of family members in Shanghai, and residential status, are also included in the model, as they are likely to influence labour market outcomes. Initial tests show that marital status is correlated with ways of finding jobs but not with wages. Moreover, year dummies of starting the job are incorporated in the wage equation to control for year-specific shocks.

Empirical results

Table 5.2 displays the results of the multinomial logit model and the wage model. Friends or relatives are the base category. The likelihood ratio test shows that the random intercept significantly improves model estimates.

Table 5.2 Results of multinomial logit model and wage model.

Independent variables	Multinomial logit model (odds)		Wage model
	Adverts vs friends/relatives	Agency vs friends/ relatives	Ln wage
Years of education	1.9239***	1.3400***	0.1046***
	(0.2506)	(0.1296)	(0.0109)
Work experience	1.1642	1.0584	0.0369***
	(0.1121)	(0.0843)	(0.0095)
Work experience squared	0.9944	0.9993	−0.0010***
	(0.0036)	(0.0027)	(0.0003)
Rural hukou status	0.3003**	2.4162*	−0.1361**
	(0.1502)	(1.1751)	(0.0534)
Female	0.5718	1.4427	−0.0329
	(0.2258)	(0.4757)	(0.0396)
Married	0.6553	0.1375***	0.0158
	(0.3384)	(0.0693)	(0.0572)
No family members	1.2561	0.6210	0.0814
	(0.5436)	(0.2356)	(0.0448)
Jobs through adverts			0.1983***
			(0.0596)
Jobs through employment agency			−0.0228
			(0.0588)
Constant	0.0003***	0.0103***	0.9850
	(0.0006)	(0.0151)	(0.3938)
Log likelihood	−648.6731		
rho			0.5671
R-sq			0.3486
Number	783	783	765

*Significant at 10%; **significant at 5%; ***significant at 1%. Omitted category is jobs through friends or relatives.

The multinomial logit model shows significantly positive effects of education on individuals' probabilities of finding jobs through the labour market. For one year's increase in education, holding other variables constant, the odds of finding jobs through job adverts versus social networks are expected to increase by 1.92 times; the odds of finding jobs through employment agency versus networks tend to increase by 1.34 times. This could be explained by the fact that individuals need certain levels of education, such as literacy and internet search skills, to get access to the open labour market. The finding is consistent with existing studies demonstrating that people with higher educational levels are more likely to seek jobs through the market (Holzer 1987). The coefficients of work experiences are positive, but not statistically significant. Being migrants originating from the countryside significantly lowers the odds of finding jobs through job adverts versus friends or relatives. However, rural migrants are 2.42 times more likely to get jobs from agencies relative to networks, than migrants from other cities. These results suggest that friends or relatives and employment agencies are two important ways for rural migrants, while urban migrants are more prone to find jobs through adverts. People with more urban experience may find it easier to access job adverts.

It seems that married people are significantly less likely to find jobs through employment agency relative to friends or relatives. One plausible explanation is that married people may have more social network resources, and tend not to pay agency fees for jobs. Gender and family members do not have significant impact on job-search methods, after controlling for other factors.

The wage model explains 34.86 per cent of variation in log wages. The intra-class correlation (rho) indicates that 56.71 per cent of the variation in the dependent variable is at the individual level. The hausman test ($\chi^2(17)=21.45$, Prob$>\chi^2=0.2067$) shows that the difference in coefficients between random and fixed effects models are not systematic. Therefore, our results of random effects are reliable.

Consistent with wage models in other studies (Knight and Song 2005), years of education significantly improve an individual's wage prospects; work experience increases wages but with a decreasing rate. Rural migrants have a wage discount compared with urban migrants, reflecting labour market discrimination against them. An important finding is that migrants who found jobs through adverts earned 19.83 per cent more than those who secured jobs through social networks. Such a wage premium is statistically significant, after controlling for unobserved individual heterogeneity and tackling the endogeneity problem. This could be explained by the fact that adverts in the labour market allow individuals to access wider information, and therefore to obtain jobs with higher levels of pay. Meanwhile, the model shows that wages of those who found jobs through agency are not significantly different from those who secured jobs through social networks, as most jobs secured through agents are low-skilled.

Discussion and conclusions

This chapter examines migrants' job-search methods and their impact on wages, using longitudinal data from a retrospective survey in Shanghai which recorded individuals' work experiences from 2001 to 2005. A multinomial logit model with random intercept is employed to investigate the determinants of job-search methods, accounting for correlation resulting from multiple observations for the same individuals. We further estimate a wage model with random effects, addressing the endogeneity problem by using predicted probabilities from the multinomial logit model as instruments for job-search methods.

Our results show that education increases the odds of finding jobs through adverts versus social networks or employment agency; moreover, finding jobs through adverts significantly improves wages, compared with the method of social networks, holding constant demographical and human capital characteristics, residential status and unobserved individual heterogeneity. One explanation is that the open labour market provides more diversified job information, and therefore jobs with better pay. Moreover, migrants' social network resources are likely to be limited. Our survey indicated that migrants tended to make friends with migrants rather than established local urban residents who might have better knowledge about well-paid local job opportunities. This is not surprising since people tend to socialize with those who have similar background (Granovetter 1995).[8] Migrants' restricted social interaction with local urban residents corresponds with findings in other studies. For example, Zhou (2000) found 'dual communities' in the Pearl River Delta where migrants and non-migrants had distinctive occupations, housing and lifestyles, with few interactions between them. As the majority of migrants conduct low-skilled jobs with low levels of pay, which has been demonstrated in various studies (e.g. Knight and Song 2005), it is not surprising to find that referrals from other migrant employees do not result in prestigious jobs with high wages. Nevertheless, our survey does support the significant role of social networks in securing migrants' jobs, especially their very first ones in Shanghai. These findings are consistent with Mitra (2010)'s study in Indian slums arguing that social networks provide migrants with job opportunities sufficient for survival in cities but that such networks are unlikely to facilitate access to prestigious occupations.

Private employment agencies provide an alternative route to urban jobs, especially for migrants who do not have social network resources. However, the empirical analysis shows that employment agencies do not have a significant effect on wages compared with social networks, suggesting that both methods lead to low-skilled jobs. Private employment agencies are a relatively new institution in China and are under-regulated. Our fieldwork revealed that some agencies charged high fees from migrant workers but failed to provide reliable job information. There is a need for regulations and monitoring procedures towards agencies, in order to minimize exploitation and poor quality of service. Moreover, it is important to expand the coverage of public employment services, and to allow migrants to access information from public job centers free of charge. This will provide the disadvantaged with a viable alternative to social networks and private employment agencies. Services provided by agencies should be more attuned to the needs of those disadvantaged.

Notes

1. Most of these discriminatory policies against migrants, such as job quotas, occupational constraints and deportation, were abolished officially in 2003, despite their continued influence.
2. These migrants account for 31.43 per cent of all respondents.
3. Some migrants were charged a fee as high as their whole month's salary.
4. The t-statistic is 7.11 when comparing average wages for jobs secured through job adverts and those through friends/relatives; the t-statistic is 7.2555 when comparing average wages for jobs secured through job adverts and those through employment agency. Both tests accept the null hypothesis of higher average wage for jobs secured through adverts.
5. The advantage of the multilevel framework is that it accounts for the dependence structure among multiple observations in a cluster by using random effects to control for unobserved heterogeneity (Rabe-Hesketh *et al.* 2004).
6. The model is estimated through the Stata program of 'GLLAMM', which integrates over the distribution of unobserved heterogeneity by using Gauss–Hermite quadrature (Rabe-Hesketh *et al.* 2004).
7. As the predicted probability is a nonlinear function of personal characteristics, they are not perfectly correlated with these characteristics and can be used as instruments (Wooldridge 2002: 624). Therefore, the standard errors of the two-stage least squares procedure remain valid.
8. Similar background could include general migration experience and does not necessarily limit to the same place of origin. The survey indicated that 59.1 per cent of migrants had migrant friends who originated from different provinces.

References

Aguilera, M. and Massey, D. (2003) 'Social capital and the wages of Mexican migrants: New hypotheses and tests', *Social Forces,* 82(2): 671–701.

Beggs, J. and Hurlbert, J. (1997) 'The social context of men's and women's job search ties: Membership in voluntary organizations, social resources, and job search outcomes', *Sociology Perspective*, 40(4): 601–22.

Bentolila, S., Michelacci, C. and Suarez, J. (2010) 'Social contacts and occupational choice', *Economica*, 77 (305): 20–45.

Bewley, T. F. (1999) *Why Wages Don't Fall During a Recession*, Cambridge, MA: Harvard University Press.

Bian, Y. (1994) 'Guanxi and the allocation of jobs in urban China', *China Quarterly*, 140: 971–99.

Bian, Y. (1997) 'Bringing strong ties back in: Indirect connection, bridges, and job search in China', *American Sociological Review*, 62: 366–85.

Blau, D. and Robins, P. (1990) 'Job search outcomes for the employed and unemployed', *Journal of Political Economy*, 98(3): 637–55.

Bridges, W. and Villemez W. (1986) 'Informal hiring and income in the labor market', *American Sociology Review*, 51(4): 574–82.

Cai, F. (1997) 'On the issue of floating population', in M. Xu (ed.) *Critical Moment: 27 Critical Problems in Contemporary China*, Beijing: Today Press, pp. 423–35.

Chan, K. W. (2009) 'The Chinese hukou system at 50 Eurasian', *Geography and Economics*, 50(2): 197–221.

Chiswick, B. (1982) 'The employment of immigrants in the United States', in W. Fellner (ed.) *Contemporary Economic Problems 1982*, Washington DC: American Enterprise Institute, pp. 1–37.

Corcoran, M., Datcher, L. and Duncan, G. (1980) 'Information and influence networks in labor markets', in G. Duncan and J. Morgan (eds.) *Five Thousand American Families*, Vol VIII. Michigan: Institute Social Research, pp. 1–37.

Datcher, L. (1983) 'The impact of informal networks on quit behavior', *Review of Economics and Statistics*, 65(3): 491–5.

Dong, X. and Bowles, P. (2002) 'Segmentation and discrimination in China's emerging industrial labor markets', *China Economic Review*, 13(2–3): 170–96.

Elliott, J. (1999) 'Social isolation and labor market isolation: Network and neighborhood effects on less-educated urban workers', *Sociological Quarterly*, 40(2): 199–216.

Frijters, P., Shields, M. and Price, S. (2003) 'Immigrant job search in the UK: Evidence from panel data', Discussion Paper No. 902, IZA Institute for the Study of Labor.

Goodkind, D. and West, A. (2002) 'China's floating population: Definitions, data and recent findings', *Urban Studies*, 39(12): 2237–50.

Granovetter, M. (1973) 'The strength of weak ties', *American Journal of Sociology*, 78(6): 1360–80.

Granovetter, M. S. (1995) *Getting a Job*, Chicago: University Chicago Press.

Green, G., Tiggs, L. and Diaz, D. (1999) 'Racial and ethnic differences in job search strategies in Atlanta, Boston, and Los Angeles', *Social Science Quarterly*, 80(2): 559–77.

Holzer, H. (1987) 'Informal job search and black youth unemployment', *American Economic Review*, 77(3): 446–52.

Ioannides, Y. and Loury, L. (2004) 'Job information networks, neighbourhood effects, and inequality', *Journal of Economic Literature*, 42(4): 1056–93.

Johnson, W. (1978) 'A theory of job shopping', *Quarterly Journal of Economics*, 92(2): 261–78.

Jovanovic, B. (1979) 'Job matching and the theory of turnover', *Journal of Political Economy*, 87(5): 972–90.

Knight, J. and Song, L. (2005) *Towards a labour market in China*, Oxford: Oxford University Press.

Knight, J. and Yueh, L. (2002) 'The role of social capital in the labour market in China', Discussion Paper Series No. 121, Department of Economics, University of Oxford.

Korenman, S. and Turner S. (1996) 'Employment contacts and minority-white wage differences', *Industrial Relations*, 35(1): 106–22.

Lee, C. K. (1998) *Gender and the South China Miracle: Two Worlds of Factory Women*, Berkeley: University of California Press.

Lin, N. (1999) 'Social networks and status attainment', *Annual Review of Sociology*, 25: 467–87.

Lin, N. (2000) 'Inequality in social capital', *Contemporary Sociology*, 29: 785–95.

Loury, L. (2006) 'Some contacts are more equal than others: Informal networks, job tenure, and wages', *Journal of Labor Economics*, 24(2): 299–318.

Ma, L. and Xiang, B. (1998) 'Native place, migration, and the emergence of peasant enclaves in Beijing', *China Quarterly*, 155: 546–81.

Marmaros, D. and Sacerdote, B. (2002) 'Peer and social networks in job search', *European Economic Review*, 46(4–5): 870–9.

Marsden, P. and Gorman, E. (2001) 'Social networks, job changes, and recruitment', in I. Berg and A. Kalleberge (eds). *Sourcebook of Labor Markets: Evolving Structure and Processes*, New York: Kluwer Academic/Plenum Publishers, pp. 467–502.

Massey, D., Alarcon, R., Durand, J. and Gonzalez, H. (1987) *Return to Aztlan: The Social Process of International Migration from Western Mexico*, London: University of California Press.

Massey, D. and Espinosa, K. (1997) 'What's driving Mexico-U.S. migration? A theoretical, empirical, and policy analysis', *American Journal of Sociology*, 102: 939–99.

Mincer, J. (1974) *Schooling, Experience, and Earnings*, New York: Columbia University Press.

Mitra, A. (2010) 'Migration, livelihood and well-being: Evidence from Indian city slums', *Urban Studies*, 47(7): 1371–90.

Montgomery, J. (1991) 'Social networks and labor market outcomes: Towards an economic analysis', *American Economic Review*, 81(5): 1408–18.

Munshi, K. (2003) 'Networks in the modern economy: Mexican migrants in US labor market', *Quarterly Journal of Economics*, 118(2): 549–97.

Pollock, G., Antcliff, V. and Ralphs, R. (2002) 'Work orders: Analysing employment histories using sequence data', *International Journal of Social Research Methodology*, 5(2): 91–105.

Rabe-Hesketh, S., Skrondal, A. and Pickles, A. (2004) 'GLLAMM Manual', Technical Report, Working Paper Series 160, U.C. Berkeley Division of Bio-statistics.

Roberts, K. (2001) 'The determinants of job choice by rural labor migrants in Shanghai', *China Economic Review*, 12: 15–39.

Rosenbaum, J. E., DeLuca, S., Miller, S. and Roy K. (1999) 'Pathways into work: Short- and long-term effects of personal and institutional ties', *Sociology of Education*, 72(3): 179–96.

Schaeffer, N. C. and Presser, S. (2003) 'The science of asking questions', *Annual Review of Sociology*, 29: 65–88.

Simon, C. and Warner, J. (1992) 'Matchmaker, matchmaker: The effect of old-boy networks on job match quality, earnings, and tenure', *Journal of Labor Economics*, 10(3): 306–30.

Smith, S. (2000) 'Mobilizing social resources: Race, ethnic, and gender differences in social capital and persisting wage inequalities', *Sociological Quarterly*, 41(4): 509–37.

Stigler, G. (1961) 'The economics of information', *Journal of Political Economy*, 69(5): 213–25.

Wooldridge, J. (2002) *Econometric analysis of cross section and panel data*, Cambridge, MA: MIT Press.

Xu, W., Tan, K.C. and Wang, G. (2006) 'Segmented local labor markets in post reform China: Gender earnings inequality in the case of two towns in Zhejiang Province', *Environment and Planning A*, 38(1): 85–109.

Zang, X. (2003) 'Network resources and job search in urban China', *Journal of Sociology*, 39(2): 115–29.

Zhang, X. and Kanbur, R. (2005) 'Spatial inequality in education and health care in China', *China Economic Review*, 16: 189–204.

Zhou, D. (2000) 'Outsiders and 'dual communities': A survey in the Pearl River Delta', *Journal of Sun Yat-sen University*, 40(2): 107–12.

6 Situating translocality in flux landscapes

Migrants and urban villages in the city of Guangzhou

Cecilie Andersson

Introduction

When you approach the urban villages[1] in the city centre, their main road entrances are often flanked by wagon bikes awaiting new assignments. The riders rest on the side roads or negotiate the conditions of the next trip with clients coming to these liminal places from both the urban village and the surrounding city (see Figure 6.1). Even though motorcycles and other light vehicles have been banned from the city centre of Guangzhou since 2006, the wagon bikes from Xian Cun and other urban villages in the area have operated within the entire financial district of Tianhe ever since. Delivery men driving on the streets at daytime can now expect heavy economic penalties. That is why, in the traffic, they act very differently from aggressive car drivers. As I have observed them, they sneak around in a humbler and more silent way, not contributing to queuing or offending pedestrians. Also to limit the risk of being caught they will limit their trips in the daytime to assignments inside or close to the village, using narrow lanes and backstreets in the city, while at night they operate across the entire financial district. This pattern is a form of time and space sharing of interests. It functions to integrate the many opposing interests of the city, the village and the many activities of their common populations within a multi-scalar urban context.

Inside the urban villages, wagon bikes are often the only option, as cars are too big to enter the narrow lanes, but they are also essential in the connections between the villages and in exchanges between the agencies of the village and the city. Their practice shows how a border is never only a border, and a boundary is never only a boundary. When the situation allows for negotiations the boundary will immediately become a border.

In the Chinese city, the migrants operate within flux landscapes, evolved through rapid urban transformation. They are seen as a temporary population within a shifting urban ambience or as a 'floating population' within a fluid urban fabric,[2] depending if time or space is to define the context. The special situation in China, with the rural–urban divide caused by the dual *hukou* classification system,[3] explains why it is obvious for both the Chinese authorities and for the people concerned to look at urban villages as rural entities within the city, and to categorize rural–urban migrants as a rural population, even though some of them

Situating translocality in flux landscapes 85

Figure 6.1 Delivery men awaiting new assignments outside Xian Cun, 2008.
Source: Photograph taken by author.

have resided in the city for decades. The divide is based on political and administrative practices, and not on concrete spatial conditions. Urban villages are for instance in many cases, the densest urban structures within the city. They are in some instances still blank spots on the urban map,[4] but in a localized context urban villages engage in multiple relations with the city and constitute an interwoven part of the urban fabric, while the migrant workforce sustains the transformation of the city from within.

With a migrant perspective on marginalized habitation in the city, urban villages and construction sites are the most visible form of migrant housing within the city. While urban villages take up approximately 20 per cent of the land of the urban area in Guangzhou, they accommodate about 70 per cent of the migrant population, which again constitutes about 40 per cent of the entire population in the city (Lin *et al*. 2011).[5] Many migrants, both residing in the urban village and visiting, find their work, network, social scene and everyday services within the urban village.[6] The urban village grants migrants an ability to sustain their basic needs and tends to become a migrant neighbourhood. As the whole city is in a process of exuviation, so are the urban villages. They are in the midst of redevelopment but also under a constant risk of being demolished. Throughout this chapter I would like to discuss the 'situatedness' of migrants within the city, as the discourse of migrants being on the move continues to affect their subjective spatial positioning within the city. In regard to situatedness, it is here relevant to question to what degree the urban village is understood or negotiated as more than a peri-urban enclave on the urban periphery and how to look at migrant perceptions of localized contexts.

For my argument I will use stories of places and people gathered through long-term observations, interviews and registrations in the urban village Xian Cun in

Zhujiang New Town in Tianhe district. Xian Cun is a village far into a demolition process, but still partly inhabited as of September 2012. To enquire into the voice of the migrants and their perceptions of relating to the urban village and the city, I will also refer to co-research with migrants in two long-term documentation projects conducted in the urban village Shigangxi Cun in Panyu district: a house rent project, collecting personal diaries from migrant residents as their tenant contribution, and a Photo Documentation Project, collecting photographic impressions and written and oral narratives that view and reflect the changes in the everyday perception of being a migrant in the city.

I choose to focus on the *situatedness* of migrants to challenge the dominant discourse stating that Chinese migrants are depicted as either 'on the move' or as 'placed' in the peri-urban areas, and in that sense can be seen as either displaced or emplaced. Some scholars clearly situate the migrants in the urban villages (Siu 2007), but in doing so fail to take into consideration how migrants themselves negotiate their relation to the urban sphere through their everyday practice on broader multi-scalar premises, including the urban neighbourhood, the whole city, their hometown and beyond. Here, I would like to argue that the dominant discourse needs to be challenged with a focus that looks at the mobile migrants as situated within a multi-sited urban landscape, and not put in place within the borders of an urban village. The migrants' locales need to be seen as multi-scalar[7] as we need to acknowledge that their spatial contextual relations bridge the hometown, family and heritage with their urban ambitions. Only then can the premises of spatial inclusion for the migrants in the city be recognized and negotiated, despite the discriminating rural–urban policy.

Out of place and put in place

With regard to the migrants' relation to the city, I find Tamara Jacka's (2006) notions of emplacement through social control relevant. She argues how social control consequently places people both in particular relationships with other people and in relation to their physical environment. In the case of China, the *hukou* system and its supplementing regulations act as this form of control, through emplacement that makes migrants feel both marginalized and 'out of place' within the urban sphere. At the same time, their spatial practice is restricted and subordinated, meaning they are 'put in place' within the city. The prelude story of the tricycles can function as an example of this, as the delivery men's activity is clearly restricted on multiple levels, explaining why they operate both in and out of place.

In general, migrants, as rural citizens temporarily residing in the city, are 'out of place'. When renting an apartment inside a confined urban village, either on the outskirts of the city or in more central areas, they find themselves in neglected, rural migrant enclaves,[8] not representing the desired image of the modern Chinese city. If the village is visible from outside, it damages the desired harmonious image of the city. If the village is hidden behind fences depicting the ideal city, it is an image that shows a modernization that does not include villages in the city.

Situating translocality in flux landscapes 87

It is not difficult to find examples of this when looking at the ways the authorities are handling the villages. During the preparations for the Asian Games in Guangzhou in 2010, for instance, we were able to witness a wide range of tactics. Some villages were demolished, some were hidden behind fences, some were hidden behind newly planted trees, or entire villages were painted in uniform pale yellow and had the same fake tilted rooftops attached.

One can see how migrants' locales are eradicated out of place, when for instance urban villages and other migrant enclaves are demolished and the forced relocation of migrants is conducted without compensation and on short notice in many cases, as part of '*clean up campaigns*'. This, according to Jacka, strengthens the highly disruptive alienation of the migrants, and the sense that they are not wanted and are 'out of place' in the city (Jacka 2006: 103).

Translocality

In this chapter, the term *translocality* is used, as conceptualized by Brickell and Datta (2011). Resisting looking at mobility and migration as uprooted, dislocated or travelling, Brickell and Datta suggest that we situate the mobile subjective.

Brickell and Datta's (2011) argument builds on Georg Marcus's (1989) and Michael Smith's (2001) works, which first called for a multi-sited transnational ethnography that looks at translocal linkages and interconnections, focusing on the multi-positionality of the migrants and their local–local connections. This suggestion is an alternative to the deterritorialized imaginings of mobility and displacement conceptualized by Appadurai (1996) and Hannerz (1998). Introduced as a way to situate the deterritorialized notion of transnationalism, it becomes an agency-oriented approach towards migrant experiences that broadens the earlier focus on social networks and economic exchange in an attempt to address the spatial processes and identities within local–local relations. Through this shift in focus they turn abstract transit spaces into tangible transit places.

In Brickell and Datta's approach, replacing the transnational focus, often used when looking at migration and mobility, with a situated translocal focus enables us to look at a multi-sited and multi-scalar situatedness that is not subsumed within a hierarchy of national or global, but rather captures the socio-spatial processes of localized contexts and everyday practices in migrant experiences. Through the translocal approach, attention is directed at the multiple and hybrid stories that go beyond economic exchange, political organizations or social networks to look into the various negotiations of space and place in between (Brickell and Datta 2011). One can then aim to provide ways to understand not just micro-processes but also macro-forces through an understanding of the local as situated in a network of spaces, places and scales, where identities are negotiated and transformed in a local site of exchange. The local is not constructed at any certain scale, but functions as a multi-local asset, constructed, politicized and relevant in everyday lives in numerous scales (Brickell and Datta 2011). This allows us to examine the connections of spaces and places related to migration as local–local journeys, and not just across spaces and scales like rural–urban or inter-regional.

88 Cecilie Andersson

On the view of migrant portraits beyond the confined peri-urban village

Through his study of migrant discourses in Chinese contemporary film, Dror Kochan shows how a new and alternative discourse is emerging. While the dominant discourse places migrants in an 'urban periphery or in peri-urban areas, socially separated from the city' (Kochan 2009: 298) the alternative discourse of the sociospatial divide is able to remove migrants from these peri-urban areas and instead place them in the city itself. Their involvement in city life, but also in their own direction of life, is evident in these expressions and can be seen in opposition to the migrants portrayed in the confined spaces of the urban village, in Kochan's argumentation.

This can perhaps explain why most of the migrants I have interviewed showed no sentiment towards the demolition of the village where they reside. They came to work in the city, not to live in a certain urban village. They say that personally they do not think it will be difficult to find another village to live in, or another cheap place to reside. The rental house management service centre for Tienhe district, Xian Cun street, said the average stay of a migrant resident in Xian Cun was six months. Most migrant residents tend to think of their stay in the village as temporary, while their urban ambition tends to be of a more lasting character. With many rumours of demolition going on for years, migrants have become used to thinking of the urban village as a place that will eventually be gone, and some even describe this as being a development for the better, resulting in a more beautiful urban environment. As individuals, most of the migrants I have talked to are not opposed to the current notion of harmonious urban development as promoted by the city authorities, and sincerely think village areas become better places when they assimilate with the modern city surrounding it. They do not resist a movement towards an urban development that has no room for the urban village (see Figure 6.2). In public, they are still seen as resistant forces against this ideal urban state. Resistance is thus in urban villages not uproar, but rather a state of disturbance (Serres 2007).

When portraying their everyday use of the city, the contributors to the Photo Documentation Project do not distinguish the urban village from the city. In their representation the village is more to be seen as an integrated neighbourhood within the urban sphere. Some portray their home in the urban village, while they in the same story of everyday practice present us with photographs of how they use public places within the city or how they relate to the absorbing work environment, sometimes located in the city, in shops or construction sites, sometimes in gated factory areas, sometimes in the village. Within the group, the participants in the Photo Documentation Project relate to very different physical and social ambiences. Living in an urban village or in some dormitory in the gated factory areas, or guarding the fences and sweeping the stone floors of the new real estate projects, all provide very different perceptions of life. Their everyday life is lived across these spatial distinctions, and the inter-connections between these sites frame their subjective and diverse life experiences as migrants in the city.

Situating translocality in flux landscapes 89

Figure 6.2 Xian Cun food market under demolition, September 2010.
Source: Photograph taken by author.

Some live in ordered, clean environments, while others are surrounded with rubbish. Still, when they zoom into the details of their immediate and subjective relations to the environment there are both more similarities and more diversity to be observed across these borders of neat/messy/village/city in the pictures of the participants in the documentation project. This can often be seen as ways of bridging the different local scales, expressed in the local–local relation orientation of the translocal approach, for instance through narratives that express their subjective relation to aspects of heritage, family, work or through more ambiguous expressions of relations to dreams and aspirations of a life in the city or contradictory relations to the modern sphere as such.

The wagon bike example at the beginning of this chapter can be linked to one of Kochan's examples of the new discourse and its potential. Kochan mentions the film *Beijing Bicycle* from 2001 by Wang Xiaoshuai. Here we see how the bicycle, rather than the *hukou*, is the means of integration into the city. Buying a bicycle is not just buying a vehicle; it is an investment in an interaction with the city, through work, through mobility and situatedness. In the film, the drama surrounds the negotiations involved in getting, keeping and using the bicycle. The character rebuilds his social identity through the use of the bike. 'The public sphere can thus be seen as an arena of discursive interaction, allowing a more accessible discussion in which participation is not limited only to the political realm, but can exist in the social and cultural sphere as well' (Kochan 2009: 303).

Obtaining a bicycle and finding a way to use it to raise an income would not be easy for newly arrived migrants if they were not attached to an urban village with its opportunities for contacts and level of reciprocity (Lin *et al.* 2011). In the

90 *Cecilie Andersson*

interviews I have conducted, delivery men describe how they bought their bicycles from contacts they established in the urban village, and when the cycle is not in use they have to either accommodate the bicycles in their own homes or store them in the guarded bicycle sheds inside the urban villages. Many delivery men provide business cards with contact information for clients coming from all over the city, but most of their clients have some relation to the activities of the village. Even though they operate on a multi-local level including the surrounding city, the facilities and opportunities created within and through the practice of the urban village are still crucial.

Urban village as the arrival city

In his book on arrival cities, Doug Saunders (2010) strongly advocates the potential of the rural–migrant neighbourhood as a tool for integration into the urban sphere. In his argument, the arrival city is a transitional space that builds on constant linkages towards the originating villages and the established city, providing a foothold in the city through its connectedness. The arrival city should thus not be seen as a static slum, an immigrant gateway or a community of primary settlement, but rather as a place for dynamic change with a transitory role vital in the urbanization process to absorb the additional 3.1 billion people that are expected to move to the cities between 2007 and 2050, worldwide. In his book, Saunders looks at arrival cities all over the world, as well as the urban village phenomenon in China. He argues that the arrival city can create and distribute social capital through its ability to create and maintain networks and to function as an entry mechanism, an urban establishment platform and a social mobility path. In this way the arrival city is linked to the surrounding urban sphere.

Although Saunders (2010) points to all this potential within the arrival city, he also addresses the factors that can turn well-functioning arrival cities into poverty traps. The physical form of the arrival city is in that respect important for its success. The presence of neutral public spaces, the ability to establish small businesses or open shops or workshops on the ground floor or to extend houses, are some examples. Also the accessibility of social services and proximity to schools and infrastructural links to city centres, workplaces and cultural activities are vital for the arrival city neighbourhood to avoid becoming a poverty trap. These are all spatial qualities that the central urban villages in Chinese cities have or easily could have had. When urban villages can only be said to be well-functioning arrival cities to a certain extent, it is because they do provide networks and partly function as entry mechanisms into the city or establishment platforms, but they hardly provide a social mobility path. This is, however, not to lay blame on the physical form, but on the policies of rural–urban division that work against the transition of migrants' integration into a full-fledged urban life.[9]

Hukou and rural–urban landscape

In this context, it is important to understand the impact of the household registration regulation (*hukou dengji tiaoli*) or *hukou* system, both as a major provider of

Situating translocality in flux landscapes 91

spatial differentiated conditions, and as a deliverer of reasons for the rural population to explain their move to the cities. It is also crucial to know about the way the system has been enforced to understand how the conditions of the rural–urban migrants have come to be as exploitative and unjust as shown in practice, with rural–urban migrant workers excluded from urban welfare and social security systems. This has shaped the biased premises favouring the local villagers and the urban population, and created the discriminating conditions of the urban villages.[10]

Traditionally, Chinese market cities like Guangzhou have been 'dynamic, cultural, economic and political spaces linking country to city', in the words of Siu (2002). This tradition has been severely challenged by the *hukou* and housing tenure systems dividing urban and rural within the expanding cities since the second part of the twentieth century. Through urban expansion and the encapsulating of rural entities in the form of urban villages, and discrimination between urban and rural residents within the cities, the border between rural and urban has moved within the city itself.

Even when focusing on the urban development in Guangzhou's Tianhe district during the 1990s, with new high-rises and urban grid, we must not forget that Tianhe was still not so much a downtown area as a big construction site surrounded by paddy fields. It was not an established urban district, but a street grid where one tall building after another was completed throughout the fields. In between the new wide, vast, urban grid, old villages and new high-rise residential neighbourhoods stood side by side with plenty of transitional spaces of fields not yet making their final urban jump. The villages were still part of the skyline, and there was visual contact between the villages, situated less than a kilometre apart: Shipai, Xian Cun, Liede, Wuyang Cun, Jiazi Cun and Yangjicun. The villages were in a transitional state of replacing old built structures of one or two floors with taller buildings of four to seven floors. The old buildings were often patio-like homes. The new buildings in the villages were massive volumes extending towards the neighbouring plots above the narrow lanes to build up an extremely dense urban structure.

We can illustrate this ambience of a paddy growing up to become the commercial centre of a mega-city with global aspirations, with the villagers still growing vegetables in their traditional way in between the bulldozers and construction sites. For instance, I did an interview in Xian Cun with two old local villagers from the Lu family who had been farmers all their lives. They told me they had kept growing vegetables all around their village until 1998, while the tallest building in Guangzhou, CITIC Plaza, was completed in their 'backyard' in 1997.

In our case, with urban villages and migrants trapped in the 'in-betweenness' of rural entities within cities, the place and time of transition is not only a state of becoming, but just as much a transition formation, a constant but shifting ambience of marginality. Turner (1967) wrote that in the liminal period a transitional being is ambiguous as he passes through a realm where he is no longer classified by the former state and not yet classified by the coming state. This in-betweenness has trapped both the urban village and the migrant population within the city, but, as I will argue, this state of in-betweenness is trespassed upon through the practice of subverting boundaries. Further, Turner built on the book *Purity and Danger* by Mary Douglas (1966) regarding how the unclear can be seen as the unclean in her concept of pollution. In this regard, the transitional beings are unclear and contradictory in a sense that makes them polluting, being liminal in regard to the cultural topography. The words and actions of the 'clean up campaigns' and the urge for 'urban harmonious development' within Chinese public discourse can be seen to perform a justification for such an unclear–unclean eradication implementation that urban villages and the migrant population have had to relate to.

The urban village as a multicultural site

The street office leader in Xian Cun said they had migrants from every province in China living in their village. 'Except perhaps from Xinjiang', he added. In my surveys I have met people in Xian Cun from most parts of China, many from Hunan, Hebei and Sichuan, but also some from more remote places such as Inner Mongolia. The Xinjiang nut sellers would also work within the village, appearing in their special hats and with their bicycles loaded with nuts, raisins or big halva-cakes. In certain periods you could see them all over the city, not only around the urban villages, but also near all metro-hubs and other crowded places. In an interview I did with one of them, he explained how they would come in groups of maybe 50 men, and then stay for a couple of months to work in the city between harvests. He told me they all lived together in an urban village, but they worked all over the city, including many urban villages. This example is not just about multiculturalism, but also concerns the character of the new arrivals and its effect on the neighbourhood through the typical annual from-the-countryside-to-the-city oscillation carried out by some migrants residing in the urban villages. This activity is also part of shaping the ambience of the urban villages as it is part of creating constant changes, since every new wave of arrivals takes part in transforming the urban village as a multicultural entity. 'Migrants and other residents of the village in the city have to negotiate their experiences both of belonging and of a perception of difference through their meeting with the changing ambience [of the village]', says Wise (2011: 96) about similar multilayered multicultural spaces in Chinese migrant neighbourhoods in Australia. This practice is 'producing in turn complex forms of translocal belonging and localized displacements'. At the same time, it constitutes the place through connections to other places further away from the locality of the neighbourhood.

On the approach of skills to subvert boundaries

In his book *The Craftsman* Sennett (2008) proposes a very constructive way to look at resistance in relation to ambiguity not only as attitudes, but also as skills. Sennett argues how resistance can be found or made. Either something blocks us or we make our own difficulties. Either way, we need techniques to work well with the obstacles; we need imagination, and we need to find ways of tolerating the frustration. He argues that the skills which allow people to productively dwell

Situating translocality in flux landscapes 93

in frustration of the resistance are ways of recasting a problem into other terms, ways of reorienting one's expectations or readjusting one's behaviour if the problem lasts longer than expected, and ways of finding the most forgiving element in a difficult situation. In my understanding, these are all techniques for handling a problem in a dynamic way that the migrants address every day, not statically identifying the problem, and not statically defining a given method for solving it, but dynamically to persist in an open form wherein neither the problem nor the solutions are definitively defined, and thus remain open for negotiations. One example of this is how the delivery men negotiate their practice or the forthcoming story of the shoe seller and her fellow migrants occupying the street to sell their goods.

When further addressing resistance, Sennett (2008) divides the sites of resistance into two types: walls and membranes. Walls can be seen as boundaries, where things end, for example a gated community. Membranes can be seen as borders or sites of exchange where organisms become more interactive. The urban village and its migrant population face resistance in sites of boundaries and borders. The urban village is handled through regulations from the city authorities defining it and reacting to it as a unity with a boundary dividing it from the city, but through the practice of its population, the borders of the village become a very active edge, reacting with the city outside the village, and letting the city react within the village.

After the urban village Xian Cun was forced inside the grid of the new city, many changes regarding its organization emerged. In the old traditional village, the inner main streets were the most important, but with adaptation to the street grid, demolishing houses that exceeded the grid, houses that used to be in the middle of the dense village fabric, were suddenly facing a 16-lane street of the city. The traditional village can be characterized as introverted, in comparison with the urban village with its extrovert character. Apart from houses blocked by fences, every house facing the street accommodates some sort of business, as many types of businesses prefer access to the surrounding road for easy transportation and contact with passing clients. Being part of the lane of houses facing the city streets allows in a way an assimilating character. Here, businesses from outside that would never locate inside the village get cheap, flexible conditions. Clients that would never enter the village will stop by and do their preferred trades here.

Sennett argues that 'Working with resistance means, in urbanism, converting boundaries into borders ... the problem is that we are better at building boundaries than borders' (Sennett 2008: 229). Often we think of the centre as a place to share, while in reality the borders are the active zones: 'the zone in which people have to deal with difficulty' (Sennett 2008: 230). That was quite apparent in Xian Cun, as the centre of the village was a quiet and introverted place for the local villagers to recuperate in the old centre, while constant negotiations with the city were taking place in the border zones where people living in the village, both local villagers and migrants, interacted with the people, practices and regulations of the city. During the demolition period the pattern I observed was, however, somewhat different, as interaction between the urban village and the city was a sensitive issue.

After months of the local villagers demonstrating for better compensation outside the main gate of the village office, facing the city street, village life has now curled up inside. The village is no longer adjacent to the urban streets but is buffered by a green belt of lawns and trees and tall fences (see Figure 6.3). The houses seen from the surrounding city appear abandoned, with windows and gratings removed, and hardly any laundry hanging out to dry. The inner streets are still lively and taking part in interactions of trade and social activities.

I argue how migrants seek to subvert the regulative boundaries of the village and city by acting as if it was a negotiable border. The story of the wagon bikes is one example of how this conversion is done in practice. In the evenings, when the rush hour traffic was calming and the enforcement of the law was less strict, they would ignore the laws and cycle all over the city, the distance depending on time and effort, and not on regulations. From time to time they would be caught. Everyone I talked to had been caught. What they then negotiated for was a fine paid directly to the policeman. This would often be considered more as bribery, as the policeman would keep the money and give them a false receipt, but leave their vehicle and the goods. If they were unlucky, the policeman would transcribe a real fine and confiscate the bike and/or the goods. A wagon bike could be bought for about 200 Yuan,[11] which was a considerable share of a month's salary for a delivery man, and it was a personal investment. During transportation, the delivery man was also responsible for the value of the goods, thus the job was risky once they broke the law. The delivery men thus negotiate and work with resistant forces using not only time and space sharing of interests, but also *soft power and minimum force* (Sennett 2008).

A different example of this attitude to a practice of resistance and spatial negotiations could be the organization of the billboard workshops along the south end street of Xian Cun. Most of these enterprises were family businesses with migrants from Hunan, and they were organized as dual private and commercial spaces, as

Figure 6.3 Xian Cun seen from northeast, September 2010.
Source: Photograph taken by author.

Situating translocality in flux landscapes 95

the family members all lived in the workshop. They were also organized as a flexible work and relaxation area, as some worked while others cooked, took care of children, watched TV or talked inside the same confined space. They often had several branches, one workshop inside the dense part of the urban village for production, and another shop and assembly hall to face the clients of the village and the passers-by on the street. Some families even had shops and workshops in several urban villages at the same time. When they opened the gate in the morning you saw into a home with a big dining table in the centre. They finished one by one, put their chairs in the corner and brought out the billboard materials and paint, temporarily occupying 'their' share of the public pavement. The big table was stored away when the rice gruel was finished, as the floor was needed for the signs and clients. The workshops were organized in a flexible way, and also the location along the main city grid provided flexibility regarding operating mode, similar to that of the wagon bikers. I believe the migrants depend on this type of flexibility provided through spatial interaction with both the city and the urban village, due to their lack of domination of space within the city. The limited resources in the village are already so densely exploited that without this flexibility in time and space sharing their limited powers would leave them no spatial latitude.

Another example is a widening of the pavement outside the old village school in the old main street of Xian Cun, now partly demolished. Until recently, the building functioned as one of a dozen bicycle sheds in the village. The couple living and working in the building used the facade facing the plaza only for a small announcement of their business and for drying clothes. However, many other activities were taking place outside the building. Together they illustrate yet another example of how the regulative boundaries become negotiable borders, through a practice of using a place, this time a plaza within the sphere of the urban village, but still with an orientation traversing the village, establishing local–local connections beyond the village.

At the widening of the street, different activities were taking place throughout the day. Occasionally, some migrant women from Kunming would come to collect cardboard and plastic in the plaza. I observed and interviewed them in this plaza two years in a row. They lived in another urban village, half an hour's walk away, but came to Xian Cun because it was a more resourceful village with better supply of material and less competition because many of the migrants living in Xian Cun were working in the service sector in the financial district and not in self-employment, as were these women. This exemplifies how different groups of migrants relate to various multi-scalar constellations within the city, among them places within different urban villages, and not only the village where they reside.

During my visit to Xian Cun in 2008, the activity at this widening of the street was an exception from the rest of the street, being calm in respect to street vendors. The plaza always displayed some sort of commercial activity. In 2009, the residents of the village had received a public announcement saying that the village would be demolished before the Asian Games in November 2010, and speculation rose about the village being demolished in February 2010. In late 2009, the

96 *Cecilie Andersson*

residents saw how patrolling became less strict as a result of the village authorities no longer focusing on the enforcement of street order, and street vendors started operating in front of the shops all along the old main street, and not just in the plaza in question. While some residents had started to move away because of the talk of demolition, the village streets were as lively as ever.

When the demolition started in late summer 2010, some shops were still operating in the old main street, but the typical street vendors were replaced by recyclers of constructional elements of gates, doors and windows. Many of the former migrant residents working in the business district had moved away, and the apartments were taken by migrants working on the demolition of the village. In my last visit in October 2011, most of the buildings had been emptied out, but small stalls and street vendors were using the space in front of the former shops to display their goods. The old school/bicycle shed was empty and roofless, but one night I saw it being used for a big banquet by the local villagers mobilizing for a continued fight for their compensation. The plaza in front of the old school was once again one of the liveliest places of the village.

In 2008, I met a migrant mother bringing her one-year-old daughter to live in Xian Cun while the father lived in a factory dormitory in another city. She would come to sell embroidered shoes in the plaza, being so conveniently placed right outside the house where she lived. The sole seller would not gain anything from claiming a right to a place to sell her soles on the street. She would be denied this both from her fellow migrants depending on the same flexible street use as her, and by the local authorities wanting the users to be of insignificant interest. She understands that when her appearance has a minimal disturbing effect on the situation of the street use, her activities are less transgressive and she can then reduce the calculated risk of being caught. Being silent and invisible is to do with minimum force.

Together, all the users of this plaza had in a way occupied it with their activity, but none of them in a total way, all of them just occasionally. Continuing their activities, despite their opposition to the law, was for them to practise soft power, as they did get to temporarily territorialize the place, but only if they were ready to move whenever they were confronted. It may be that the local authorities could also be said to practise 'soft power' in this case, as they did allow the activity to persist as long as it did not get too formalized. It was accepted as long as it had a temporary character. And, taking this line of argument further, this could even be said about the whole existence of urban villages and migrants in the urban realm; they have to use soft power and minimum force in their negotiations and are only allowed to indicate a vague and temporary territorializing of a place in the city.

Conclusion

If this vague territorializing was their whole latitude however, migrants' situatedness would be miserable, as it could be said that they were 'placed' in a liminal peri-urban inbetween state. The migrants are, however, not just a mirage, vaguely

Situating translocality in flux landscapes 97

positioning themselves within the temporality and liminality of the city. On the contrary, through the subjective stories I have presented in this chapter, I hope I have shown how the urban village in the city is an arena where the migrant residents, through their everyday practices and attitudes, subvert diverse boundaries, not only that of the urban–rural divide, but equally important that of their own subjective experience of belonging and connecting to various multi-scalar urban spheres, through local–local relations, within and beyond the urban village.

Bridging the thoughts of temporary territorializing a place as a means to subvert diverse boundaries, and not only that of the urban–rural divide, with thoughts of situating within the multi-sited and multi-scalar localities enables us to see how migrants through their negotiations can be said to trespass boundaries just as much through their ability to connect and interlink. Thus, through their practice, migrants challenge the massive temporality of the urban ambience through a multi-local situatedness, relating to the urban village, the city and beyond. With this as a premise, one can find a starting point to ground a spatial inclusion for the migrants in the city.

Acknowledgement

I would like to thank Migrant Workers Documentation Centre, Panyu, Mr Zeng and participants in the Photo Documentation Project, Chen Jie Lin and Ping Shen; and students from South China University of Science and Technology: Xian Peining, Gong Cheng, Weng Xuan, Han Meng Jie, Chan Yiran, Peng Weiqing, Wang Xi, Liu Yayuan, Lin Ying Hao, Li Hong and Deng Li Ying for helping me on this project.

Notes

1. When I use the term 'urban village', I refer to the same condition as Chinese scholars when they use the term 'chengzhongcun' or 'village in the city'. A condition characterized by the villages' dual rural–urban structure, emerging when the agrarian village loses its farmland to urban expansion and is left with the residential areas and thus starts an approach to gaining an income from housing (Lin *et al.* 2011).
2. Fluid, as in Gutierrez and Portefaix's (2003) explanations of the state of the Pearl River Delta in their 'lean planning approach'.
3. On the hukou or household registration regulation (*hukou dengji tiaoli*), see later in this chapter.
4. While some urban villages have kept their rural status, many are administered as urban neighbourhoods.
5. Only migrants staying for more than 6 months in the city are included in official population estimates.
6. There are more invisible forms of migrant housing than the urban villages, further strengthening the migrants' marginality within the city. Jacka (2006: 104) accounts for this when she describes how migrant women working as maids are isolated in their employers' apartments and waitresses sleep on the restaurant floors or tables at night, while cleaners in the large offices live in dormitories in the basements of the office blocks.
7. In this chapter, I use the term 'multi-scalar locality' as theorized by Brickell and Datta (2011). The term is contextualized later in this chapter.

98   Cecilie Andersson

8. Xian Cun had, in 2005, a population of 51,868 residents. Among them 38,650 were migrant residents, while the remaining were local villagers and urban residents according to Tianhe District Document Department.
9. Among the more successful arrival cities, operating as upward mobility clusters, are some neighbourhoods in the UK, where the main difference from other failing arrival cities is that 85 per cent of the arrival city migrant residents have UK citizenship, according to Saunders (2010).
10. For a broader discussion on the effects of the system, see the retrospective analysis of the hukou system by Kan Wing Chan (2009) in *The Chinese Hukou System at 50*, and Tamara Jacka's book from 2006, about the many causes and effects of rural population becoming and staying migrant residents in the city, exemplifying the subjective experiences of the hukou regulation.
11. In December 2008.

References

Appadurai, A. (1996) *Modernity at Large: Cultural Dimensions of Globalization*, Minneapolis: University of Minnesota Press.

Brickell, K. and Datta, A. (2011) (eds) *Translocal Geographies. Spaces, Places, Connections*, Farnham: Ashgate Publishing Limited.

Chan, K. W. (2009) 'The Chinese Hukou System at 50', *Eurasian Geography and Economics*, 50(2): 197–221.

Douglas, M. (1966) *Purity and Danger: An Analysis of Concepts of Pollution and Taboo*. London: Routledge.

Gutierrez, L. and Portefaix, V. (2003) 'Pearl River Delta: Lean Planning, Thin Patterns Urban Flashes Asia', *Architectural Design*, 73(5), Sussex: Wiley-Academy.

Hannerz, U. (1998) 'Transnational research', in H. R. Bernard (ed.), *Handbook of Methods in Cultural Anthropology*, London: Altamira Press.

Jacka, T. (2006) *Rural Women in Urban China. Gender, Migration, and Social Change* Armonk, New York: M. E. Sharpe.

Kochan, D. (2009) 'Visual representation of internal migration and social change in China', *China Information*, 23: 285–316.

Lin, Y., Meulder, B. and Wang, S. (2011) 'Understanding the "Village in the City" in Guangzhou: economic integration and development issue and their implications for the urban migrant', *Urban Studies*, 48(16): 3583–98.

Marcus, G. E. (1989) 'Imagining the whole: ethnography's contemporary efforts to situate itself', *Critique of Anthropology*, 9 (3): 7–30.

Saunders, D. (2010) *Arrival City. How the largest migration in history is shaping our world*. London: William Heinemann.

Sennett, R. (2008) *The Craftsman*, London: Penguin Books.

Serres, M. (2007) *Parasite*, Minneapolis: University of Minnesota Press.

Siu, H. F. (2002) 'Redefining the market town through festivals in South China', in David Faure and Tao Tao Liu (eds.) *Town and Country in China: Identity and Perception*, Basingstoke: Palgrave.

Siu, H. F. (2007) 'Grounding displacement: Uncivil urban spaces in postreform South China', *American Ethnologist*, 34(2): 329–50.

Smith, M. P. (2001) *Transnational Urbanism: Locating Globalization*, Oxford: Blackwell.

Turner, V. W. (1967) *The Forest of Symbols: aspects of Ndernbu ritual*, Ithaca, NY: Cornell University Press.

Wise, A. (2011) 'You wouldn't know what's in there would you? Homeliness and "Foreign" signs in Ashfield, Sydney', in: Brickell, K. and Datta, A (2011) *Translocal Geographies. Spaces, Places, Connections*. Farnham: Ashgate Publishing Limited.

7 Migrant integration in China
Evidence from Guangzhou

Bart Wissink, Arjan Hazelzet and Werner Breitung

Introduction

While migrants have played a crucial role in China's economic growth since the 1980s (Zhang 2001; Fan 2008), their reception in urban centres has not been easy. National and municipal governments have reacted to migration with repeated regulatory strategies (Zhang 2001). Local residents and the media perceive migrants negatively: allegedly, they overload urban infrastructures, engage in criminal activities, and violate birth control regulations (Solinger 1995; Zhang 2002; Fan 2008). In this hostile atmosphere, the general response to migration has been separation: institutionally, socially and spatially. The continuation of the hukou system, with its negative consequences for migrant urban life, forms just one case in point. This system might fit the official rhetoric of a temporary 'floating population'. But while many migrants have returned to their home towns and more will follow, others seem to have longer-term ambitions (Liu *et al.* 2012). Meanwhile, institutional and other barriers seriously hinder their integration. With huge numbers of migrants, limited integration in the long run can threaten social stability.

While migrant integration in Chinese cities is an urgent research topic, English language research so far is remarkably limited. Against this background, this chapter presents an exploratory study of migrant integration in Guangzhou. On the basis of a household survey in Guangzhou in 2010 and 2011, we analyse the characteristics of the social networks of 599 migrants (out of 919 total respondents). Especially, we will answer the following research questions: *Where do migrants in Guangzhou live? What are the characteristics of their social networks? And to what extent does this relate to characteristics of the receiving neighbourhood?* Our analysis shows that migrants in Guangzhou have very diverse characteristics. Some have a local hukou while others have a temporary registration. Many live concentrated in urbanised villages, but others are scattered across the city. And while the social networks of some are homogeneous, others have mixed social networks. The findings imply that in Guangzhou a substantial part of the migrants integrate, reinforcing the idea that migration for them has a permanent character.

In this chapter, we reach these conclusions in seven sections. First we take a closer look at migration within China. Then we discuss the international literature

100   *Bart Wissink, Arjan Hazelzet and Werner Breitung*

on migrant integration. Together, these sections form the theoretical background for our discussion of the empirical material. This discussion starts with an explanation of the assumption of our study, followed by an overview of the characteristics of migrants in our Guangzhou sample. Next, we discuss the characteristics of migrant social networks, before analysing the existence of different migrant groups. The concluding section answers the research questions.

Attitudes towards migrants in China

Migration obviously is not unique to China. But Chinese institutional, sociocultural and economic practices, together with the related interpretation of migrants as a temporary 'floating population', do give it a specific local reality (Zhang 2001: 23). While many of these practices emerged during the recent reforms, others have a longer history. One crucial example is the household registration (hukou) system, enacted in 1958 in response to rapidly growing migration to cities. The system registers people in a hukou location (*hukou suozaidi*) with a rural or urban hukou classification (*hukou leibie*). It binds migration to cities to strict rules of approval (Fan 2008; Chan 2010). Additionally, communist rule gradually replaced commercial consumption in shops and restaurants with collective consumption in communes and work-units (*danwei*) (Davis 1995). Together, these practices radically diminished mobility (Solinger 1995: 5). The remaining migration consisted of relatively rare formal placements with hukou change (mainly between cities), and of political migration to rural areas for 're-education' or to populate regions. This helped to contain urban growth, and contributed to sharp boundaries between city and countryside (Douglas *et al.* 2012). In 1976, more than 80 per cent of China's population was rural.

All this dramatically changed after 1980 (Douglas *et al.* 2012; Breitung 2012). Concentrated Maoist cities transformed into huge urban fields, while the mixed functions of work-unit urbanism made way for networks of specialised urban enclaves like gated commodity housing, urbanised villages, shopping streets and malls, university towns, and special economic zones. Citywide infrastructure networks now organise everyday life, and transportation flows are extensive. Migration was one of the cornerstones of this amazing transformation. Between 1980 and 2000, 268 million Chinese entered the cities and the urbanisation rate grew from 19.6 per cent in 1980 to 42.9 per cent in 2005 (Yusuf and Nabeshima 2008: 1). According to the latest census, it has now surpassed 50 per cent. The precise contribution of rural–urban migration is difficult to determine (Davis 1995: 1), but estimates hold it to 70 per cent of urban population growth (Zheng *et al.* 2009: 425) or 140 million people (NBS 2010).

The rural exodus has multiple causes: rural labour surplus through agricultural de-collectivisation, demand for cheap labour in industrialising cities and large income disparities between rural and urban areas (Tian 2008). The growth of a market economy in cities and the end of food rationing in the 1980s further supported migration (Du and Li 2010:1). But migrants put stress on urban infrastructures and resources, and despite their economic contribution, they were soon

Migrant integration in China 101

considered a problem. Initially, local governments blocked or repressed migration, resulting in recurrent expulsions (Zhang 2002). Regulations in 1984 and 1985 introduced a more permissive approach through the creation of registration as temporary resident. But hukou regulations stayed in place, excluding temporary residents from urban services; only rich migrants with 'blue stamp' resident cards escaped this institutional exclusion.

The new regulations pictured migrants as a uniform floating population that would not settle down and integrate in cities (Zhang 2001: 26–38; Wang 2004; Li 2006). The majority of the migrants proved to be young, male, unmarried, with relatives in the same city, and with low education although higher than those staying behind. They engaged in unpopular low skilled jobs, while earning lower wages than local residents (Solinger 1995; Wang 2004; Fan 2008; Zheng *et al.* 2009). Nonetheless, migrants make up a diverse group (Solinger 1995; Zhang 2001) with different backgrounds and different plans for their future. The recent observation of a 'new' generation of migrants underlines these differences (Fan 2008; Liu *et al.* 2012). Born after 1980, these migrants have a higher education, a lower endurance for hardship and a stronger tendency towards individualism and consumerism, and they want to obtain an urban hukou. While migrants share a structurally disadvantaged position, they identify as diverse groups, and rarely picture themselves as part of a uniform 'floating population' (Zhang 2001; Li 2006).

Research suggests that the residential situation of migrants mirrors the differences between these groups (Wu *et al.* forthcoming). While Chinese households have been given the freedom to choose their preferred dwellings, tenure and neighbourhoods for the first time in decades, and some migrants have made it into commodity housing estates, for most this is impossible due to economic and institutional factors. Subsidies help to bring commodity housing within the reach of urban residents, but these subsidies are not available for migrants without a local hukou. With bureaucrats generally indifferent to migrant housing, and housing reforms generally overlooking the needs of migrants (Du and Li 2010), the result is enormous housing inequality (Tian 2008; Logan *et al.* 2009; Huang and Jiang 2009; He *et al.* 2010).

So where do migrants live? Generally, this depends on the employment situation (Wang 2004; Gransow 2010). Construction workers live in on-site barracks; dormitories house factory workers; and private households accommodate domestic workers. All others rent an apartment on the private market. Between 1998 and 2008, this sector rose from 25 per cent to 50 per cent of all migrants (Gransow 2010). Because of budget constraints, only a few places provide viable options: former work-units, old-street neighbourhoods and urbanised villages. And there are clear differences between cities, with rural migrants in Shanghai and Beijing dispersed in different housing categories, and migrants in the South concentrated in urbanised villages (Wu *et al.* forthcoming). These are former villages that have been swallowed by cities as result of urban sprawl. In 2003, such 'villages' accounted for 80 per cent of Guangzhou's migrants (Tian 2008). While migrant villages in Beijing – partly through chain migration – display a strong provincial

102 *Bart Wissink, Arjan Hazelzet and Werner Breitung*

selection, those in the South house mixed resident groups (Zhang 2001; Tian 2008; He *et al.* 2010; Wu *et al.* forthcoming). These housing solutions, however, are far from secure as city governments pursue redevelopment (Wu *et al.* forthcoming; Li and Li 2011).

Theories on migrant integration

Over the last decades, migration – both domestic and international – has become a global phenomenon (Massey *et al.* 1993). Traditional host societies like Australia, Canada, and the United States saw a shift from European immigrants towards immigrants from Asia, Africa and Latin America. Europe saw first the emergence of Mediterranean immigration to the North, while Southern countries became immigrant countries themselves more recently. And rapidly developing economies like India, Brazil, and China triggered unprecedented rural-to-urban migration.

The social sciences have paid considerable attention to the integration of these migrants. Initially, theories were mainly based on US experiences with European migrants. They were as much inspired by 'desirable' social developments, as they were by migrant realities (Rumbaut 1997). This is clearly reflected by the *classical assimilation theory*, for a long time the dominant theory on integration (Alba and Nee 1997; Brown and Bean 2006). Introduced by the Chicago School in the 1920s, it conceives of assimilation as a progressive, linear process in which migrants shed their former identity and after two or three generations fully integrate into mainstream America. Gordon (1964) argues that this process consists of several independent stages, starting with acculturation in terms of language, dress, and daily customs, and eventually involving all aspects of social life, including socioeconomic status, language attainment, intermarriage and residential location (Waters and Jiménez 2005).

For a long time, assimilation theory structured both scientific and popular narratives. But from the 1960s, migrant experiences created doubt about its predictive power, while the desirability of integration in the majority culture was criticised as ethnocentric (Rumbaut 1997). First, attention focused on the structural barriers to integration of African-Americans (Glazer and Moynihan 1963). More recently, the relevance of assimilation theory for second-generation migrants was questioned (Portes and Zhou 1993). This resulted in the *racial or ethnic disadvantage model*, which stresses that discrimination and institutional barriers block the assimilation of many migrant groups after acculturation (Brown and Bean 2006).

Further research, especially into assimilation of migrants after 1965, confirmed that some migrant groups were confronted with structural barriers, resulting in permanent poverty and assimilation into the 'underclass'. However, at the same time, other groups still follow the straight line of assimilation into the white middle class, while a third group of migrants managed to achieve structural integration while residing in ethnic enclaves. In order to explain these differences, Portes and Zhou (1993) introduced the *segmented assimilation model*. Migrant groups have different experiences as a result of different 'modes of incorporation', which are determined by a combination of types of government policies (receptive, indifferent or hostile), a prejudiced or non-prejudiced societal reception, and a weak or strong co-ethnic community. For example, migrants that face indifferent or hostile government policies and prejudiced societal receptions can still manage assimilation through strong co-ethnic networks in migrant enclaves that help migrants to find jobs.

Assimilation also has a spatial dimension. The classic assimilation theory interprets diminishing segregation as one form of migrant assimilation (Zhou and Logan 1991; Allen and Turner 1996). Initially, migrants settle together for mutual support, but with increased assimilation they leave the ethnic enclaves. Residential segregation would thus be a temporary phenomenon that disappears over time. But in recent decades this linear view has been criticised. Allen and Turner (1996: 153) suggest that 'research has confirmed a general association between spatial assimilation and other types of assimilation, but it has raised questions about the variables and groups that do not fit the expected patterns'. In their view, these can be explained with additional hypotheses regarding 'access to the migrant enclave' and 'spatial decentralization of earlier migrants'. Others, following the *ethnic disadvantage model*, stress that migrants can get 'stuck' in segregated neighbourhoods (Wilson 1987). And the *segmented assimilation model* argues that migrant enclaves are crucial for some, but irrelevant for others, depending on their 'modes of incorporation' (Portes and Bach 1985; Portes and Zhou 1993).

These often hotly debated theories are based on political rhetoric as well as the realities of migrant integration in the USA. For the discussion on migrant integration in China, European experiences are interesting as well. In a context of diverse national migrant policies, controversy here especially focused on political attitudes regarding migrant integration (De Palo *et al.* 2007). In France, in line with assimilation theory, integration used to be interpreted as assimilation to French culture. In Germany, migrants initially were seen as 'temporary' visitors and not expected to integrate. The Dutch followed a multicultural model: resisting separation, it was critical of integration into Dutch culture as well.

With growing numbers of migrants, heightened cultural awareness of receiving communities and second-generation migrants, and increased pressures on national resources, these ideologies have changed dramatically. While the French have had to accept that migrants are heterogeneous and that assimilation might be limited, Germany came to realise that migrants do stay, and Dutch society has become highly critical of the multicultural model. Stressing the importance of mixed neighbourhoods, segregation came to be seen as a political problem (Hudson *et al.* 2007). In response to these empirical realities, government policies began to stress migrant resettlement, neighbourhood development, compulsory language training, and acculturation through national tests. European experiences thus show that societies disregard migrant integration to their detriment. Robust responses to migration do not start from political rhetoric alone, but keep an eye on empirical realities as well.

Researching migrant integration in Guangzhou

Notwithstanding some exceptions (Du and Li 2010; Liu *et al.* 2012), migrant integration in China has received little attention in the English language literature. In view of the extensive literature on migrant integration in the USA and Europe, and the potentially hazardous effects of limited integration, this state of affairs is striking. A considerable number of migrants seem to be in Chinese cities to stay, and with the existing institutional barriers, their integration and the integration of their children could soon become a huge social issue. In line with the adage 'practice is the sole criterion for judging the truth' it is high time to trade political rhetoric for research into facts about migrant integration in Chinese cities.

In contrast to the above, migration in China is mainly domestic, and migrants generally share a Han-Chinese background with other urbanites (Liu *et al.* 2012). But the hukou system creates barriers to integration, and especially rural-to-urban migrants compare to international migrants in terms of citizenship entitlement, cultural distinction, settlement pattern, and intergroup contacts (ibid.). At the same time, there are considerable differences in modes of incorporation for Chinese migrants. Governments are receptive to some but indifferent or hostile to others; societal reception is prejudiced to some but not to others; and many migrants arrive in co-ethnic enclaves with strong ties, while others live scattered in cities. In line with the *segmented assimilation model* we would expect related variations in assimilation outcomes.

Against the background of these observations, we analyse a dataset on social networks and the neighbourhood that we collected in 2010 and 2011 in Guangzhou, China (Wissink *et al.* 2011). Over the last decades, this economic centre of Southern China has been a prime migrant destination, and saw its urban population grow from 3.2 million in 1985 to more than 10 million registered inhabitants in 2009, and an estimated floating population of 2 million.

Following the social network research of Wellman and Fischer, we collected data on aspects of the social networks of our respondents. In line with Fischer (1982) we initially focused on friendship relations. However, 'friendships' get a very broad interpretation in China and, as one respondent in the testing stage remarked, 'everybody is your friend once you have met them'. Therefore, we made a more detailed distinction between four important types of relationships in urban China: 'good friends', colleagues, classmates and kin. Our research set out to study characteristics of these relations within Guangzhou as a whole, including spatial diffusion and homogeneity of contacts. We made a closed-question questionnaire, and we used four neighbourhood types as entrances to our respondents: old-street neighbourhoods, former *danwei* compounds, commodity housing estates and urbanised villages (see Wissink *et al.* 2011 for more information on methodological choices). Eventually, we randomly selected 16 research neighbourhoods (see Figure 7.1).

So far, we have analysed this dataset on the role of the neighbourhood for social networks (Wissink *et al.* 2011), and on the differences between 'old' and 'new' migrants (Liu *et al.* 2012). In view of the limited knowledge of migrant life in Chinese cities, our dataset provides interesting material for an exploratory

Migrant integration in China 105

Figure 7.1 Research neighbourhoods in Guangzhou, China.

study of migrant integration. Of course, this study cannot tell the whole story of migrant lives in cities, but it can contribute to a general idea of migrant integration in Guangzhou.

In line with the literature on international migration, we expect that different migrant groups have different social networks, with new migrants having more

106 *Bart Wissink, Arjan Hazelzet and Werner Breitung*

local and homogeneous networks than long-term migrants, and temporary migrants having more local and homogeneous networks than permanent migrants. We also expect that migrants in urbanised villages have more local and homogeneous networks, while other migrants have more heterogeneous networks. Additionally, we expect that migrants in commodity housing estates have more non-local networks in view of their higher incomes. In line with the literature on *segmented assimilation* we expect to find different migrant groups with differences in social networks that cannot be directly explained through individual migrant characteristics alone.

The migrants in our sample

Our definition of migrants as respondents born outside of Guangzhou, or living in Guangzhou with a non-local hukou amounts to a total of 599 or 65 per cent of our 919 respondents (Table 7.1). While migrants live in each of the neighbourhood types, they are most present in urbanised villages (82 per cent), and their proportion is higher in commodity housing estates (66 per cent) than in old-street neighbourhoods (47 per cent) and former work-unit housing (49 per cent).

Of the migrants in our sample, 66 per cent are 'temporary migrants' without Guangzhou urban hukou registration, while the remaining 34 per cent have obtained a local Guangzhou hukou. If we look at the presence of both types of migrants in the four neighbourhood types, we can see a clear differentiation. The urbanised villages and old-street neighbourhoods house more migrants with a temporary registration than commodity housing estates. The migrants in our sample also differ according to their province of origin. In all neighbourhood types, most migrants originate from outside Guangdong province. This percentage is highest in urbanised villages (72 per cent) and lowest in commodity housing estates (57 per cent) and work-unit housing (53 per cent).

In work-unit compounds, a relatively large proportion (39 per cent) of migrants have lived in Guangzhou for more than 30 years. They moved to the city before the start of the reforms and are generally older than migrants in other neighbourhood types. Migrants in urbanised villages have been living in Guangzhou for a much shorter time than all others. They have considerably fewer children (37 per cent) than migrants in commodity housing estates (58 per cent).

Table 7.1 shows differences in the monthly household expenses *per capita*, with migrants in urbanised villages spending significantly less and migrants in commodity housing estates considerably more than those in other neighbourhood types. Location choice thus seems to be structured by budgetary constraints. Table 7.1 also suggests that migrants in commodity housing estates and former work-unit compounds are much better educated than migrants in urbanised villages and old-street neighbourhoods. This differentiation in spending power and educational attainment is also reflected in migrants' occupations. Migrants in the urbanised villages (54 per cent) and old-street neighbourhoods (50 per cent) are mostly employed as industrial, commercial or service workers. Migrants in former work-unit housing (44 per cent) and commodity housing (39 per cent) are more likely to be professionals, managers and entrepreneurs.

Migrant integration in China 107

Table 7.1 Migrant characteristics (by neighbourhood type).

	Urbanised villages	Old-street	Work-unit	Commodity	Total
Total number of migrants	298	95	78	128	599
In percentages	50	16	13	21	100
Type of migrant					
Temporary	74	68	59	48	66
Permanent	26	32	41	52	34
Place of origin					
Guangdong	28	36	49	44	35
Outside Guangdong	72	64	51	56	65
Length of residence in Guangzhou					
0–5 years	36	25	17	26	30
5–10 years	27	31	15	20	24
10–20 years	30	24	15	35	28
20–30 years	5	10	14	13	9
More than 30 years	2	10	39	6	9
Age (years)					
<30	24	35	11	18	23
30–40	33	25	12	38	30
40–50	25	22	21	17	22
>50	18	18	56	27	25
Children <16 in the household	37	43	50	58	44
Family monthly expense per head					
0–500 Yuan	19	2	1	1	10
500–1000 Yuan	36	30	35	17	31
1000–1500 Yuan	26	39	27	29	29
1500–2000 Yuan	9	14	20	16	13
>2000 Yuan	9	15	17	37	17
Education					
Primary or lower	23	10	13	13	18
Junior secondary	45	42	21	14	35
Senior secondary	24	36	15	24	25
Tertiary	8	12	51	49	23
Occupation					
Never worked	4	2	3	4	3
Agricultural	3	1	4	9	4
Industrial workers	26	16	14	8	19
Commercial or service workers	28	34	17	19	25
Self-employers	25	21	8	12	20
Clerks	2	9	10	9	6
Professionals	10	14	42	29	19
Managers or entrepreneurs	2	3	2	10	4

It is also interesting to compare migrants to local residents. Table 7.2 suggests that migrants are generally younger and that men are overrepresented. Migrants have more children under 16 in their household, probably due to their lower average age. While monthly expenses *per capita* are generally higher among local Guangzhou residents, there is no significant difference in levels of educational attainment. Table 7.2 shows that migrants are more likely to have a job than locals,

108 *Bart Wissink, Arjan Hazelzet and Werner Breitung*

partly because the local population includes more retirees, and partly because migrants leave the city when losing their job.

Characteristics of migrant social networks

Migrants in Guangzhou make up a very diverse group with a differentiation in demographic and socioeconomic characteristics. The international literature suggests that this translates into varying social networks (Hazelzet and Wissink 2012). In order to pursue this assumption for migrants in Guangzhou, we follow Fischer *et al.* (1977) and distinguish between three characteristics of social networks: network composition, network dispersion and dominant source. We relate *network composition* to the social mix (or heterogeneity) of social networks on two levels. First, we identify network composition based on the origin of migrants' contacts. Second, we determine network composition by the question whether respondents' social networks transcend levels of occupational status. *Network dispersion* refers

Table 7.2 Migrants versus locals

	Migrants	*Locals*	*Total*
Total number	599	320	919
In percentages	63	37	100
Age (years) in %			
<30	23	10	19
30–40	30	12	24
40–50	22	23	22
>50	25	55	25
Gender in %			
Male	74	68	48
Female	26	32	52
Children <16 in the household in %	44	40	43
Family monthly expense (per head) %			
0–500 Yuan	10	5	9
500–1000 Yuan	31	29	30
1000–1500 Yuan	29	35	31
1500–2000 Yuan	13	15	13
>2000 Yuan	17	17	17
Education in %			
Primary or lower	18	20	18
Junior secondary	35	26	35
Senior secondary	25	34	25
Tertiary	23	20	23
Work status in %			
Part-time/full-time	66	35	56
Unemployed	5	13	8
Retired	13	40	22
House-keeper	12	8	10
Other	4	4	4

Migrant integration in China 109

to the locality of social networks: do residents have most of their contacts inside their neighbourhood, in an adjacent neighbourhood, or elsewhere? *Dominant source* refers to the context through which respondents have met most of their social contacts: at the workplace, at school, by being neighbours, through kin, through other social relations, through one's children, through hobbies or clubs, or through the army.

Composition, dispersion and dominant source

Table 7.3 shows that 57 per cent of all migrants primarily have contacts with people from their own province. However, migrants in urbanised villages have significantly more mixed social networks than in old-street neighbourhoods and commodity housing estates. For network composition based on occupation, there is a relatively similar distribution among the four neighbourhood types. For all neighbourhoods, most migrants have a mixture of occupational status within their social network. Migrants in commodity housing estates, however, have significantly more heterogeneous social networks than those in all other neighbourhood types, and migrants in urbanised villages more social networks than in old-street neighbourhoods.

For network dispersion, Table 7.3 shows that 59 per cent of the migrant population have contacts mainly outside their neighbourhood. However, our sample indicates a significant difference between neighbourhood types. In commodity

Table 7.3 Composition, dispersion and dominant source of migrant social networks

	Overall (%)	Urbanised village (%)	Old-street (%)	Work-unit (%)	Commodity housing (%)
Composition (origin)					
Same province	57	54	65	53	64
Different province	13	12	12	15	18
Mixed	30	34	23	32	18
Composition (occupation)					
Homogeneous	25	24	37	31	13
Heterogeneous	75	76	63	69	87
Dispersion					
Neighbourhood	27	35	23	30	2
Adjacent neighbourhood	14	12	22	14	13
Elsewhere	59	53	55	56	85
Dominant source					
Work	57	57	60	60	56
School	17	14	11	25	22
Neighbours	10	8	17	4	11
Other social relations	6	10	4	3	4
Kin	5	6	4	6	1
Hobbies/clubs/military/ children	5	5	4	2	6

110   *Bart Wissink, Arjan Hazelzet and Werner Breitung*

housing estates, this proportion is significantly larger than in all other neighbourhoods. This seems to support the common view that higher income groups have less localised networks.

By asking for the dominant source of social contacts, we can see if the neighbourhood is the actual source of local social networks. Table 7.3 shows that the workplace is by far the most important primary source of contacts for migrants (57 per cent), with school (17 per cent) and neighbours (10 per cent) distant second and third sources. Among the four neighbourhood types, there are relatively similar distributions in dominant source categories.

Determinants of network composition, dispersion and dominant source

These outcomes suggest that the majority of the migrants in our sample primarily have contact with people from their own province. Their network is heterogeneous based on the occupation of their good friends, for the majority of social networks transcend the local residential area and the majority of new relations are formed with colleagues. However, at the same time our data show big differences in the characteristics of social networks. Do these variations relate to differences in the social characteristics of migrants?

Table 7.4 shows predictors with a significant influence on social network characteristics. For the social network composition based on origin of contacts, three predictors have a significant impact: migrant type, educational attainment and neighbourhood type. Migrant type has the biggest impact on the probability of having contacts primarily from one's own province. While there are no differences between permanent and temporary migrants, migrants from Guangdong (permanent or temporary) are more likely than migrants from elsewhere to have contacts with people from their province. For educational attainment, only tertiary education has a significant impact. Migrants who kept on studying after middle school are less likely to have social networks exclusively with people from their own province. Inversely, migrants in commodity housing estates are more likely to have contact primarily with people from their own province.

For homogeneity of social network based on occupational status of good friends, educational attainment is the only statistically significant predictor. Migrants with only primary education or less are more likely to have homogeneous social networks.

The dispersion of migrants' social networks is influenced by average monthly spending, length of residence in the neighbourhood, and children under 16 in the household. Household expenditure has the biggest influence on network dispersion. Migrants who spend more than 1,000 Yuan a month per household member are more likely to have their social network primarily outside the local residential area. Length of residence has a negative impact on network dispersion. With increasing duration, it becomes more likely that migrants' networks are exclusively local. Migrants with children under 16 in their household are also more likely to have localised social networks.

The dominant source for new social relations varies according to social factors. Table 7.4 shows that the probability of developing social networks primarily with colleagues is highly influenced by the duration of stay in Guangzhou. Migrants who have lived in the city for more than 10 years are much more likely to have colleagues as their contacts. Men and people of higher age are also more likely to have contacts primarily with colleagues. The most important predictor for schoolmates as good friends is educational attainment. Also, those living in the city for more than 10 years are more likely to have schoolmates constitute an important part of the network. The probability of developing social networks among neighbours is high for migrants with no more than primary education, for women, and for those who do not work (any more). Some migrants develop most of their new contacts through already existing network members. Table 7.4 indicates that this is especially the case for migrants from Guangdong with a temporary registration. Migrants with an educational attainment above senior secondary level are less likely to develop new contacts through other social relations.

Five migrant groups

While the characteristics of social networks of migrants and the most important determinants give a first impression of migrant integration in Guangzhou, their interrelatedness is even more interesting. By combining these characteristics, relatively coherent migrant groups can be distinguished on the basis of their integration in Guangzhou (see Wissink and Hazelzet 2012 for a comparable clustering of residents in Tokyo). We have clustered the migrants for network composition based on origin of contacts as well as occupational status of contacts, dispersion and migrant type. For practical reasons, our analysis could only include migrants from other provinces than Guangdong, leaving a dataset of 354 migrants.

With a focus on network composition based on the migrant type, our analysis results in a five-cluster outcome (Tables 7.5 and 7.6). The first group, the *Local hukou migrants*, consists entirely of migrants with a Guangzhou hukou. This is the smallest group of the sample (13 per cent). Members of this group are more likely to be integrated into Guangzhou life on the basis of our identifiers. Contacts primarily exist outside their own residential area (60 per cent) with people who originate from other provinces (69 per cent). Based on occupation of contacts, their social network is heterogeneous. These contacts have primarily been formed at work (65 per cent) and through education (31 per cent). 'Local hukou migrants' are strongly represented in former work-unit housing (59 per cent) and commodity housing (39 per cent), but nearly absent in urbanised villages (1 per cent).

The remaining four groups are entirely made up of migrants with a temporary registration. The 65 *Integrated temporary registration migrants* (18 per cent of the sample) have contacts with people from a wide variety of occupational levels and not primarily with those from their own provinces. Most of their contacts live outside their neighbourhood, and were met through work (68 per cent) or other social relations (15 per cent). 'Integrated temporary registration migrants' have an equal presence in all neighbourhood types (around 20 per cent).

Table 7.4 Predictors for social network composition, dispersion and dominant source.

	Composition (origin)		Composition (occupation)		Dispersion		Dominant source							
							Work		School		Neighbours		Social relations	
	B	WALD	B	WALD	B	WALD	B	WALD	B	WALD	B	WALD	B	WALD
Age							−0.02*	4.15						
Gender (1 = female)							−0.70**	15.7			1.30**	11.8		
Children under 16 years in the household (1 = yes)					−0.40*	4.68								
Employment (1 = working)											−0.80*	6.45		
Educational attainment														
Primary or less (reference category)		13.1		12.6						30.3		20.4		8.74
Junior secondary	0.01	0.00	0.89**	9.53					1.49	3.42	−0.94**	7.11	−0.59	2.92
Senior secondary	−0.30	1.01	0.99**	9.58					2.59**	10.6	−1.39**	9.85	−0.50	1.83
Tertiary	−1.06**	9.42	0.66*	3.87					3.45**	17.4	−3.49**	11.4	−1.85**	7.81
Monthly average spending *per capita*														
0–500 Yuan (reference category)						19.0								
500–1,000 Yuan					0.33	1.13								
1,000–1,500 Yuan					0.86**	7.39								
1,500–2,000 Yuan					1.13**	9.08								
More than 2,000 Yuan					1.15**	10.2								
Years in neighbourhood					−0.03**	13.3								
Years in Guangzhou														
Less than 5 years (reference category)								18.4		14.5				

	B (1)	Wald (1)	B (2)	Wald (2)	B (3)	Wald (3)	B (4)	Wald (4)	B (5)	Wald (5)	B (6)	Wald (6)	B (7)	Wald (7)
5–10 years							0.09	0.14	−0.39	1.35				
10–20 years							0.58*	6.40	−1.13**	9.31				
20–30 years							1.29**	11.5	−1.85**	8.20				
More than 30 years							1.34**	9.15	−2.67**	8.41				
Migrant type														
Temporary migrant (reference category)		34.4												8.76
Permanent migrant Guangdong	0.99**	15.2											−0.79	0.52
Permanent migrant	−0.33	0.66											−0.29	0.68
Temporary migrant Guangdong	1.65**	15.5											0.83*	4.66
Neighbourhood type														
Urbanised villages (reference category)		7.79												
Old–streets neighbourhoods	0.35	1.63												
Work–unit housing	−0.62	0.03												
Commodity housing	0.81**	5.46												
χ^2	59.1**		22.4**		36.2**		45.2**		88.6**		68.7**		20.3**	
Nagelkerke R^2	0.15		0.06		0.09		0.11		0.26		0.25		0.11	

Note: χ^2: *$p<0.05$, **$p<0.01$.

The Wald-statistic indicates the relative weight of a predictor on the probability of having a specified attribute (composition/from the same province; composition/same occupational status; dispersion/contacts outside local residential area; dominant source/work, school, neighbours or other social relations); a higher value indicates a larger impact. The B-statistic indicates the direction of the relationship between a predictor and having this attribute. The probability of having the attribute, as shown in the table, may increase (positive value) or decrease (negative value).

Table 7.5 Composition, dispersion and dominant source for resident groups (%).

Migrant groups	No.	Migrant type		Composition (origin)		Composition (occupation)		Dispersion	
		Permanent	Temporary	Same province	Other province/mixed	Homogeneous	Heterogeneous	Local	Distant
Local hukou migrant	48	100	0	31	69	27	73	40	60
Integrated temporary registration migrants	65	0	100	0	100	0	100	0	100
Home-towners	70	0	100	100	0	0	100	0	100
Neighbourhood workers	87	0	100	48	52	0	100	100	0
Socially non-mobiles	84	0	100	52	48	100	0	48	52

Migrant integration in China 115

Table 7.6 Distribution of resident groups over neighbourhoods (%).

	Local hukou migrants	Integrated temporary registration migrants	Home-towners	Neighbourhood workers	Socially non-mobiles
Urbanised village	1	20	21	32	26
Old-streets	10	18	15	23	34
Work-unit	59	20	5	8	8
Commodity	39	22	19	9	11
Overall	13	18	20	25	24

For the other three groups of migrants with temporary registration, local integration is less distinct. *Home-towners* are 70 migrants (20 per cent) who have contacts primarily from their own province. At the same time, their contacts span diverse occupational statuses. Contacts live primarily outside their neighbourhood. The workplace is an important source for contacts (45 per cent), but considerably less so than for the previous two groups. The presence of 'Home-towners' in work-unit neighbourhoods is very small.

Neighbourhood workers are the largest group of migrants, with 87 members (25 per cent). They mainly have contacts within their neighbourhood, and the workplace is the main source of these contacts (63 per cent). The contacts are evenly from their own and other provinces. At the same time, contacts are heterogeneous in terms of occupation. 'Neighbourhood workers' constitutes the largest group of migrants in urbanised villages (32 per cent), and is well represented in old-street neighbourhoods (23 per cent). Their presence in work-unit and commodity housing estates is marginal (respectively 8 per cent and 9 per cent).

Socially non-mobiles constitute the final group of 84 members (24 per cent). As for the 'Neighbourhood workers', the contacts of this group are almost equally from their own and other provinces. Unlike all other groups, 'Socially non-mobiles' primarily have contact with people from similar occupational level. The workplace is the primary source of contacts for 49 per cent of this group, and about half of them (48 per cent) have their contacts mainly within the neighbourhood. 'Socially non-mobiles' are the largest group within old-street neighbourhoods (32 per cent) and are common in urbanised villages (26 per cent). They are rare in work-unit (8 per cent) and commodity housing estates (11 per cent).

Table 7.7 provides a better insight into these five groups through a number of variables. These suggest a striking difference between 'Local hukou migrants' and the four groups of migrants with temporary registration. The former on average have lived in Guangzhou and their neighbourhood much longer, are about 10 years older, are more likely to have a child in the household, have much higher *per capita* expenditure and have higher education levels. These factors may all contribute to a higher degree of integration.

The differences between the 'Integrated temporary registration migrants' and the three other migrant groups that are less integrated are very interesting. 'Integrated temporary registration migrants' are more often working men with a higher household expenditure and educational attainment. At the same time, length of residence is strikingly similar to the other temporary registration migrants. Apparently this is not an important discerning factor for integration. Furthermore, there are only small differences between the social profiles of the three less integrated migrant groups. 'Home-towners' have been in Guangzhou for a slightly shorter time, while 'Neighbourhood workers' have lived there slightly longer. They are also somewhat more likely to have children in the household. 'Socially non-mobiles' are more often women with lower spending and educational attainment. But the similarities between the social profiles of these groups are perhaps more striking. The main differences seem to relate to the neighbourhood in which they live.

Conclusion

This chapter provides an exploratory study of migrant integration in China, on the basis of a resident survey in Guangzhou. Specifically, we asked the following questions: *What are the characteristics of migrants in Guangzhou? Where do they live? What are the characteristics of their social networks? And to what extent does this relate to the receiving neighbourhood?* With the dramatic growth of Guangzhou over the last 30 years, it is not surprising that 63 per cent of the respondents in our sample turned out to be migrants and that these have very diverse characteristics. While some migrants have a local hukou, others have a temporary registration. Some arrived recently, while others have been in the city for a long time. This underlines that at least a part of the migrant population is here to stay. The migrants in our sample also display extensive variations in other characteristics like age, occupation, and household expenditure that in other researches are shown to correlate to social network characteristics.

As for the residential location of migrants, our sample shows a remarkable dispersal of migrants over different neighbourhood types. There is a strong correlation between residential location and household expenditure, suggesting that budgetary constraints play an important role in location choices. As expected, our sample shows that migrants are the overwhelming majority in urbanised villages, but migrants have a significant presence in other neighbourhood types as well. Migrants in old-street neighbourhoods have similar characteristics to those in urbanised villages; these neighbourhoods are viable alternatives for recent labour migrants. Migrants in former work-unit compounds are much longer in Guangzhou – often over 30 years – and most have a local hukou. Many of these are pre-reform migrants who came to Guangzhou as work-unit employees. Migrants in commodity housing estates generally have higher incomes and many have a local hukou. These are more privileged migrants, who received their 'blue stamp' hukou registration. But each of the neighbourhoods also houses migrants with different characteristics.

Table 7.7 Characteristics of the four resident groups: mean values.

Group	Years in Guangzhou	Years in the neighbourhood	Age	Gender (female)	Child	Monthly expense	Educational attainment	Work
Local hukou migrant	22.0	14.3	49	0.48	0.62	3.64	3.60	0.56
Integrated temporary registration migrants	7.4	4.2	36	0.35	0.32	3.05	2.52	0.84
Home-towners	6.6	4.0	39	0.43	0.33	2.88	2.34	0.78
Neighbourhood workers	7.7	5.4	36	0.47	0.45	2.64	2.24	0.78
Socially non-mobiles	7.3	5.0	39	0.52	0.33	2.49	2.12	0.75
Overall	9.3	6.0	39	0.45	0.40	2.86	2.47	0.76

In view of the diverse characteristics of migrants, it is not surprising that their social networks also vary a lot. Our analysis of the determinants of these variations did not result in a distinct picture. But there are some interesting conclusions: while educational attainment, neighbourhood type and source of contacts were good predictors, length of stay in Guangzhou and household expenditure were not. Apparently, there are different modes of integration, and work and neighbourhood seem to be the driving forces, an indication that seems to fit in with the segmented assimilation model.

The variation of characteristics of migrant social networks was further explored through the distinction between five migrant groups. 'Local hukou migrants' have been in Guangzhou for a long time, and have heterogeneous social networks. The other four migrant groups do not have a Guangzhou hukou. Among them, the 'Integrated temporary registration migrants' have heterogeneous networks as well, which they form mainly through work. 'Home-towners' mainly have contacts with people from their own province and 'Neighbourhood workers' mainly in their own neighbourhood. 'Socially non-mobiles' mainly have contacts with people from their own occupation level. Our analysis showed clear differences in the presence of these groups in the different neighbourhood types, and relatively small differences in the social profiles of the four groups of migrants with temporary registration.

The factors that determine differences in integration are quite clear, but length of residence and household expenditure influence migrant integration less than education, source of contacts and neighbourhood type. These relations will have to be further explored through detailed ethnographic research. But it is safe to assume that many migrants are in Guangzhou for a long time, and that they are integrating in society. So while government agencies frame migration as a temporary phenomenon, many migrants themselves have very different ideas. Given the large numbers of migrants, persisting institutional barriers for migrants with temporary registration this might have serious consequences for the social future of cities. Unfortunately, the Chinese government does not seem eager to change this situation any time soon (Logan *et al.* 2009).

Acknowledgement

The authors gratefully acknowledge the funding received from the German Science Foundation (DFG) as part of their Priority Programme "Mega Cities, Mega Challenge" (project number BR 3546/2-1).

References

Alba, R. and Nee, V. (1997) 'Rethinking assimilation theory for a new era of immigration', *International Migration Review*, 31(4): 826–74.

Allen, J. P. and Turner, E. (1996) 'Spatial patterns of immigrant assimilation', *Professional Geographer*, 48(2): 140–55.

Breitung W. (2012) 'Enclave urbanism in China: Attitudes towards gated communities in Guangzhou', *Urban Geography*, 33(2): 278–94.

Brown, S. K. and Bean, F. D. (2006) 'Assimilation models, old and new: Explaining a long-term process', *Migration Information Source*, Washington DC: Migration Policy Institute. Online. Available: http://www.migrationinformation.org/Feature/display.cfm?id=442 (Accessed 21 January 2012).

Chan, K. W. (2010) 'The Chinese household registration system and migrant labor in China: Notes on a debate', *Population and Development Review*, 36(2): 357–64.

Davis, D. S. (1995) 'Introduction: Urban China', in Davis, D. S., Kraus, R., Naughton, B. and Perry, E. J. (eds), *Urban Spaces in Contemporary China: The Potential for Autonomy and Community in Post-Mao China*, Cambridge: University of Cambridge Press, pp. 1–20.

De Palo, D., Faini, R. and Venturini, A. (2007) *The Social Assimilation of Immigrants*, SP Discussion Paper No. 0701, Washington DC: The World Bank.

Douglas, M., Wissink, B. and Van Kempen, R. (2012) 'Enclave urbanism in China: Consequences and interpretations', *Urban Geography*, 33(2): 167–82.

Du, H. and Li, S. (2010) 'Migrants, urban villages, and community sentiments: A case of Guangzhou, China', *Asian Geographer*, 27(1–2): 93–108.

Fan, C.C. (2008) 'Migration, hukou, and the city,' in Yusuf, S. and Saich, T. (eds), *China Urbanizes: Consequences, Strategies, and Policies*, Washington DC: The World Bank, pp. 65–89.

Fischer, C. (1982) *To Dwell Among Friends: Personal Networks in Town and City*, Chicago, IL: University of Chicago Press.

Fischer, C. S., Jackson, R. M., Stueve, C. A., Gerson, K., Jones, L. M. and Baldassare, M. (1977) *Networks and Places: Social Relations in the Urban Setting*, New York: The Free Press.

Glazer, N. and Moynihan, D. P. (1963) *Beyond the Melting Pot: The Negroes, Puerto Ricans, Jews, Italians, and Irish of New York City*, Cambridge, MA: MIT Press.

Gordon, M. (1964) *Assimilation in American Life*, New York: Oxford University Press.

Gransow, B. (2010) 'Slum formation or urban innovation? Migrant communities and social change in Chinese megacities', paper presented at 'Rural-Urban Migrations in Mega Cities and Mega Slums', Our Common Future, Essen, Germany, 5 November, 2010.

Hazelzet, A. and Wissink, B. (2012) 'Neighbourhoods, social networks and trust in post-reform China: The case of Guangzhou', *Urban Geography*, 33(2): 204–20.

He, S., Liu, Y., Wu, F. and Webster, C. J. (2010) 'Social groups and housing differentiation in China's urban villages: An institutional interpretation', *Housing Studies*, 25(5): 671–91.

Huang, Y. and Jiang, L. (2009) 'Housing inequality in transitional Beijing', *International Journal of Urban and Regional Research*, 33(4): 936–56.

Hudson, M., Phillips, J., Ray, K. and Barnes, H. (2007) *Social Cohesion in Diverse Communities*, York: Joseph Rowntree Foundation.

Li, B. (2006) 'Floating population or urban citizens? Status, social provision and circumstances or rural-urban migrants in China', *Social Policy and Administration*, 40(2): 174–95.

Li, L. H. and Li, X. (2011) 'Redevelopment of urban villages in Shenzhen, China: An analysis of power relations and urban coalitions,' *Habitat International*, 35(3): 426–34.

Liu, Y., Li, Z. and Breitung, W. (2012) 'The social networks of new-generation migrants in China's urbanized villages: A case study of Guangzhou', *Habitat International*, 36(1): 192–9.

Logan, J. R., Fang, Y. and Zhang, Z. (2009) 'Access to housing in urban China', *International Journal of Urban and Regional Research*, 33(4): 914–35.

Massey, D. S., Arango, J., Hugo, G., Kouaouci, A., Pellegrino, A. and Taylor, J. E. (1993) 'Theories of international migration: A review and appraisal,' *Population and Development Review*, 19(3): 431–66.

NBS [National Bureau of Statistics of China] (2010) *2009 Report On Migrant Workers Monitoring Survey*. Available online at: http://www.stats.gov.cn/tjfx/fxbg/t20100319_402628281.htm (Accessed 19 March 2010).

Portes, A. and Bach, R. L. (1985) *The Latin Journey: Cuban and Mexican Immigrants in the United States*, Berkeley: University of California Press.

Portes, A. and Zhou, M. (1993) 'The new second generation: Segmented assimilation and its variants,' *Annals of the American Academy of Political and Social Science*, 530(1): 74–96.

Rumbaut R. G. (1997) 'Assimilation and its discontents: Between rhetoric and reality,' *International Migration Review*, 31(4): 923–60.

Solinger, D. J. (1995) 'The floating population in the cities: chances for assimilation?', in Davis, D. S., Kraus, R., Naughton, B. and Perry, E. J. (eds), *Urban Spaces in Contemporary China: The Potential for Autonomy and Community in Post-Mao China*, Cambridge: University of Cambridge Press, pp. 113–39.

Tian, L. (2008) 'The chengzhongcun land market in China: Boon or bane? A perspective on property rights,' *International Journal for Urban and Regional Research*, 32(2): 282–304.

Wang, Y. P. (2004) *Urban Poverty, Housing and Social Change in China*, London: Routledge.

Waters, M. C. and Jiménez, T. R. (2005) 'Assessing immigrant assimilation: New empirical and theoretical challenges', *Annual Review of Sociology*, 31(1): 105–25.

Wilson, J. (1987) *The Truly Disadvantaged: The Inner City, the Underclass, and Public Policy*, Chicago: The University of Chicago Press.

Wissink, B. and Hazelzet, A. (2012) 'Social networks in "Neighbourhood Tokyo",' *Urban Studies*, 49(7): 1527–49.

Wissink, B., Hazelzet, A. and Breitung, W. (2011) 'Social networks and the neighbourhood in China: Evidence from post-reform Guangzhou,' Paper presented at the 2nd International Conference on China's Urban Transition and City Planning, Cardiff, UK, 27–28 May 2011.

Wu, F., Zhang, F. and Webster, C. (forthcoming) 'Informality and "slum clearance": The development and demolition of urbanized villages in the Chinese peri-urban region', *Urban Studies*.

Yusuf, S. and Nabeshima, K. (2008) 'Optimizing urban development', in Yusuf, S. and Saich, T. (eds,) *China Urbanizes: Consequences, Strategies, and Policies*, Washington DC: The World Bank, pp. 1–40.

Zhang, L. (2001) *Strangers in the City: Reconfigurations of Space, Power, and Social Networks within China's Floating Population*, Stanford, CA: Stanford University Press.

Zhang, L. (2002) 'Urban experiences and social belonging among Chinese rural migrants', in Link, P., Madsen, R. P. and Pickowicz, P. G. (eds,) *Popular China: Unofficial Culture in a Globalizing Society*, Lanham: Rowman and Littlefield Publishers, pp. 275–99.

Zheng, S., Long, F., Fan, C. C. and Gu, Y. (2009) 'Urban villages in China: A 2008 survey of migrant settlements in Beijing,' *Eurasian Geography and Economics*, 50(4): 425–46.

Zhou, M. and Logan, J. R. (1991) 'In and out of Chinatown: Residential mobility and segregation of New York City's Chinese,' *Social Forces*, 70(2): 387–407.

8 Migrant integration in China's urban villages

A case study of Beijing, Shanghai and Guangzhou

Zhigang Li and Fulong Wu

Introduction

China is becoming a country of migrants. Millions of rural migrants have resettled in large coastal cities such as Beijing, Shanghai and Guangzhou in the last three decades. According to the official statistical report, the number of migrants dramatically enlarged to 211 million in 2009 from 6.57 million in 1982 (Editorial 2010). A large proportion of rural migrants are now counted as urban people in the national survey. Accordingly, for the first time in China's history, the number of the urban population exceeded that of the rural population in 2011.

Nevertheless, rural migrants in large cities are still characterized by floating. For instance, in early 2011 a number of books, magazines and newspapers published papers or articles with the titles of 'leaving away/escaping from Beijing-Shanghai-Guangzhou', and the disadvantages of living in large cities such as expensive living costs, a snobbish social atmosphere, challenging competition and so on have been highlighted (Su and Min 2010). Misunderstandings and conflicts between local urbanites and migrants were so intense in Zengcheng Town, the northern suburb of Guangzhou, in June 2011 that friction turned into a riot so severe that it actually involved the army (BBC 2011). Will rural migrants successfully integrate or assimilate into local urban society? Or are they going to be sociospatially segregated? This chapter will try to answer these questions with a case study of Beijing, Shanghai and Guangzhou, three of the largest Chinese cities that have attracted millions of migrants, using a database collected from about 60 informal settlements – so-called urban villages – in a large-scale survey conducted in 2010. For two reasons, we choose urban villages as a target. First, urban villages are the most conspicuous sites where rural migrants accumulate in these cities. For instance, in Sanyuanli Village in Guangzhou, the local population is only 8,985, while there are 40,000 rural migrants (Project-team 2007). Urban villages are typical cases for examination of the lives and daily practices of rural migrants. Second, urban villages are normally sites where rural migrants start their urban lives, i.e. the starting point of migrant integration into cities. An examination of urban villages will provide an opportunity for us to further understand the mechanism of migrant integration.

122 *Zhigang Li and Fulong Wu*

In the following sections, we will first review the theory of migrant integration and assimilation together with the study of rural migrant integration in urban China. After that, we will make an effort to understand the situation of China's urban villages and migrant integration. A case study of urban villages in Beijing, Shanghai and Guangzhou will be reported, and detailed information from our survey and the results of empirical study will comprise the major part. In the final session, we will discuss the implications of this study and make concluding remarks.

Theories of migrant integration

A well-established literature has been developed, particularly in immigrant-receiving countries such as the USA and the Netherlands, in relation to the issue of migrant integration/assimilation. Integration and assimilation are two words mainly used by scholars to address the host–migrant relationship. 'Integration' is often taken to be the same as 'assimilation', though the latter is mainly used in the USA (Portes and Zhou 1993; Alba and Nee 2003), while the former has become a key word in both Canada and European countries such as the Netherlands. The concept of assimilation, which is closely associated with the melting pot ideal (Alba and Nee 2003), stems from the Chicago School of the 1920s. Park and his colleagues (Park *et al.* 1925: 735) use it to describe 'a process of interpenetration and fusion in which persons and groups acquire the memories, sentiments, and attitudes of other persons and groups and, by sharing their experience and history, are incorporated with them in a common cultural life'. Assimilation is a process of establishing conformity to the host society (Gordon 1964; Alba and Nee 2003). In contrast, integration refers to more specific domains, such as the extent to which migrants are integrated or participate in the socioeconomic domains of the host society, e.g. the labour market and education, or in social–cultural domains. In addition, integration indicates the level of interaction between migrants and local residents. As such, we use integration as the main term to delineate migrant–local interactions in Chinese cities. Nevertheless, it is difficult to develop a plain distinction between the literatures of assimilation and integration, and they will both be reviewed below.

First, there are multidimensional formulations of integration in the literature, such as the well-known seven steps of cultural, behavioural, structural, marital, identification, attitude reception, behaviour reception and civic assimilation (Gordon 1964). This sees integration as a largely linear process, in which migrants make progress from the very basic to the most advanced. In this model, the beginning of integration is cultural integration, an acquisition of local language, values and cultural practices; complete assimilation to the host society requires biological integration through interracial marriages, to enable migrants to be no longer distinguishable (Gordon 1964). Nevertheless, this theory is criticised not only for its White-centralism but also for its misrepresentation of the integration process – the process is by no means linear. That is, the interaction between migrants and local residents is two-way rather than one-way, and will reshape both sides.

Migrant integration in China's urban villages 123

Accordingly, the demographics of immigrants and the patterns of integration will be diverse (Portes and Zhou 1993; Alba and Nee 2003).

In more detail, two dimensions of integration, the socioeconomic as well as the spatial, are important. First, as to the socioeconomic integration of migrants, occupational mobility and economic upgrades are two key dimensions. The increase in life chances within the host society is a critical indicator of the decline of social boundaries, and entry into the occupational and economic mainstream has undoubtedly provided migrants with a motive for social integration. Socioeconomic mobility will create the social conditions conducive to other forms of integration, as it will bring about contacts between different people. In essence, integration rests on equality of attainment or position and equates to the attainment of average or above average socioeconomic standing, as measured by indicators such as education, occupation, and income (Alba *et al.* 1997). When migrants participate in institutions such as the labour market and education on the basis of parity with native groups of similar backgrounds, the emphasis on socio-economic integration may upgrade to equality of treatment – migrants have the same life chances as local people in the pursuit of such scarce values as high-status jobs and higher education. Nevertheless, socioeconomic integration allows for 'segmented' assimilation (Portes and Zhou 1993): some labour migrants, such as Mexicans, may end-up on the lower rungs of the stratification order, while human capital migrants, such as Asians or Russian Jews, experience rapid social mobility. This suggests that the socioeconomic integration of migrants is ethni-cally contingent as well as historically contingent, as various groups of migrants may have very different outcomes of integration. There will be a variety of options for migrants to achieve socioeconomic integration: acculturating to the middle-class values of the dominant white society, gravitating towards an underclass, or advancing socially while maintaining strong ties with one's ethnic or racial community and its values.

Moreover, migrant integration is also spatially contingent. That is, the social integration of migrants contains an important spatial dimension. There are three major theoretical frameworks that have been generally accepted for the formation of migrant neighbourhoods: the spatial assimilation model, place stratification theory and the theory of choice (Logan 2006; Brown and Chung 2008). According to the spatial assimilation model, residential segregation or concentration is linked with socioeconomic status. With a low status at the bottom of the social ladder, migrants, at least at the earlier stage of migration, are restricted to poor neighbour-hoods where affordable accommodation, kinship or birthplace-tied social capital is available. When migrants obtain greater economic resources, they access higher quality housing, neighbourhoods and improved amenities through moving away from ethnic enclaves to communities of local majorities – a process of spatial assimilation (Massey and Denton 1985). However, spatial assimilation is by no means a one-way upgrading process, as racial/ethnic prejudice or discrimination may be a force that maintains segregation through housing markets, institutional behaviour, societal values and the like (Logan *et al.* 2002). That is, local residents may prefer to maintain social distance between themselves and migrants.

Therefore, place stratification theory noted the constraints and restrictions imposed on migrants' residential choices by more advantaged groups through various discriminatory practices (Alba and Nee 2003). It implies that group membership, in addition to income and other sociodemographic characteristics, affects the integration of migrants.

The third theory, choice theory, turns to highlight the own-group preference in choosing neighbours: migrants may prefer to stay in proximity to each other; local residents may prefer to practise avoidance of migrants; and therefore preserve residential segregation (Schelling 1971; Clark 1991). This framework further highlights the impacts of racial/ethnic preference. For instance, Logan, Zhang and Alba (2002) found that African and Hispanic immigrants who reside in more affluent areas of New York and Los Angeles are often without cultural assimilations such as language skills. They argue that these racial/ethnic settlements could be better understood as ethnic communities driven by preference and choice, rather than as immigrant enclaves driven by economic and cultural constraints. In this sense, in-group attraction generates segregation or concentration, even when sociospatial integration is feasible.

Accordingly, the function of migrant enclaves is disputed (Kempen and Ozuekren 1998). On the one hand, the ethnic enclave is a place of social isolation that may fix or lock migrants into poor economic status. On the other hand, ethnic enclaves also provide advantages such as social capital, informal jobs and high productivity. That is, migrant enclaves represent group preferences, common interests, social networks and cultural–religious needs, serving as the basis for migrant integration into the mainstream society. As such, migrant enclaves are a form of voluntary segregation, not an instrument or product of overt discrimination. In addition, there are scholars who argue that there is a diminishing role for neighbourhoods in people's daily lives, as contemporary society witnesses an ever-expanding spatial scale of social relations (Bolt 2002). People now are able to function in different social networks that are not strongly limited by physical barriers and spatial obstacles. Social ties and economic opportunities are no longer attached or confined to the neighbourhood. As such, the impacts of migrant enclaves have a reduced influence on the socioeconomic integration of migrants.

In sum, the integration of migrants is not only contingent on the socioeconomic, cultural and spatial contexts of the host society; it is also shaped by the subjective choices of migrants. Moreover, the demography, spatiality and functions of migrant villages/enclaves will be diverse. In this regard, to understand migrant integration we should pay attention to the local context. Current studies of migrant integration have largely concentrated on cities of the developed economies, the melting pot of international immigrants, while far less is known about the situation of developing countries. Even less is known about the situation of transitional economies. Most studies focus on international immigrants, but less attention has been paid to the settlements of unrestricted migration flows within one state boundary. To fill this gap, we need to produce more empirical studies to examine migrant integration in other contexts such as large Chinese cities.

Understanding China's informal settlements and migrant integration

In the last three decades, urban China scholars have produced abundant knowledge to aid in understanding the situation of informal settlements such as urban villages as well as migrants in Chinese cities. In the earlier 1980s, for instance, Xiang (1999), together with Gu and Kesteloot (2002), investigated Zhejiang Village in Beijing to understand its residents, social networks and economies. Such 'non-state' spaces indicate that marginalised migrants have been authorised to make a living in post-reform urban China. In the same vein, millions of rural migrants have poured into large cities, in particular coastal cities such as Shanghai, Guangzhou and Shenzhen, to work in factories, shops, companies, restaurants, hotels and so on (Fan 2008). Migrants resort to survival strategies related to the self-organisation of housing, employment and education (Lin *et al.* 2011). Constructed on collective-owned lands rather than state-owned lands, urban villages provided rural migrants with affordable accommodation to sustain a specific urbanism (Zhang 2011). In a case study of Guangzhou, Tian (2008) found that the retention of collective land ownership in urban villages allowed low-rent affordable housing for migrants, but the maintaining of collective land ownership also resulted in high social and economic costs. In this regard, there are both positive and negative impacts of urban villages (Liu *et al.* 2010; Song and Zenou 2012).

Urban villages have been transformed into functional but unregulated migrant enclaves (Zhang 2011). To save money and living costs, a higher proportion of rural migrants prefer to stay in affordable but very small spaces. Based on a survey of migrant settlements in Beijing in 2008, Zheng *et al.* (2009) found that though migrant workers are willing to pay the same or higher rent per unit of space, they consume smaller dwelling spaces than local residents, as they prefer to save their earnings from work in the city. That is, migrants consider the city as a place to work rather than a home to live. On the other hand, to maximise the size of rental space, villagers will increase the density of their houses to an extreme extent, and the rental market becomes a major resource – sometimes even the only one – for villagers or collective companies to earn income.

Second, the issue of migrant integration has also received much attention among urban China scholars. It is assumed by some that rural migrants may integrate into urban society, i.e. become urbanites, so that the term 'civilisation', or *shiminghua* in Chinese, has often been applied (Wang *et al.* 2008; Ren and Qiao 2010). For instance, Ren and Qiao (2010) took social integration as the process in which different people interact with each other. Wang *et al.* (2008) asserted that integration means that migrants obtain the same identity as well as the social rights as urban citizens. Ma and Tong (2008) termed social integration as the result of migrants transforming into urban residents, in which their residences, jobs and values became the same as those of urbanites. They argued that there are three stages for migrant integration: at the first stage when migrants are very different from local residents in areas such as social welfare, employment, entertainments, consumption, residence and psychological issues, the community of migrants and local residents is a dual community. Interactions between migrants and local residents bring about communication as well as understanding towards each other, so that the development of the community will enter the second stage and become cordial; and in the end, migrants will obtain formal rights of urban residence and citizenship, so that the community becomes integrated.

There are various dimensions or variables that may mould the integration of migrants in urban China. Zhu (2002), for example, focused on economic, social and psychological facets, and claimed that there will be a gradual process of integration, from a low extent to a high extent. In a case study of Shanghai, Zhang and Lei (2008) found that the identity of migrants is largely rural – few see themselves as 'Shanghainese': the mobility of migrant housing is high, and only a few prefer to settle in Shanghai. In a comparison of sole migration, couple migration and family migration, Fan *et al*. (2011) examined the practice of split households among rural migrants in Beijing, and found that migrants' decision to leave their children behind or to bring them depends on the children's age and whether migrants' parents are available to help. They highlighted the significance of including circular migration as a consideration, and asserted that the number of household members in the city has no relation to the level of social integration. Zhang and Wang (2010) claimed that the granting of urban *hukou* (household registration) to migrants is based largely on migrants' contribution to, rather than on their presence in, the host city. Urban citizenship is used by city governments to exclude some members of society from accessing urban welfare, and also to make the urban economy more competitive by grabbing capital and human resources possessed by migrants.

Nevertheless, most of these studies focus on the social dimension of migrant integration, while few pay attention to the spatial issue. In particular, few studies shed light upon specific communities such as urban villages. It is unknown what the process of social integration is on the microscopic scale, yet a careful study of such places may disclose intriguing mechanisms. For example, Liu *et al*. (2012) examined the sociospatial pattern of migrant networks in Guangzhou through an examination of specific urban villages, and found that new generation migrants prefer to draw on cross-class, non-kin, and non-territorial networks when seeking support. They argued that new generation migrants construct colleague and friendship ties that transcend the boundaries of migrant enclaves. Tomlinson (2012) asserted that there are no slums in Shanghai. The absence of slums is attributed to specific reasons such as the pace and scale of urban redevelopment, together with the incorporation of urban villages, both set against Shanghai's slow increase in household formation. In essence, studies of migrant integration and urban villages to date are largely separate – the spatial dimension has only recently been considered by a few scholars of migrant integration in Chinese cities, whilst the study of urban villages has largely concentrated on the issues of demographic features of the residents, land use, property rights, social networks, and so on, and little is known about the social integration of migrants in these enclaves. In sum, as a specific sociospatial outcome of rural–urban dualism in China, urban villages may provide us with a unique opportunity to articulate the dynamic relation between rural migrants and local residents, to decipher the mechanism of migrants' local integrations, and to deepen our understanding of China's urbanisation.

First, as China's informal settlements, urban villages are *de facto* the ethnic-like enclaves of rural migrants that pave the way for integration into urban society. Thousands of Hubei migrants have accumulated in Datang Village in Guangzhou, working in the clothing industry, enjoying convenient 'ethnic' enclave economies – restaurants for Hubei foods, transportation run by Hubei migrants, middlemen for Hubei migrants, etc. In this regard, urban villages provide migrants with not only affordable housing, but also a convenient route to emerging urbanism. Previously arrived rural migrants make it easier for later migrants to find a social environment. Based on migrant social networks, rural migrants can easily find shelter shortly after their arrival. Moreover, settlements of migrants also create important development opportunities for local villagers. The accumulation of migrants in urban villages provides local villagers with huge amounts of rental income. For instance, the annual rent in some urban villages of Guangzhou such as Sanyuanli has reached about 100 million Yuan (Project-team 2007). The arrivals of rural migrants contribute not only to their own integration, but also to that of the local villagers.

Second, the urban village is de facto a dual community, as its main residents – rural migrants and local villagers – are largely divided. In particular, the identities of local villagers are built on formal institutions, i.e. collective committees, which provide their members with collective dividends, social welfare, and other identity-based profits. More often than not, urban villagers hold urban hukou, so that they can also take advantage of the benefits of urban citizens, such as social security, pensions, medical treatment, etc. Urban villagers take advantage of both urban and rural institutions. In contrast, rural migrants have been largely ignored by both village collectives and urban governments, and they can access none of the local welfare benefits. Moreover, though the population of rural migrants may dwarf the numbers of villagers, all the managers of urban villages are local villagers; no rural migrants can obtain a seat on a collective committee. In this regard, the relation between migrants and the local regime is weak, and this may impair their integration into urban villages. Moreover, villagers and migrants have different demographic features. Many villagers who stay and choose to remain living in the village will be old persons, while most rural migrants are either young persons or working labourers. The division can be even more remarkable if we take into account the young group of post-1980s/1990s migrants. In many cases, urban villagers and migrants even stay in different spaces. Migrants will aggregate in rental houses, with several households sometimes sharing one house or room, while a villager household may either hold on to the top floor of the building, to enjoy the spacious living space or even move out of the village. These two groups will have different facilities – urban villagers may own cars, well-equipped private kitchens, bathrooms, and so on, while the living conditions of migrants are just on the edge of surviving. Will migrants integrate into urban villages? What are the relations between migrants and local villagers? What factors will impact the integration? All these questions remain to be answered.

128 *Zhigang Li and Fulong Wu*

According to the literature, the resulting neighbourhood integration of migrants may link to their demographic features, such as ethnicity, age, educational attainment, etc., and also to their socioeconomic status such as income, employment or occupation. For instance, rural migrants of different generations in China may have different results for neighbourhood integration. Going beyond existing studies, we argue that the integration of migrants is largely dependent upon local contexts or conditions. That is, in order to understand the mechanism of migrant integration, we need to examine specific local contexts, migrants and communities. For example, in the Chinese context, two factors, hukou status and property rights, i.e. owned or rented housing, with or without formal housing contracts, may be the determinants of integration. Moreover, the varying strength of local controls on migration in different cities will also shape the outcome of integration. In this sense, the extent or dynamics of migrant integration in different cities or urban villagers will be different. To examine these hypotheses, we need in-depth empirical studies, and the following sections will use Beijing, Shanghai and Guangzhou as study cases to examine migrant integration in urban villages.

A case study of Beijing, Shanghai and Guangzhou

We selected Beijing, Shanghai and Guangzhou as case studies mainly because these three cities are the major destinations of rural migrants. According to the sixth national census in 2010, the numbers of migrants in Beijing, Shanghai and Guangzhou reached 7.04, 8.97 and 4.76 million, respectively. Moreover, migrants in these three cities have been extensively studied, including migrant villages such as the 'Zhejiang Village' (Ma and Xiang 1998). Second, urban villages in these cities have been extensively rebuilt into higher densities but include important variations. In Guangzhou, for example, high-rise 'hand-shaking' buildings are built with more than five floors. In Shanghai, many households still live in subdivided apartments. In Beijing, underground spaces are used for private rental housing for migrants. Third, there are differences in terms of the development models of the three cities. For instance, Guangzhou is known for its market-oriented approach (Xu and Yeh 2003). Shanghai is more regulated with strong legacies of the centrally planned economy, and maintains control over migrants. Beijing, in terms of development models, is between Guangzhou and Shanghai. As a result, villages in Guangzhou represent highly developed collective village economies, whereas in Shanghai villages are much weaker and do not usually provide shares and benefits to villagers. These cases may provide a good sample of various urban villages in China.

The survey was conducted in 2010, simultaneously in Beijing, Shanghai and Guangzhou. This seasonal control is to provide comparability as the survey was done well before the Spring Festival when many migrants return to the countryside. The survey used structured questionnaires completed through face-to-face interviews, which consisted of six sections: sociodemographic attributes, income and spending, housing characteristics, employment, and neighbourhood features. The sampling approach uses the list of urban villages to randomly select 20 villages

Migrant integration in China's urban villages 129

for each city; from each village, 20 households are randomly selected through a random start address with fixed intervals. This address-based approach is widely used in Chinese household surveys because there is no official list for migrants. The address-based approach is able to numerate the migrant population better than other household registers. In total, 1,208 valid questionnaires were collected. The strength of this survey is that it is a multi-city survey with a relatively larger spread of surveyed villages (20 villages), rather than several case villages. The development of the list of villages is critical. Fortunately, for Beijing and Guangzhou, through contacts with local governments, the 'official' lists were made available, because both cities intend to redevelop urban villages as a priority. For Shanghai, the survey was co-incident with the municipal planning bureau's pilot study. The name list of villages was congregated from district planning offices.

Because villages are randomly selected from the lists, their distribution reflects the characteristics of urban villages in the city in general. Figure 8.1 shows that they are located mostly in the peri-urban areas. In Beijing, villages within the fourth ring road will soon be demolished. The majority of urban villages (over 80 per cent) are located between the fourth and sixth ring roads. In Shanghai, the number of villages is smaller and mainly concentrated in a few districts such as Putuo, Xuhui, Minghang, Zhabei and Pudong. In Guangzhou, villages are more spread out in the central areas and more widely distributed than in Shanghai.

Measuring migrant integration

The Index of Integration (referred to as Index in the following) is calculated as Sum (Scores)/60. As shown in Table 8.1, for all the samples, the mean of the Index is about 61.54; the figure for local residents is 69.80 and that for migrants is 59.41. It is not surprising that local residents in these three cities are more integrated into the community than migrants. For instance, in Shanghai, the mean for local residents is 67.07, while that for migrants is just 62.61. Second, according to our fieldwork observation, the living conditions of migrants in Shanghai are far worse than in Beijing and Guangzhou. It may be expected that the Index of Guangzhou would be higher than that of Shanghai. However, that contrasts with the empirical result: the Index mean of Shanghai (62.61) is larger than that of Guangzhou (57.79), and that of Beijing is the smallest (52.26). The assumed linkage between migrants' living conditions and their integration may thus be rejected, as the improvement of migrants' living conditions may not create higher levels of integration. This will be further examined in the following regression models. Third, it is interesting to further compare the indices of new generation and old generation migrants. It turns out that the mean of all of the old generation migrants is larger than that of new generation migrants. Some literature argues that compared with the old generation, new generation migrants are more suited to urbanism, prefer more to stay in cities, and are more likely to integrate into cities (Zhang and Lei 2008). Yet this does not mean that the level of integration of new generations is higher than for the old generation. In detail, in both Beijing and Shanghai,

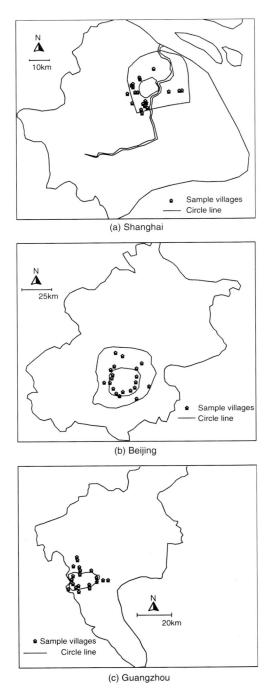

Figure 8.1 The sample villages in (a) Shanghai, (b) Beijing and (c) Guangzhou (2010).

Migrant integration in China's urban villages 131

Table 8.1 Migrant integration of the samples.

	Beijing		Shanghai		Guangzhou		All	
	Mean	*Std. E.*	*Mean*	*Std. E.*	*Mean*	*Std. E.*	*Mean*	*Std. E.*
All samples	60.44	0.75	63.22	0.50	61.01	0.67	61.54	0.37
Local residents	72.04	1.45	67.07	1.53	69.57	1.17	69.80	0.79
Migrants	52.26	0.76	62.61	0.52	57.79	0.73	59.41	0.39
Old generation	57.61	1.09	63.40	0.59	50.19	1.02	60.30	0.51
New generation	56.84	1.08	61.04	1.04	57.31	1.04	58.17	0.62

the mean for old generation migrants is larger than for new generation migrants. However, in Guangzhou, the Index for the old generation is just 50.19, while that for the new generation is as high as 57.31, indicating a higher level of neighbourhood integration. Such differences among the three cities indicate that there may be different mechanisms of migrant integration in these three cities.

Determinants of migrant integrations

A total of 18 variables were selected to examine the effects on migrant integration. First, there are several demographic variables such as age, gender, marriage status, and child/children. For example, it is assumed that the development of family in the cities will contribute to the integration of migrants. Second, in order to examine the lingering impacts of institutional forces, we also examine the impacts of hukou status. The ownership of urban hukou may largely increase the level of migrant integration. Third, several socioeconomic variables will also be examined, such as educational attainment, occupation status, employment status, working contract, working stability, social welfare (Index of social welfares), and income, as an upgrade of socioeconomic status may have significant impacts upon migrant integration. Moreover, the length of residence has also been considered, as it often has positive impacts upon the integration of migrants. In addition, several housing variables are considered, such as property rights, self-use areas, house construction time, facility conditions (Index of facilities) and housing rents, as it is generally assumed that the obtaining of property rights or the improvement of housing may increase the level of integration.

Table 8.2 reports the result of the linear regressions to examine factors that may impact the integration of migrants for all samples. To decrease the impacts of data collinearity, we undertook the regression approach of 'forward' in SPSS. Above all, for migrants in general (Table 8.2), only a few variables are found to be associated with neighbourhood integration, such as marriage (married), employment (staff), income (income 4,000–5,999 Yuan, income 6,000–7,999 Yuan), length of residence (0–3 years), housing quality (construction time of house 1950–1979) and consumption (rent). Some findings confirm the theories of the literature. For example, the development of families will push forward the

Table 8.2 Linear regressions for the determinants of migrant integration for all samples.

	All		Old generation		New generation	
	B	*t*	*B*	*t*	*B*	*t*
(Constant)	57.43	51.88	58.59	63.52***	58.37	58.72***
Age						
Female (dummy)						
Married (dummy)	2.69	2.68**				
Child (dummy)					5.05	3.54***
Hukou status (reference: other rural)						
HK local–urban						
HK local–rural						
HK other urban						
Educational attainment (ref: college and above)						
Primary school and below						
High school						
Occupation (ref: others)						
State-owned enterprise						
Collective-owned enterprise						
Private enterprise						
Retired						
Employment status (ref: others)						
Manager						
Technician						
Staff	4.47	2.96**	5.42	2.74**		
Industrial worker						
Service worker						
Peasant					−12.17	-2.15*

	B (1)	t (1)	B (2)	t (2)	B (3)	t (3)
Working status						
Working contract (dummy)						
Working stability (dummy)			3.18	2.99**	−2.75	-2.17*
Social welfare index						
Income (ref: 8,000 and above)						
Income 0–1,999						
Income 2,000–3,999						
Income 4,000–5,999	−3.11	−2.75**	−3.27	−2.21*		
Income 6,000–7,999	−5.77	−2.39*	−6.32	−2.12*		
Length of residence (ref: above 30)						
0–3 years	−2.69	−3.31**	−2.55	−2.52*		
4–10 years						
11–30 years						
Housing status						
House ownership (dummy)						
House self-use area						
Built-up time of house (ref: after 2000)						
before 1949						
1950–1979	3.71	3.19**	3.91	2.81**		
1980–1999						
Rent	0.00	2.92**	0.00	2.87**		
Index of facilities						
R^2	0.81		0.11		0.06	

Note: *Significant at 5%; **significant at 1%; ***significant at 0.1%; variables without data indicate that these variables have been excluded from the models during the regression process. B = coefficient; t = t-test.

integration of migrants, as married migrants report a higher level of integration than those not married. Second, a successful upward movement on the socioeconomic ladder will contribute to neighbourhood integration, such as working as enterprise staff or white collar, increase in income, as well as the input of consumption (rent). Third, long-term residence will also contribute to integration. In all, it confirms that a successful upgrade of socioeconomic status will improve migrant integration into the local society.

The deficiencies of the assumed impacts of the variables of hukou status, social welfare, property rights (house ownership) and facility conditions (index of facilities) are important. First, this indicates that the impact of institutional forces such as hukou and its related welfare arrangements upon migrant integration is decreasing. After market reforms as well as recent hukou regime reforms that transformed the close relation between hukou status and social welfare, the institutional barriers to gaining an urban livelihood imposed on rural migrants have been removed. Instead, market factors such as income, consumption and employment status are taking the place of institutional arrangements to be the determinants of migrant integration. Second, neither property rights nor facility conditions are found to be important. For migrants in general, the spatial dimension is not important to their neighbourhood integration. As such, the integration of migrants in post-reform urban China is a 'floating' and largely social process – it may not be attached to any specific spaces.

Moreover, the determinants of neighbourhood integration for old generation migrants and new generation migrants are by no means the same (Table 8.2). The factors that impact the integration of old generation migrants include the variables of employment status (staff); stability of working (working contract); income (income 4,000–5,999 Yuan, income 6,000–7,999 Yuan); length of residence (0–3 years); housing quality (construction time of house 1950–1979) and consumption (rent). In contrast, the determinants for new generation migrants only include three variables: demographic features (one or more children), employment status (peasant) and working stability (working contract). At the earlier stage of migration, only a few socioeconomic variables such as employment status may shape migrant integration. Along with the increase in the length of residence, new factors such as income, property rights and consumption will start to contribute to integration.

It is important to note the deficiency of the assumed impacts of several factors. The impact of hukou status upon migrant neighbourhood integration is not found. This suggests that the institutional barriers placed upon migrants in the past are disappearing. Hukou is no longer a significant factor that will shape the integration of rural migrants. In the same vein, the impact of social welfare upon integration also has not been identified. Moreover, the variable of 'index of facilities' has also been found to be insignificant. This indicates that the improvement of living conditions will not directly contribute to migrant integration.

Variations between Beijing, Shanghai and Guangzhou

These three cities show a similar trend in that the significance of institutional factors such as hukou status is diminishing, while that of market factors such as income, employment and housing status is increasing. Nevertheless, there are also variations in terms of the determinants of migrant integration for the three cities (Tables 8.3, 8.4 and 8.5). As mentioned in the last section, Shanghai's development model is relatively more state-oriented, whilst that of Guangzhou is largely market-oriented, and that of Beijing is more often in-between the last two cities. Such differences have significant impacts upon the integration of migrants. First, the determinants of integration in Shanghai are more diverse than for Beijing and Guangzhou (Table 8.4). Demographic variables, hukou status, employment and length of residence are found to be important factors in Shanghai. For instance, migrants with urban hukou are more integrated than rural hukou holders, i.e. rural migrants; those working as staff – white collar – are more integrated than other groups. Both institutional factors and market factors contribute to the integration of migrants.

Fewer variables are found in Beijing and Guangzhou (Table 8.3 and Table 8.5). In contrast to Shanghai, housing status and income are most important to the integration of migrants in Beijing and Guangzhou. In Beijing, the identified variances show that the determinants of migrant integration are largely housing-related variables such as house ownership, house self-use areas, and so on. Specifically, the ownership of housing in Beijing will largely increase migrant integration. For new generation migrants, the development of family and the increase in income are also important, while the integration of old generation migrants is mainly dependent on their housing status. Third, Guangzhou's migrant integration is even more market-oriented – the income variable is found to be a major determinant – a high income will greatly enhance the integration of both new generation and old generation migrants. In addition, an increase in rent, i.e. consumption, will also contribute to integration. Moreover, living conditions such as well-equipped facilities are also important, in particular to new generation migrants.

Discussion and conclusions

A growing number of studies have shed light upon both rural migrants and urban villages in urban China. Little, however, is known about the integration of migrants in urban villages. In this study we examined the integration of migrants in the urban villages of Beijing, Shanghai and Guangzhou, the three largest cities in China. It is found that for all the samples the mean of Integration Index is 61.54 on a scale of 0–100, suggesting that migrants' integration in urban villages is not low. It confirms that urban villages provide opportunities for the further integration of migrants in Chinese cities. Moreover, the impact of institutional factors such as hukou status is by no means remarkable, whilst those of income, property rights and consumption are increasing, suggesting that market factors are taking the place of institutional factors to become the determinants of migrant integration in urban China. The diminishing of institutional barriers may pave the way for the future integration of migrants into urban China.

Nevertheless, the process of integration will be a gradual, tough and largely contextualised process. For instance, the effects of the length of residence upon

Table 8.3 Linear regressions for the determinants of migrant integration in Beijing.

	All		Old generation		New generation	
	B	t	B	t	B	t
(Constant)	53.20	39.36***	53.86	36.08***	54.08	40.15***
Age						
Female (dummy)						
Married (dummy)						
Child (dummy)	3.40	2.12*			7.99	3.27**
Hukou status (reference: other rural)						
HK local–urban						
HK local–rural						
HK other urban						
Educational attainment (ref: college and above)						
Primary school and below						
High school						
Occupation (ref: others)						
State-owned enterprise						
Collective-owned enterprise						
Private enterprise						
Retired						
Employment status (ref: others)						
Manager						
Technician						
Staff						
Industrial worker						
Service worker						
Peasant						

	B	t	B	t	B	t
Working status						
Working contract (dummy)						
Working stability (dummy)						
Social welfare index						
Income (ref: 8,000 and above)						
Income 0–1,999					5.71	2.15*
Income 2,000–3,999						
Income 4,000–5,999						
Income 6,000–7,999						
Length of residence (ref: above 30)						
0–3 years						
4–10 years						
11–30 years						
Housing status						
House ownership (dummy)	29.53	2.48*	27.55	2.28*		
House self-use area	0.19	3.26**	0.23	3.05**		
Built-up time of house (ref: after 2000)						
before 1949						
1950–1979						
1980–1999						
Rent						
Index of facilities						
R^2	0.08		0.12		0.12	

Note: *Significant at 5%; **significant at 1%; ***significant at 0.1%; variables without data indicate that these variables have been excluded from the models during the regression process. B = coefficient; t = t-test.

Table 8.4 Linear regressions for the determinants of migrant integration in Shanghai.

	All		Old generation		New generation	
	B	*t*	*B*	*t*	*B*	*t*
(Constant)	58.00	25.00***	63.50	86.82***	38.78	4.50***
Age	0.17	3.12**			1.19	3.63***
Female (dummy)	−3.72	−2.27*				
Married (dummy)						
Child (dummy)						
Hukou status (reference: other rural)						
HK local–urban						
HK local–rural						
HK other urban	5.32	3.63***			5.39	2.05*
Educational attainment (ref: college and above)						
Primary school and below						
High school						
Occupation (ref: others)						
State-owned enterprise						
Collective-owned enterprise						
Private enterprise	−2.73	−2.48*				
Retired						
Employment status (ref: others)						
Manager						
Technician						
Staff	4.93	2.83**	8.79	4.65***		
Industrial worker						
Service worker						
Peasant						

	B	t	B	t	B	t
Working status						
Working contract (dummy)					−5.31	-2.50*
Working stability (dummy)						
Social welfare index						
Income (ref: 8,000 and above)						
Income 0–1,999						
Income 2,000–3,999						
Income 4,000–5,999						
Income 6,000–7,999						
Length of residence (ref: above 30)						
0–3 years	−2.87	−2.68**	−3.06	−2.47*		
4–10 years						
11–30 years						
Housing status						
House ownership (dummy)						
House self-use area					−0.56	-2.23*
Built-up time of house (ref: after 2000)						
before 1949						
1950–1979						
1980–1999						
Rent						
Index of facilities						
R^2	0.15		0.11		0.27	

Note: *Significant at 5%; **significant at 1%; ***significant at 0.1%; variables without data indicate that these variables have been excluded from the models during the regression process. B = coefficient; t = t-test.

Table 8.5 Linear regressions for the determinants of migrant integration in Guangzhou.

	All		Old generation		New generation	
	B	t	B	t	B	t
(Constant)	50.42	25.71***	54.12	33.02***	47.13	15.63***
Age						
Female (dummy)						
Married (dummy)						
Child (dummy)						
Hukou status (reference: other rural)						
HK local–urban						
HK local–rural						
HK other urban						
Educational attainment (ref: college and above)						
Primary school and below						
High school						
Occupation (ref: others)						
State-owned enterprise						
Collective-owned enterprise						
Private enterprise						
Retired						
Employment status (ref: others)						
Manager						
Technician						
Staff						
Industrial worker						
Service worker						
Peasant						

	B	t	B	t	B	t
Working status						
Working contract (dummy)			5.96	2.71**	−6.18	−2.81**
Working stability (dummy)						
Social welfare index						
Income (ref: 8,000 and above)						
Income 0–1,999						
Income 2,000–3,999						
Income 4,000–5,999	−5.23	−2.74**	−8.57	−3.37**		
Income 6,000–7,999	−13.50	−3.43**	−11.07	−2.45*	−16.26	−2.13*
Length of residence (ref: above 30)						
0–3 years						
4–10 years						
11–30 years	4.18	2.09*	5.03	2.24*		
Housing status						
House ownership (dummy)						
House self-use area						
Built-up time of house (ref: after 2000)						
before 1949						
1950–1979						
1980–1999						
Rent	0.00	2.88**				
Index of facilities	1.50	3.31**			3.06	4.23***
R^2	0.13		0.16		0.20	

Note: *Significant at 5%; **significant at 1%; ***significant at 0.1%; variables without data indicate that these variables have been excluded from the models during the regression process. B = coefficient; t = t-test.

142 *Zhigang Li and Fulong Wu*

the integration of migrants are by no means the same for the three cities. In contrast to Guangzhou, old generation migrants are more integrated than new generation migrants in both Beijing and Shanghai. Moreover, there are differences in terms of the determinants of the integration for new and old generation migrants. Many factors such as income, property rights and consumption will impact the integration of old generation migrants. However, only a few socioeconomic variables such as employment status are important to new generation migrants. This may suggest that the routes of integration for old generation migrants are diverse, whilst for new generation migrants they are limited. In this sense, the possibility of migrant integration is diminishing.

Moreover, our case study indicates that most of the determinants are socioeconomic variables, i.e. social factors, rather than spatial factors. It indicates that the integration of migrants in urban villages is short of a spatial dimension, i.e. it is largely rootless and superficial, and it maintains the mobility of migrants. The redevelopment of urban villages during recent years makes this problem worse (Lin *et al.* 2012). For example, Hin and Li (2011) examined the 'power relation' in the redevelopment of two urban villages in Shenzhen and confirmed the existence of formal urban coalitions in which local authorities play a determining role. Lin and De Meulder (2012) examined the roles and partnerships of various stakeholders in the process of redevelopment, and worked out that migrants have almost no impact on it. As a result, the demolition–redevelopment approach adopted by the local government would be devastating not only for rural migrants but also for the city's economy, which is largely based on labour-intensive sectors (Hao *et al.* 2011).

Fourth, this study confirms that migrant integration is largely a localised process. There are differences among the three cities. In detail, the determinants for Shanghai include both institutional and market factors, while that for Beijing is mainly housing status, and for Guangzhou mainly income. Clearly, there are various mechanisms of migrant integration in different places. Moreover, only in Shanghai is it found that hukou status is important to the integration of migrants. It is a consensus that the authorisation of localised identity may contribute to the integration of migrants, and more often than not this is taken as the strategy for integrating rural migrants in many Chinese cities. Our studies suggest that the application of integration policies or strategy should be concerned the variation between different contexts, so that the local geography of social integration has to be taken into account.

References

Alba, R. and Nee, V. (2003) *Remaking the American Mainstream: Assimilation and Contemporary Immigration*. Cambridge, MA: Harvard University Press.

Alba, R. D., Logan, J. R. and Crowde, K. (1997) 'White neighborhoods and assimilation: The greater New York region, 1980–90', *Social Forces*, 75: 883–909.

BBC (2011) *China Migrant Workers clash with Police for third Night*. Online. Available: http://www.bbc.co.uk/news/world-asia-pacific-13746989 (Accessed 15 June 2012).

Migrant integration in China's urban villages   143

Bolt, G. (2002) 'Window on the Netherlands. Ethnic segregation in the Netherlands: New patterns, new policies?', *Tijdschrift voor Economische en Sociale Geografie*, 93(2): 214–20.

Brown, L. A. and Chung, S. Y. (2008) 'Market-led pluralism: Rethinking our understanding of racial/ethnic spatial patterning in US cities', *Annals of the Association of American Geographers*, 98(1): 180–212.

Clark, W. A. V. (1991) 'Residential preferences and neighbourhood racial segregation: A test of the Schelling segregation model', *Demography*, 28(1): 1–19.

Editorial (2010) *2010 Report on China's Migrant Population Development*. Beijing: China Population Press.

Fan, C. C. (2008) *China on the Move: Migration, the State, and the Household*. London: Routledge.

Fan, C. C., Sun, M. and Zheng S. Q. (2011) 'Migration and split households: A comparison of sole, couple, and family migrants in Beijing, China', *Environment and Planning A*, 43(9): 2164–85.

Gordon, M. M. (1964) *Assimilation in American Life: The Role of Race, Religion, and National Origins*. New York: Oxford University Press.

Gu, C. and Kesteloot, G. (2002) 'Beijing's socio-spatial structure in transition', in Schnell, I. and Ostendorf, W. (eds), *Studies in Segregation and Desegregation*, Aldershot: Ashgate, pp. 12: 285–311.

Hao, P., Sliuzas, R. and Geertman, S. (2011) 'The development and redevelopment of urban villages in Shenzhen', *Habitat International*, 35(2): 214–24.

Hin, L. and Li, X. (2011) 'Redevelopment of urban villages in Shenzhen, China – An analysis of power relations and urban coalitions', *Habitat International*, 35(3): 426–34.

Kempen, R. V. and Ozuekren, A. S. (1998) 'Ethnic segregation in cities: New forms and explanations in a dynamic world', *Urban Studies*, 35(10): 1631–56.

Lin, Y., de Meulder, B. and Wang, S. (2011) 'Understanding the "village in the city" in Guangzhou: Economic integration and development issue and their implications for the urban migrant', *Urban Studies*, 48(16): 3583–98.

Lin, Y. and de Meulder, B. (2012) 'A conceptual framework for the strategic urban project approach for the sustainable redevelopment of 'villages in the city' in Guangzhou', *Habitat International*, 36(3): 380–7.

Liu, Y., He, S., Wu F. and Webster, C. (2010) 'Urban villages under China's rapid urbanization: Unregulated assets and transitional neighbourhoods', *Habitat International*, 34: 135–44.

Liu, Y., Li, Z. and Breitung, W. (2012) 'The social networks of new-generation migrants in China's urbanized villages: a case study of Guangzhou', *Habitat International*, 36(1): 192–200.

Logan, J. R. (2006) 'Variations in immigrant incorporation in the neighborhoods of Amsterdam', *International Journal of Urban and Regional Research*, 30(3): 485–509.

Logan, J. R., Zhang, W. Q. and Alba, R. D. (2002) 'Immigrant enclaves and ethnic communities in New York and Los Angeles', *American Sociological Review*, 67(2): 299–322.

Ma, X. and Tong, X. (2008) 'Looking after others: The road to the integration of new migrants', *Jianghai Academic Journal*, 2: 16–22.

Ma, L. J. C. and Xiang, B. (1998) 'Native place, migration and the emergence of peasant enclaves in Beijing', *The China Quarterly*, 155: 546–81.

Massey, D. S. and Denton, N. A. (1985) 'Spatial assimilation as a socioeconomic outcome', *American Sociological Review*, 50: 94–110.

144 *Zhigang Li and Fulong Wu*

Park, R. E., Burgess, E. W. and McKenzie, R. D. (1925) *The City*. Chicago: Chicago University Press.

Portes, A. and Zhou, M. (1993) 'The new second generation: segmented assimilation and its variants', *The Annals of the American Academy of Political and Social Science*, 530: 74–96.

Project-team (2007) *The Redevelopment Planning of Urban Villages around Baiyun Airport (2007–8)*. Guangzhou: Sun Yat-sen University.

Ren, Y. and Qiao, N. (2010) 'Social integration for migrants: Process, measurement and determinants', *Population Research*, 34(2): 11–19.

Schelling, T. (1971) 'Dynamic models of segregation', *Journal of Mathematical Sociology*, 1: 143–86.

Song, Y. and Zenou, Y. (2012) 'Urban villages and housing values in China', *Regional Science and Urban Economics*, 43(2): 495–505.

Su, Y. and Min, W. (2010) *Escaping from Metropolis*. Nanjing: Jiangsu People Press.

Tian, L. (2008) 'The Chengzhongcun land market in China: Boon or bane? – A perspective on property rights', *International Journal of Urban and Regional Research*, 32(2): 282–304.

Tomlinson, R. (2012) 'Does Shanghai have slums?' *International Development Planning Review*, 34(2): V–XVI.

Wang, G., Shen, J. and Liu, J. B. (2008) 'Citizenization of peasant migrants during urbanization in China-A case study of Shanghai', *Population and Development*, 14(1): 3–23. (in Chinese).

Xiang, B. (1999) 'Zhejiang village in Beijing: Creating a visible non-state space through migration and marketized networks', in Pieke, F. N. and Mallee, H. (eds), *Internal and International Migration: Chinese Perspectives*, Surrey: Curzon.

Xu, J. and Yeh, A. G. O. (2003) 'City profile: Guangzhou', *Cities*, 20(5): 361–74.

Zhang, L. (2011) 'The political economy of informal settlements in post-socialist China: The case of chengzhongcun(s)', *Geoforum*, 42(4): 473–83.

Zhang, L. and Wang, G. (2010) 'Urban citizenship of rural migrants in reform-era China', *Citizenship Studies*, 14(2): 145–66.

Zhang, W. and Lei, K. (2008) 'The urban new immigrants' social inclusion: Internal structure, present situation and influential factors', *Sociological Research*, 5: 117–41.

Zheng, S. Q., Long, F. J., Fan, C. C. and Gu, Y. (2009) 'Urban villages in China: A 2008 survey of migrant settlements in Beijing', *Eurasian Geography and Economics*, 50(4): 425–46.

Zhu, L. (2002) 'The urban integration of migrants', *Jianghai Academic Journal*, 6: 82–8.

Part 3

Migrants' habitat in urban China

9 A tale of Foxconn city

Urban village, migrant workers and alienated urbanism

Daniel You-Ren Yang

Introduction: new-generation migrant workers' urbanism

Since mainland China started its economic reform and adopted an open-door policy in 1978, there has been a huge influx of labour from rural areas into the coastal cities. Due to the urban–rural dichotomous *hukou* system (the household registration), these migrant workers were called 'peasant workers' or *nong min gong*. Nowadays, with the number over 100 million, the 'new generation migrant workers' born since the 1980s have become the mainstream of the floating population (Development Research Centre of the State Council, 2011; see also Chapter 2 of this book). Many young, new-generation migrant workers disassociated from their familiar hometown places and left for workplaces with which they were unacquainted. The labour conditions they faced seem to have been harsh, and there was little social support available to them. As the tip of an iceberg, the serial fell-from-building suicides of Foxconn factory workers in 2010 shocked the world, and revealed the difficulties and risks of migrant workers' lives in urban China.

Classical urban sociologist Louis Wirth stressed the broad implications of the statement '*urbanism is a way of life*' (Wirth 1938). The characteristics, shape and the effects of transforming urbanism in the Western context became one of the focuses of the urban studies tradition (Butler and Robson 2001; Gottdiener and Hutchison 2010; LeGates and Stout 2011; Park 2006; Savage *et al.* 2003). People should not limit China's urbanism to that of the Shanghai Pudong Oriental Pearl Tower. The migrant workers' ways of life are forms of urbanism as well. What kinds of lives do migrant workers – especially the new-generation ones – live in these workplace cities? There have not been many studies on this topic.

For example, the lives in Dongguan's migrant villages are unquestionably patterns of urbanism to which some scholars refer as 'peri-urbanism' (Fan 2006; Lin 2006; Pannell 2006). We observe the new-generation migrant worker's way of life typifies, to a certain extent, the *alienated urbanism* of contemporary Chinese cities. In our field survey with Shenzhen Foxconn's young employees, the evidences of 'social alienation' (Seeman 1959)[1] were common. For instance, 316 copies of the questionnaire survey showed that 34.4 per cent of interviewees

148 *Daniel You-Ren Yang*

felt there was almost nobody close to them, while another 33.3 per cent felt there were few people close to them. The following field journal entries recorded some of this:

> The only friends who would talk to each other are the few co-workers I know on the production line. Off work, we would gather only on Sunday, when we have the opportunity and the time to meet. We hardly know our dormitory-mates; we would nod to one another; we don't even know each other's names ....

> Xiao Xu says he feels pressured working here in Shenzhen, but the pressure does not come solely from work; it is the personal relations. He states, to work in Shenzhen by himself, all he knows are the co-workers at the factory, but the interactions with them are formal, superficial; few of them would help out if one was caught with difficulties.

Table 9.1 describes a day's routine for Foxconn workers; it clearly shows how migrant workers' everyday lives are spatially restricted in the lack of social interaction opportunities.

For the purpose of inquiry, we define the 'alienated urbanism' commonly observed among Foxconn's new-generation migrant workers as the *lack of social support networks in the workplace cities*. Here, social support refers to both affective and instrumental support, and networks including those of the family, relatives, friends, classmates, countrymen and co-workers, etc. (Lin 2001). What is the causal mechanism that shapes such alienated urbanism in the city? What is its implication for new-generation migrant workers? Taking the case of Foxconn's employees in Shenzhen, this research aims to further elaborate the problematic.

The conceptual context of alienated urbanism

The perspectives of classical urban sociology (Williams 1973; Wirth 1938) help us to realize the alienation among people subject to the forces of a monetary economy in a modern metropolis. For more and more people, life in a modern metropolis is not dominated by traditional bonds as in rural society; it is like living in a 'world of strangers'. Ferdinand Tönnies' (1855–1936) commented on this transformation as the vast inconsistency between the interest-exchanging modern 'society' (*Gesellschaft*) mediated by 'rational will' (*Kürwille*), and the 'community' (*Gemeinschaft*) predominated by 'natural will' (*Wesenwille*, referring to the natural will of instinct, the affected entity) and shaped by blood-ties, neighbourliness and a mental sense of belonging (Tönnies 2001). One incessantly meets crowds of people in modern cities, where one knows essentially nothing about the other. For Simmel (1950), cities have a dual effect upon the disorder. On the one hand, there is the individual's isolation amid rapid changes and fragmented social experiences. On the other hand, the city life stimulates residents' new social experience.

A tale of Foxconn city 149

Table 9.1 Living parameter of a day of a Foxconn pugong (ordinary worker).

Time	Behaviour	Venue	People contacted	Conversation content
6:00–8:00	Get up, breakfast get dressed, walk to work	Dormitory, factory canteen, rented room, road	Dormitory-mates	Brief greetings
8:00–12:00	Work	Workshop	Co-workers at workshop	Mainly about work; not able to chat freely for worries of having to do the poorly-done work again
12:00–14:00	Meal, rest, nap	Factory canteen, workshop	Co-workers at workshop, or alone	Brief chat
14:00–17:00	Work	Workshop	Co-workers at workshop	
17:00–18:00	Meal, rest	Factory canteen	Co-workers at workshop, or alone	Chat when work schedules are not tight
18:00–21:00	Work	Workshop	Co-workers at workshop	Chat when work schedules are not tight
21:00–24:00	Getting off work by walking, chat on phone, internet browsing, listening to music, watching TV, strolling on street	Road, dormitory, rented room, neighbourhood	Room-mates, fellows from the same home place, classmates, former co-workers, or alone	Contacting far-away family members and friends, communicate with local friends
23:00–6:00	Sleep	Dormitory, rented room	Nil	Nil

Source: Author.

The breaking of social ties between rural society and the metropolis has been a major topic of classical sociology. There is, for instance, Durkheim's macroscopic discussion of the breaking and reconstruction of social ties (Durkheim 1893, 1897). Further, Simmel (1950) considered as social space expands, so the growth of modern cities promotes the development of personal character, autonomy and freedom. However, it also leads to isolation and alienation among people. These classical insights suggest that bonding networks among people relate structurally to societal development. In other words, the alienated condition of migrant workers is not caused by some problem to do with their personal mental well-being. Rather, it is closely linked with the transformation of the social structure wherein these workers are embedded.

The social network school underlines the critical role of the network in social integration and mobility (Bian 1997; Burt 1992; Calvó-Armengol 2003; Campbell and Barrett 1992; Granovetter 1973; Montgomery 1992; Lin 2001). The social network is crucial to one's accumulation of *social capital*, broadly defined as *the resources embedded in the social-relational networks that could be mobilized to benefit the purposive action* (Lin 2001). Social capital also contributes to the trustworthiness and norms of reciprocity that eliminate opportunism in collective action and facilitate cooperation and the establishment of formal institutions (Putnam 1994, 2000). Putnam (2000) distinguished two interrelated though different mechanisms of social capital in enhancing social–economic development: bonding and bridging. These were not seen as 'either-or' categories to which social networks can be neatly assigned, but as 'more-or-less' dimensions along different forms of social capital (Putnam 2000).[2] Bonding capital is more inward-looking and has a tendency to reinforce exclusive identities and homogeneous groups. Bridging capital is more outward-looking, spans diverse social cleavages, and connects people across different divides.

In short, the social network is not merely 'affective', but also 'instrumental' in nature. Not only does the network affect migrant workers' way of life and socio-psychological state in workplace cities, it also affects their social mobility. However, social capital should not be conceptualized only as an independent variable giving rise to various results; it is also influenced by the broader political, legal, legitimate and institutional environment. Moreover, prevailing groups can take advantage of the privileged resources gathered from the institutional framework and shape the exclusive network to consolidate their power, as suggested by 'bonding social capital'. For example, in highlighting the 'social reproduction' mechanism of the dominant class, sociologist Pierre Bourdieu defined social capital as 'the aggregate of the actual or potential resources which are linked to possession of a durable network of more or less institutionalized relationships of mutual acquaintance or recognition' (Bourdieu 1986). In this sense, social capital is 'privileged-good' as well.

The problematic of 'alienated urbanism' – defined as the lack of social support networks for new-generation migrant workers – is apparently relevant in the theses of social integration and social capital. However, 'constraint conditions' that shape the opportunity structure (North 1990) for social networks have not been adequately investigated. To further elaborate the alienated urbanism in question, we would like to ask: *how are the expansion and repression of the social support networks of the workers in Shenzhen's Foxconn city affected by the 'migrant labour regime'?*

Based on an institutionalist perspective (Scott 2001), we define the 'migrant labour regime (MLR, dagong regime)' as 'a set of dynamic systems operating in various scales that comprises the formal institutional arrangements and informal rules regulating and normalizing the migrant workers' social relations of production and reproduction, as well as providing those agents with the recognitive foundation'. Especially, these interacting institutional constituents in question include spatial disparities, the hukou system, housing policy, the labour market, work organization and the factory regime.

This framework assumes that migrant agents are embedded in the broader institutional environment, and possess the relational-rationale (Lin 2001). We conceptualize the labour market with the 'internal labour market' thesis, instead of that of neo-classical economics (Fan 2002). Internal labour markets refer to a set of 'institutional rules and procedures', such as recruitment, training skill specificity and the work customs, which govern the employment relationship, in contrast to the external labour market, where such decisions are controlled directly by economic variables (Doeringer and Piore 1971; Althauser and Kalleberg 1981). In this regard, the labour market in China would be differentiated with respect to those institutional rules and procedures of the enterprise (e.g. MNCs, SMEs), industrial sector (e.g. informal sector, electronic manufacturing) and locality (e.g. the Pearl River Delta, the Yangtze River Delta).

The main concerns of the 'factory regime' concept are workers' various social relations in direct production activities in the workplace, as well as 'workplace politics' that evolved around 'labour control' (Buraway 1985). Studies have shown that various kinds of spatial-temporal tactics are employed by the management for the subjugation of and dominance over employees. For example, Pun (2005, 2007) proposes the concept of the 'dormitory labour regime' in deciphering how dormitories are used by mainland factories run by Hong Kong capital as a form of 'total institution' (Goffman 1961; Foucault 1975). The workers' labour and everyday life are subjected to near-total, systematic control by arrangements of effective labour control and managerial configurations that shape the workers' way of life.

The research subjects of this essay are employees in Foxconn's Longhua and Guanlan campuses in suburban Shenzhen. In 2010, the employees in the Longhua campus – called here 'Foxconn city' – numbered 300,000, more than the population of Newcastle. The research methods used were quantitative analysis and qualitative in-depth interviews. Purposive sampling[3] was used for the collection of samples in field investigations conducted in July 2010, March 2011 and July 2011; each took around two weeks. The questionnaires were distributed near Foxconn's Longhua plant in Shenzhen, where the follow-up in-depth interviews also took place. With the limitations of funding and time, the present study had issued 316 questionnaires at the time of writing. Twenty-six (person-time) in-depth interviews were completed, and interviewees included Foxconn base-level operators, technicians, and mainland as well as Taiwanese managers. They were reached by snowballing friends' referrals.

Basic socioeconomic conditions of Foxconn's employees in Shenzhen

The parent company of Foxconn is Hon Hai Precision Industry Co. Ltd., established in 1974. Since 1988, the founder and CEO Terry Gou Tai-Ming has been

152   *Daniel You-Ren Yang*

investing in establishing manufacturing plants in mainland China. The group's global operations have extended to over a dozen countries, including Czechoslovakia, Hungary, Denmark, the Netherlands, Finland, the UK, Turkey, Russia, the USA, Brazil, Mexico, India, Vietnam, Thailand, Malaysia, Singapore, Japan and Australia, with 1,300,000 employees around the world, over 1,000,000 of whom are in China.[4]

Established in 1988, Foxconn's manufacturing base in Shenzhen Longhua district (formerly called Longhua town, renamed since Shenzhen's administrative restructuring of districts in 2004) has seen rapid expansion. In 2001, Hon Hai became Taiwan's largest corporation, and Foxconn is at present the world's largest subcontract manufacturing company. In 2003, Foxconn became China's largest exporter, and its revenue reached US$61.8 billion in 2008, US$55.6 billion of which came from export, accounting for 3.9 per cent of China's entire export. Foxconn ranked 110th in the Fortune 500 in 2010. During the period from 2005 to 2008, the scale of the Longhua campus multiplied, with the number of employees rising from 50,000 to over 300,000. It was not until 2011 that the scale of the production base reduced for the first time, owing to the strategy of relocation to the hinterland (especially Henan and Sichuan) after the suicide incidents (Chan and Pun 2010).

Over 85 per cent of Foxconn workers are *pugong*, i.e. basic workers or base-level production line operators. Foxconn *pugong's* average age is 21.9 in the survey. The average age of *non-pugong* (non-basic workers, including production line managers, technicians, middle to top level supervisors, etc.) is 27.8, that is, around 5.8 years older than *pugong*. The first-time employment age for workers who are employed as *pugong* is 17.7, whereas for *non-pugong* it is comparatively older, at around 20.8. The average years of schooling for Foxconn's *pugong* is 11, which means they received approximately two more years of education after graduating from junior high school. The average years of schooling for *non-pugong* is 13.7, which is 2.7 years more than the average for *pugong*. The time spent in further education could account for the older first-time employment age of *non-pugong*.

In terms of salaries, the average monthly income for *non-pugong* at Foxconn is 4,862 Yuan and 2,051 Yuan for *pugong*. Average monthly expenses for *non-pugong* are 2,321 Yuan, and 1,049 Yuan for *pugong* – around 45 per cent of that of *non-pugong*. Monthly expenses take up around 48 per cent of *non-pugong's* monthly income and around 51 per cent of *pugong's*. *Non-pugong* send 13.5 per cent of their income home on average, with 27.9 per cent for *pugong* (Table 9.2). In actual figures, Foxconn's *non-pugong* would send 657 Yuan home each month, and *pugong* would send 571 Yuan each month.

For the duration of employment, the average seniority for *pugong* is about 25.6 months, whereas for *non-pugong*, it is about 64 months. Evidently, the job mobility of *pugong* is higher than for *non-pugong*. The high mobility of Foxconn's *pugong* conforms to the general feature of Pearl River Delta's labour market, particularly for non-skilled workers without advanced technical capacities.

Table 9.2 Statistics of Foxconn employees' wages, expenses, work hours, days-off and wages sent home.

	Mean	Min.	Max.	Number of answers	Standard deviation
Non-pugong					
Monthly income	4,862.0	1,400	100,000	167	7,724.9
Monthly expenses	2,321.3	150	8,000	169	1,426.8
Daily work hours	8.62	8	15	181	1.0
Day-off per month	5.43	1	9	181	2.1
Percentage of the income sent home	13.5	0	75	113	19.9
Pugong					
Monthly income	2,050.7	1,200	4,000	115	455.3
Monthly expenses	1049	0	3,000	103	535.6
Daily work hours	9.4	8	12	116	1.1
Days-off per month	4.8	1	10	116	1.9
Percentage of the income sent home	27.8	0	100	89	26.2

Source: Author.

Some scholars consider that they are essentially hired as 'short-term contract workers' (Huang 2008). In other words, the relationship between these people and their jobs is that of a changing and unstable nature.

The *pugong's* opportunities for promotion in the company are limited, with education being one of the major constraints. The corporate organization of Foxconn is highly hierarchical. The 'top-down' power relations in the hierarchy are exceedingly rigid; even the engineering departments which prioritize technical capacities are no exception. They are managed in a pyramid model where managers are on the top, below which there are section managers, who oversee team leaders of various departments, with line leaders as the lowest management tier. The hierarchical group of line leaders comprise mostly 'operator I' and 'operator II' by rank whose main task is to manage base-level operators. Most of them are promoted from base-level operators. The probable route of promotion for the majority of *pugong*, who lack qualifications in education and technical capacities, is to start from a base-level operator to become a 'full-operator',[2] then a line leader, and at last a team leader. The glass ceiling of such a promotion channel is obvious and the increase in salaries for such posts is not substantial either. The monthly income of a full operator is above that of *pugong* by 150 Yuan, whereas the monthly incomes of a line leader and a team leader are above that of *pugong* by 300 Yuan and 400 Yuan, respectively. Being a line leader does not require much technical expertise, since Foxconn's knowledge requirement for the post is not high. What matters most is the individual's interpersonal management capabilities.

154 *Daniel You-Ren Yang*

Chengzhongcun as the informal settlement

In the area nearby Foxconn, as well as in the whole industrial area of suburban Shenzhen, the unauthorized construction of peasant housing in '*chengzhongcun*' is very common. These peasant houses could easily reach over 10 storeys high with a high density. Such informal settlements of *chengzhongcun* are the fundamental system of migrant workers' housing supply, owing to the absence of an affordable housing policy in Shenzhen.

As for Foxconn's employees, in comparison with staying in disciplinary, strictly managed dormitories (Pun 2005, 2007), they obviously prefer the choice of renting a place in *chengzhongcun*, where living conditions are generally better. Furthermore, employees often regard the *chengzhongcun* as a more 'human' space with more individual freedom, unchained from management authority. Our survey shows that 90.5 per cent of the respondents prefer living in *chengzhongcun's* rented rooms to dormitories. The *relative freedom* of living was cited as the main reason. For those who prefer to stay in dormitories, the most often cited reason is *lower costs*.

The questionnaires indicate that the proportion of *non-pugong* staying in peasant housing in *chengzhongcun* comprises 85.1 per cent. On the other hand, *pugong* living in rental peasant housing take up only 48.2 per cent. Here, we would like to stress that the *pugong's* choice of staying in dormitories is largely a result of economic limitations. The questionnaires show the average rental expense for *pugong* living in *chengzhongcun* is 296.4 Yuan, whereas the expense for *non-pugong* reaches 574.1 Yuan. *Non-pugong* spend much more than *pugong* and at the same time consume more residential space. We further analysed the correlation of work type and residential expenses via a *T*-test. The result is significant; it indicates the influence of different work type (*pugong/non-pugong*) on the amount of residential spending (Table 9.3). In other words, *non-pugong* are generally more inclined to spend on residential consumption, which also matches our observation that the economy is the major constraint in terms of Foxconn workers' choice of residence.

The marital status of *pugong* and *non-pugong* differs noticeably since 50 per cent of the *non-pugong* in our survey are married while only 10 per cent of *pugong* are married. Staying single is the general condition of new generation migrant workers. However, a substantial portion of married *non-pugong* work in Shenzhen without the company of their spouses. These 'singles in Shenzhen' cases are common among technicians we interviewed; their children are left behind in their home places with family elders, while some of their spouses stay home or go elsewhere for work.

Lastly, on the prospect of settling in Shenzhen in the future, 31 per cent of *non-pugong* intend to stay in Shenzhen for work, while 17 per cent of them would choose to get married in Shenzhen – that is to say 14 per cent of *non-pugong* intend to work in Shenzhen and get married in their home places. The 'chance of marriage' in Shenzhen is generally low. We have similar findings with *pugong*, 15.7 per cent of whom intend to get married in Shenzhen, which is lower than

A tale of Foxconn city 155

Table 9.3 Independent sample *T*-test on pugong/non-pugong's expenses on housing.

		Levene's test for equality of variances		T-test for equality of means	
		F	Sig.	T	Sig. (2-tailed)
Housing rents (including water, electricity and gas)	Equal variances assumed	3.464	0.064	−6.086	0.000
	Equal variances not assumed			−6.312	0.000

Source: Author.

the 23.5 per cent who intend to stay working in Shenzhen (Table 9.4). With further statistical analysis, there seems to be no correlation between work type (*pugong/non-pugong*) and whether one plans to settle in Shenzhen. The barrier to settling in Shenzhen for work or marriage is very high for both *pugong* and *non-pugong*.

The barriers to settling

There are many restrictions on hukou transfer if workers wish to settle in Shenzhen. Under the 'point-based hukou granting system', the local government's requirements for hukou transfer involve a set of assessment indices. The individual's 'human capital' as well as 'economic contribution to Shenzhen' are the main concern. We noticed that Foxconn corporation would assist application for

Table 9.4 Foxconn employees' choices for working and marriage in Shenzhen for the future.

Options	Number	%
Non-pugong	53	31.0
Stay in Shenzhen for work		
Not stay in Shenzhen for work	118	69.0
Total	171	100.0
Stay in Shenzhen for marriage	29	17.0
Not stay in Shenzhen for marriage	142	83.0
Total	171	100.0
Pugong		
Stay in Shenzhen for work	24	23.5
Not stay in Shenzhen for work	78	76.5
Total	102	100.0
Stay in Shenzhen for marriage	16	15.7
Not stay in Shenzhen for marriage	86	84.3
Total	102	100.0

Source: Author.

transfer only if the applicant's hukou was an urban one and the applicant was aged under 35 – on a quota. Other requirements include the male migrant's spouse being a non-rural hukou holder; he has to obtain a 'single child privilege card', which means he would have no more children, or none without a fee. In short, strict hukou restrictions and population control together with high housing prices are major reasons for migrant workers' continuous roaming with no prospect of settling and putting down roots.

An issue closely related to hukou is schooling for children. Having a local hukou is by regulation one of the admission requirements for some schools in Shenzhen, especially public ones. With limited resources, there are few public schools in the Shenzhen region. In comparison, resources (school fees to be paid, teachers' qualification and experience, school facilities) in public schools are better than in private ones. Although there are many private schools available for the migrants' children, the tuition fees are much higher than for public ones.

In addition, we found that buying a house no longer secures a hukou in Shenzhen as before; it is, however, an admission requirement for public schools. As the technician Xiang Ge describes:

> First, if there is a public school in this area, you are to live in this area the first thing. You have the 'hukou ben' (household registration record) of this area, and that is the first requirement. The second is that you have bought a flat in the area; you have your own housing. These two are the most crucial. If you don't have a flat and your hukou here, then it depends upon whether you have signed a contract of lease, which proves that you rent a place here. And you need one with at least a year's contract.

Housing in urban villages, such as those in the workers' villages of suburban Shenzhen, are self-built by farmers on homesteads belonging to village collectives. They are mostly unlicensed, without a Property Ownership Certificate. Therefore, it is very hard for the migrant workers staying in these villages to provide a contract of lease for their children's admission to public schools.

Xiang Ge has a colleague who has already bought a house in Shenzhen. He bought it because there are primary and secondary schools in the area so that his children could attend in the future. In other words, this colleague of Xiang Ge is regarded as a successful case of settling in Shenzhen, with a local hukou and his own housing in Shenzhen. Yet Xiang Ge told us there is only one such case in his department, and this colleague is actually his superior, whose rank equals that of a section manager in Foxconn. When the researcher asked, 'Do people have to be at least a section manager or above to get married, make a career and settle in Shenzhen?' Xiang Ge thought it was generally the case, or else one had to have high income. For a post like section manager, one earns 7,000 to 8,000 Yuan monthly at Foxconn. However, Xiang Ge believes that one needs over 10,000 Yuan per month. In that case, the economic barrier to settling in Shenzhen is over four times the average monthly income of *pugong*.

Migrant workers who are married with children mostly lead some form of separated lives. This is particularly common with mid-level management personnel and technicians. For instance, Xiang Ge was married in 2007; his wife is presently staying in Hunan. With a monthly income of four thousand Yuan, he cannot afford to buy a flat. Has Xiang Ge considered renting a more spacious place in Longhua that would accommodate his small family? He expressed his disinclination for such a mode of settling. In brief, Xiang Ge has been living with a sense of insecurity and roaming about; as he mentioned, working status like his is something where 'each day counts for itself'.

Strangers in a foreign place

Many workers in Foxconn city just hang around pointlessly when off work. They are *xiaguang zhe* ('aimless strollers'). Unlike Walter Benjamin's notion of *flâneur*[5] or Italo Calvino's *traveller of a winter's night*, these *xiaguang zhe*, or aimless strollers, are situated in different urban milieus. They are more like a 'proletariat having a scheduled break in prisons', when they can get some air in a restricted place. They can walk about, move a bit and look at people, or at times smoke a cigarette or breathe some fresh air.

In Foxconn city, it is hard for workers to simply find somewhere to sit down and have a rest. They hang around in Longhua Square, the only park square in Longhua, in supermarkets or at the small indoor skating-ink and dance floor compound, or else they spend their off-work hours browsing the internet. As the technician Xiao We described:

> For introverts and those who are not particularly used to socializing, it could be empty and lonely. They might just stay in the dormitory, go out for meals and come back to the dormitory to sleep. There are many of them. Of course, maybe he is not used to socializing... and then, especially when they go out, they are merely walking from one place to another, and from there they walk back here, or else they would just surf the internet.

Xiao Wu felt that a working life like his has no *spiritual enjoyment*. The place he is now renting is a typical 'handshake house' in an urban village. In his words, it is merely a *space for sleep*. When his wife and child occasionally come to visit him, they would sleep there together and go out for meals, or go to find a place like a supermarket or square where they can take a walk. For him, residence does not have a sense of homeliness; it is more like a *tool for rest*.

Further, Xiao Wu thinks the people living there (in the migrant village around Foxconn) have a strong sense of defensiveness, through fear of being cheated. He feels as though everyone is cold to one another, and would only be familiar with someone they knew from before or who came from the same home place. Xiao Wu's friends are basically limited to his co-workers or classmates. It is rare that he knows someone from the neighbourhood. This highlights the loneliness and isolation of workers in a foreign place, where they are dislodged from their network of friends and relatives.

158 *Daniel You-Ren Yang*

Compared with workers from outside, local hukou people in Longhua are wealthier. Their income largely comes from leasing their land and houses, as well as dividends from village collectives, etc. In general, they do not have to work and comprise a typical 'rent recipient class'. The area nearby Longhua Renmin Road, which local hukou people frequent, is a prosperous district with higher consumption levels in contrast with the districts where the workers reside. For most grassroots workers, everyday needs are settled in the cheap stalls in the migrant neighbourhood near the factory.

Labour control strategy

An employee tends to have at least a few friends here, but it is hard for these new acquaintances to become closer friends. The friendship of co-workers on the shop floor is a major communal channel for the Foxconn *pugong's* otherwise limited social network. And yet, the major barrier to this form of network development is the company's labour control strategy.

With each production line counting as a unit for calculation of efficiency, IE or industrial engineering personnel assign productivity indices with reference to the work speed of the most skilled workers. Base-level supervisors (such as Full Operator, Line Leader and Team Leader) pressurize the grassroots workers to keep up with the efficiency requirements.[6] If the workers lag behind, they might be subject to censure of various forms (such as punishment by standing in the corner, scolding them, etc.). The phenomenon was serious before the serial fell-from-building incidents, and has continued to exist since then.

An interviewee, Xiao Wang, states that the way Foxconn manages its production lines has not seen much change since the serial suicides. It has been more or less the same, he mentions:

> Foxconn wants you to finish a certain product within a certain number of seconds, and from that they give an expected count of finished items per hour and lay out what would happen if you couldn't finish them on time. I feel like it is still the way it was before. I think I can't make it, I really can't... to do things according to that sort of standard is unbearable; it's unbearable.

Besides base-level monitors, a harsh system of peer review is employed to ensure efficiency and quality. For instance, if there were 10 production lines manufacturing the same product, the management would rank their performance. Such mutual review among production teams for productivity inducement is a regular practice in Foxconn's corporate culture. If a production line fails to achieve a satisfactory placing, the Team Leader would ask for the Line Leader, and the Section Manager would put pressure on the Team Leader, whereas supervisors at a higher level would put pressure on the Section Manager over the unsatisfactory performance. There might be meetings to call for a 'critical review' of specific personnel. The mechanism is premised on competition between individuals, lines, groups, and departments. In this way, a top-down hierarchical system of pressure and supervision is facilitated, by which ongoing performance assessment instils the goal of increased productivity.

The effectiveness of this system is closely related to the promotion and appraisal of managerial personnel. Promotion within the Foxconn factory depends upon the recommendation of one's superior; *having a good relationship with the superiors* thus determines whether a base-level monitor will be positively assessed. In general, senior managers give orders to monitors directly, as in the military. Base-level monitors must obey their seniors, or they risk unfavourable assessment. Afterwards, they press upon the grassroots workers various indexes of production plans or similar requirements, the implementation of which are enforced by the monitors' tactics, cohesive or otherwise. An interviewee Xiao Huang explains:

> If you can't make it or can't get used to it, you will have to go. In time, they will just make you go; they will be harsh on you, or set traps for you, and you will have to go. In such a working environment, most base-level operators could only take care of their own business. They could not afford to think, or to act for others.

Also, Foxconn's management policies contrive to break down the possible social ties of grassroots workers, rendering them in a disconnected state and thus preventing them from self-organizing for resistance. These considerations are implicit in the 'interest-rationality' of productivity. As we learnt from interviews, workers' resistance occurs on the production lines from time to time, particularly in defiance of base-level monitors' disciplinary measures for the attainment of production indexes. For instance, they would deliberately slow down their work, increase the product defect rate or steal raw materials, etc.

To deal with workers' possible resistance, Foxconn constantly carries out a company-dominant 'workplace politics' (Buraway 1985). Workplace resistance of individual workers cannot spread without the support of fellow workers; instead it can be reported. In this sense, Foxconn's selection of base-level monitors largely depends on their abilities in 'manipulating workplace politics'. The company considers such abilities as productivity correlated, and they are thus to a large extent encouraged by Foxconn's corporate culture. Since the company is a typical flexible production enterprise with frequent work schedule changes as well as working overtime the corporation appreciates how management personnel exercise their power in handling workers to accommodate production contingencies.

With these considerations, Foxconn deliberately breaks down the social ties between workers, rendering them into a state of isolation. 'Compartmentalization' as such provides a foundation for the monitors' exercise of power and manipulation of workplace politics, making workers' resistance difficult to embed, let alone collective organization. As Xiang Ge describes it:

> Let's say some of you came from the same place; it won't group you together, not in the workshops, because many are recruited from schools [via staff recruitment programmes]. For instance, if there were 40 from the same class of a school, it won't assign 40 of you on the same production line; it would

160 *Daniel You-Ren Yang*

> break you up and send you to different places. This is because you would act in consolidation if they put you on one production line. To separate you all, you will find no way to get together, and you won't form small organizations.

The heavy workload at Foxconn itself also poses limitations on the collective organization of workers. As the case of interviewee A-Chang shows, there are frequent changes in work shifts at their department to accommodate changes in the production plan. Morning shifts become night shifts, and there are times when the shift schedule changes every two weeks. It causes huge difficulties for workers to adapt 'biologically'. When work is exhausting, one only wants to sleep after work. There is literally no time for social relationships when one cannot even get enough sleep. Some interviewees point out that the workload in some departments requires a scheme of 'Rest 1 for 13', that is, one day of rest for a consecutive 13 days of work. Foxconn repeatedly claims that overtime work is voluntary and consented to by workers, and there are overtime agreements signed by workers as required by labour law. However, our investigations found workers are pressed to work overtime with a 'compulsory consent'. Due to the tactful manipulation of work politics on the part of base-level management, it is difficult for workers to refuse monitors' requests for overtime work. As interviewee Xiao Zhou states:

> It is impossible to say 'No.' If you say no, he will get even with you later. If you want to do overtime work as regulations permit, he won't let you. He'd say something like it is only for your health concerns.

In short, using base-level workplace politics Foxconn manipulates grassroots workers' 'forced consent' to exploit loopholes in labour law, and continues to claim that the company is thoroughly law-abiding.

Conclusion

From the analysis above, we arrive at a clearer picture of the new-generation migrant workers in the Foxconn city. *Pugong* generally leave their home places for work at the age of 18, and stay at the company for no more than two years before they leave. Promotion channels for them are very limited, difference in education level causes disparity in career opportunities. There are few opportunities for gaining knowledge at work. On the production lines, they are faced with base-level management's supervisory pressure, as well as manipulation of workplace politics that strives for productivity. Off work, the *pugong* could be a *xiaguang zhe* without much chance for social interaction. They cope with huge disadvantages with regard to their economic status and the hukou system if they want to settle in Shenzhen – they will have to earn at least 10,000 Yuan, or four times the salary of *pugong*. Besides the disciplinary dormitory, *chengzhongcun* rentals are the only housing resources available for them. Most *pugong* do not settle and get married in Shenzhen. Moreover, those married employees' family status is usually the 'split household' with members live in two defferent places.

In this case study, we illustrate the 'migrant labour regime' not only shapes the alienated urbanism in Foxconn city, with the compression of the social network being a key cause; it also sets up huge barriers to upward mobility for workers. In other words, the regime has led to drastic spatial flow of workers, yet considerably limits their social flow. Constrained by structural limitations, migrant workers are characterized by 'circular migration' (Fan 2008; Wang and Zuo 1999). They are not recognized as citizens by the authorities and the local population, and not even included in city planning as a part of the population for whom public services should provide. The drastic disparity in educational resources make numerous new-generation workers come into society with insufficient human capital accumulation, which limits their possibilities regarding career prospects. Furthermore, the company's labour control strategies further split workers' social ties, worsening their state of alienation in the city.

The basic principle of mainland China's economic reform, namely, '*uneven development*', has left behind a huge historical legacy after 30 years. The suicides of the new-generation migrant workers of Foxconn are, to a certain extent, a cry of protest (Chan and Pun 2010) that pledge the world to remember the existence of 'unequal developments'. Echoing the critique, this study further reminds us of another issue relevant to urban development: how to enhance workers' social support networks compressed by the migrant labour regime.

Acknowledgement

The author would like to thank R.O.C. 99' National Science Council Research Project (NSC-99–2410-H-029–047) for funding this study.

Notes

1. This text adopts the classical definition of 'alienation' by Seeman (1959), which refers to socio-psychological states including powerlessness, meaninglessness, normlessness, isolation and self-estrangement.
2. For a critical assessment of social capital, see Fine (2001).
3. A non-random selection of participants on purpose. The variables to which the sample is drawn up are linked to the research question.
4. *Source*: Foxconn's homepage, http://www.foxconn.com.cn/quanqiushiliangbujutu/000.html
5. For the notion of flâneur, please refer to Parker (2006).
6. We would like to stress that management practices vary among Foxconn departments.

References

Althauser, R. P. and Kalleberg, A. L. (1981), 'Firms, occupations, and the structure of labor markets: a conceptual analysis', in I. Berg (ed.), *Sociological Perspectives on Labor Markets*, New York: Academic Press, pp. 119–49.

Bian, Y. (1997) 'Bringing strong ties back in: Indirect ties, network bridges, and job searches in China', *American Sociological Review*, 62(3): 366–85.

Bourdieu, P. (1986) *Outline of a Theory of Practice*, Cambridge: Cambridge University Press.

162 Daniel You-Ren Yang

Buraway, M. (1985) *The Politics of Production: Factory Regimes under Capitalism and Socialism*, London: Verso.

Burt, R. (1992) *Structure Hole*, Cambridge: Harvard University Press.

Butler, T. and Robson, G. (2001) 'Social capital, gentrification and neighbourhood change in London: A comparison of three south London neighbourhoods', *Urban Studies*, 38(12): 2145–62.

Calvó-Armengol, A. (2003) 'Job contact networks', *Journal of Economic Theory*, 115(1): 191–206.

Campbell, K. E. and Barrett, A. L. (1992) 'Sources of personal neighbour networks: Social integration, need, or time?' *Social Forces*, 70(4): 1077–100.

Chan, J. and Pun, N. (2010) 'Suicide as protest for the new generation of Chinese migrant workers: Foxconn, global capital, and the state', *The Asia-Pacific Journal*, 37: 2–10.

Development Research Centre of the State Council (2011) *Civilianizing the Rural Migrants*, Beijing: China Development.

Doeringer, P. and Piore, M. (1971) *Internal Labour Markets and Manpower Analysis*, Lexington, MA: Heath.

Durkheim, E (1893); Coser, L. A. (trans.) (1997) *The Division of Labor in Society*, New York: Free Press.

Durkheim, E (1897); Spaulding, J. A. and Simpson, G. (trans.) [1951] (1997) *Suicide: A Study in Sociology*, New York: Free Press.

Fan, C. C. (2002) 'The Elite, the Natives, and the Outsiders: Migration and Labor Market Segmentation in Urban China', *Annals of the Association of American Geographers*, 92(1): 103–24.

Fan, C. C. (2006) 'Comment on "Peri-urbanism in Globalizing China" and Pannell's critique', *Eurasian Geography and Economics*, 47(1): 58–60.

Fan, C. C. (2008) 'China on the move: Migration, the state and the household', *The China Quarterly*, 196: 937–8.

Fine, B. (2001) *Social Capital versus Social Theory: Political Economy and Social Science at the Turn of the Millennium*. London: Routledge.

Foucault, M. (1975) *Discipline and Punish: The Birth of the Prison*, New York: Random House.

Gottdiener, M. and Hutchison, R. (2010) *The New Urban Sociology*, 4th edn. New York: Westview Press.

Goffman, E. (1961) *Asylums: Essays on the Social Situation of Mental Patients and Other Inmates*, Oxford: Doubleday (Anchor).

Granovetter, M. (1973) 'The strength of weak tie', *American Journal of Sociology*, 78: 1360–80.

Huang, D. B. (2008) *Dang Dai Zhong Guo Gu Yong Gong Ren Zhi Yan Ziu (The Study of China's Contemporary Wage Workers)*, Taipei: Weber. (in Chinese).

LeGates, R. T. and Stout, F. (eds) (2011) *The City Reader*, 5th edn. New York: Routledge.

Lin, N. (2001) *Social Capital: A Theory of Social Structure and Action*, Cambridge: Cambridge University Press.

Lin, G. C. S. (2006) 'Peri-urbanism in globalizing China: A study of new urbanism in Dongguan', *Eurasian Geography and Economics*, 47(1): 28–53.

Montgomery, J. D. (1992) 'Job search and network composition: Implications of the strength-of-weak-ties hypothesis', *American Sociological Review*, 57: 586–96.

North, D. C. (1990) *Institutions, Institutional Change and Economic Performance*. New York: Cambridge University Press.

Pannell, C.W. (2006) 'Peri-urbanism in globalizing China: A critique', *Eurasian Geography and Economics*, 47(1): 54–7.

Parker, S. (2006) *Urban Theory and the Urban Experience: Encounter the City*, London: Routledge.

Pun, N. (2005) *Made in China: Women Factory Workers in a Global Workplace*, Burham, NC: Duke University Press.

Pun, N. (2007) 'Gendering the dormitory labour system: Production, reproduction, and migrant labour in south China', *Feminist Economics*, 13(3/4): 239–58.

Putnam, R. D. (1994) *Making Democracy Work: Civil Traditions in Modern Italy*. Princeton, NJ: Princeton University Press.

Putnam, R. D. (2000) *Bowling Alone: The Collapse and Revival of American Community*. New York: Simon and Schuster.

Savage, M., Warde, A. and Ward, K. (2003) *Urban Sociology, Capitalism and Modernity*, 2nd edn. London: Palgrave Macmillan.

Scott, R. (2001) *Institutions and Organizations*. Thousand Oaks, CA: Sage.

Seeman, M. (1959) 'On the meaning of alienation', *American Sociological Review*, 24(6): 783–91.

Simmel, G. and Wolff, K. (1950) *The Sociology of Georg Simmel*, New York: Macmillan.

Tönnies, F. (2001) *Community and Society*, transl. by Harris, J. and Hollis, M. (*Gemeinschaft und Gesellschaft*, first published in 1887), Cambridge: Cambridge University Press.

Wang, F. and Zuo, X. (1999) 'Inside China's cities: Institutional barriers and opportunities for urban migrants', *The American Economic Review*, 89(2): 276–80.

Williams, R. (1973) *The Country and City*, London: Chatto and Windus.

Wirth, L. (1938) 'Urbanism as way of life', *American Journal of Sociology*, 44: 1–24 (as reprinted in Albert J. Reiss, Jr. (ed.), *Cities and Social Life*. Chicago, IL: University of Chicago Press, 1964, pp. 60–83).

10 Shanghai's urban villages

Migrants, temporary residence and urban redevelopment

Mingfeng Wang, Xiaoling Lin and Yuemin Ning

Introduction

According to the 2010 population census data, the population of China has reached 1.37 billion, among which the urban population accounts for 660 million, taking up 49.68 per cent (National Bureau of Statistics of China 2011). Compared with the data from the 2000 population census, the urban population has risen 13.36 per cent. The urban labour force transfer and rapid economic growth have encouraged migration. The number of migrants has reached 221 million, 100 million more than in 2000, rising by 82.89 per cent. In this huge migrant group, most are rural migrant workers from the countryside and the suburbs. They live in the city and form special settlements and landscapes (Zhou and Cai 2008). The urban village (*Chengzhongcun* in Chinese), which is also called 'villages-in-the-city', is emerging as a distinct kind of settlement, catching wide attention among local and international scholars (Chung 2010).

Chinese urban villages are formed through rapid urbanization, dual management institutions, dual land ownership institutions, and the inflow of migrants during the process of urban restructuring (Feng *et al.* 2008; Song *et al.* 2008; Tian 2008). According to several known studies, house rents in urban villages are very low, but the living conditions are very poor and there is a lack of public infrastructure, with some social problems such as poverty concentration and high crime rate (Wu, F. 2004; Zhang *et al.* 2003; Zheng *et al.* 2009). Therefore, the redevelopment of urban villages has become a major issue during the urban development process in many Chinese megacities. But during the planning and construction of cities, local governments pay more attention to the benefit of real estate developers and local residents, while ignoring the demands of dwellers, who are mainly rural migrants (Hao *et al.* 2011). In fact, with the rapid growth of migrants, how to effectively provide affordable housing for them is becoming a challenge for local governments.

This study aims to explore the development and redevelopment of urban villages through investigation in Shanghai, which is the largest Chinese city. Compared to Guangzhou, Shenzhen, Beijing and some other cities, few studies have concentrated on the urban villages in Shanghai. In the last decade, the main research interest in Shanghai from academia has focused on how to make a global city or world city (Chen 2009; Ning *et al.* 2011; Yusuf and Wu 2002). However, the current population in Shanghai has reached 23 million, among which the migrant population is almost 8 million, taking up 39 per cent (Shanghai Municipal Statistics Bureau 2011). Rural migrants' survival in cities, especially their living conditions, needs urgent attention. Hence, in the process of Shanghai's urbanization, the question is whether urban villages are also an agglomeration of rural migrants as in other Chinese megacities. Meanwhile, in the process of urban redevelopment and restructuring, what part does the urban village play and what is its future? This study will try to reveal the living conditions of residents, the main factors of living in urban villages, and residents' attitudes towards the redevelopment of urban villages in Shanghai. In addition, we attempt to provide some beneficial ideas and policy suggestions for Shanghai's urban development from the perspective of rural migrants' housing demands.

The urban village as a distinct space in Chinese cities

The rapid economic growth and restructuring have increased social and living space differentiation in Chinese cities (Madrazo and van Kempen 2012), especially in several international metropolises such as Beijing, Shanghai and Guangzhou (Feng *et al.* 2008; Li and Wu 2006, 2008; Yeh *et al.* 1995). All kinds of gated communities are on the rise (Pow 2007; Pow and Kong 2007; Wang and Lau 2008; Wu 2010), while living spaces such as the urban village, shanty town, factory dormitory and migrant apartment have formed in the city (Zhou and Cai 2008). Due to their special geographical location and social background, urban villages have become the major settlements for low-income migrants (Wu, W. 2004; Zhang *et al.* 2003). Urban villages are closely related to migrant settlements, but somewhat different. Furthermore, urban villages serve as temporary residences for migrants, attracting floating population due to their low housing costs (Liu *et al.* 2010; Song *et al.* 2008; Wu 2009; Wang *et al.* 2009).

In early research on urban villages, scholars mainly focused on cities located in the Pearl River Delta (Chan *et al.* 2003; Zhang *et al.* 2003) and Beijing's suburbs (Liu and Liang 1997; Ma and Xiang 1998). Soon, however, almost every city in China with urban villages started to attract the attention of both academia and the public. Among studies inside China, more attention has been paid to changes in urban morphology and their formation mechanism. Particular focus has been given to the dual land ownership institution and policy recommendations for redevelopments (Zhu 2002). Some researchers suggest that the government should clear up all urban villages in a swift and determined manner. However, during the redevelopment process, local governments tend to give more consideration to the interests of developers and prospective residents, whilst generally ignoring the housing demands of the migrants who form the main share of existing residents of urban villages (Hao *et al.* 2011). In fact, migrants do not care about land ownership or compensation from redevelopment or how good the development will be. Migrants simply regard urban villages as affordable residences and a low cost living space (Zhang *et al.* 2003). With the urban village clearance approach being encouraged nationwide, most residents in urban villages are facing the threat of losing their living space.

166 *Mingfeng Wang, Xiaoling Lin and Yuemin Ning*

Urban villages are an important part of Chinese urbanization, and they play a vital role in two ways: on the one hand they provide house owners with a stable income, and on the other hand they offer tenants cheap housing. Both aspects are important for Chinese urbanization, and consequently any excessive redevelopment should be carefully considered (Wang *et al.* 2009). Loose regulations, cheap rents and good accessibility have enabled a flourishing business environment in urban villages, which in turn provides numerous employment opportunities for rural migrants. Moreover, these advantages have also turned urban villages into popular gathering spots for the informal sector (Xue and Huang 2008). Compared to migrants in other countries, migrants in Chinese urban villages have higher mobility and are exposed to a higher level of instability (Wehrhahn *et al.* 2008). Housing conditions have a significant impact on the migration intentions of the floating population. Conversely, it is possible to state that factors such as the housing selection process, the temporary identity of migrants and other restrictions contribute significantly to their harsh living conditions (Logan *et al.* 2009; Wu and Wang 2002). The demands of the floating population for affordable housing have made urban villages difficult to replace. However, these informal housing neighbourhoods have also brought many social problems such as a dilapidated environment, security problems, unfair income distribution and financial losses to the government (Li and Wu 2008; Zheng *et al.* 2009).

This study of Shanghai's urban villages focuses on migrant settlements, which can be considered as an entry-level housing alternative that also offers employment opportunities to migrants (Luo and Wang 2009). Thus, it will be meaningful to understand the development mechanism and the trend of urban villages from the migrant's own perspective. Based on the above mentioned theoretical framework and the current background of redevelopment, this study investigates the living conditions and housing demands of residents in Shanghai's urban villages, and provides some useful suggestions for the government on migrants' housing policy.

Methodology and data

The data resource comes from the investigation of the ESRC/DFID project of 'The Development of Migrant Villages under China's Rapid Urbanization'. During August and September in 2010, we conducted a survey of residents in Shanghai's urban villages. At present it is still hard to find a commonly acknowledged definition of 'urban village'. This study defines it from a spatial perspective. The urban village is a rural area that has been encroached upon by rapid urban development and surrounded by urban land. According to this definition we conducted a series of interviews with related government bodies and set up a list of urban villages in Shanghai. Then from the list, we chose 23 villages as the survey target.

The 23 villages are distributed throughout the city, primarily situated in outer central districts and nearby suburbs (see Figure 10.1). Eleven of them are situated between the inner ring and the middle ring, the other nine between the middle and the outer rings. A further three villages are located in nearby areas outside the outer ring of the city. Furthermore, these villages are mostly located nearby elevated highways and well-connected street networks, which allows for high levels of accessibility.

In terms of Shanghai's urban spatial structure, the area within the inner ring has been highly urbanized for a long time and has experienced a decrease in population since the 1990s. On the other hand, the areas between the inner ring and the outer ring have been undergoing rapid urbanization for the last two decades and also have the highest concentration of migrants in Shanghai (Li and Ning 2007). Lastly, the areas beyond the outer ring are mostly suburban and are thus significantly different from all other parts of the city.[1] It can be seen that urban villages in Shanghai are mainly located in the area outside the inner ring in the suburban areas, which is the result of increasing urban sprawl.

In each selected village, households were selected for investigation based on their addresses, using a fixed interval approach. The investigation collected not only information about the tenants but also about the landlords, with which we can conduct a comparison between different types of residents. Questionnaires were distributed

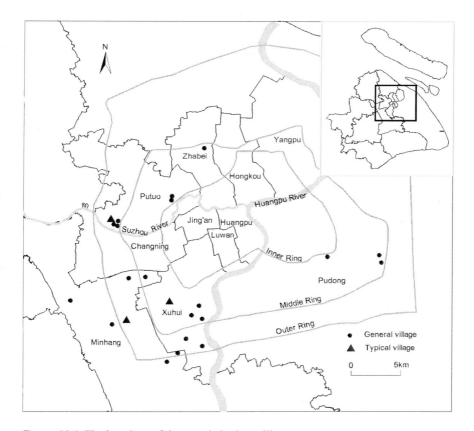

Figure 10.1 The locations of the sampled urban villages.

168   *Mingfeng Wang, Xiaoling Lin and Yuemin Ning*

to heads of households, and we conducted face-to-face interviews, involving information such as basic information on family members, household income and expenditure, living conditions, employment situation, and so on. We distributed 20 questionnaires to 20 general villages respectively, and for the three typical villages, we allocated 100 questions to each village. We generated 700 valid questionnaires in total,[2] including the related information of 1,778 urban village residents.

Who is living in urban villages?

According to the statistical analysis on the questionnaires, the properties of samples are shown in Table 10.1. The sex ratio of residents in the survey is almost equal, while the educational level is relatively low. The average age is 33, and the marital status is mainly married. Moreover, the residents in the survey show significantly similar features in aspects such as identification, employment situation, and income and expenditure.

Rural migrants

A major part of residents in urban villages are rural migrants. According to the survey data, local residents in the survey account for 16.8 per cent, while migrants account for 83.2 per cent (Figure 10.2). Native families account for 13.7 per cent, while migrants take up 86.3 per cent. The family size in the survey is 2.54 persons per household, of which local ones have 2.92 persons per household, while migrant ones have 2.48 persons per household, which corresponds to Shanghai's

Table 10.1 Basic information about the sample.

Variable	*Properties*	*Number*	*%*	*Per cent of Shanghai*
Gender ($n = 1,778$)	Male	922	51.9	51.5
	Female	855	48.1	48.5
Educational attainment	Uneducated/preschool	237	13.5	7.1
($n = 1,758$)	Elementary school	318	18.1	13.5
	Junior high school	660	37.5	36.5
	Senior high school/ secondary technical school	395	22.4	21.0
	College/university/ postgraduate and above	146	8.3	22.0
Age distribution ($n = 1,772$)	14 and under	246	13.9	8.6
	15–59	1,397	78.9	76.3
	60 and above	128	7.2	15.1
Marital status ($n = 1,774$)	Unmarried	454	25.6	N/A
	Married	1,287	72.5	N/A
	Divorced or widowed	33	1.9	N/A

Source: Authors' survey; Shanghai Municipal Statistics Bureau (2011).

Shanghai's urban villages 169

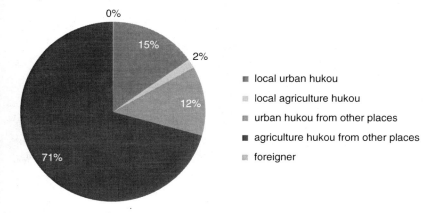

Figure 10.2 Hukou status of residents.
Source: Authors' survey.

2.49 persons per household. The questionnaire data indicates that 85 per cent of spouses also live in the same household, from which we can suggest that migrants in Shanghai show a relatively high proportion of 'family immigration'. Furthermore, the data shows that the average age of migrants is 31.1 years old. The group aged 17 and below accounts for 16 per cent, and the group aged 18–34 accounts for 42 per cent, while the group aged 60 and above accounts for 3 per cent. Compared to Shanghai's permanent population, migrants present the feature of rejuvenation (Figure 10.3).

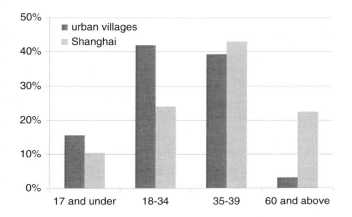

Figure 10.3 Comparison of age distribution of urban villages' residents with that of Shanghai's permanent population.
Source: Authors' survey; Shanghai Municipal Statistics Bureau (2010).

Informal employment

The employees in urban villages are mainly engaged in informal employment. Among 700 households, 17 per cent are engaged in temporary jobs without contracts, 22 per cent are self-employed, 14 per cent of employees have short-term contracts of less than a year, and only 3 per cent of employees have a permanent job (Figure 10.4). The low level of employment contract suggests that most households are engaged in informal employment. Among 1,209 employees, private employment account for 48 per cent, while the self-employed account for 18 per cent (Figure 10.5). As for occupation, 60 per cent of employees are engaged in commercial services (Figure 10.6). The employed are mostly shopkeepers in wholesale markets. Some urban villages are located nearby large-scale wholesale markets, thus serving as a vital source of housing for employees as well as the self-employed vendors in these markets. Furthermore, Figure 10.7 shows that the social insurance rates of the residents in the survey are obviously lower than the average of Shanghai, among which pension insurance, unemployment insurance, and injury insurance rates are only half the average. The lower social insurance rate is mainly attributed to two factors, namely the high proportion of migrants and the informal employment in which most employees are engaged, especially migrants.

Low income and expenditure

The residents in our survey are mainly in the low income group. As shown in Table 10.2, the urban average *per capita* disposable income in Shanghai is 2,403 Yuan per month in 2009, while the average *per capita* income of residents and

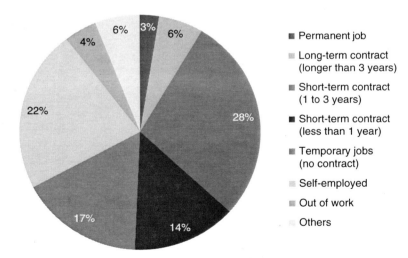

Figure 10.4 Contract situations of householders.
Source: Authors' survey.

Shanghai's urban villages 171

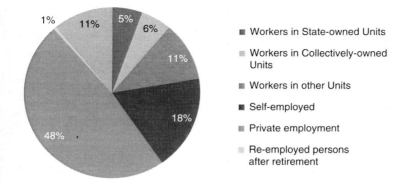

Figure 10.5 Employment situations of the employees.
Source: Authors' survey.

migrants in the survey is 2,061 and 2,003 Yuan per month, respectively, which is lower than urban residents. The urban average *per capita* consumption expenditure is 1,749 Yuan per month, while those of residents and migrants in the survey are 842 and 843 Yuan per month, respectively, less than half those of urban residents. The ratio of urban residents' expenses to income reaches 72.8 per cent, while that of residents and migrants is only 40.9 per cent and 42.1 per cent, respectively, much lower than for urban residents.

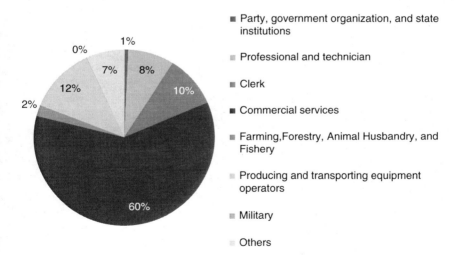

Figure 10.6 Occupation situations of the employees.
Source: Authors' survey.

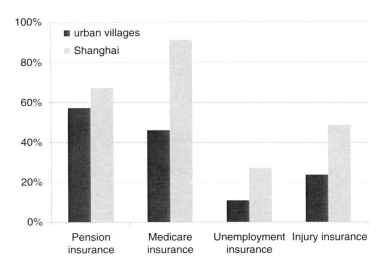

Figure 10.7 Comparison of social insurance of urban villages' residents with that of Shanghai's permanent population.
Source: Authors' survey; Shanghai Municipal Statistics Bureau (2010).

The features described above are significant for the migrants in the survey. In the migrants' composition of *per capita* consumer expenditure, the proportion of food expense accounts for 37.6 per cent, and other expenses for living accounts for 28.7 per cent, reaching 66.2 per cent in total. Rather than spend earnings in the city, migrants would be more likely to send money to their home town for children and parents or to deposit it in the bank. Migrants have a fairly low desire to

Table 10.2 Comparison of migrants' incomes and expenditures with those of Shanghai's permanent population.

	Per capita income (Yuan per month)	*Per capita consumption expenditure (Yuan per month)*	*The ratio of expenditure to income (%)*
Urban resident	2,403	1,749	72.8
Residents in survey	2,061	842	40.9
Migrants in survey	2,003	843	42.1

Note: Urban average *per capita* disposable income refers to the average income with individual income tax and payment on social insurance deducted. The average income of residents and migrants in the survey refers to all the income including salaries, net income from household, business property income and transferred income. So the average income of urban residents may be higher than what is presented in the table.
Source: Authors' survey; Shanghai Municipal Statistics Bureau (2010).

Shanghai's urban villages   173

consume compared with urban residents. The city is more a space to work than a place to live for them. Their consumption standard in this city is to maintain basic needs.

Living conditions in urban villages

Generally, the housing conditions of rural migrants in Shanghai's urban villages are rather poor and much worse than those of permanent residents in Shanghai.

Small living space

The survey shows that the living space of residents in urban villages is very small. The *per capita* living space of residents in the survey is 7.1 square metres, while that of house owners is 26.1 square metres and that of tenants is 4.7, only one-sixth that of house owners. Most families occupy an independent room, few of them sharing a room. The rental ratio is very high at 87 per cent. But the signing rate for rental contracts is very low, with only 18 per cent of tenants signing rental agreements. The housing structure is mainly only one bedroom without a living room. The family owns 1.2 bedrooms and 0.1 living rooms per household.

The *per capita* living space of urban residents in Shanghai was 17.5 square metres in 2010, while that of residents in the survey is less than a half of the average. The house owner's per capita living space is 1.5 times the average, but that of tenants is only a quarter of the average, which is equivalent to the average in 1978.

Insufficient facilities

The housing facilities in urban villages are insufficient. As shown in Table 10.3, the availability of liquefied gas is highest, reaching 76 per cent; the availability of private kitchens, private toilets, air conditioners and the Internet is relatively low, about 20 per cent; and the availability of bathrooms is even lower, only 11 per cent; the lowest availability is pipeline gas, which is only 5 per cent.

Compared to the average for urban residents, the availability of housing facilities in urban villages is much lower.[3] Per 100 urban households, the possession of a personal computer in Shanghai is 129, while the availability of the Internet in

Table 10.3 Housing facilities of residents.

	Independent kitchen	Private toilet	Water heater	Liquefied gas	Pipeline gas	Air conditioner	Internet
Facilities availability (%)	20	16	11	76	5	21	17

Source: Authors' survey.

urban villages is only 17 per cent,[4] which is almost one-eighth of the average. Per 100 urban households, possession of a household air conditioner is 200, while the availability of that in urban villages is 21 per cent, which is nearly one-tenth of the average. Per 100 urban households the possession of a water heater is 98, while the availability of that in urban villages is only 11 per cent, which is nearly one-ninth of the average. Through the comparison above, it can be seen that the housing facilities in urban villages are much worse than for urban residents.

Dilapidated housing

The housing in urban villages is dilapidated. As revealed in survey data, most housing was built before the 1990s, of which 37 per cent was built before 1980 and 40 per cent was completed in the 1980s. Housing built in the 1990s accounts for only 19 per cent and that built after 2000 accounts for only 4 per cent. It can be seen that few housing in urban villages was built after 1990s, and the housing construction almost stopped after 2000. The need for housing is met by housing extensions.

In Shanghai, the total floor area of completed residential housing is 476.2 million square metres, of which 80 per cent was completed after the 1990s, and nearly a half was completed after 2000 (Shanghai Municipal Statistics Bureau 2010). The floor area of residential housing completed before 1980s is 28.5 million square metres, or only 6 per cent; that completed in the 1980s is 66.7 million square metres, or 14 per cent; that completed in the 1990s is 157.3 million square metres or 33 per cent; and that completed after 2000 is 222.3 million square metres or 47 per cent. As shown in Figure 10.8, most of the residential housing in

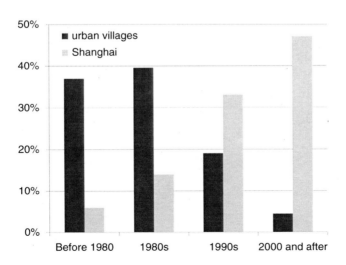

Figure 10.8 Comparison of urban villages' housing built time with that of Shanghai city.
Source: Authors' survey; Shanghai Municipal Statistics Bureau (2010).

urban villages was completed before the 1980s, while most of that in the city as a whole was completed after the 1990s. The city has been proceeding with large-scale construction since 2000. In contrast, housing construction in urban villages has remained stagnant.

Why live in urban villages?

Through comparisons of living space, housing facilities and time of construction, it can be seen that the living conditions of the residents in the survey are much worse than those of urban residents. So why do urban village residents choose to live in such places? For house owners, what are the main reasons for them to stay? And for tenants, what are the factors that attract them to live in urban villages?

House owners' perspective

As shown in the survey of 92 house owners, from the perspective of individual aspiration, 97 per cent of house owners believe that 'inherited private housing' is the main reason to stay, while other people choosing 'incidental' and 'convenient for children's schooling'. As indicated in the survey data, the average year when a house owner started to live there is 1965, and the average age of house owners is 47.7 years, while people 60 years and above account for 29 per cent. It can be concluded that house owners have been living there for a long time and the age structure has revealed an aging tendency. So for the owners in urban villages, familiarity with the old neighbourhood and long-term living habits are important factors for staying in urban villages.

Rental income is another reason for house owners to stay. As suggested in the survey data, on average house owners have 6.7 rooms to rent and earn 2,798 Yuan per month. The average income of a household is 8,447 Yuan per month, of which rental income takes up one-third. Rental income is a rather important source of income for house owners, thus they stay in order to operate their rental housing better.

Tenants' perspective

As indicated in the survey data of 608 tenants, 46 per cent give the reason of 'close to workplace' and 'cheap rent, respectively'. People choosing 'incidental', 'convenient for children's schooling', 'living here for a long time' and other reasons, is 4, 2, 1 and 1 per cent, respectively. It can be concluded that a location close to the workplace and cheap rent are two major factors attracting tenants to live in urban villages.

According to the survey, the average distance from home to workplace is 5.7 kilometres, and the average time spent on the way is 19 minutes. As for the means of commuting, 62 per cent of tenants ride a bicycle, 26 per cent walk, 6 per cent take the public bus and 3 per cent take the metro or a private car, respectively. It can be seen that most tenants use the cheapest way of commuting. Meanwhile, in order to further reduce the cost of commuting, they choose to live near the

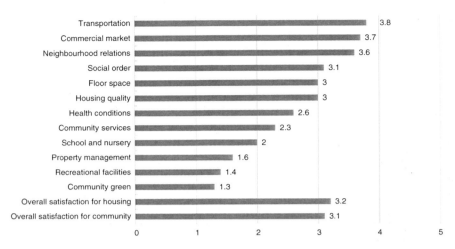

Figure 10.9 Residential satisfaction of tenants.
Source: Authors' survey.

workplace. The survey data shows that the average rent in urban villages is 518 Yuan per unit per month, which is much lower than the average for Shanghai.[5] So it can be concluded that minimizing the cost of living is the major reason for the tenant to live in an urban village.

As indicated in the tenants' satisfaction data (Figure 10.9) with their housing and environment, the four indicators of recreational facilities, school and nursery, community green, and property management score 2 points and below; the other four indicators of floor space, such as housing quality, community services and health conditions score 2–3 points; and another six indicators of neighbourhood relations, commercial market, transportation, social order, overall satisfaction for housing and overall satisfaction for community, score above 3 points. It can be seen that convenient transport, a prosperous commercial market, a harmonious neighbourhood and good social order are the favourable factors that attract tenants. Meanwhile, the lack of recreational facilities, community green, property management and school and nursery does not discourage tenants from living in urban villages. It can be concluded that for tenants the most important principle in seeking residence is minimizing the cost of living rather than having a comfortable and liveable environment.

Impacts of village redevelopment

Nowadays, Shanghai's urban villages are facing large-scale redevelopment, and many of them are disappearing. Between the start of the investigation and the

Shanghai's urban villages   177

completion of this study, some of the villages surveyed have been demolished, and others are facing the fate of being redeveloped. So when these urban villages disappear, where should residents go and what does the redevelopment mean for them?

House owners' perspective

As suggested in the survey data for house owners, 99.6 per cent of house owners believe that their residence will be redeveloped, and 84 per cent of them agree with the government's compensation standards; only 16 per cent do not. The survey data show that the average building cost is 24,000 Yuan, and the estimation of redeveloped housing at the site would be 2,300,000 Yuan per unit. Redevelopment is important for house owners. Some of them say that they have been waiting for redevelopment all the time. They consider it a chance for getting major benefits.

Tenants' perspective

As indicated in the data for tenants, 92 per cent of them believe that their residence will be redeveloped and only 8 per cent believe not. When asked where they would go if their residence were to be redeveloped, 11 per cent would choose to live in 'the redeveloped residence in better living condition, regardless of the higher rent', and 34 per cent would choose 'the residence with convenient transport, regardless of the higher rent', while 55 per cent would choose 'the further residence, keeping the low rent'. The tenants believe that the highest average rent rise they can afford is 266 Yuan. Out of this range, they would leave the city. Urban villages have provided them with a place with a low cost of living. It can be seen that for tenants how to find a residence with cheap rent and convenient transport is the most important thing if their residence is redeveloped.

Conclusion

Through the survey, we have found that there still exist some urban villages in Shanghai, which are mainly located near suburbs outside of the inner ring. This is the result of Shanghai's rapid urbanization. Compared with Guangzhou and Shenzhen, the scale is smaller and the number is much lower. In fact, urban villages are just one kind of migrant settlement. The proportion of migrant population in urban villages is not high.[6] But as a special urban social space, urban villages are important settlements for migrants in Shanghai and other cities, and can be considered as a vital part of China's process of social transition and rapid urbanization.

This research discusses the formation mechanism and development state of urban villages from the migrants' own perspective. From the evidence listed in this study it is possible to state that the urban–rural dual institution is the major factor influencing the formation of urban villages. Moreover, the survey also suggests that residents in urban villages are engaged in informal and low income employment. Therefore, to some extent, the formation of urban villages is also the result of increasing social differentiation in Chinese megacities. Compared with those of urban residents, living conditions in urban villages are much worse, with smaller living space, insufficient facilities and dilapidated housing. Nonetheless, urban villages are also a vital income source for owners and an affordable accommodation option for migrants. However, as the product of rapid urbanization, urban villages are just a temporary residence for both house owners and tenants. For house owners, it is only a matter of time until their property will be subjected to redevelopment. As for tenants, the convenient location, proximity to workplace and cheap rent offer them lower commuting costs and living costs. Therefore, the urban village is more of a dormitory than a home for them.

With the promotion of large-scale redevelopment, Shanghai's urban villages are gradually disappearing. Once they have all perished, where should the residents, especially the tenants, go? Most of them are low-level labour force, engaged in occupations that urban residents would not like to take on, and providing cheap labour for urban development. How to provide an affordable and applicable housing alternative effectively has become one of the issues that the government should take into account, otherwise major Chinese cities and the growth machine of China will soon come to suffer from the lack of significant amount of low-cost labour force.

Acknowledgement

The research is supported by the ESRC/DFID Grant 'The Development of Migrant Villages under China's Rapid Urbanization: Implications for Poverty and Slum Policies' (RES-167–25–0448). The authors also would like to acknowledge the funding of the Chinese Ministry of Education (11JZD028; 11JJD840015).

Notes

1. The survey suggests that many urban villages in Shanghai are formed by historical factors. They are mainly located in the suburbs, which have become the migrant's main location since the 1990s. The number of migrants in outer suburban districts did not go up until recent years. It is impossible for a new urban village to form due to the current rigorous regulation from urban government.
2. All of the questionnaires were finished with the face-to-face help of the investigator to ensure quality.
3. The data for the entire city are adopted from per 100 urban household year-end possessions of durable consumer goods in the *Shanghai Statistical Yearbook 2010*. The data for urban villages are adopted from the availability of housing facilities in the questionnaire. Such a comparison may be less accurate. But considering that most families have one or even less than one facility, it can still affect the actual situation.
4. According to the survey, the rate of accessing the Internet is 17 per cent, which is in accordance with the ownership rate of computers.
5. According to 2010 White Papers from SouFun Net, the average rent in Shanghai is 2,825 Yuan per unit per month, while that of a two-bedroom apartment is 2,857 Yuan per unit per month and a three-bedroom is 3,881 Yuan.

Shanghai's urban villages 179

6. In fact, the proportion of migrants in urban villages is not high in Shanghai. For example, the permanent resident population in Putuo District is 1.29 million, among which the number of migrants is 0.36 million. Through the survey, the number of migrants in urban villages is estimated to be 20,000. We can take Zhabei District as another example: the permanent resident population is 0.83 million, among which the number of migrants is 0.2 million, taking up 24 per cent. In our survey, there is only one urban village in Zhabei District, which has already been redeveloped in 2011. Therefore, rural migrants in Shanghai live in other urban areas as well as in urban villages. Except for factory and construction dormitories, most of them live dispersedly.

References

Chan, R. C. K., Yao, Y. M. and Zhao, S. X. B. (2003) 'Self-help housing strategy for temporary population in Guangzhou, China', *Habitat International*, 27(1): 19–35.

Chen, X. (ed.) (2009) *Rising Shanghai: State Power and Local Transformation in a Global Megacity*. Minneapolis, MN: Minnesota University Press.

Chung, H. (2010) 'Building an image of village-in-the-city: a clarification of China's distinct urban spaces', *International Journal of Urban and Regional Research*, 34(2): 421–37.

Feng, J., Zhou, Y. and Wu, F. (2008) 'New trends of suburbanization in Beijing since 1990: from government-led to market-oriented', *Regional Studies*, 42(1): 83–9.

Hao, P., Sliuzas, R. and Geertman, S. (2011) 'The development and redevelopment of urban villages in Shenzhen', *Habitat International*, 35(2): 214–24.

Li, J. and Ning, Y. (2007) 'Population spatial change and urban spatial restructuring in Shanghai since the 1990s', *Urban Planning Forum*, (2): 20–4. (in Chinese).

Li, Z. and Wu, F. (2006) 'Socio-spatial differentiation and residential inequalities in Shanghai: A case study of three neighborhoods', *Housing Studies*, 21(5): 695–717.

Li, Z. and Wu, F. (2008) 'Tenure-based residential segregation in post-reform Chinese cities: a case study of Shanghai', *Transactions of the Institute of British Geographers*, 33(3): 404–19.

Liu, X. and Liang, W. (1997) 'Zhejiangcun: social and spatial implications of informal urbanization on the periphery of Beijing', *Cities*, 14(2): 95–108.

Liu, Y., He, S., Wu, F. and Webster, C. (2010) 'Urban villages under China's rapid urbanization: unregulated assets and transitional neighbourhoods', *Habitat International*, 34(1): 135–44.

Logan, J. R., Fang, Y. and Zhang, Z. (2009) 'Access to housing in urban China', *International Journal of Urban and Regional Research*, 33(4): 914–35.

Luo, R. and Wang, D. (2009) 'Types and characteristics of migrant communities in Shanghai', *City Planning Review*, 33(2): 31–7. (in Chinese).

Ma, L. J. C. and Xiang, B. (1998) 'Native place, migration and the emergence of peasant enclaves in Beijing', *The China Quarterly*, 155: 546–81.

Madrazo, B. and van Kempen, R. (2012) 'Explaining divided cities in China', *Geoforum*, 43(1): 158–68.

National Bureau of Statistics of China (2011) *Communiqué of the National Bureau of Statistics of People's Republic of China on Major Figures of the 2010 Population Census (No. 1)*. 28 April. Online. Available: http://www.stats.gov.cn/english/newsandcomingevents/t20110428_402722244.htm (Accessed 28 April 2011].

Ning, Y., Zhao, X., Li, X., Shi, D., Deng, L. and He, T. (2011) 'A study on the trend and policy of population of Shanghai', *Shanghai Urban Planning Review*, (1): 16–26. (in Chinese).

180 *Mingfeng Wang, Xiaoling Lin and Yuemin Ning*

Pow, C.-P. (2007) 'Securing the "civilized" enclaves: gated communities and the moral geographies of exclusion in (post-) socialist Shanghai', *Urban Studies*, 44(8): 1539–58.

Pow, C.-P. and Kong, L. (2007) Marketing the Chinese dream home: gated communities and representations of the good life in (post-) socialist Shanghai, *Urban Geography*, 28(2): 129–59.

Shanghai Municipal Statistics Bureau (2010) *Shanghai Statistical Yearbook 2010*. Beijing: China Statistics Press.

Shanghai Municipal Statistics Bureau (2011) *Communiqué of the Shanghai Municipal Statistics Bureau on Major Figures of the 2010 Population Census*. 3 May. Online. Available: http://www.stats-sh.gov.cn/2005shtj/tjgb/node94/userobject1ai14655.html (Accessed 3 May 2011].

Song, Y., Zenou, Y. and Ding, C. (2008) 'Let's not throw the baby out with the bath water: the role of urban villages in housing rural migrants in China', *Urban Studies*, 45(2): 313–30.

Tian, L. (2008) 'The Chengzhongcun land market in China: boon or bane?—A perspective on property rights', *International Journal of Urban and Regional Research*, 32(2): 282–304.

Wang, J. and Lau, S. S. Y. (2008) 'Forming foreign enclaves in Shanghai: state action in globalization', *Journal of Housing and the Built Environment*, 23(2): 103–18.

Wang, Y. P., Wang, Y. L. and Wu, J. S. (2009) 'Urbanization and informal development in China: urban village in Shenzhen', *International Journal of Urban and Regional Research*, 33(4): 957–73.

Wehrhahn, R., Bercht, A. L., Krause, C. L., Azzam, R., Kluge, C. L., Strohschön, R., Wiethoff, K. and Baier, K. (2008) 'Urban restructuring and social and water-related vulnerability in mega-cities – the example of the urban village of Xincún, Guangzhou (China)', *Die Erde: Zeitschrift der Gesellschaft für Erdkunde zu Berlin*, 139(3): 227–49.

Wu, F. (2004) 'Urban poverty and marginalization under market transition: the case of Chinese cities', *International Journal of Urban and Regional Research*, 28(2): 410–23.

Wu, F. (2009) 'Land development, inequality and urban villages in China', *International Journal of Urban and Regional Research*, 33(4): 885–9.

Wu, F. (2010) 'Gated and packaged suburbia: packaging and branding Chinese suburban residential development', *Cities*, 27(5): 385–96.

Wu, W. (2004) 'Sources of migrant housing disadvantage in urban China', *Environment and Planning A*, 36(7): 1285–304.

Wu, W. and Wang, H. (2002) 'As immigrant in metropolis: the analysis on housing condition of the floating population in Beijing and Shanghai', *Sociological Studies*, (3): 92–110. (in Chinese).

Xue, D. S. and Huang, G. Z. (2008) 'Regulation beyond formal regulation: Spatial gathering and surviving situation of the informal sectors in urban village case study in Xiadu Village of Guangzhou City', *Geographical Research*, 27(6): 1390–8. (in Chinese).

Yeh, A. G. O., Xu, X. and Hu, H. (1995) 'The social space of Guangzhou City, China', *Urban Geography*, 16(7): 595–621.

Yusuf, S. and Wu, W. (2002) 'Pathways to a world city: Shanghai rising in an era of globalization', *Urban Studies*, 39(7): 1213–40.

Zhang, L., Zhao, S. X. B. and Tian, J. P. (2003) 'Self-help in housing and Chengzhongcun in China's urbanization', *International Journal of Urban and Regional Research*, 27(4): 912–37.

Zheng, S. Q., Long, F. J., Fan, C. C. and Gu, Y. (2009) 'Urban villages in China: a 2008 survey of migrant settlements in Beijing', *Eurasian Geography and Economics*, 50(4): 425–46.

Zhou, M. and Cai, G. (2008) 'Trapped in neglected corners of a booming metropolis: residential patterns and marginalization of migrant workers in Guangzhou', in Logan, J. R. (ed.), *Urban China in Transition*. Oxford, UK: Blackwell, pp. 226–49.

Zhu, J. M. (2002) 'Urban development under ambiguous property rights: a case of China's transition economy', *International Journal of Urban and Regional Research*, 26(1): 41–57.

11 Urban villages as local economic clusters

The case of the Zhongda cloth market in Guangzhou

Uwe Altrock and Sonia Schoon

Introduction

Mega-urban regions in China show first signs of consolidation. A need for restructuring of the urban fabric and the socioeconomic structures starts to complement the strong focus on growth and expansion related to office and retail development in urban cores and high-tech parks in the periphery. Higher value-added manufacturing, service industries and a more knowledge-based economy in the Pearl River Delta are increasingly focusing on the upgrading of under-used or neglected old town areas, urban villages and older manufacturing sites under the heading of the so-called "three olds regeneration" policy.

Upgrading approaches are not limited to changes in the physical fabric. Studies about the upgrading of economic clusters recommend a careful consideration of the functioning of global value chains to derive appropriate innovation and investment strategies. While those strategies seem promising at the regional level and find the establishment of industrial zones or other spatial arrangements useful, one may ask if they are still worthwhile when it comes to upgrading very densely built-up older manufacturing and trade clusters in urban China. Increasing land values in the course of continued urbanization seem to have severe impacts on them. Urbanization theory would suggest that the clusters may be relocated and replaced by other land uses or even dissolved. Thus, the physical and spatial aspects of cluster organization also have to be taken into account in a discussion about their possible upgrading.

Surprisingly, clusters of light industry and trade are not always simply replaced by office clusters or high-end residential towers. Their upgrading often follows a different model: we can observe *in situ* and – to a certain extent – self-restructuring of those clusters. However, this type of upgrading is ridden with political and economic prerequisites. This chapter will focus on one such example in Guangzhou, the Zhongda cloth market (referred to in the following as: ZDCM) in Haizhu District.

The objective is to explore the modes of on-going urban restructuring processes as the interplay of physical redevelopment and economic upgrading policies carefully adapted to local constraints and making use of the locational advantages of the urban cores (see Table 11.1). While the importance of manufacturing and

Table 11.1 Stages of urbanization and upgrading of ZDCM.

	Stage 1 (1988–95)	Stage 2 (1996–2000)	Stage 3 (2001–04)	Stage 4 (2005–12)	Stage 5 (hypothetical)
Physical development					
Drivers of change and influential reforms	Establishment of market, temporary shops	Urban problems	Urban problems, land auctions and availability of land for large-scale projects	Improvement of Ruikang road and Yijing road	Improvement of road infrastructure and public open spaces
Important results	Growth of urbanized villages, increase in density and height in village cores	Greenfield development, increase in density and height in southern part, replacement of temporary shops	Small-scale upgrading, increase in density and height in south-eastern part	Construction of new integrated centers, increase in density and height in market area	(Redevelopment of urbanized villages, revitalization of brownfields and under-used buildings)
Economic development					
Drivers of change and influential reforms	Establishment of open market	Integration with manufacturing	WTO accession	Increasing competition in the textile sector, cancelling of quotas, large-scale private investment	Competition in wholesale
Important results	Trade center	Trade and processing center	Establishment of low-rise wholesale markets	Establishment of new trade platforms, branding, banking and electronic transactions	(Stabilization of international role)

(Continued)

Table 11.1 Stages of urbanization and upgrading of ZDCM. (cont.)

	Stage 1 (1988–95)	Stage 2 (1996–2000)	Stage 3 (2001–04)	Stage 4 (2005–12)	Stage 5 (hypothetical)
Political and organizational development					
Drivers of change and influential reforms	Relocation of market	Regulation of informal market by district government	Transformation of urbanized villages, upgrading ideas, preparation of national and Asian games	Foundation of management committee, development plan	Negotiations about restructuring and compensation
Important results			Overcoming of most pressing urban problems	ZDCM as part of agglomeration of regional headquarters in district	(Commodification and regularization of urbanized villages and economic activities, increase in tax base)

Urban villages as local economic clusters 185

small-scale trade gradually decreases giving way for a greater share of integrated services, the entire cluster continues to operate in the textile sector. Despite its location embedded in urban villages and workers' neighborhoods in central Guangzhou, it is thus able to adapt to the changing needs of a highly competitive sector and to the rapid growth of the market in which the companies operate.

Background: the upgrading of economic clusters

In this chapter, it is not possible to give a comprehensive account of cluster theory. Some introductory remarks will outline the context for an understanding of the upgrading of ZDCM. Introduced by Michael Porter (1990, 1998), the notion "cluster" was quickly taken up and discussed controversially (for a critical appraisal, see Martin and Sunley 2003). For China and the Pearl River Delta, a regional organization in clusters was both observed analytically (Enright *et al.* 2005; Zhang and Cao 2004; Li and Fung Research Center 2006; Lin *et al.* 2011) and used as a metaphor in the strategic planning for Guangzhou and Haizhu district (Zhang 2008).

There is evidence that clusters offer small companies crucial advantages for market entry due to their options to overcome problems in access to loans in an environment of fine division of labor (Ruan and Zhang 2008). This observation is interesting for newly industrializing countries, where large amounts of capital are scarce and there is a high need for generating new employment.

However, after the successful establishment of clusters, their adaptation to increasing competition and the need to climb up the value chain with decreasing cost advantages requires economic upgrading strategies. Here, the textile clusters formed by small and medium-sized enterprises in China may pose serious obstacles as the companies are often not innovative enough, and lack the ability to create internationally competitive brands and to implement other measures that help tap the profits made in the global value chain in the textile sector (Gu 2006; Zhu 2008). Given the fact that small-scale economic clusters in China embedded into cities are sometimes extremely densely built-up and therefore pose serious challenges for physical upgrading, it is interesting to note that studies on clusters, especially when it comes to lower value-added sectors such as the textile sector, focus almost exclusively on economic issues (Humphrey and Schmitz 2000; Humphrey 2002; Shao and Chi 2006). Thus, the physical aspect will be discussed in the following.

The formation of the ZDCM area as economic cluster

ZDCM is located immediately south of Sun Yat-sen University Campus in Haizhu, one of Guangzhou's districts, located on an island in the Pearl River south-east of the historic center of the city and south of the new Central Business District (CBD) in Tianhe district. After the opening under Deng Xiaoping in the late 1970s, the hinterland of Hong Kong quickly grew into one of the major mega-urban regions and economic centers in China. Despite strong regional competition,

Guangzhou has regained its original position as one of the centers of international trade. Besides its role as provincial capital and trade center, Guangzhou gained strength in manufacturing sectors such as car production and textile processing. The importance of the city is underlined by the fact that it is now home to the largest trade fair complex in the world, built in the eastern part of Haizhu district.

ZDCM came into life in 1988, as a consequence of the displacement of informal mobile vendors selling knitting wool and other textile fabrics (Haizhu District CCPC 2009). Those had been relocated from closer to downtown to the area in the urban periphery around a wool plant (*Private Economy News* 2005). The small market grew steadily in the 1990s and became more professional when iron sheet sheds and later brick shops were introduced for the storage of goods.

Although ZDCM seems to have developed mainly as a huge market, it had grown into an economic cluster by the turn of the century. The rather elusive term "cluster" is applied because it intuitively grasps the nature of the area: a complex agglomeration of diverse companies, linked to each other via demand and supply chains, partially or even mutually depending on each other, allowing for a flexible yet integrated system of production, assembly and services around a diversified family of products in an environment of severe competition.

The core market area around what is today Ruikang road was originally arranged around the residential core areas of the original villages and developed a variety of specialized markets (see Figure 11.1) and spatial layouts over time

Figure 11.1 Older low-rise wholesale center in Wufeng village.
Source: Photograph taken by Uwe Altrock.

Urban villages as local economic clusters 187

(Yuan *et al.* 2007: 7ff.). At the southern edge of the villages, a great number of garment processing and accessory factories were established with support from the markets in the mid-1990s on former agricultural land, taking orders from all over Guangzhou (see Figure 11.2). They are responsible for about 30 percent of the turnover of the market area and live in a close symbiotic relationship to it, giving feedback to the markets about the latest trends in demand. They are located in compact, most often four- to five-story buildings with a variety of services on the ground floor. Their huge product range comprises dye printing, clothing, embroidery, bead bearing, knitwear mills, thread mills, zipper factories, etc. (Yuan *et al.* 2007: 7).

Even the core areas of the urban villages are used as production spaces, not only for cheaper migrant workers living in "kissing buildings". The ground floors of residential buildings are flexibly used for various complementary work steps to serve the markets (accessory-related finishing, mounting of zippers, etc.); upper floors sometimes for storage purposes (Cai 2010: 59; Interview with Haizhu District Regeneration Office 2011). Smaller craftsmen's workshops, educational facilities related to the textile business, and services complement the picture. Besides, a number of related businesses such as designers, advertisement agencies, hotels, restaurants, retail shops, employment agencies, banks, and real estate agencies as well as shops serving daily consumer needs, have developed. More than 1,000 carriers (see Figure 11.3) transport the goods locally (Yuan *et al.* 2007: 20).

Figure 11.2 Processing factory near Ruikang road.
Source: Photograph taken by Uwe Altrock.

Figure 11.3 Carrier in front of CJCTC.
Source: Photograph taken by Uwe Altrock.

The special nature of the cluster lies in the proximity of a whole range of different companies or individuals working and living in the same place, allowing for great flexibility and speedy supply of goods. For instance, a lot of big shops selling fabric produced elsewhere have warehouses in the urban villages nearby, whereas printing factories are sometimes located close to the shops allowing for immediate finishing of orders, and factories in the urban villages place their orders in the cloth market and subcontract some of their work to specialized processing factories nearby (Cai 2010: 59ff.).

Approaches towards upgrading over time

The rather unplanned growth of the market led to disorganized development. Around the turn of the century, the scale of the workshops, factories and stalls had developed according to the needs of the rather small-scale units. High profits for individual market traders were possible, but there was hardly any organizational structure or elaborated planning concept that guided development. The high density allowed for great flexibility in an economy based on individualized physical transactions of money and goods. A lot of space was used for storage areas.

Urban villages as local economic clusters 189

The lack of strategic planning and investment into larger markets made the entire cluster vulnerable to the short-sighted interests of key stakeholders. Streets were sometimes partly built over, and parking facilities, logistics centers, and an effective road infrastructure were missing (Yuan *et al.* 2007: 26). The density seems to have caused environmental problems and overstrained the available sanitary facilities. Despite the role of the area as an entry port for the accommodation of migrants, it was seen as a multiple security risk due to fire hazards and the fear of crime.

Some of these issues were addressed after a transformation of the residential, political and economic status of urban villages in the early 2000s. It stabilized the role of the villagers in the restructuring process (Guangzhou Government Sui Office 2002; Guo and Wu 2007; Lin and De Meulder 2011); gave them the status of urban residents, integrated their self-administration structures into the formal municipal hierarchy (Fengyang street office); transformed collectively owned land into state-owned land without changing land use rights, and formed joint-stock companies to administer villagers' assets. Joint stock companies and professional companies became the major market operators in the area. Large-scale developers bought land use rights and thus accelerated a concentration process with the help of capital from Zhejiang, the leading province in the textile business (Yuan *et al.* 2007: 24; Cai 2010: 20). The management of the market area was handed over to a special-purpose association founded in 2004, the so-called Management Committee of the ZDCM Area, to address urban problems.

A major effort towards modernization and upgrading came after China's accession to the WTO in 2001 and the rise of national competitors such as the China Textile City in Keqiao in the Yangtze River Delta, especially in the middle of the 2000s (see for instance Yuan *et al.* 2007: 13f; Yue and Everett 2010). Despite the opportunities for China in international markets, the textile sector faces increased competition. Low-end manufacturing is increasingly being transferred to the Chinese hinterland and neighboring countries, whereas coastal centers can continue to act as hubs for international trade and regional headquarters. A simple comparison between aerial views of China Textile City and ZDCM, however, shows that clusters embedded in urban villages such as ZDCM face severe infrastructural disadvantages compared to artificial centers built in urban peripheries next to motorways and free to determine the size and layout of specialized markets.

In this situation, it would have been possible to give up the ZDCM cluster completely. However, the favorable location next to the trade fair, the firm position the textile market had already achieved, and the ideal cluster advantages with the processing centers and the small-scale companies nearby seemed to make an upgrading strategy feasible, based on a shift of the management mode of the cluster away from more localized small-scale transactions towards the establishment of a textile hub of international importance. It required the management of much bigger deals and depended on technological modernization, concentration, and specialization (Yuan *et al.* 2007: 14).

Since the established advantages of the cluster were not to be abandoned, an "urban" strategy seemed appropriate. Although it would require an increase in

190 *Uwe Altrock and Sonia Schoon*

size of the wholesale centers, the complicated land use distribution and poor infrastructure did not allow the construction of centers similar to the peripheral one in Keqiao. While the "urban" strategy seems to have a lot of advantages, with attractive centers, functional blending of different elements integrating the wholesale center into a new type of urban entertainment center, proximity to potential end users, to urban village structures allowing for fast and flexible processing and to trade fairs, etc., it depended on a complex interaction of economic, political and physical upgrading elements whose implementation was needed to make the modernization possible. The prerequisites for the strategy were only at hand in the mid-2000s when land in the periphery of the urban villages was opened to land auction, main roads could be built and developers saw a perspective in investing into the markets. Still, the strategy was highly selective, focused strongly on intervention in some key areas, and worked well since there was still some complementary space in the southern periphery available.

Necessary steps were taken with the "Development Plan for a Commodity Network in Guangzhou (2003–2010) [Guangzhou shi shangye wangdian fazhan guihua (2003–2010)]," a "working program" for the upgrading of Guangzhou's wholesale markets by the city (Yuan *et al.* 2007: 16), the Eleventh Five-Year Plan for Economic and Social Development of Haizhu District CCPC (2006), stating the attempt to create a "diverse and dynamic Haizhu" based on the exhibition area in the eastern part of the district and the market area itself, and the Haizhu district government's "Development Plan for ZDCM [Zhongda bupi shichang zhengzhi guihua fang'an]" (Yuan *et al.* 2007; Chen 2003: 49). The so-called "Commercial Belt of South Guangzhou Road" (Chen 2003: 49) making up more or less the eastern part of Haizhu district is of strategic importance in this context.

Interestingly, Haizhu district still relies strongly on manufacturing (Yuan *et al.* 2007: 10; see also Zhang 2008). It is seen as a trading cluster with different specializations (auto parts, building materials, hardware, piece goods, hotel articles, footwear (see also Li 2006; Haizhu District CCPC 2006) in a "middle ring" between the inner city and its periphery. Provided that major links to a modern transportation and telecommunication network were available, the cluster advantages were thought to be kept by reorienting the area away from a mere unstructured agglomeration of wholesale booths. The goals are to turn it into a center of regional headquarters of international companies, to make it a center of wholesaling clothes instead of textiles, to integrate logistics functions, to build on the location close to the trade fair, and to establish further-reaching business and e-commerce facilities (Chen 2003: 51–2; Interview with HETB 2010; Yuan *et al.* 2007: 29ff). With this approach, the district is also trying to increase the disappointing tax revenues from a market that used to depend on cash transactions without invoices, making the estimation of actual turnovers difficult (Yuan *et al.* 2007: 18; Interview with HETB 2010).

However, the 9th National Games in 2003 and the Asian Games in 2010 ultimately spurred some upgrading even in urban villages (Yuan *et al.* 2007: 21f). The further upgrading of the area aims at the regeneration of the urban villages and a relocation of the clothes processing factories. For the time being, neither

Urban villages as local economic clusters 191

can be achieved easily, as compensation issues are difficult to negotiate, villagers resist expropriation of collective land for infrastructural purposes, migrant workers are still living in the urban villages, and there is hardly any space for relocation of existing factories. Thus, the economic modernization of the markets will also contribute to the upgrading of the urban villages as it may gradually release the close ties between wholesale markets and processing factories, which today are still important customers (Interview with Haizhu District Regeneration Office 2011).

In-situ upgrading

When analyzing how the upgrading of the ZDCM area took place in practice, it becomes clear that physical, economic and political restructuring closely depend on each other, and gradual progress in one of the three serves as a prerequisite for further steps in the respective two others. To show how these factors influence development in detail, three major wholesale centers that have fundamentally changed the area will be looked at. Due to their different strategic locations, they represent contrasting models of development that are of comparative interest. For the analysis, we are going to look at physical structures (infrastructure, functional patterns, density and scale, and symbolic architecture), economic challenges (structural changes, concentration processes, specialization and division of labor, and technological modernization) and political conditions (land issues, urban integration of villages, and management institutions).

One-stop shop: Guangzhou International Textile City (GITC)

The first wholesale center, located in close proximity to the key area around the south gate of Sun Yat-sen University opened in 2004/05. Its floor area of 300,000 m^2 offering room for more than 4,000 shops significantly changed the economic and physical character of the ZDCM area. GITC offers a wide range of functions for national and international customers and serves as a "one-stop fabric and accessories center" in an era of liberalized international textile trade. Its enormous size made it one of the most important textile trade centers in all of China. It could only be established when the district government decided to improve Ruikang Road, thereby linking the ZDCM to the major roads in Haizhu district.

Obviously, the construction of additional east-west roads that would have a grave impact on the existing urban fabric in the villages could only be implemented later. The first waves of reform of urban villages that brought major parts of the agricultural land under effective control by the state in the 1990s laid a clear priority for redevelopment away from the built-up areas in the cores of the urban villages. There, redevelopment would depend on the political will to engage in complicated negotiations about compensation with the villagers. Areas in the periphery of the villages (brownfield sites formerly used as bigger factories, Greenfield sites formerly used as agricultural land) could be equipped with good access to road infrastructure and more easily re-used within a reasonable time.

The dramatic increase in building height compared to the older low-rise markets seems atypical for trade centers around the world. It is due to the lack of space for quick development in the area. The integration of the market area into national and international networks seems to justify the proliferation of more globalized symbolic architecture. Considering its cost, one may question the usefulness of its application in the context of large-scale wholesale trade in textiles. The logic behind it lies in the competition among similar centers throughout China, making the establishment of unique selling propositions worthwhile. Here, the bright and well-lit courtyard of GITC is an invitation for the wider public to visit the center and its facilities in the basement and on the lower floors where very small stalls with high direct turnover dominate. The supporting services for the textile trade such as banks, a hotel and other services that do not rely on high frequencies of customers on top of the trade areas made the high density possible and turned the market into a complex specialized wholesale center. With the help of fashion shows by local school graduates and other events, the center has been able to create new forms of linkages with its environment (Guan-yin 2011; Algren 2011).

The will and the economic need to undergo a concentration process of the textile markets in the area is seen as a matter of increasing efficiency, proliferating new technologies and improving the urban fabric. This was possible as village-based market operators were complemented by more professional operators that have gradually taken over a great part of the business. Wider-reaching supply and sales networks are made possible with the help of technological modernization, banking and telecommunications facilities (Yuan *et al.* 2007). This can only be realized by an influx of concentrated capital. It therefore requires a change in the operational model and an increase in unit size and thus in the physical structure of the entire market cluster.

The sheer size of the new center has the potential to act as a valve to channel overspill demand and to bring down the rents of market stalls. This deliberately enforces competition between the different wholesale markets and increases pressure on villagers' assets. The formation of joint-stock companies with stocks held by the original villagers (Guo and Wu 2007; Interview with Haizhu District Regeneration Office 2011), professional management of those assets, and negotiations between city governments and villagers have been made easier. In this understanding, the competition by modern wholesale centers and the establishment of joint-stock companies are to push the modernization of the economic structures of the urban villages, although there is as yet no scope for a comprehensive urban integration of the villages. A modernization of the urban fabric, the redevelopment of some of the older residential buildings, and the improvement of leisure facilities could enhance the attractiveness of an internationally competitive wholesale cluster. However, compensation issues, the importance of the urban villages as reservoirs for cheap labor and the functioning of the textile cluster do not yet allow the outright redevelopment of the physical structures in the villages, although all planning documents show the will for it in the long run.

Specialized business center: Chang Jiang (China) Textile City (CJCTC)

After the completion of GITC, business activities have concentrated spatially around Ruikang Road leaving other parts of the market area behind. A clear center–periphery gradient has started to evolve related to economic function and dominance when other new centers and especially CJCTC, an even bigger center than GITC, were built. They are located along Ruikang Road and the newly opened Yijing Road, which passes the ZDCM area to the south of the adjacent villages and creates a major link towards the new Guangzhou fair in the eastern part of the district.

Size, design and concept of CJCTC are striking and dominate the area even more than GITC (see Figure 11.4). It consists of two parts, north and south of Yijing Road, connected by a pedestrian bridge and a car underpass. The center has a diversity that is similar to GITC, while its huge size of more than 400,000 m² for more than 6,000 shops on five floors above and two below ground, its sophisticated access from a multi-story parking deck, its underground and roof terrace parking and its truck yards make it a highly efficient logistics center linking it trans-regionally.

It differs significantly in appearance and concept from GITC. Its size shows the ambition of the area and its major stakeholders to turn ZDCM into a major wholesale center. However, despite its favorable location in the heart of Haizhu district and at a major intersection of transportation arteries, it does not resemble a suburban wholesale center. Its decidedly urban height and density and its functional concept indicate that the area is to be seen as part of the inner city in the future. Being located close to the Guangzhou fair, there seems to be a lot of potential in turning it into a multifunctional trade center. For professional visitors, specialized services like a "VIP customer club" are created. With its linkages to the Guangzhou fair and abroad, it tries to attract international companies and offers them opportunities to enter the Chinese market, thereby creating a competitive advantage over other centers. Additional facilities, such as hotels, restaurants, supermarkets, leisure and recreational clubs aim to make it a "city in the city".

The construction of GITC and CJCTC has started to turn Ruikang Road into a representative boulevard. This is stressed by a more explicit and visible outward orientation of the whole textile-related product chain and eventually thematic design features that represent complementary lifestyle-related elements. Wholesale-specific flagship design features gradually evolve and become increasingly sophisticated. However, the interior does not always show the same ambitions. Very introverted, dark and functional stalls in CJCTC cater to the needs of specialized wholesale transactions and stress its business specialization. The latter can even be observed by looking at facilities like restaurants on the upper floors: while GITC has popular fast food restaurants and even a McDonald's restaurant obviously addressing a wider general public, in CJCTC there are some simple traditional restaurants and large high-end restaurants obviously mainly for business meetings.

Contrary to Greenfield developments, GITC and PRTC had to be embedded into the inherited physical structure of urban villages that could not be redeveloped

Figure 11.4 Main façade of CJCTC.
Source: Photograph taken by Uwe Altrock.

Urban villages as local economic clusters 195

as the core market area. This is reflected in their layout adapting to the availability of land and the congestion problems that were by no means solved by improving Ruikang Road, a context that distinguishes them remarkably from the last case study.

Mixed-use wholesale city: Pearl River Textile City (PRTC)

The southern periphery of the urban villages became the spill-over area for the latest, biggest and most elaborate form of wholesale center when the infrastructural conditions were ripe with the construction of Yijing Road, connecting Ruikang Road to Guangzhou Road further east. There, the local stakeholders could resort to free space for development more easily and systematically than further north. A first conversion of agricultural and marsh land into city space is now integrated into something like a post-industrial newly urban area. It represents a completely different mode of development than the ones analyzed above. A division of labor between the local state and developers acting in the southern periphery is clearly visible and follows a typical path. The state, limiting itself to providing key infrastructures such as new roads and thus improving location factors, leaves it to developers to implement a more detailed vision of how the adjacent plots are to be subdivided and built upon.

For the area of PRTC, the availability of huge plots and the proximity of green open space further south were determining factors. The political and physical situation at the urban fringe allows for development almost unaffected by existing plot structures: PRTC has a very rational layout influenced only by an improved creek crossing Yijing Road. Yet there was no guarantee that a center of such dimensions would work, as it cannot build on the established environment and the incorporation of displaced shops that could be attracted with the help of improved services and a guaranteed high concentration of visitors. It represents the belief in the mainstreaming and risky extrapolation of the model applied to turn the ZDCM into a hub competitive on the world market (Yuan *et al.* 2007). This has important consequences for its urban design and functional concept.

With a total size of 900,000 m², a 46-story office tower, a six-story food court, a hotel, business apartments, and 5,000 parking stands, the PRTC stands for larger and even more integrated developments on Greenfield areas enforcing economic concentration (PRTC 2012). As the size and especially the height of the new centers require appropriate uses in the upper floors, obviously not guaranteed in CJCTC, relying mainly on its role as logistics center, PRTC has a layout that seems even better suited for exhibitions and leisure activities around the marketing of international brands.

While GITC and CJCTC face the street with huge billboards and the means of advertising, further-reaching urban design options at PRTC have been translated into a differentiated relationship between street and buildings, even though it seems to be out of scale when compared to its environment. Its northern part is organized around a huge open plaza that offers a spectacular access to the complex. The consequences of the spatial diversification can also be seen in the

196 *Uwe Altrock and Sonia Schoon*

organizational patterns. The plaza serves as a multi-purpose open space reserved as an access area, representative gathering point or leisure space for open-air events. It offers a lot of advertising space on its façades, but it could also host shows and presentations related to the textile business. High-rise buildings erected on both sides of the road accentuate the complex, creating a gate situation visible from a distance. The combination of high-rise building typologies for hotel, office and residential purposes with wholesale-related functions makes it a new type of integrated center. Particularly when compared with older buildings nearby, formerly embedded into the cluster in the green periphery of the textile center, it symbolizes a stark increase in modernity symbolized by size, height, and material (steel and glass). One may assume that the self-contained concept is to attract a globalized clientele differing even further from the one frequenting traditional markets or earlier-built centers.

Contrary to GITC and CJCTC, the development of PRTC clearly shows the dominance of the long-term idea of restructuring the entire urban fabric of the urban villages: mega-structures gradually convert the suburban periphery into a densely built-up area, cutting off the villages from the open green areas further south, obviously countering the idea of integrating the villages into the city. With the help of the new centers, though, not only individual buildings and façades have been face-lifted but also some of the storage-oriented sites have been redeveloped or re-used. Thus, the reforms that brought farmland in urban villages under the control of the state ultimately led to the first spin-off effects.

Conclusion

This chapter tried to link the upgrading of urban villages and economic clusters. It looked at the prominent phenomenon of manufacturing or trade agglomerations in urban villages in a way that differs significantly from either the planning or the economic discourse on upgrading. It illustrated that despite the political importance of the integration of urban villages into Chinese coastal mega-cities and the respective transformations that have been implemented so far, upgrading is by no means a simple undertaking. The need to respect villagers' rights, the hindrances when it comes to investment into economic modernization, the limits in the availability of space for a reorganization of the physical structures of the local economies, and the importance of complicated cluster relations require a strategic coordination of physical, economic and political reforms. However, the process of modernization can be implemented only with the help of external developers' investment and a careful selection of intervention measures that allow for a favorable relation between profits gained from establishing new structures, compensation, and the costs for a modernized infrastructure.

So far, the restructuring has made enormous progress. The construction of important artery roads and the modernization of the market area with the huge wholesale center developments have proven to be successes in the context of *in-situ* upgrading of the economic cluster without destroying the urban fabric that

Urban villages as local economic clusters 197

forms its hinterland and fertile ground. However, a comprehensive restructuring of urban villages and ideas to replace some of the older and more modest housing complexes and handshaking buildings in villages by higher-standard residential areas, complemented by improved public open spaces and attractive destinations for visitors, is still only a distant goal. For now, the new wholesale centers have affected the markets and some former factories, while most of the villages have kept complementary processing activities and remained important reservoirs of cheap labor (Ling and Xing 2008a,b) due to the importance they still have for the economic cluster. In this situation, redevelopment approaches are flexibly applied and depend on the strategic importance of the site, its location, land use type, availability of land, and overall upgrading strategy.

The upgrading of markets builds on technological modernization and an operational mode that turns them into "comprehensive commercial facility clusters" (Yuan *et al.* 2007: 47) and will allow them to compete with other mega-centers. Recreation and entertainment play a greater role, and "facility integration" turns them into veritable wholesale-based CBDs. However, this type of integration requires much larger units than traditional markets, a lot of capital, good infrastructure and high densities.

The upgrading of infrastructure, that is, the construction of main roads and the modernization of the wholesale centers changed the attractiveness of adjacent sites. This opened up new possibilities for property-led development and thus the realization of potential rent gaps. Not only did attractive locations in the periphery become potential sites for commodity housing, but some markets along major roads were also replaced by residential towers allowing for much higher building densities.

The restructuring of urban villages and their complex and heterogeneous stock of buildings as well as, of course, the closely connected sociocultural fabric is by no means easy to achieve. It requires complex negotiations between villagers, developers and district government agencies. Decision-makers at the village level come to different conclusions with respect to the possible transformation strategies for their urban villages (Interview with Haizhu District Regeneration Office 2011). In this period of uncertainty, some of the existing buildings are thus adapted to changing needs even when they do not represent a long-term vision for the area.

A similar short-term rationality in improving living conditions while the future of the entire area is not yet completely certain can be identified: a large amount of funds was allocated to improving the state of local ponds and creeks and their immediate environment by the municipality in preparation for the Asian Games in 2010. This city-wide program led to the improvement of the water quality in the urban villages and to the demolition of adjacent buildings to create better access and tree-lined boulevards next to them. For the first time since the urbanization of the villages, they reduced the ever-increasing building density in some parts, improved poor hygienic conditions in important open spaces, and created attractive yet relatively small promenades along a minor network of canals and waterways.

198 *Uwe Altrock and Sonia Schoon*

Table 11.2 Cluster upgrading in comparison.

	ZDCM before upgrading	*"Ideal" cluster*	*ZDCM 2012*
Physical features			
Density	High	Medium	Very high
Scale of key cluster elements	Small	Very large	Small to large
Small-scale functional mix	Highly diverse	Low diversity	Highly diverse
Architectural quality of cluster elements	Poor	Medium	Poor-High
Quality of living in environment	Poor	Heterogeneous	Heterogeneous
Location factors and economic features			
Road infrastructure	Very poor	Excellent	Medium
Telecommunication, IT infrastructure	Not developed	Powerful	Developing in important nodes
Economic and organizational features			
Mode of transactions	Informal, direct	Formalized, indirect	Variety of different forms
Operation	Unregulated, chaotic	Integrated, innovative	Integrated, highly flexible
Management and services	No management, services lacking	Highly developed	Centralized management committee, decentralized services, limited by physical structure
Global value chain integration	Low-end trade	R&D orientation, branding, logistics	Logistics, branding only starting
Integration			
Local integration	High (workforce, processing)	Low	Medium (workforce, processing)
City-wide integration	Medium	Low to high	High (market orders, trade fair)
Regional, national and international integration	Low to medium	High (supply and demand networks)	High (supply and demand networks)

They stand for the pursuit of livability issues during the transformation process even before the ultimate concepts for comprehensive transformations, whether they ever take place or not, have even been decided on.

There are some shortcomings threatening the success of the upgrading process. Despite the construction of trunk roads, increasing density and trade have created an amount of traffic that cannot be managed easily. Congestion is overstraining the existing infrastructure. The planned grid pattern of main roads would ease the situation but at the same time require reorganizing the entire urban fabric

Urban villages as local economic clusters   199

in the urban villages. Although the modernization of the cloth market area intended to improve the local traffic situation, the necessity of concentrating powerful wholesale markets has worked against a more rigid solution. The future will have to show whether the advantages that lie in the proximity of other cluster elements in the market area and the trade fair will be able to balance those disadvantages. However, a further-reaching transformation will have to resort to areas for temporary relocation of some factories and markets to initiate redevelopment processes, and may have significant negative effects for the great number of migrants that work in the area. As central Haizhu district is close to being built out after waves of progressive urbanization, one may doubt whether they will be easily at hand.

The upgrading of inner-city clusters is a complex governance issue that incorporates a number of stakeholders such as municipal and district governments, joint stock companies, villagers and developers. The key element to reassure the importance and future existence of the textile cluster is the comprehensive wholesale center that provides a strategic linkage between an internationalizing demand management, manufacturing and flexible local companies. Although the orientation of the new centers towards marketing, leisure, trade fairs and fashion shows means a gradual adaptation to local opportunities and needs, their success builds on location factors deeply rooted in the nature of the urban villages in central Guangzhou. The centers stand for an urban type of textile center that is competing with more suburban centers elsewhere. The municipal and district governments seem to be aware of the changed needs of the centers and their adjacent cluster elements. Only gradually, they are improving the respective hard and soft location factors. This is due not only to the well-known weaknesses of low-end clusters when it comes to innovation and integration into the global value chain, but also to the dense urban fabric in which they are embedded. So far, flexibility and the advantages of the proximity of inner-city services make up for disadvantages. However, it is not known yet whether ZDCM will become a stable and internationally relevant player in the textile trade. The upgrading strategy seems to follow a convincing analysis of the local economy that nevertheless builds on the opportunities of the district to transform its local economy partly into a headquarters economy. The chapter showed that the methods used in this direction necessarily differ strongly from the establishment of both conventional CBDs and suburban industrial districts, both maximizing scale in different ways, while the presented strategy relies rather on retaining the complexity of the cluster and building on it (see Table 11.2).

References

Algren (2011): *Graduation Show of Guangdong Baiyun University*. Online. Available: http://news.everychina.com/wz4139a7/graduation_show_of_guangdong_baiyun_university.html (Accessed September 25, 2012).
Cai, J. (2010) "The Linkage between Urban Formal Economy and Informal Economy: a Case Study on Clothes-Making Industry Near Guangzhou Textile Market," Unpublished PhD Dissertation, Zhongshan University, Guangzhou.

200 Uwe Altrock and Sonia Schoon

Chen, X. (2003) *Thoughts on the Advancement of Constructing the Commercial Belt of Guangzhou Road South* (in Chinese). Online. Available: http: //www.haizhu.gov.cn/tj2/UploadFiles/2005124192321947.pdf (Accessed March 4, 2011).

Enright, M. J., Scott, E. E., Chang, K. M. (2005) *Regional Powerhouse: The Greater Pearl River Delta and the Rise of China*. Singapore: John Wiley & Sons (Asia).

Gu, Q. (2006) *Promoting the Upgrading of China Industrial Clusters up the Global Value Chain*, Paper presented at Global value chains workshop at Duke University, November 9–10, 2006. Online. Available: http: //www.cggc.duke.edu/pdfs/workshop/20061110.pdf (Accessed March 6, 2012).

Guan-yin (2011) *2010 Graduate Fashion Show by South China Agriculture University Art & Design Institute*. Online. Available: news.everychina.com/wz41399c/2010_graduate_fashion_show_by_south_china_agriculture_university_art_design_institute.html (Accessed September 25, 2012).

Guangzhou Government Sui Office No.17 (2002) *Several Instructions on the Transformation of Urbanized Villages*. Guangzhou: the Guangzhou Municipal Government.

Guo, Q. and Wu, H. (2007) "Study of problems and feasible modes for urbanised village redevelopment in Guangzhou," *Sichuan Building Science*, 33(3): 182–6. (in Chinese).

Haizhu District CCPC (2006) *Eleventh Five-Year Plan for Economic and Social Development of Haizhu District*. Online. Available: http: //www.haizhu.gov.cn/upload/200608/20060821145032945.doc (Accessed September 25, 2012).

Haizhu District CCPC (2009) *The Forming and Development of Zhongda Textile District. Guangzhou History Web*. Online. Available: http: //www.gzzxws.gov.cn/gzws/gzws/ml/69/200902/t20090206_11348.htm (Accessed March 4, 2011).

Humphrey, J. (2002) "Opportunities for SMEs in developing countries to upgrade in a global economy," *SEED Working Paper*, No. 43. *ILO Series On Upgrading in Small Enterprise Clusters and Global Value Chains*.

Humphrey, J. and Schmitz H. (2000) "Governance and Upgrading: Linking Industrial Clusters and Global Value Chain Research," *IDS Working Paper*, No. 120. Brighton: IDS.

Interview with Haizhu District Regeneration Office's Administrative Office of Urban Village Redevelopment staff. Interviewed by Schoon (July 13, 2011).

Interview with HETB (Haizhu Economic and Trade Bureau staff). Interviewed by Schoon (December 28, 2010).

Li, Q. (2006) *The current status of headquarters economy in Haizhu district and the strategies for its future development* (in Chinese). Online. Available: www.haizhu.gov.cn/site/tjj/upload/633705663640738750150.doc (Accessed March 6, 2012).

Lin, Y. and De Meulder, B. (2011) "The role of key stakeholders in the bottom-up planning processes of Guangzhou, China," *Journal of Urbanism*, 4(2): 175–90.

Lin, H., Li, H., Yang, C. (2011) "Agglomeration and productivity: Firm-level evidence from China's textile industry," *China Economic Review*, 22(3): 313–29.

Li and Fung Research Center (ed.) (2006) "Textile and apparel clusters in China," *Industrial Cluster Series*, Issue 5, May.

Ling, H. and Xing, Q. (2008a) "Kangle Village: The Logistics Department of the Textile District" (in Chinese) *Information Times* (in Chinese) Online. Available: http: //house.focus.cn/newshtml/420682.html (Accessed March 4, 2011).

Ling, H. and Xing, Q. (2008b) "Kangle Village: The Logistics Department of the Textile District" (in Chinese) *Information Times* (in Chinese), January 14, 2008. Online. Available: http://news.xinhuanet.com/house/2008–01/14/content_7418211_1.htm (Accessed March 6, 2012).

Urban villages as local economic clusters   201

Martin, R. and Sunley, P. (2003) "Deconstructing clusters: chaotic concept or policy panacea?" *Journal of Economic Geography*, 3: 5–35.

Porter, M. E. (1990) *The Competitive Advantage of Nations*. London: Macmillan.

Porter, M. E. (1998) "Clusters and competition: New agendas for companies, governments, and institutions," in Michael E. Porter (ed.), *On Competition*. Boston: The Harvard Business School Publishing, pp. 197–287.

Private Economy News (2005) "Textile District: Stalls of Peddlers Have Been Developed into International Supermarkets" (zhong da bu shi: xiao fan bai chu guo ji da mai chang), June 13, 2005.

PRTC (2012) *Pearl River International Textile City*. Online. Available: www.prttc.com/markets/show-htm-itemid-32.html (Accessed September 25, 2012).

Ruan, J. and Zhang, X. (2008) "Finance and cluster-based industrial development in China," *IFPRI Discussion Paper*, 00768. Washington DC: IFPRI.

Shao, X. and Chi, R. (2006) "Integrating textile industry into global value chain stage – case study from Shaoxing textile sector in Zhejiang province," in Henry Z., Rui-M. Z., Chen L. (eds), *Orient Academic Forum: Proceedings of the Eighth West Lake International Conference on SMB*, Hangzhou: Aussino Academic Publishing House, pp. 1028–34.

Yuan, Q., Qiu, J., Lin, G., Xu, S.; Haizhu Branch of Guangzhou Municipal Urban Planning Bureau and Geography and Planning School of Sun Yat-sen University, Guangzhou, China (2007) "Development plan of Zhongda cloth market" (Zhong Da Bu Pi Shi Chang Zheng Zhi Gui Hua Fang An), Guangzhou, *Technical paper*.

Yue, P. and Everett, S. J. (2010) *Moving Up the Value Chain: Upgrading China's Manufacturing Sector*. Online. Available: http: //www.iisd.org/pdf/2010/sts_3_moving_up_the_value_chain.pdf (Accessed February 25, 2012).

Zhang, G. (2008) "Government Work Report (Excerpt) of the Mayor of Guangzhou," February 17, 2008. *White Paper on Guangzhou Foreign Trade and Economy 2008*.

Zhang, Z. and Cao, N. (2004) "How do industry clusters succeed: A case study in China's textiles and apparel industries," *Journal of Textile and Apparel, Technology and Management*, 4(2): 1–10.

Zhu, H. (2008) "A Study of the Development of China's Textile Industry – Upgrading the Competitiveness of Industrial Clusters in the Process of Globalisation," Master's thesis, Aalborg Universitet.

12 Spatial evolution of urban villages in Shenzhen

Pu Hao, Stan Geertman, Pieter Hooimeijer and Richard Sliuzas

Introduction

In the past three decades, urbanization has changed China's spatial and social landscape dramatically. Led by a large urban–rural income gap, the rural population have been flooding into cities for jobs and better lives. However, urban policies discriminate against rural migrants and exclude them from various amenities including subsidized housing. Outside the welfare scheme, the booming commodity housing market is largely beyond the reach of rural migrants due to their low purchasing power. In many cities, however, the great majority of migrants are accommodated by so-called 'urban villages' – villages that are encircled by urban expansion, forming enclaves within an area of formal urban development. The lucrative room renting business in urban villages motivates the indigenous villagers to build as many housing units as they can on their land. Consequently, these villages grow physically and vary functionally, enabling an increasing housing stock and a variety of social and economic activities. The spatial evolution of these urban villages, although having mostly occurred in the last decade, represents a very large share of urban growth and significantly shapes the cities' residential profiles. Urban planning and management should therefore recognize the important roles that urban villages play within contemporary Chinese urban development.

Although the urban village phenomenon attracts wide attention, most literature focuses on exploring the theoretical mechanisms of their emergence (Zhang *et al.* 2003; Zhang 2005; Tian 2008) or studies specific villages to illustrate their physical and social status (Wang *et al.* 2009; Bach 2010; Liu *et al.* 2010; Hao *et al.* 2011). Most of these authors acknowledged the supportive role of urban villages, and they suggested that in the short run, the urban village would remain as a realistic and effective solution for affordable housing. Despite their interesting insights and important implications, there is a tendency to view the urban village as a simple, static and homogeneous stereotype of a migrant enclave. Consequently, the lack of attention to the spatial evolution of urban villages hinders our understanding of their dynamics and diverse nature, and in so doing perhaps misleads the pursuit of sustainable urban village policies.

This chapter provides empirical analyses of the spatial evolution of urban villages in Shenzhen, a booming migrant city where half the population live

Spatial evolution of urban villages in Shenzhen 203

in urban villages. Rapid urban development since 1979 has created 320 urban villages spread over the entire city. Due to their large numbers and wide distribution it is possible to observe and compare their different development trajectories, and learn more about the role of locational factors in their development. Moreover, a relatively long time scope of study from 1999 to 2009 allows different phases of urban village development to be readily examined. Based on fieldwork and using building-level data for all 320 urban villages, this study reveals that the growth of urban villages exhibits spatial and functional diversity that is to an extent driven by the planned development of the formal city. The spatial evolution of the villages manifests organic growth and high levels of adaptability that is responsive to their individual surroundings. The chapter finally suggests that urban development programmes concerning urban villages should be case-specific and arbitrary demolition-redevelopment should be avoided.

Urban villages in Shenzhen

Shenzhen is probably the fastest growing city in the world: from 1979 to 2009, its population rose from less than half a million to 14 million, and its urban built-up land expanded from 20 square kilometres in 1983 to 813 square kilometres in 2009. The Shenzhen Municipality has an area of 1,969 square kilometres with six districts. Four of them, Luohu, Futian, Yantian and Nanshan, comprise the Shenzhen Special Economic Zone (SEZ) occupying 410 square kilometres. The other two districts, Baoan and Longgang, cover 714 square kilometres and 845 square kilometres, respectively. In 2009, the 320 urban villages covered 101 square kilometres, equivalent to 12 per cent of the built up land (Figure 12.1). They were composed of over 300,000 buildings, making a total living space of 159 million square metres of floor area for an estimated 7 million inhabitants or almost 23 square metres per person.[1]

From 1979 to 2008, the annual growth rate of the floating population was 33.5 per cent, almost five times higher than that of the population with local *hukou*, which was a mere 7.1 per cent per annum. Consequently, the proportion of the floating population in Shenzhen had been constantly increasing, greatly outweighing its permanent population. Meanwhile, with the dramatic change of the environs of villages towards urbanization, these urban villages became favourable places for migrants by virtue of their affordability and accessibility to jobs. The total floor space of urban villages grew by 105 million square metres throughout 1999–2009. In contrast, the total floor space of commodity housing completed in this period was only 58 million square metres (Shenzhen Statistics Bureau 2010), which clearly indicates the contribution of the spatial evolution of the urban villages to the housing provision of the booming city.

The data employed in this analysis were primarily from the Shenzhen Municipal Building Survey 2009, which contained all building records with attributes including address, ownership, function, plot area, built-up area, floor space, height and number of storeys. At the level of the administrative village, the Shenzhen Urban Planning and Design Institute (UPDIS) collected data about the physical status of

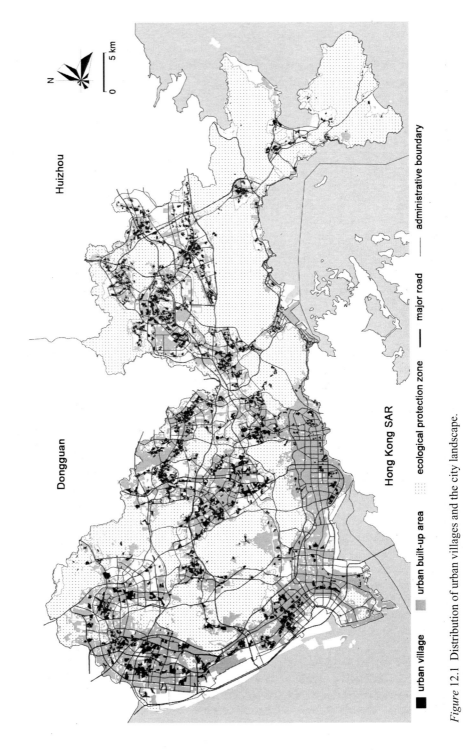

Figure 12.1 Distribution of urban villages and the city landscape.
Source: Shenzhen Urban Planning Bureau.

all urban villages in Shenzhen in 1999, and then again in 2004. These data include gross land area, the number of buildings, total built-up area, and total floor space. Contextual data, provided by the UPDIS and the Shenzhen Urban Planning and Research Centre (SUPRC), were used to examine factors that may influence urban village development. These data included administrative boundaries, road network, metro lines, industrial parks, various city planning documents, and the locations of city centres, sub-centres, and checkpoints to the SEZ. Employment data of mid- and large-scale manufacturing enterprises (annual gross turnover above five million RMB) were provided by Shenzhen Trade and Industrial Development Bureau (STIDB). ASTER Digital Elevation Model (DEM) data was used to produce a general terrain slope map of the whole area of Shenzhen.

Development process and patterns

The spatial evolution of the urban village is a progressive process, which is enabled by China's land institution. Under the regime of collective land ownership, a rural village has direct power over its land use rights and development control. The urban village inherits this power, allowing its housing development to continue institutionally outside the city's urban planning and land management system. The indigenous urban village residents, as *de facto* landlords, exploit their land via highly profitable room rental to migrants. Large quantities of substandard housing units provided in villages not only enable low rent, but also satisfy the massive and increasing housing demand from migrants. Under such circumstances, the development of urban villages differs greatly from planned urban development patterns.

The centuries-old presence of rural villages provides the initial spatial setting for their transformation and evolution into urban villages, i.e. original size, layout, natural and man-made landscape. In the beginning, encroachment on adjacent agricultural land is relatively cheap and easy. New houses are built on the vacant land around the village settlements, causing the village to expand. Over time this expansion becomes increasingly difficult as it is in competition with formal urban development. However, inside the village there may still be potential for more houses to be built. Consequently, new houses are constructed within the village, e.g. yards are occupied by extensions and new houses, open spaces are developed, roads are narrowed, all of which increase the village's density. As developable land inside the village becomes scarce, continued pressure gives rise to upward expansion. By replacing traditional low-rise houses with concrete high-rise apartment buildings, the growth of floor space can be further sustained. Eventually, by maximizing the usage of available land and the height of buildings, possibly to their limits, an urban village can become extremely over-developed (Hao *et al.* 2012) (Figure 12.2).

When faced with increasing natural and institutional constraints over time, this development path, namely expansion, densification and intensification, is a logical response for the indigenous villagers to continue exploiting the economic potential of their land. The three phases of growth can be examined with three

Figure 12.2 Gangxia urban village in the city centre of Shenzhen, 2009.

empirical measurements respectively: the growth of land area, the growth of built-up density, and the growth of floor area ratio (FAR).

Urban villages follow the same general development path but each has a specific development phase at any moment in time; their overall growth was neither uniform across the city nor stable through 1999–2009. The land occupied by urban villages grew greatly from 73 square kilometres to 94 square kilometres in 1999–2004, but their expansion slowed and reached only 101 square kilometres in 2009. The speed of expansion of urban villages outside the SEZ exceeded those within the SEZ, while their densification rates were more or less identical. In 1999, the built-up density was already high in the villages within the SEZ, further increasing in the villages in Futian and near-by areas during 1999–2004, and stabilizing at a high level in 2004–09. Outside the SEZ, built-up densities were low in 1999, but rose quickly in 1999–2004, and rose further still in 2004–09. During the whole 1999–2009 period, urban villages in the SEZ exhibit significant intensification, exceeding the intensification rates of villages outside the SEZ.

In addition there is also a tendency for the growth of urban villages to be clustered in space. Spatial autocorrelation analysis reveals that their development in terms of expansion, densification and intensification is clustered (Table 12.1). The Moran's *I* coefficient of the expansion of urban villages for the period 1999–2004 is 0.36, indicating a significant positive spatial autocorrelation. This implies that urban villages with a similar geographic location tend to expand at similar scales and that expansion is spatially clustered. As the expansion significantly slowed

Spatial evolution of urban villages in Shenzhen 207

Table 12.1 Spatial autocorrelation in terms of expansion, densification and intensification.

	Expansion		Densification		Intensification	
Period	99–04	04–09	99–04	04–09	99–04	04–09
Moran's I	0.3617	0.0813	0.1590	0.1453	0.4274	0.3439
p-value	0.001	0.037	0.001	0.004	0.001	0.001

in the subsequent period 2004–09 due to diminishing land availability, the clustering of the expansion also diminishes. The Moran's I coefficient of 0.08 indicates an almost random distribution of expansion.

As village expansion is confined by different levels of land availability in different locations, constructing more houses through infilling became an opportunity for many villages. In terms of densification, the growth of urban villages exhibits mild positive spatial autocorrelation for both periods. The Moran's I coefficient for intensification is respectively 0.43 and 0.34, revealing significant positive spatial autocorrelation for both time periods, implying that the production of floor space by increasing building heights is highly clustered in certain locations.

These results demonstrate that in general urban village development tends to concentrate in certain locations. The distribution of these concentrations should coincide with the growth centres of migrant population. The three processes (expansion, densification and intensification) are the means to provide more housing units for migrants. However, expansion is the least sustainable form due to diminishing land availability in the surroundings of urban villages. As expansion becomes increasingly difficult over time, its clustering pattern also diminishes. Similarly the densification process also faces increasing difficulties due to diminishing land availability inside urban villages. However, as intensification is not constrained by the lack of land, a highly clustered distribution of intensification may be sustained for a longer time.

At local level, the spatial clustering of urban village development exhibits distinct patterns between different development modes and time periods. Local Indicators of Spatial Association (LISA) (Anselin 1995), which allows the identification of development clusters independent from classification schemes, were used to identify development hotspots (high–high units, i.e. high development villages surrounded by other high development villages) and cold spots (low–low units, i.e. low development villages surrounded by other low development villages) (Figure 12.3). Such hotspots and cold spots are village clusters that experience either the most or the least growth, reflecting the changing distribution of migrant housing demand.

In 1999–2004, hotspots of expansion were two clusters: one in Baoan and the other in Longgang, both having good access to the city centre. Cold spots were clustered in the SEZ where vacant land can barely be found. Hotspots of densification were found in locations that were very close to the city centre, while cold

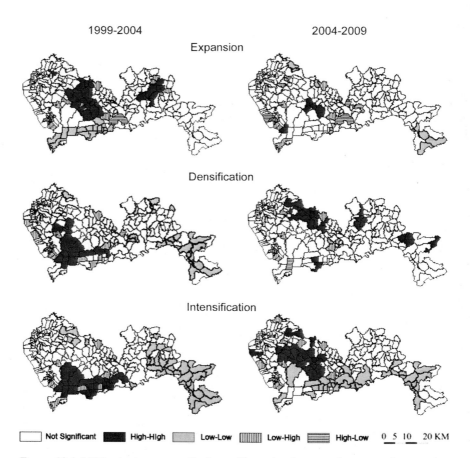

Figure 12.3 LISA cluster maps of urban village development in terms of expansion, densification and intensification, respectively.

spots were mostly found in the eastern part of Longgang. For intensification, hotspots were inside the SEZ and most cold spots were in the eastern part of the city, distant from the city centre.

In 2004–09, as land expansion was much more confined, hotspots were more concentrated than those in the previous period. Cold spots were found in Dapeng Peninsular at the remote east end of the city. Hotspots for densification were close to the hotspots for land expansion in the first period, but more peripheral. Hotspots for intensification corresponded to the hotspots for expansion and densification in the first period. In the SEZ, urban villages had gone through a dramatic intensification process and were fully developed, so they thus lacked potential for further intensification. Outside the SEZ, urban villages had followed the same general development path as those in the SEZ to produce more housing units.

The analyses show that there is great variation in urban village development across the city. The speed and scale of an urban village's development is related to its location in the urban fabric, and the development phases of different villages vary across urban space. At the city scale, the development of urban villages tends to be clustered and village development manifests itself as a spillover effect from inside to outside the SEZ. These patterns imply the spatial clustering of the growth of migrant population and the possible diffusion of migrant employment out of the SEZ. These patterns manifest themselves in the three development stages at the city scale, which temporally and spatially overlap each other. Initially the development of urban villages in the outer districts lagged behind those in the SEZ, but they have been catching up rapidly. These stages represent a very rational strategy for villagers to first maximize their land holdings at minimal cost and then use the accrued rents to finance more capital-intensive high-rise development. Such patterns may also be found in other rapidly developing Chinese cities and the analysis suggests that urban villages in or close to central development zones are likely to be growth centres for high density migrant housing in the absence of formal low-cost housing programmes.

Explaining the spatial variation

The continued urban development and the growth of migrant population are major driving forces for the development of urban villages. As the city's development is not uniform, housing demand from migrants should also vary across the city. Different places experience different levels and types of development. The growth of any village thus depends on the nature of development in its surroundings, as well as its position in the city. Both the provision of jobs in an urban village's immediate environs, and the accessibility to job locations from the village are expected to exert a huge influence on its development. Besides, institutional and natural constraints may hinder the development of the village. Consequently, the development of an urban village can be seen as a function of the combination of the three main factors: job opportunities in the vicinity,[2] accessibility to job locations and development constraints.

The relationships between urban village development and possible driving factors were analysed using multivariate analysis. Separate models were built for the SEZ and the outer districts as a reflection of the significant heterogeneity of the urban development and population in the two areas. In order to have a representative reflection of job opportunities in each village's environs, the employment of large- and medium-scale industrial enterprises, the scale of industrial development, tertiary development and construction projects were considered. To indicate the accessibility to job locations, road distance to metro stations, road distance to industrial parks, and distances to major and minor roads were measured. Further, village land area, the ratio of non-residential land use, land slope, and the presence of ecological protection zone, restricted development zone or water protection zone were considered as variables that reflect development constrains. Outside the SEZ, in addition, road distance to the SEZ, road distance

210 *Pu Hao, Stan Geertman, Pieter Hooimeijer and Richard Sliuzas*

to commercial sub-centres, and road distance to the Guangzhou–Shenzhen expressway were considered, but employment of large- and medium-scale industrial enterprises and road distance to metro stations were dropped, because outside the SEZ employment is largely represented by the scale of industrial development and the metro is not available.

In the SEZ, the proximity to a metro stop has a positive impact on the development of urban villages, and it is the most influential of all factors. Metro stops are often located in activity centres. Besides, accessibility benefits from metro lines and nodes of other public transport modes that are linked to the metro. Consequently, urban villages close to metro stops are very attractive living places and are thus intensively developed. In the outer districts, the proximity to the SEZ has the greatest positive impact on the development of urban villages, reflecting the enormous number of job opportunities provided in the SEZ. However, proximity to sub-centres is not significant, an indication of the strong mono-centric nature of Shenzhen.[3]

The industrial sector in Shenzhen is characterized by labour-intensive manufacturing and a substantive proportion of informal developments, both of which provide great numbers of jobs for migrants and drive urban villages to develop. The development of the tertiary sector also drives the development of urban villages. Its effect is more significant in the outer districts than in the SEZ, reflecting the different development status of tertiary development in and outside the SEZ. In the outer districts tertiary development is relatively low key and composed of substantial informal activities, while their SEZ counterparts serve mid- and high-end markets and employ a better skilled and better paid labour force. Consequently, tertiary sector employees in the outer districts are more likely than their SEZ counterparts to depend on urban village housing.

In the SEZ, the number of jobs generated by mid- and large-scale manufacturing enterprises does not have a positive influence on village growth. This might be explained by the fact that employees in these enterprises, which are likely to be state-owned or foreign-owned enterprises, are more likely to obtain a local *hukou* and were likely to be economically better off (Gravemeyer *et al.* 2011; Huang 2003). These enterprises are also more likely to provide housing facilities for their workers, who are therefore less likely than the employees of small-sized enterprises or informal sectors to reside in urban villages.

With Shenzhen transforming from fields and forests to a teeming metropolis of millions in barely one generation, the need for construction labour has been enormous. For a long time, construction workers have formed a substantial proportion of the migrant population. A positive, though insignificant, influence was found between construction projects and the development of urban villages. The lack of significance can be explained by the fact that construction workers are often provided with temporary shelters on the construction sites. Even for those who have to find rooms in nearby urban villages, room sharing with co-workers is common because of their low wages, reducing their demand for housing space in urban villages.

Proximity to industrial parks positively influences urban village development, though this effect is not significant in the outer districts. This can be explained by the fact that in the outer districts, industrial parks are often equipped with workers' dormitories, making them less dependent upon housing from neighbouring urban villages. However, their SEZ counterparts seldom provide housing facilities for workers due to the higher land value and their relatively smaller size. Within the SEZ industrial workers thus have to find other cheap housing, making a significant impact on nearby urban villages.

Distances to major and minor roads represent accessibility from various parts of an urban village to the city road network. It was expected that the development intensity of urban villages would be higher closer to the road network. In the SEZ, the road network can be accessed at every location, therefore no effect was detected. In the outer districts, positive though insignificant contributions of both major and minor roads are found. More importantly, the Guangzhou–Shenzhen expressway has a great impact on the development of urban villages. Villages with better access to the expressway have a significantly higher built intensity than other urban villages.

In the SEZ, smaller urban villages have a significantly higher built intensity, while in the outer districts bigger urban villages show higher intensities. This difference is a reflection of the different development stages and conditions between the SEZ and the outer districts. In the SEZ, urban villages are under pressure from formal urban development and face urban renewal processes that threaten them with total redevelopment. Through partial redevelopment many urban villages are becoming smaller. In the outer district, urban villages are in their early phases of development so that formal urban development has not exerted direct pressure for large-scale redevelopment. Bigger urban villages may imply stronger political and financial power, both of which positively influence urban village development.

The ratio of non-residential floor space is negatively related to the built intensity of urban villages, an effect that is significant in both the SEZ and non-SEZ. This implies that the development of the formal city not only drives the development of the residential components of urban villages, but is also encroaching on urban villages. The collectively owned parts of a village that is characterized by multiple non-residential functions tend to be converted first, leading to a lower ratio of non-residential use and higher built intensity in the village's residential part.

Both natural and institutional constraints may curtail urban village development. High land slope generally increases the construction cost of houses and is thus expected to negatively impact urban village development. Although some effect is detected, it is not significant because in general the land slope of urban villages is quite low.

Ecological protection zoning shows the expected negative impact, but only in the SEZ. Restrictive zoning does not show up as significant, while water body protection actually has a positive rather than a negative effect on urban village growth. This indicates that only the ecological protection zone legislation entailed some control on urban village development and this only happened in the SEZ where development control enforcement was much stricter. Meanwhile, proximity to a water body actually increases the environmental quality of the urban village and thus increases its attractiveness for development. These results imply that

212 *Pu Hao, Stan Geertman, Pieter Hooimeijer and Richard Sliuzas*

general city planning regulations have failed to control developments in urban villages.

To sum up, accessibility (as suggested by proximity to the metro, the SEZ and industrial parks), local employment (as suggested by local industrial and tertiary development), along with development constraints (given by encroachment of formal development, land slope and ecological protection zoning), are the most important determinants for the development of urban villages.

Land use evolution

Traditional rural village societies in China are family-based and largely self-sufficient in conducting daily activities, i.e. living, working, and various social amenities. Most villagers are farmers who work in the fields and obtain services based on their own family needs. Dedicated public facilities such as kindergartens, supermarkets, or factories, which are common in cities, are rare in rural villages. Village land use is dominated by farms and dwellings, showing little diversity in functionality. However, in their transformation to urban villages, besides extra housing units, various other facilities are also developed: factories, supermarkets, schools, medical centres, etc., which together create a niche place for migrants to work and live that is radically different from a traditional rural village.

The land of an urban village is subject to the fundamental subdivision of village land use: individual-family-controlled land for housing, referred to as *zhaijidi*; and collectively owned and managed land for streets, public facilities and premises used for businesses. When the city government acquires agricultural land for development, they usually leave some spare land to the villagers. This increases the area of collectively owned village land, allowing villagers to retain proper infrastructure and enabling them to develop collective economic activities that can partly solve the unemployment problem created by the loss of agricultural land (Wang *et al.* 2009). On this land, village collectives can build industrial or commercial buildings for lease, but they are not allowed to sell the land or use it for residential development (Zhao and Webster 2011). It is the development of non-residential facilities on the collectively controlled land that changes the land use mix in urban villages.

With urbanization, the land use of the villages evolves, catering for the changing demands of the indigenous and migrant population and their requirements for urban institutions (Table 12.2). In the beginning, as a rural village is transformed into an urban village, village enterprises are established to promote village industries as an alternative livelihood to farming (Smart and Smart 2001). Some villages start industrial activities themselves, but more villages rely on developing dedicated, low-cost industrial space for external entrepreneurs. Meanwhile, the population of migrant tenants dramatically increases and greatly exceeds the indigenous population. Consequently, a great demand for commercial and service facilities is generated, which enables such facilities to flourish. As migrant housing, employment and services all develop, the villages become a niche

Spatial evolution of urban villages in Shenzhen 213

Table 12.2 Main aspects in the evolution from rural village to urban village.

Aspect	Rural village	Early-phase urban village	Mature urban village
Environment	Agricultural land	Low-density urban development	High-density urban development
Residents	Indigenous villagers	Indigenous villagers and migrants	Mostly migrants
Main employment	Agricultural activities	Non-agricultural work inside and outside the village	Non-agricultural work outside the village
Areal size	Original size	Expanding	Shrinking
Built density	Low	High	Very high
Open space	Common	Few	Rare
Population density	Very low	High	Very high
Land use diversity	Low	High	Low
Collective common land	Original composition	Increased	Decreased
Service	Little	Increased	Decreased
Leadership	Village committee	Village committee and shareholding company	Village committee and shareholding company

location for migrants to enjoy an "urban life", resulting in land use diversity within these urban villages.

As the environs of the urban villages develop, the underlying conditions to maintain certain land uses change. Industries may be driven away from villages in central locations because of their relatively low returns and rising land values. As land is relatively more abundant in suburban areas and transport and other infrastructures are improving, more peripheral villages may become more attractive industrial locations over time. Similarly, the development of commercial activities and public services may also change, in order to meet local demand and to suit the prevailing local conditions for development. Such changes lead to an adjustment of the land use structure of urban villages over time. Meanwhile, the surrounding areas also become commercially well established and provide increasing numbers of jobs and services. This is also in accordance with an increase in the educational level of migrant tenants. Thus, village residents become less reliant on jobs and services inside villages, and consequently the multifunctionality of their village is likely to decrease.

Besides, the development of formal urban areas requires more land, so that both market-driven and government-led redevelopment starts to encroach on urban village land. In this process, the land to be redeveloped is expropriated from village land and converted to state-owned urban land. When faced with such forces, villagers are more likely to give up their collectively controlled land than their *zhaijidi* for three reasons: first, most of the indigenous villagers rely on their private properties on *zhaijidi* for their own accommodation and as their most important source of revenue; second, property rights over collectively owned properties are not clearly defined, and thus indigenous villagers feel less secure over their collectively owned land compared to their *zhaijidi*; and third, the cost of redeveloping the collectively owned part of the village is considerably less because the compensation standard is lower (Zhao and Webster 2011) and quite often the village committee or shareholding company can make decisions on behalf of the collective, thereby negating the need to negotiate with numerous village families. These reasons lead to a decrease in the non-residential part of the villages and consequently to a radical decline in land use diversity.

In Shenzhen, given the distinctive characteristics of the SEZ, differences in land use diversity are found between the SEZ and non-SEZ. Urban villages in the SEZ are in a more advanced development phase. Their environs are more economically established and intensively developed, providing sufficient jobs and services, and thus the urban villages have less need to develop multiple functions themselves. Typically their tenants also tend to have attained a higher level of education and acquired jobs in the formal urban sectors. Moreover, as municipal policies are more focused on redeveloping the SEZ villages, they are likely to have experienced more extensive redevelopment and land acquisition. Consequently, SEZ urban villages are likely to have less non-residential land use and relatively low land use diversity. In the non-SEZ districts, urban villages are generally still in an earlier development phase. Urban encroachment is less common and the provision of jobs and services is still largely in the villages themselves. Consequently, urban villages located outside the SEZ are generally affected by market-driven land use development and thus far have been less affected by large-scale redevelopment.

In the course of their evolution urban villages across the city exhibit different land use structures based on their location in the urban fabric, their development phase, and the development of their surroundings. To examine these empirically, Shannon entropy measurement was used to examine the overall diversity level of each urban village. The entropy values for the villages vary greatly, ranging from 0.012 (very low land use diversity) to 0.953 (very high land use diversity). The low diversity villages are found in both the most central and developed area (Futian district) and the most peripheral areas (northwest of Baoan and Dapeng Peninsular in the east of Longgang). Urban villages having high diversity were mainly found in the middle zone of the city.

To explore the driving factors of land use diversity, we use a spatial regimes model. This model uses a disaggregated modelling strategy by estimating separate models for predefined spatial regimes, in our case, the SEZ and the non-SEZ. It results in more precise standard error estimates and also evaluates whether there is a statistical difference between the coefficients in each regime. Seven factors are considered, including road distance to city centre, distance to road network, road distance to industrial park, village size, development intensity, intensification rate and development intensity in the environs. To account for spatial dependency we use a spatial lag model and a spatial error model.

Spatial evolution of urban villages in Shenzhen 215

The heterogeneity of the effect of independent variables between the SEZ and non-SEZ is significant, suggesting that the effects are not stable across the two regions. Moreover, an examination of the tests of individual coefficients reveals that several of the explanatory variables exhibit significantly different effects between the SEZ and non-SEZ. These results support the hypothesis that different causal processes operate across urban villages.

The areal size of the urban village is positively related to land use diversity for both regimes. This positive effect was expected because bigger villages have advantages in developing multiple land uses. Abundant land resources are important for developing dedicated facilities, especially industrial buildings; a bigger village implies more political and economic power of the village collective, and a bigger village is also more likely to establish a self-sufficient community. All these aspects contribute to greater land use diversity. However, between villages in the SEZ and those in the non-SEZ, the magnitude of the effect is significantly different. The much greater impact in the SEZ implies that redevelopment processes, which include land acquisition leading to an immediate drop in land use diversity, play an important role in determining the current land use pattern. However, in the non-SEZ, this effect is less evident because large-scale land requisition has not yet taken place, though the implications of such a policy for land use diversity are evident.

As expected, location is an influential determinant of the land use of urban villages. Locations close to the centre are more economically vibrant and thus urban villages in those locations attract a larger variety of development. Away from the centre, urban villages do not readily establish a diverse land use structure. The proximity to the city centre thus positively influences land use diversity. The proximity to an industrial park is also positively related to land use diversity throughout the city. This positive relationship is due to the fact that industrial parks are mono-functional but attract migrant workers who generate demand for multiple functions in the neighbouring villages. The effect is not significant in the non-SEZ area because there many industrial parks provide their own living compounds and other service facilities for workers inside the parks, reducing the demand for such services in the nearby urban villages. The proximity to the road network is not significant, but an opposite effect is detected for the two regimes. The negative effect in the SEZ reflects the higher frequency of redevelopment in places close to roads inside the SEZ. On the other hand, a positive effect is seen in the non-SEZ districts because proximity to roads is an advantage for villages to develop multiple functions and redevelopment is yet to occur.

The built intensity of the residential part of an urban village reflects its development phase. Villages in a later phase of development usually have a greater built intensity and are also more likely to have experienced redevelopment. Consequently, these villages have a lower proportion of non-residential land and lower land use diversity. Moreover, in the SEZ, urban villages that have recently experienced rapid intensification on their residential land tend to have lower land use diversity. In many cases, they have sold their collective land though a second round of public land acquisition, providing a new source of capital for further residential construction and intensification. Thus, less land is used for non-residential functions and their land use diversity is lower. However, in the non-SEZ, housing development is positively related to land use diversity as a result of market-driven land use development and less redevelopment.

The built intensity of the urban village's environment gives opposite effects between the two regimes. In the SEZ, a greater built intensity reflects greater development pressure and higher land value. Property development in such locations is thus more profitable and villages are more likely to face redevelopment offers. Where redevelopment does occur it generally first targets the collectively owned village lands which tend to be used for non-residential purposes. Consequently, SEZ urban villages located in more intensively developed urban areas tend to have a lower proportion of non-residential land and lower land use diversity than those found elsewhere. Outside the SEZ, a greater built intensity indicates a more active level of development in the surroundings, and therefore a positive influence on the land use diversity of the village.

Despite the effects given by the previous factors, significant spatial autocorrelation was detected, suggesting the possibility of diffusion. Villages that successfully develop multiple functions may influence their neighbouring villages through the diffusion of entrepreneurship, experience and investment, leading to similar multifunctional development in the neighbouring villages. However, spatial autocorrelation could also result from the effect of other unmeasured factors related to cultural or socioeconomic characteristics, or it could be a reflection of the local policy environment shared by villages that are close to one another.

Multiple economic and social functions have developed on the collective village land, which was initially proportional to the village size. However, as the urban villages are diverse in terms of location, development phase and the level of surrounding development, their land use patterns also vary greatly. Besides the factors examined, an urban village's local culture, socioeconomic status, collective collaboration and leadership, networking and the ability to attract investment are other important factors that contribute to the shaping of its land use structure. Some of these factors, especially those that are rooted in historical legacy, are intangible and difficult to directly observe or measure. However, these factors almost certainly play an important role in the land use development of urban villages and deserve further research.

Conclusions

Urban villages in Shenzhen have been evolving rapidly throughout the most recent decades, resulting in their current diversity in physical development and land use patterns. This study suggests that a view of urban villages as static and uniform migrant enclaves is not valid. The growth of urban villages through expansion, densification and intensification, has been continuously producing large quantities of low-cost housing units for the enormous migrant population. Although the lack of demographic data prevented a direct measurement of the population density of urban villages, based on the assumption that there is a very

Spatial evolution of urban villages in Shenzhen 217

quick response to demand, low vacancy rate and little variation of floor space per person, the development intensity could be used as a suitable proxy for population density. Based on this assumption, our rich and fine-resolution data at building level enables an analysis of the complete population of urban villages in Shenzhen. The development of an urban village is determined by its location in the urban fabric and the development in its surroundings. Major density concentrations of urban village development are found in the city's prime development areas, but the pattern also shows a spillover effect from the SEZ to Shenzhen's outer districts. It is expected that urban villages in other large, fast growing Chinese cities might also show similar dynamics and diversity in their development patterns.

The evolution of urban villages is also associated with the growth and decline of multiple economic and social functions, reflecting the changing local demand and conditions for the development of different land uses as well as the competitive pressure from formal urban development in their environs. Variation in land use diversity is explained by each urban village's location in the urban fabric, its phase of development, and the surrounding level of urban development. The different patterns apparent inside and outside the SEZ reflect the dominant role that is played by large-scale land acquisition and redevelopment in the SEZ. Formalized urban redevelopment programmes are leading to a reduction in the land use diversity of centrally located villages, while more peripheral villages experience a rise in land use diversity. These trends will definitely have an influence on the overall land use development of the city.

Severe competition in the land development market has been reshaping the urban landscape in Shenzhen and other Chinese cities. Land leasing and development take place on an enormous scale, including lands in the vicinity of urban villages. Driven by market demand, land use efficiency has improved significantly in those places. However, because landlords cannot transfer their property rights to private developers, land values in urban villages are usually substantially lower than those of neighbouring formal urban areas (see Figure 12.2). Property development by indigenous villagers, although comprised largely of unauthorized constructions and modifications, is the only possible means to exploit the potential land value. The spatial evolution of these villages is thus inevitable. However, the government-led redevelopment that is under way in many cities has become an increasingly influential factor for the spatial evolution of urban villages. Redevelopment reduces a great deal of urban village housing-stock, results in a declining land use diversity, and pushes the remaining villages to become even more intensely developed. Cities that adopt urban village redevelopment policies should therefore consider the fluidity of the migrant housing system and search for means to address low cost housing improvement in a way that does not simply relocate the problem it is attempting to address.

It is worth noting that the evolution of urban villages works on the just-good-enough principle, rather than a perfecting principle. On the one hand, the urban villages cater for migrants' housing needs in terms of quantity and affordability, implying that the current policies to redevelop urban villages are likely to disrupt this niche housing market. On the other hand, left unattended urban village development often generates far from ideal living environments. The insecure property rights of urban village land tend to induce short-term investments, leading to a sub-optimal utilization of scarce land resources and to various negative externalities. The lack of standard regulations, professional guidance for urban village development options, and enforcement of building codes in urban villages result in many of the physical problems found in urban villages today. In a situation where market forces undermine development regulations, over-development seems an inevitable destination of the urban village's spatial evolution. Thus enforcing building codes in urban villages is critical to ensure proper construction and the provision of adequate infrastructure so that the villagers' capital investments may enjoy a longer life span and redevelopment may be postponed or perhaps even become superfluous.

This study has examined the situation in Shenzhen, a city whose size and scale of urban villages are not comparable to most other cities. However, the relationships resulting from the analysis and its policy implications are almost certainly not limited to Shenzhen. With our cross-sectional approach it is not possible to fully capture the interactions between the evolution of urban villages and the overall urban growth, because the development of urban villages is determined not only by the present conditions and constraints for development, but also subject to past experience. There is also a time lag for formal urban development to have an impact on urban villages. Repeating the municipal building survey at regular intervals may allow interactions between these factors to be determined and reveal how changes in formal urban development influence the built intensity and land use of urban villages over time. Besides, more detailed studies of the interplay among factors such as socio-economic characteristics, leadership, and implementations of redevelopment programmes will also be needed to understand fully the factors and mechanisms that drive the further evolution of urban villages.

Notes

1. Considering much larger room space is used by the landlords, the average room space used by migrants was considerably smaller. Besides, room vacancy was not taken into account.
2. A radius of 2 kilometres was defined as the immediate vicinity of each urban village.
3. Multiple city centres have been planned and developed since the early 1980s; however, all the centres are in the SEZ.

References

Anselin, L. (1995) 'Local indicators of spatial association – LISA', *Geographical Analysis*, 27(2): 93–115.
Bach, J. (2010) '"They come in peasants and leave citizens": urban villages and the making of Shenzhen, China', *Cultural Anthropology*, 25(3): 421–58.
Gravemeyer, S., Gries, T. and Xue, J. (2011) 'Income determination and income discrimination in Shenzhen', *Urban Studies*, 48(7): 1457–75.

Hao, P., Geertman, S., Hooimeijer, P. and Sliuzas, R. (2012) 'Spatial analyses of the urban village development process in Shenzhen, China', *International Journal of Urban and Regional Research*, DOI: 10.1111/j.1468–2427.2012.01109.x (Online).

Hao, P., Sliuzas, R. and Geertman, S. (2011) 'The development and redevelopment of urban villages in Shenzhen', *Habitat International*, 35(2): 214–24.

Huang, Y. (2003) 'A room of one's own: housing consumption and residential crowding in transitional urban China', *Environment and Planning A*, 35(4): 591–614.

Liu, Y., He, S., Wu, F. and Webster, C. (2010) 'Urban villages under China's rapid urbanization: unregulated assets and transitional neighbourhoods', *Habitat International*, 34(2): 135–44.

Shenzhen Statistics Bureau (2010) *Shenzhen Statistical Yearbook 2010*, Beijing: China Statistics Press.

Smart, A. and Smart, J. (2001) 'Local citizenship: welfare reform urban/rural status, and exclusion in China', *Environment and Planning A*, 33(10): 1853–69.

Tian, L. (2008) 'The chengzhongcun land market in China: boon or bane?: a perspective on property rights', *International Journal of Urban and Regional Research*, 32(2): 282–304.

Wang, Y. P., Wang, Y. and Wu, J. (2009) 'Urbanization and informal development in China: urban villages in Shenzhen', *International Journal of Urban and Regional Research*, 33(4): 957–73.

Zhang, L. (2005) 'Migrant enclaves and impacts of redevelopment policy in Chinese cities', in L. J. C. Ma and F. Wu (eds.), *Restructuring the Chinese City: Changing Society, Economy and Space*, New York: Routledge, pp. 218–33.

Zhang, L., Zhao, S. X. B. and Tian, J. P. (2003) 'Self-help in housing and chengzhongcun in China's urbanization', *International Journal of Urban and Regional Research*, 27(4): 912–37.

Zhao, Y. and Webster, C. (2011) 'Land dispossession and enrichment in China's suburban villages', *Urban Studies*, 48(3): 529–51.

Part 4

Migrants' transient urbanism

Village redevelopment

13 'Three olds redevelopment'
Advances in urban upgrading in Guangzhou

Sonia Schoon and Uwe Altrock

The emergence of urban villages

As is well known, China has been witnessing tremendous changes in all spheres of society, politics and economics since it started opening up to the world in the late 1970s. During the first stages of rapid development, the Chinese government first and foremost gave attention to economic growth and – in the realm of urban planning – to urban expansion, making use of the easy approach of green-field development on former agricultural land expropriated from peasants living in villages surrounding the city. Only built-up residential areas were left to those expropriated farmers – usually consisting of around 10 per cent to 12 per cent of the former territory of the whole village – and further managed by the village committee and the village collectives. The villagers, in this way deprived of their sources of agricultural income, had to strike new paths in order to make a living. According to the land regulations promulgated by the provincial government of Guangdong in 1989 in the 'Regulations of Guangdong Province on Administration of Planning and Construction of Townships (Towns) and Villages' (Guangdong Province People's Government No. 134, 1989), the utilization of rural land can be decided upon collectively by the rural population. In 1993, the State Council issued Regulations on Village and Town Planning and Construction Management (State Council PRC No. 116, 1993), suggesting that village and town governments take on the responsibility for planning land utilization. However, despite these regulations, village committees usually ignored the guidelines. As a matter of fact, there is no formally established land planning in rural areas. How the land is utilized is wholly decided by village committees and the villagers themselves. In order to cope with their new circumstances as a jobless and low educated population, the villagers took the opportunity of renting out their residential property to the migrant workers streaming into the villages seeking for cheap accommodation. The more the migrant population increased, the more the villagers arbitrarily enlarged their houses to accommodate more people and get more income. This way, densely built-up areas emerged, with extremely narrow passages, 'hand-shaking houses' (*woshoulou*) or 'kissing houses' (*louwenlou*) that lie closely next to or even touch each other, and are of poor quality. With the passing of time, the urban area grew incessantly until many of the former villages were totally

224 *Sonia Schoon and Uwe Altrock*

surrounded by the city, now being transformed into collective enclaves. Thus, the so-called phenomenon of 'urban villages' emerged. For a long time, this unwelcome outcome of massive urban growth and its related problems was ignored and neglected by different governments, as the benefits of urban villages providing housing for urgently needed floating workers outweighed the negative effects.

The need to redevelop

Only since around the beginning of the new century has the problem of urban villages become a major concern for the municipal government of Guangzhou City. Some serious incidents such as fires in several urban villages with dozens of victims, a high crime rate and a lack of efficient security and control mechanisms (e.g. population, fire and urban management control) led to the need for redevelopment. In addition, and to be considered perhaps, as an even stronger driving force, only extremely scarce land resources were left for development. Up to 2020, the areas that the Central Department of Urban and Rural Construction have approved for Guangzhou's urban construction amount to 170 square kilometres of the total urban area of 3,843 square kilometres. But Guangzhou Municipal Government realized that it has already consumed nearly 160 square kilometres of construction land by 2011 (Interview with A., GZ 3OO 2010). This problem of limited available land resources is faced not only by Guangzhou City, but the entire Guangdong Province needs to cope with the issue of ineffective land use. One hundred and thirty-eight urban villages in Guangzhou's core area and their redevelopment would offer a tremendous opportunity to gain much needed land resources for urban development. By regaining full control over those areas, the local government intends to implement redevelopment schemes that may allow for better buildings and also improving general living conditions by inserting much needed open space.[1] Besides urban villages, old town areas that have been neglected for a long time and large, old manufacturing sites that can be converted could make up the deficiency. Accordingly, at the 2009 People's Congress, the provincial government appointed Guangzhou City as a precedent for the so-called 'second land reform' and for solving land problems 'left over by history' during the process of land redevelopment. As an urban redevelopment pioneer, Guangzhou drew up a work programme to promote renovation in Guangzhou as a model (Altrock and Schoon 2011a,b).

(Re)Development and its drivers

The main drivers for urban village redevelopment can be summarized. Even so, they are all intricately intertwined and therefore constitute a complex structure of interdependencies and consequences. These drivers are location factors, mega-events (such as the Asian Games in Autumn 2010), and the economic and management strengths of the various urban villages. Furthermore, they include bilateral willingness (government and urban village), intensity of existing problems and political interest and tasks.

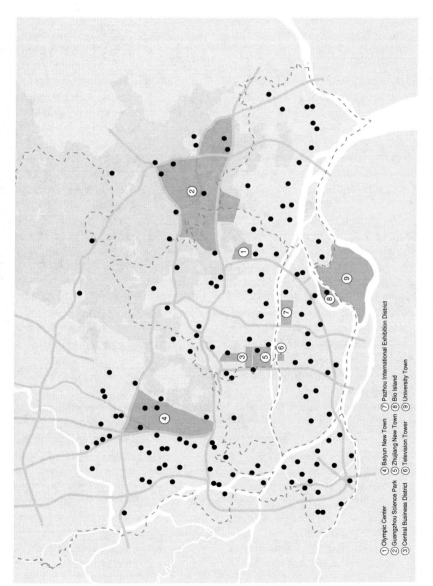

Figure 13.1 Urban villages in Guangzhou and important planning projects.

Source: Author's map 2009, based on the 138 urban villages defined by Guangzhou Municipality and a survey of important projects.

Location factors always play a crucial role when it comes to urban village redevelopment (cf. Figure 13.1). The lands of the urban villages in the city core, such as Liede, Shipai, Linhe, Xian and Yangji villages lying in and directly around the heart of the newly erected central business district of Zhujiang New Town, are of an extremely high value. Here, economic interests are notable, and the need to restructure or demolish the old villages in order to make possible comprehensive planning for the whole area is pushing forward the process of negotiation and finally implementation. Other urban villages that are situated in the area of certain planning projects also enjoy preferential treatment, so as to smooth the restructuring process. Prominent examples are Pazhou and Huangpu villages, located in the vicinity of the new Pazhou Exhibition Centre, that are being accordingly redeveloped to attract visitors. Also in Baiyun District a new city centre is planned on and around the area of the old abandoned airport, Baiyun New Town. As in Zhujiang New Town, villages disturbing the appearance of a totally newly designed centre, namely Tangxia, Xiaogang and Sanyuanli, are put forward to be redeveloped first.

Next to the location factors triggering developments, the aspect of an attractive urban image is very important for the municipal government. In particular, a mega-event such as the Asian Games 2010, which could be seen as being as important to Guangzhou as the Olympic Games and the World Expo were to Beijing and Shanghai respectively, forces the municipal government to make huge investments in infrastructure improvement, city beautification, and greening (Qin 2010; Xinkuai Net 2010; Zeng 2010). The endeavour to project the image of an emerging Chinese mega-power to the whole world releases accelerated processes that, in respect of urban villages, lead to massive governmental incentive policies and concessions, but also to the clear intention to urgently push forward (re)developments. In this respect, the concerned municipal bureaus had a mission to at least pull down or begin to pull down the selected urban villages under their responsibility before the Asian Games (Interview with M., GZ BY UPO 2009). Guangzhou has now selected nine urban villages as redevelopment test sites, or pioneers. The first village that was fully demolished and restructured is Liede. Others are following.

One indispensable prerequisite for redevelopment is the villagers' will to support the redevelopment efforts, which means that the urban village needs to have a strong economic standing with enough assets to realize the upgrading, and, equally important, to have a financially strong and competent leadership enjoying the villagers' full trust (Schoon 2012). Therefore, the renovation will be carried out and the pace of restructuring accelerated in those selected villages where the cadres are enthusiastic, where the village itself is economically developed, and where the villagers are very eager to go through the renovation process (Interview with C., GZ UPO 2009; Interview with Z., GZ BY UPO 2010). If just the government or only one village is willing to redevelop, desperately needed agreements between the two influential players in the governance arrangement cannot be reached. The famous saying 'the crying baby gets the milk' (*hui ku de haizi jiu you nai he*) quite neatly displays the situation of urban villages – those that are strong and know how to articulate their interest may achieve a lot.

The intensity of problems also triggers redevelopment. For example, most of the urban villages suffer from a severe danger of fire due to the high building density. If no comprehensive mutual agreements for redevelopment can be reached, at least such problems will be combated as quickly as possible, installing fire passages, etc. to meet minimum security standards.

A further intriguing driving force is political as well as personal prestige interest. Suppose a newly assigned commission or bureau secretary is commissioned with certain tasks from higher authorities or led by personal ambitions and sets up new milestones or goals, they will be immediately carried out by the appointed organization (Interview with Z., GZ BY UPO 2010) and nobody would be too surprised even if this could mean a change of course.

Coping with the leftovers from history

As for the problems left over from history (*lishi yiliu de wenti*), the main problems the government has to cope with are land-use-related problems concerning land ownership; the transfer from agricultural or collectively owned land to state-owned land, and the change in use of different kinds of small pieces of lands below three *mu*, called 'marginal land' (*bianjiao di*), sandwich land (*jiaxin di*) and wedged land (*chahua di*) that have not yet been assigned for use. (Guangdong Province People's Government No. 78, 2009; Interview with A., GZ 3OO 2010). Dealing with the first two leftovers poses the biggest challenges, because identifying land ownership in urban villages is extremely difficult due to villagers' arbitrary construction habits, and because the transfer from collective to state-owned land needs the official consent of more than 90 per cent of the village collective and is dependent on satisfactory compensation which the government itself cannot provide. In order to first and foremost eliminate these problems as a milestone on the way towards sustainable and comprehensive urban planning, the Three Olds Redevelopment concept has been established.

The concept: 'three olds redevelopment'

The formation of the Three Olds Redevelopment policies can be seen as a great leap forward in the field of experimental urban governance (Schoon 2011b). It is, on the one hand a result of long-lasting experimentation processes in dealing with built-up areas that are perceived as ineffectively used or as disturbing factors within the planned urban fabric within the cities. The aim is to regain full control over them, to make better use of those spaces, and to integrate them into comprehensive municipal planning schemes. On the other hand, Three Olds Redevelopment can also be seen as a starting point for a continuous and coordinated experimentation process in urban development under legal guidance.

The main objective of the three olds policies is described in Guangdong Province's provisions as follows:

> We should strictly balance the requisition and compensation of cultivated land, complete the state-assigned tasks of protecting cultivated land and basic

228 *Sonia Schoon and Uwe Altrock*

farmland by quantity and quality, and make Guangdong province become a model province for economic and intensive land use with a strong economy, a harmonious society, a beautiful environment, and a sound ecological environment.

(Guangdong Province People's Government No. 16, 2009).

The key phrase of 'economic and intensive land use' simply refers to the main objective of optimizing land resource allocation and usage, since land has become an extremely scarce resource over recent decades.

Challenges

The ambitious goal of this new policy, though short and clear, entails a complex set of challenges.

Many different villages with different conditions

In Guangzhou's central districts alone, 138 urban villages have been officially declared as such, although the problem of villages being more and more urbanized and lacking professional guidance and control concerns many more than just those 138. For historical reasons, location factors, social and physical structures, the partially exorbitant compensation demands of the local population, sanitation and environmental problems, and the different economic strengths and leadership qualities of urban village joint stock companies, it is impossible to find a one-for-all solution with which to comprehensively approach redevelopment (Schoon 2012).

Imperfect law and lack of experience

The problem of urban village development is a new phenomenon. In a country that has no rule of law tradition to resort to and no experience to build on, a unified legal foundation that determines approaches towards urban villages in general and their redevelopment in particular must first be cautiously generated, which poses a huge challenge.

Get approval from villagers. Pay attention to people's will

The government usually does not dispose of the ability and capacity to convince the villagers to redevelop. This should be the will of the village and be led by the village's joint stock company. How to find a way to match all individual interests to reach 90 per cent consent to redevelopment, which especially means consent to the compensation schemes, needs a very strong and persuasive collective leadership. Since it happens that some individuals (among the 10 per cent) resist until the very end, the phenomenon of nail houses (*dingzi hu*) occurs every once in a while, where in most cases the owners struggle for a maximum individual benefit from the compensation process.

Guangzhou's government policy is 'giving supportive policy but not providing funds' (Interview with H., GZ UPE 2009/02)

Closely related to the challenge mentioned above is the need to promote redevelopment, to raise villagers' interest to support the change and invest in the redevelopment themselves or to find a developer who is willing to invest, because the municipal and district governments are far from being financially capable of taking care of urban regeneration. Therefore, the only possibility the government has is to provide preferential policies and facilitate the process of redevelopment.

Safeguarding a successful redevelopment process

The government learned its lesson from previous attempts at developer involvement where it failed to implement sufficient supervisory measures. This often led to bankruptcy and half-way project terminations with many individuals suffering from the lack of risk protection. In a nutshell, the challenge now is to carefully involve developers, safeguard villagers' profits, minimize risks and supervise developers. Therefore, the government now has to walk the tightrope of balancing political, economic, social and technological aspects and trying to achieve a perfect combination of all of them (Interview with H., GZ CC 2009).

The government is fighting to balance economic and environmental interests (Interview with C., GZ UPO 2009)

The whole process of urban village redevelopment needs to be carried out in the market according to the law of supply and demand. Since real estate companies are responsible for the reconstruction work, it is very important whether they accept the redevelopment plans or not, because they eventually represent the response from the market and the money invested also finally comes from them (Interview with L., GZ SYSU UPE 2009). It is impossible for the government to invest the large amounts of money needed for redevelopment. Therefore it has to make concessions, but at the same time adhere to its principles. The challenge of balancing interests leads to extensive rounds of bargaining.

Institutionalization of the whole process

In times of continuous changes and amendments in terms of policies, official responsibilities and redevelopment implementation approaches and procedures, the biggest challenge is the aggregation of experiences, the translation of positive or assertive experiences into institutionalized processes, and the successful and immediate elimination of negative or non-assertive experiences. Until just recently, the renovation of urban villages was still an unpredictable process. Sometimes, the departments in charge changed due to the adjustment of functions or the replacement of staff. This changed with the establishment of urban regeneration offices.

Important innovations

Although the policies of Three Olds Redevelopment are still in the maturing stage, some remarkable approaches to cope with the challenges of old village, old town and old factory redevelopment have been formulated so far.

These can be summarized as follows:

Incentive policies

The municipal government, willing to actively push forward the process of urban regeneration and to stimulate the affected stakeholders and the market as well, worked out the most effective ways to formulate incentives for self-redevelopment or third-party investment. Not equipped with enough financial ability to invest directly into urban upgrading, tax reductions, preferential policies, facilitated processes, prioritized public auctions, etc., disburden the involved actors and may even allow for new opportunities that were not given before.

Agreements and concessions

Further, the government emphasizes the openness of processes and its willingness to compromise. Pro-active public and stakeholder participation is welcomed to a certain degree in order to find the best solutions for the challenges that are to be mastered. This does not mean that there is extreme freedom or the possibility of uncontrolled development for the non-governmental participants in the process, but an 'open ear' for new and reasonable ideas and room for bargaining, discussion and compromises.

Compensation schemes and profit sharing

In order to standardize compensation requirements and schemes, the municipal government detaches them from individual bargaining powers and appoints certain rules that cannot be overcome or preconditions that have to be fulfilled by all parties. A new voting mechanism is introduced according to which houses can only be removed if 90 per cent of villagers agree to carry out redevelopment in a first official vote at the shareholders' congress of the urban village. These shareholders' congresses are held until agreements have been reached. In the course of the discussions, negotiations and bargaining, the village joint stock company and mainly the head of a village and his fellow cadres are responsible for reaching the necessary 90 per cent. They are commissioned with this difficult task, because due to familial and clan ties within the village community, they have much stronger and more effective means to pursue their fellows than any governmental body. They are supported by developers (in respect of providing convincing arguments for future economic benefits) and by the local government (as guarantor for the village cadres' honesty and therefore as a control mechanism). The district government that is responsible for implementing the redevelopment process now also receives fixed compensation related to the land auction value added in the proportion 2:8 shared with the municipal government, in order to become a motivated driving force. Before, districts were reluctant to carry out land auctions, as they did not profit from it, because all value added was gained by the municipal government (Interview with H., GZ UPE 2009/02). Now, the district government is required to establish a special fund for the reconstruction of urban villages as well as for investment in infrastructure and public facilities (Guangzhou Municipal Government No. 56, 2009).

Transparency

One prior condition for redevelopment formulated by the Central State mentioned above is 'social harmony'. Therefore, much attention is paid to the transparency and fairness of processes, even if this entails a slowing down of processes (Interview with C., GZ UPO 2009). Villagers have to be clearly informed all the way through the renovation and everyone has to be able to express their own ideas. Public hearings have to be held in order to explain for example why a renovation scheme cannot be approved or in order to inform people about ongoing decisions and progress made. Also, compensation schemes have to be made transparent, as well as all other facts and figures of public interest.

Professional support

The newly established Urban Regeneration Offices in Guangzhou's urban districts are assigned with clear tasks and are under the clear guidance of the municipal Reconstruction Bureau. This is the first time that urban village redevelopment has been put under the structured umbrella of 'urban regeneration'. Before, it was supervised by the municipal Construction Committee, and then for a short time by the Land Bureau. Now, responsibilities and duties are clearly defined, and urban planning and land use can be combined and structured more easily by relevant experts working closely together in one office. During the renovation, the district government plays the leading role in accelerating renovation by providing professional organization, planning, management, supervision and information, whereas the municipal government supports the process mainly through issuing preferential treatment and guiding policies, through supervision and approval of processes reported from below (see Figure 13.2).

Invitation of developers

From 1999 until 2006, developers were not allowed to participate in urban village redevelopment. After 2006, they were not interested due to massive restrictions. These policies changed because the government needs their financial power and experience to successfully initiate restructuring, and accordingly formulated new preferential treatment. Since they represent the market, they are perceived by villagers as much more persuasive than governmental bodies. Moreover, their

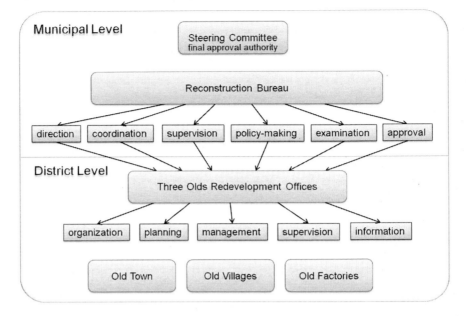

Figure 13.2 Guangzhou 'Three Olds Regeneration' duty allocation on municipal and district levels.
Source: Schoon (2011).

practical experience is said to better assist villagers to develop successful planning documents, find acceptable relocation opportunities and organize the whole process (Interview with M., GZ BY UPO 2009). Besides, land prices in the urban cores have risen significantly. With the price for a piece of land determined not only by the market but also by land use designation, the new will for making concessions also offers profit maximization opportunities for the developers involved (Interview with L., GZ SYSU UPE 2009).

Safeguarding and supervision

During a pro-growth oriented phase of urban development until the end of the 1990s, the government did not put enough emphasis on urban construction regulation. The results were not only those land use problems left over from history, but also unfinished and abandoned building construction, where developers ran out of money and where not only many loans could not be paid back, debts grew, and ugly ruins now disturb the urban image, but also many private investors were ruined through bankruptcy. As a consequence, developers were restricted in their actions. Now, after letting developers again participate in regeneration, the government is enforcing a '100 per cent sure policy', because a whole village population could not be put at risk, jeopardizing the 'harmonious society construction'.

Accordingly, the developers have to deposit the full amount of their redevelopment investment in a government bank account to provide security. If they go bankrupt during the renovation, this will no longer have a negative effect on the regeneration measure (Interview with H., GZ CC 2009).

Uncoupling the regeneration process from external and unpredictable push factors

A common consensus among planners and urban governments is the perception that redevelopment measures should not be carried out under time pressure or under immature conditions that could cause conflicts. As a result, the government will not agree to proceed faster or even exclusively when the real estate market is at high tide. Unpredictable external push factors like real estate prices are said to be irrelevant to decisions made concerning urban village redevelopment. Also, an open ending is favoured for Three Olds Redevelopment. The wish is to finish the policy-making process within a five year period, but regeneration measures could nevertheless be slowed down if concerns about sustainability were to arise.

The modes of 'old village' redevelopment

The following redevelopment modes so far concern only the 52 urban villages located within the designated Three Olds Redevelopment area of 54 square kilometres or those that have been added with official approval. Only those urban villages can be redeveloped that possess clearly defined land use rights and where more than 90 per cent of the original members of the village collectively agree to redevelopment. Usually, two different modes are applied: one is 'comprehensive redevelopment', the other 'integrated improvement'. Whereas the former mode consists of a systematic transformation normally fully demolishing and reconstructing the core area of the urban village, the latter mode aims mainly at improving the living environment, roads and fire protection facilities and refers to inefficiently used old factories or stores within the villages. In the first mode, the redevelopment will be carried out by the economic organization of the village itself, and the land is openly auctioned. In the second mode, a change in the collective construction land use rights is applied for. The land used in comprehensive redevelopment is mainly the land of the old villages. It will be redeveloped as a contiguous piece along with the surrounding land resources, including collective economic land, deserted factory sites and state-owned land. The procedures and steps are quite complex, especially since the transfer from collectively owned land to state-owned land has to be achieved, and quite a lot of traditional and emotional factors as well as interest disagreements come into play here. Anyway, the government found ways to make urban village redevelopment much more attractive for collectives (Guangzhou Municipal Government No. 56, 2009).

In fact, the first mode of 'comprehensive redevelopment' has its weaknesses. It imposes a lot of pressure on the government and requires a huge input of resources and money, namely transaction costs. Only the urban villages that are

234 *Sonia Schoon and Uwe Altrock*

located in the urban core are encouraged to follow this path. As a matter of fact, there are also only a few villages that would choose the removal and reconstruction mode, about 20 per cent of all urban villages. The remaining 80 per cent are not enthusiastic about the first mode since the lower land values in their villages do not allow for such a comprehensive restructuring. Thus, generally speaking, the second mode of 'organizing and managing renovation' is clearly more requested and encouraged by both government and villagers (Interview with H., GZ CC 2009).

No matter what mode of redevelopment is chosen, it should follow the principle called 'transformation first and reconstruction second': changing farmers into urban citizens, changing village committees into residents' committees, changing village collective economic organizations into shareholding companies, changing collective-owned land into state-owned land and converting it to be under urban management and security system supervision (Guangzhou Municipal Government No. 56, 2009: Enclosure 2 (Art. 3 (5)). The reality, though, drags behind this principle. While the transformations of villagers into citizens and collective organizations into shareholding companies have been realized, the other three tasks are difficult to enforce, one the one hand because the traditional village system is hard to overcome due to its persistent durability, and on the other hand because of multiple conflicting interests when it comes to questions of land ownership and land use rights. If the urban village keeps its land collectively, then its properties and rights are also collective and villagers' houses and buildings can only be capitalized by renting them out. However, if it changes its land to state-owned land, villagers can sell and buy their houses and buildings after they have paid 15 per cent of the land assigning fees. Even though it is the villagers' choice, the government generally encourages urban villages in the downtown areas to change their land to state-owned status, whereas this is not compulsory for urban villages in the suburbs (Interview with A., GZ 3OO 2010). Here again, traditional thinking and emotional relationships to family-owned land that can be passed down from generation to generation play a crucial role when it comes to negotiation processes. The government, still acting as a flexible pathfinder open to compromises, also does not necessarily and always stick to all principles in order to push forward or to allow redevelopment in the first place. The mayor of Guangzhou, Zhang Guangning, provides a vivid description concerning the role his government plays during the process of renovation: 'We offer a bucket of water, which is an offer of conditions; how to share the bucket of water is up to the village. Of course, we will try to offer a large bucket, so that the water will not be used up so quickly' (Interview with H., GZ CC 2009). The image of a bucket full of water is quite an ostensive illustration of the incentive policies the government offers; how they are distributed and how they are used can be decided according to the situation and by the urban village itself. This leads us to the practice of experimental urban governance.

Experimental urban governance

The Three Olds Redevelopment policy is both a great leap forward in comprehensively governing urban (re)development, and an experimental approach working out the most appropriate solutions for urban regeneration in a highly fragmented urban space (Schoon 2013). The situation and nature of the process of finding feasible modes to cope with the high diversity of the urban villages that finally culminated in the three olds policies can be described in the words of two high ranking urban planners:

> Guangzhou has defined 138 villages as urban villages. Therefore, the government is very cautious in dealing with them, groping to find out a perfect policy. For example, it tries to pick those villages as experimental sites that have unique and serious problems. Since the urban villages in Guangzhou are usually very large, the renovation must be accordingly carried out in large scale. After some time of groping and probing, Guangzhou proposes "one village one policy" (*yi cun yi ce*). It is the most important general policy of Guangzhou. There is no fixed or specific policy for the renovation. Every village has to carry out the renovation in accordance with its practical situation.
>
> (Interview with C., GZ UPO 2009)

> "One village - one policy" (*yi cun yi ce*) is very useful. Every village has its situation.... There are thousands of different situations in the urban villages in Guangzhou. Therefore, we treat every renovation as a research.... We have to combine the policy with the reality.'
>
> (Interview with H., GZ CC 2009)

'One village one policy' was the first step to become able to take into account the complexity and diversity of the existing problems and at the same time to tighten the urban village redevelopment to official regulations. Nowadays, redevelopment is all about 'balancing the interests': the government represents the interest of a better environment, better control and management, the villagers represent the interest of maximizing the collective benefits, and the developers stand for maximizing economic profits. Therefore, all interest groups are constantly struggling in redevelopment schemes. This process needs coordination, negotiation, and to a large extent, bargaining capacities. The balance of interests in a stage of research, experimentation and coordination is very time-consuming. Therefore, from the time when awareness of urban village problems was raised around the beginning of the new century until the three olds policy was introduced, nearly ten years passed. Chen Yun's slogan: 'groping for stones crossing the river' is perceived as the guiding theme throughout the reform and opening-up era and reflects the uncertainty and openness of the process to reach the intended goal. Pushing something forward in a rush could end up in drowning, whereas reaching the safe side has top priority. The most interesting aspect of experimental governance is the fact that the government by no means loses control. If developments or redevelopments run counter to objective targets or have negative impacts, the government is at all times able and willing to exert coercive measures. But since the Chinese government sees itself as a 'learning authoritarian system' (Heilmann 2008: 13; Heilmann and Perry 2011) following a 'scientific outlook on development'

236 *Sonia Schoon and Uwe Altrock*

(*kexue fazhan guan*), ratified at the 17th Chinese Party Congress in October 2007, it proclaims its willingness to put people first and aim at comprehensive, coordinated and sustainable development. The 'putting people first' approach can definitely be found in the stage of experimenting with urban village redevelopment. Taking villagers' interests as a matter that has to be safeguarded is a big step forward towards taking not only economic and pro-growth interests as first priority, but also as a way of restructuring the city in a more environmentally friendly manner, carrying out the redevelopment process in a comprehensive and more sustainable way.

This leads to the question of what happens to all the other people living in urban villages who are not original villagers; are they put first as well?

The missing part: migrant population

Generally, a large migrant population lives in urban villages, usually far outnumbering the local population. According to a small non-representative quantitative survey conducted by the authors and their research team in three urban villages in Guangzhou in November and December 2007 ($n = 447$) the main reasons for the floating population interviewed to move to the selected case study areas were first, that housing was arranged by their employers (39.4 per cent); second, that they liked the living environment (30 per cent); third, that good opportunities to do business (29.8 per cent) were offered; fourth, that friends, relatives and hometown fellows recommended the urban village to them (24.2 per cent); and fifth, that they also work in the urban village (21.3 per cent) (multiple answers were possible). More than 50 per cent of the respondents spend most of their daytime within the urban village. These figures indicate the importance of urban villages as living and also working environments for them. Over the years, a multifaceted social structure has developed within urban villages consisting of the original population and floating workers (who mainly see the urban village as a cheap residential area and/or a good business environment, planning to earn as much money as possible and to spend as little as possible to later take back accumulated savings and knowledge to their hometowns), but also of young white-collar workers (who use the urban village as their first residential quarter before being able to afford to rent more expensive housing or buy their own apartment), and of course of the local urban poor (who can only afford to live in these low-income areas). How to (re) arrange these urban village residents' structures when demolishing and rebuilding the whole area is an issue that needs careful consideration and planning. The government has adopted some measures to solve the problem, such as constructing low-rent housing or economically affordable houses. Accordingly, the Circular of the State Council on Promoting the Economical and Intensive Land Use (State Council of PRC 2008: No. 3, Article 3 (15)) mentions:

> The structure of the land used for housing shall be optimized. The land used for housing shall be apportioned properly ... to ensure that 70 per cent of the housing land can be used for the construction of subsidized houses, economically affordable houses, price limited houses and the ordinary

medium-small commodity houses with an area less than 90 m^2 and avoid the big commodity houses occupying too much land.

As can be perceived, the cited passage consists of two 'shalls' lacking any binding character, in a 'circular' which as well promulgates phrases that are more or less 'wishes' and function as information material rather than guiding principles. This is also owing to the fact that not enough experiences concerning the management of urban village restructuring with all its implied consequences have so far been collected, so governments are still in the phase of experimenting. In the words of one responsible urban planner: 'We are in the stage of experimentation: it is inevitable that there are defects in it' (Interview with C., GZ UPO 2009).

A sketchy explanation for the disregard of the floating population could be the fact that the three old policies are primarily designed to solve land issues in urban redevelopment. The floating population, not owning properties in the city, therefore tends to be neglected in such processes and is not even considered in participation schemes (Interview with Y., GZ SYSU UGE 2011). Another argument is that migrants' concerns have no direct relation with the GDP of the city, which is said to be the focus of the government. Moreover, their administration is under the responsibility of each migrant's hometown government. Therefore, 'the municipal government does not want to take responsibility for them. In the meantime, they are the 'weak masses' (*ruoshi qunti*) in the city, and lack the rights to stand in for their interests' (Interview with M., UPE SZU 2011). A further definition of floating population and migrant workers says that this population is like 'floating water' and that they consequently cannot share the same rights as the local urban population. They are perceived as just low-paid and temporary workers in the city who will go back to their hometowns taking with them the money earned and knowledge gained anyway.

Some urban planners argue that implementing the second mode of redevelopment will not imply a drastic increase in rents, and the construction of low income residences and affordable housing will allow the urban poor to still live there. But the reality shows that migrants move to other urban villages rather than accepting higher living expenses. It is somewhat obvious that a fundamental structural change will take place after renovation, whether full redevelopment or only partial. The newly built boarding houses in the villages are envisaged to be mainly rented by white-collar workers if the urban village has new commercial buildings, which will increase the villagers' income and is therefore highly welcomed. Besides, at present the population setup in the urban villages is complicated and hard to track, and after the urban villages are transformed into urban communities with a structured and streamlined administration it is expected that 'the whole environment and social order will be better' (Interview with M., GZ BY UPO 2009). Here again, the catchy phrase of 'balancing the interests' can also be interpreted in an ambiguous way: on the one hand the migrants are seen as needed workers, and the urban villages 'undeniably have contributed to the provision of low-cost housing for the mass of rural-to-urban immigrants, thus somewhat alleviating the problems of housing affordability' (Li 2008: 297), while on the other hand migrants are perceived as disruptive factors. What is more important: getting a powerful workforce or getting rid of the lowest class?

238   *Sonia Schoon and Uwe Altrock*

Summing up, in terms of urban management in China, local governments are working in two directions. The priority is to develop the economy of the cities, that is, plainly, to increase GDP and the tax base of the government; the second is the restructuring of the physical environment, mainly to implement the most effective land use, with the protection of ecological environment following. The improvement of incomes, living standards and social welfare of the local residents will not be considered until the tasks above are completed. This can also be traced back to Jiang Zemin's dictum that China first needs the right to develop, only after that can the rights of individuals be improved. Therefore, speaking from the financial and economic angle, compared to the central government, local governments rarely take into account employment, housing and living conditions or the social welfare of the floating population and migrant workers. Those aspects are still more rhetoric than reality. Until now, mostly when workers are urgently needed the government encourages enterprises, companies or other employers to hire the floating population; and usually only when conflicts between employers and migrant employees come up or migrant workers organize strikes that might lead to social unrest, does the government become engaged in favour of workers.

In recent years (starting around 2005), the social problems introduced by migrant workers and the floating population have become noticeably severe with more and more strikes, demonstrations and conflicts between workers and their companies. This is when the governments started to recognize the workers' precarious situation and when accordingly the social welfare conditions and salaries of workers began to improve. In 2011, severe conflicts between the floating and local population in Chaozhou, Shantou and Xintang Town in Zengcheng in Guangzhou marked a turning point in government consideration of floating workers' problems. They are attempting to provide social services for migrant workers in the future, but no official work has been done so far (Interview with W., GZ SYSU SSE 2011).

In conclusion, consciousness of the migrants' and floating population's problems exists and is growing, also in the field of urban planning, but so far the experimental approaches towards finding sustainable solutions for all spheres of economic, political, physical and social problems associated with urban villages are not mature enough to comprehensively solve them. Until appropriate solutions are found, urban villages continue to make significant contributions to settling and managing the floating population despite the various kinds of trouble they cause. Therefore, urban villages in this respect also play a positive role in urban development and there is no need to rush or urge on this particular process of urban regeneration.

Note

1. The districts of Panyu, Huadu, Zengcheng and Conghua are excluded.

References

Altrock, U. and Schoon, S. (2011a) 'The Politics of Upgrading the PRD's Urbanized Villages. [Zhujiang sanjiaozhou diqu chengzhongcun zengzhi de xiangguan zhengce]', *Design Community Zhuqu*, 5: 44–8.

'Three olds redevelopment': advances in urban upgrading in Guangzhou   239

Altrock, U. and Schoon, S. (2011b) 'The Governance of Urban Regeneration in Southern China', *The Governance of Urban Upgrading in Southern China – The Example of Urbanised Villages*. DISP 2011.

Guangdong Province People's Government No. 78 (2009) *Opinions on Promoting "Three-old" Redevelopments and Advancing Intensive and Economic Land Use*.

Guangdong Province People's Government No. 16 (2009) *Notice on Issuing the Working Plan of Establishing Guangdong Province to an Experimental and Demonstration Province for Economical and Intensive Land Use*.

Guangdong Province People's Government No. 134 (1989) *'Regulation of Guangdong Province on Administration of Planning and Construction of Townships (Towns) and Villages'*.

Guangzhou Municipal Government No. 56 (2009) *Opinions of People's Government of Guangzhou City on Accelerating and Promoting the "Three Olds" Redevelopment*.

Heilmann, S. (2008) 'China als lernendes autoritäres System: Experimentierende Staatstätigkeit und wirtschaftliche Modernisierung', *China Analysis* 63, July 2008, in: Sonderseite (Special edn) 'Themen und Thesen der Wirtschaft (Topics and Thesis of the economy)', *Neue Zürcher Zeitung*, Saturday/Sunday, 28–29 June 2008, p. 13. Online. Available: www.chinapolitik.de (Accessed 29 June 2008).

Heilmann, S. and Perry, E. J. (eds) (2011) *Mao's Invisible Hand. The Political Foundations of Adaptive Governance*. Cambridge, MA: Harvard Contemporary China Series 17.

Li, T. (2008) 'The Chengzhongcun Land Market in China: Boon or Bane', *A Perspective on Property Rights' in: International Journal of Urban and Regional Research*, 32(2): 282–304.

Qin, H. (2010) '"Three old" office has been promoted to bureau-level (In Chinese)', *Nanfang Dushibao*, 12 January 2010. Online. Available: http://gcontent.nddaily.com/6/eb/6eb6e75fddec0218/Blog/7ec/fdfb7c.html (Accessed 12 January 2010).

Schoon, S. (2011a) 'The challenges of redeveloping urbanized villages (In Chinese)', *Zhuqu Design Community*, vol. 5: 49–51.

Schoon, S. (2011b) 'The power of conceded informality. Experimental modes of urban restructuring', Conference paper. International Conference on Urban and Regional Development in the 21st Century and Lingnan Forum, Guangzhou, December 2011.

Schoon, S. (2012) 'Niche authority in urbanized villages. Bottom-up codetermination of megacity development', in N. Perera, W. S. Tang (eds), *Transforming Asian Cities: Intellectual impasse, asianizing space, and emerging translocalities*. Abingdon, London: Routledge.

Schoon, S. (2013) 'Three olds redevelopment – an introduction to experimental urban restructuring with Chinese characteristics', in Altrock, U., Schoon, S. (eds), *Maturing Megacities. The Pearl River Delta in Progressive Transformation*. New York: Springer.

State Council of PRC No. 3 (2008) *Circular of the State Council on Promoting Economic and Intensive Land Use*.

State Council of PRC No. 116 (1993) *'Regulation on the construction of villages and market towns'*.

Xinkuai Net (2010) 'Guangzhou "Three-old" Redevelopment Office Opened. Nine Urbanized Villages will be Demolished or Relocated before the Asian Games', (in Chinese) *Xinkuai Net*. Online. Available: http://www.xkb.com.cn/html/xinwen/guangzhou/2010/0225/44839_2.html (Accessed 26 February 2010).

Zeng, N. (2010) 'Administrative structure has just been reformed in Guangzhou. Another organization, the "Three-old" redevelopment office was set up' (in Chinese), *Nanfang Daily Net*, 12 January 2010. Online. Available: http://news.southcn.com/g/2010–01/12/content_8067618.htm (Accessed 12 January 2010).

14 The symbiotic relationship between urban villages and the city

Implications for redevelopment strategies

Yanliu Lin, Bruno De Meulder and Shifu Wang

Introduction

Dynamic urbanization in Guangzhou has led to the emergence and proliferation of "urban village" (chengzhongcun) or "villages in the city" (ViCs). Due to its unique position as the provincial capital and its designation as one of the 14 coastal open cities back in 1984, Guangzhou has attracted a considerable share of capital and mass migrants for labor intensive industries and service sectors. The urban area has expanded markedly in the past 30 years, and consequently, a great number of villages at the fringes of the city have been swallowed up by urban development. Urban villages are created when agricultural land is used for urban development while village settlements remain untouched in order to avoid costly compensation and relocation programmes. Deprived of their traditional agricultural resources, the villagers "illegally" construct their houses to accommodate mass migrants, who are institutionally and economically excluded by the urban system. Although the total area of 138 urban villages in Guangzhou only amounts to 20 percent of the total urban area, they house around 70 percent of migrants who comprise 40 percent of the total urban population (Li 2004). Consequently, urban villages become informal settlements, characterized by overcrowding and high density.

Most scholars have treated urban villages as migrant enclaves, which supply affordable housing for rural migrants (Jie and Taubmann 2002; Zhang *et al.* 2003; Zhang 2005). Some scholars have examined the nature of urban villages as transitional neighborhoods (Lan 2005; Liu *et al.* 2010). A few scholars have paid attention to the relationship between urban villages and urban areas. Huang and Li (2007) analyzed the influence of urban expansion on the sociospatial evolution of Shipai Village in Guangzhou. Hao *et al.* (2011a) studied the land use diversity of urban villages in Shenzhen. They suggested that the land use patterns of urban villages are linked to their locations in the urban fabric, development phases and the surrounding urban development. However, there is a lack of in-depth analysis of the interplay between specific urban villages and urban areas and its implication for redevelopment strategies.

The symbiotic relationship between urban villages and the city   241

This chapter is an attempt to fill this gap. First, it explores the relationships between urban development and the dynamics of urban villages in Guangzhou. Second, it analyzes the proximity between urban villages and urban areas in contemporary Guangzhou. Third, it studies two typical urban villages, with an emphasis on spatial and socioeconomic connections between the urban villages and their surrounding urban environments. This chapter concludes that a vision at the city scale is required for the integration of urban village redevelopment, poverty reduction strategies, economic restructuring and infrastructure networks in the city scale. It suggests that development strategies should strengthen existing connections and emphasize the coproduction of various stakeholders in strategic locations. The findings are based mainly on data collected during four periods of fieldwork (February–April in 2007 and 2008; August–September in 2009, and November in 2010). In order to obtain an integrated picture of urban villages in Guangzhou, we visited several different categories of urban villages in terms of geographical setting, spatial structure, development processes, planning practices and socioeconomic context. Case studies are performed through a combination of literature study and fieldwork (including collection of plans and documentations, observation, in-depth interviews, mapping, photographs, etc.).

The interplay between urban villages and urban areas

Urban development and the dynamics of urban villages

Guangzhou has a long history of more than 2,100 years. Because of its location at the northern tip of the PRD, which is fed by more than a thousand miles of waterways, Guangzhou possesses exceptional advantages as a port, and has been nicknamed the "Silk Road on Water." As a traditional commercial city, there were few industrial areas in the city before 1949. Villages were far away from the city center and were surrounded by a large amount of farmland. They usually had dense and compact spatial structures, which had developed for several hundred years and were organized by clan authorities (Lu and Yang 2004).

From 1949 to 1978, the city emphasized the development of secondary industries and consequently, some industrial areas emerged at the urban fringe (Zhou 2005). The city government requisitioned farmland from villages located at the urban fringe for this development. In close proximity to urban industrial areas and with the improvement of accessibility, these villages started to develop collective industrial sectors. For example, due to the construction of industrial areas, workers' dormitories, and an urban road in the surrounding urban areas, several collective industrial enterprises were established in Lijiao village in the 1970s (Li 2004). However, a majority of villages were left untouched by urban development and experienced little change during this time.

In 1984, Guangzhou was designated as one of the 14 coastal open cities. The new status offered an exceptional opportunity for the city to revitalize its former role as a commercial center and trading port, which in turn stimulated the expansion of tertiary activities (Xu and Yeh 2003). Consequently, the city has markedly

242 *Yanliu Lin, Bruno De Meulder and Shifu Wang*

expanded over the past 30 years. It doubled its urbanized territory from 136 km^2 in 1980 to 276 km^2 in 1998 (Huang and Li 2007). This rapid urbanization was mainly promoted by the 14th and 15th master plans of Guangzhou. In the 1980s, the 14th master plan of Guangzhou was initiated to control the growth of the historical city center and to encourage eastward development along the northern bank of the Pearl River. A new district of Tianhe, which administered a number of villages and towns, was established on the east side of Guangzhou in 1985. Using the opportunity of the 6th National Games held in Guangzhou in 1987, the city started to construct the Tianhe Sports Center in 1984 and the Guangzhou East Railway Station. About 5.2 km^2 of agricultural and storage lands surrounding the Tianhe Sports Center and the railway station were designated for the new CBD development in the late 1980s (Zhao 2004). In order to compete for international investment with other metropolises in the Pearl River Delta, the 15th master plan of Guangzhou (1991–2010) was formulated. Unlike previous plans, this new blueprint abandoned the compact city idea and proposed an enlargement of the built up area to 225 km^2 and 555 km^2 in 2010. The city was divided into three large clusters: the center cluster for political, economic, cultural and external communication uses, the eastern cluster for industrial, port and warehouse development, and the northern cluster for residence and non-polluting industry. Consequently, the city structure has gradually changed from a compact model to one of leapfrogged urban sprawl. A large number of villages at the urban fringe were swallowed by urban development (Figure 14.1). However, the city government usually requisitioned farmland for new development, while leaving village settlements which demanded a high level of compensation and relocation programmes. Consequently, many villages have become "villages in the city", characterized by their dual urban–rural structure.

To deal with the problem of unemployed peasants and facilitate land requisition, a special policy was developed in Guangzhou, called the "Reserved Land Policy" (*liuyongdi zhengce*) (Huang and Li 2007). According to this policy, 8–12 percent of requisitioned farmland has to be reserved for collective industrial and commercial developments. Urban villages have the ownership and the usage rights of this land, but they are not allowed to sell it. Many collective industrial and commercial projects have developed on this land and other collective lands. However, the developments of collective projects are largely influenced by their surrounding environments (Lin *et al.* 2011b; Lin and De Meulder 2011). As the city goes through economic restructuring and social transition, which result in diverse development themes and social restructuring at the city scale, urban villages evolve differently in response to the specific demands of the local and migrant population (Hao *et al.* 2011b).

Although urban village farmland in Guangzhou declined sharply, their total built-up land increased by 18.4 square kilometres between 1990 and 2000 (Li 2004). A considerable amount of the increased built-up land was used for industrial and commercial sectors. Secondary industry was largely developed between 1990 and 1995. Although industrial land amounted to only 2.39 percent of total urban village land in 1990, it had almost doubled and reached 4.59 percent of total

The symbiotic relationship between urban villages and the city 243

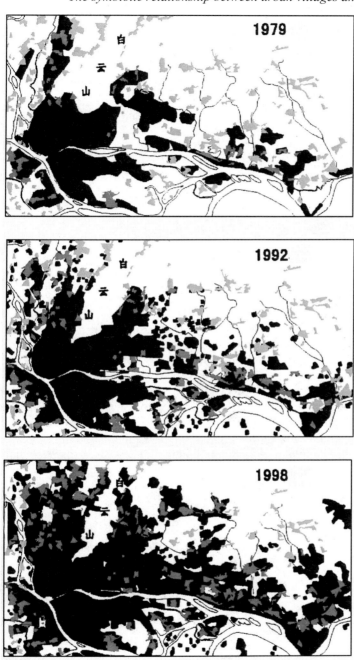

Figure 14.1 Urban development and urban villages.

244   *Yanliu Lin, Bruno De Meulder and Shifu Wang*

urban villages land in 1995 (Li 2004). At the end of the 1990s, there was a boom-ing real estate market. Consequently, new commercial and residential buildings were constructed to replace the aged industrial sites and dilapidated neighbor-hoods in the city center. This process was often accompanied by the relocation of industries to the periphery and residents to new housing estates at the edge of the city (Xu and Yeh 2003). As a result, the tertiary industry of Guangzhou was greatly developed. In 2000, tertiary activities constituted 52.6 percent of the GDP of Guangzhou, surpassing the secondary sector to become the main driving force of the urban economy. These economic and spatial restructuring in urban areas impacted on the development of urban villages. One of the results was that indus-trial land increased slowly, while commercial land increased rapidly (Li 2004). Nevertheless, labor-intensive industries were still the main economic activity of many urban villages, particularly those located at the urban fringe. In 2000, 4.92 percent of urban village land was industrial land, while only 2.27 percent of urban village land was used for tertiary activities (Li 2004).

With the development of urban areas and urban villages, very large numbers of migrants have come to work in labor-intensive industries and service sectors in both urban areas and urban villages. Without citizenship, migrants are excluded from urban low-income public housing. The commercialization of urban housing has also not helped, resulting in no provision of homes for the vast majority of rural migrants who are employed in urban low-paid positions (Zhang 2005). Consequently, villagers "illegally" construct houses to meet the housing demand of migrants. Urban villages provide housing and services at a relatively low stand-ard but at rents which are affordable to low-income households. Thus, the low cost of living makes it possible to keep the wages of the employees of industrial and service sectors low (Hao *et al.* 2011b). In this sense, the development of urban villages greatly contributes to the urban economy.

The above analysis shows that the dynamics of urban villages in Guangzhou have been affected by urban development. In turn, urban villages have responded quickly to the new demand and socioeconomic dynamics of the surrounding urban areas. The development of labor-intensive industries and service sectors in urban villages has complex relationships with the development of the surrounding urban areas. With the rapid development of urban areas and the increasing number of migrants, the demand for residential and service space has significantly exceeded the formal supply in the city. Therefore, urban villages provide alterna-tives to the rigid urban system. They act as low-income neighborhoods for the city, which is incapable of providing a large amount of cheap accommodation for mass migrants during the rapid urbanization process.

The proximity of urban facilities and economic activities

With investment from public and private sectors, the geographies of urban villages changes, from a remote position to a central position in the functioning of the city (Lin *et al.* 2011a). As a result, many urban villages in Guangzhou are in close proximity to urban roads, commercial office complexes, industrial areas, warehouses and public buildings. First, some urban villages in the new city center (such as Shipai village and Xian village) are mixed with commercial office complexes, expensive apartment buildings, universities, and other urban buildings (Figure 14.2). They are well connected to urban road systems and have access to public transportation (such as bus and subway stations). As a result, these urban villages have well-developed tertiary industry which provides services to the surrounding urban areas. Second, most urban villages in Guangzhou are dispersed at the urban fringe, in close proximity to external transportation lines (Figure 14.3), urban industrial areas (Figure 14.4), and warehouses (Figure 14.5). They contain a considerable amount of industrial areas. However, urban villages in the suburbs are less explored, as they are far from urban areas.

In close proximity to urban areas, some urban villages function as service centers in the city. For example, Sanyuanli village, which is close to the central railway station, has developed a wholesale trade in leather and fur; Yangji village which is close to the new CBD has developed a fabrication plant for wood processing and a large market for furniture; and Shipai village, which is close to several universities and science research institutions, has developed several computer towns and numerous IT product shops, which have a national reputation for the scale of their services. These suggest that the development of urban villages

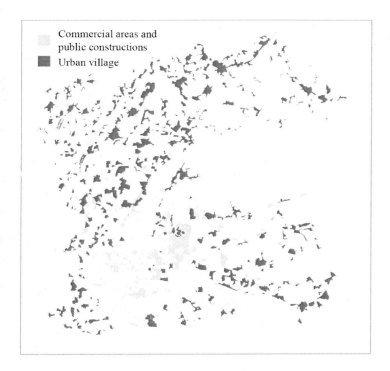

Figure 14.2 Urban villages and commercial areas/public constructions.

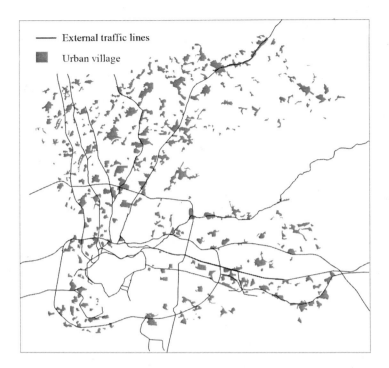

Figure 14.3 Urban villages and external traffic lines.

contributes to urban development. Rather than being "islands," urban villages are part of urban systems and have complex relationships with the surrounding urban areas.

The proximity of urban facilities, amenities, and economic activities is probably one of the most important qualities of urban villages (Lin *et al.* 2011a). "Externalities" (such as state-financed investment in urban roads/public transportation) have greatly enhanced the land value of urban villages. With the increased land use, villagers cooperate with the private sector in the development of collective industrial and commercial projects on reserved land and other collective land. The proximity and accessibility of public services and economic activities also provide job opportunities and living convenience for habitants in urban villages. On the one hand, villagers become "landlords." On the other hand, the majority of migrants work in the manufacturing and service sectors in the surrounding areas, generally within half an hour's walking distance. Both villagers and migrants also use public transport and other urban facilities at the periphery of urban villages. As they have not paid taxes for the use of public services in urban area, it could be argued that the proximity of jobs and public facilities actually cross-subsidizes them and serves to integrate them in market exchange and redistribution spheres (Lin *et al.* 2011a).

The symbiotic relationship between urban villages and the city 247

Figure 14.4 Urban villages and industrial areas.

Two case studies

The above shows that there are complex spatial, social, and economic relationships between urban areas and urban villages. We will examine this argument by studying two specific urban villages (Shipai Village and Tangxia Village) in Tianhe District. Shipai Village is a fairly typical urban village in Guangzhou. Located in the center of Tianhe District, it is one of the oldest urban villages in Guangzhou and was formed in the 1980s (Lan and Guo 2006). It also has the highest building and population density. Tangxia village is another famous urban village in Guangzhou, due to its rich historical legacies and remarkable development. Located at the edge of Tianhe District, Tangxia Village has been greatly transformed in the past 30 years. These two urban villages are different in terms of location, industrial development, spatial structure, land use pattern, and social complex.

Shipai village

Shipai village once occupied an area of 14 km², including 3.2 square kilometres of farmland and other land uses at the beginning of the twentieth century

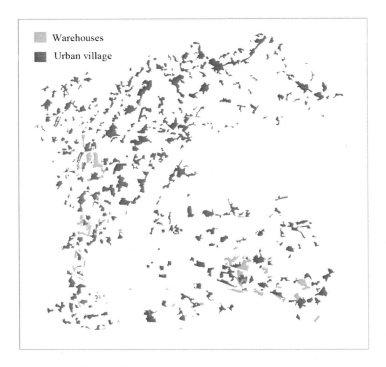

Figure 14.5 Urban villages and warehouses.

(Guangzhou Tianhe District Tangxia Committee 2003). For several hundred years, it remained a traditional village, where villagers were mainly engaged in agriculture. This remained so until 1985, when Tianhe district was established, and the village began to experience a great sociospatial transformation. From 1985 to 1994, an area of 254 hectares (ha), 79.2 percent of the total farmland of Shipai village, was requisitioned by the city for new developments, including urban roads, high-tech zones, software parks, scientific research centers, universities, real estate projects, hospitals, banks, hotels, shopping malls, etc. (Guangzhou Tianhe District Tangxia Committee 2003). Since 1994, Shipai village has become an urban village without farmland. It is now located 1.5 kilometres away from the new city axis. Mixed with urban land uses, tertiary industry has been greatly developed. Most commercial activities are concentrated along two commercial streets (Shipai Western Street and Shipai Eastern Street).

With the improvement of accessibility, two technology streets close to a technology university and several research institutions started flourishing at the end of the 1980s (Guangzhou Tianhe District Shipai Committee 2003). The collective organizations of Shipai village have cooperated with developers in the construction of many small shops, which exhibited and sold the products of universities

The symbiotic relationship between urban villages and the city 249

and institutions. In the 1990s, these small shops were upgraded and integrated into formal urban areas. Such developments also spread into Shipai Western Street. The collective organizations cooperated with the private sector in development projects on both sides of the street. This informal cooperation creates a win-win situation (Lin *et al.* 2011b). On the one hand, for investors, constructions on collective lands are much cheaper than those on urban land that have to pay urban service and facility fees. They also can use cheap peasants' houses inside Shipai village for warehouses and dormitories. On the other hand, the collective's income increases amazingly without taking any investment risk. As a result, many computer towns and numerous IT product shops have been constructed on both sides of Shipai Western Street, the north borderline of the village, and the surrounding urban areas. Shipai village become the biggest computer distribution center in Guangzhou and South China. The services appear to extend beyond the boundary of Shipai village, covering a large area of the city and even a region. In close proximity to several universities and urban roads, Shipai Eastern Street has also become a flourishing commercial street, with more than 100 small shops (clothing shops, restaurants, etc.). This inferior quality development provides cheap services for urban areas, as most of the customers are university students.

With the rapid urbanization and self-development of Shipai village in the 1990s, large numbers of migrants came to work in the computer towns and the surrounding service sectors. Most of them lived in Shipai village, which provides them with cheap accommodation and is in close proximity to their working places. In 2008, 45 percent of tenants in Shipai village were engaged in the IT industry; 35 percent serviced restaurants and shops in the surrounding urban areas; 15 percent serviced the village; and 5 percent were unemployed (Ling and Xing 2008). With continuous migration, the pressure for densification of the village became extreme. Three-story brick concrete structure buildings were replaced by seven- to eight-floor beam-post frame structure buildings, with cantilever floors. As a result, Shipai village become the densest urban village in Guangzhou. Although the total area of the village is less than 0.7 square kilometres, it provides dormitories for 70–80,000 tenants and about 10,000 villagers. Due to overexploitation, the "handshake and kissing buildings" street profile has become the new prototypical morphological condition. Many village main roads and alleyways are also blocked and narrowed by newly added constructions. A considerable number of houses lack sufficient sunlight and ventilation.

With increasing migration, strong demand for commercial services is generated. There are more than 1,000 small shops concentrated in four open markets and several village main roads. These shops not only offer opportunities for migrant entrepreneurs, but also provide cheap services for the daily lives of migrants and villagers. Over the past few years, we have observed that many new shops have been established along the village main roads and provide services for people who work in computer towns and other service sectors at the periphery of Shipai village. Consequently, these roads tended to be overcrowded. It appears that these are strategic places, where specific actions to deal with economic opportunities and problems (poor infrastructure, overcrowding, and so on) could take place.

250 *Yanliu Lin, Bruno De Meulder and Shifu Wang*

Tangxia village

Similar to Shipai village, Tangxia village was once a traditional village surrounded by a large amount of farmland. Due to the rapid development of the surrounding urban areas in the past 30 years, the village has dramatically changed. Six kilometres away from the new CBD center, much of the farmland of Tangxia village was requisitioned for the construction of urban infrastructure, several urban neighborhoods, and a high-technology industrial park. Up to 2000, the remaining total area of Tangxia village shrank to less than 2 square kilometres, while farmland reduced to less than 33 ha (Guangzhou Tianhe District Tangxia Committee 2003). Mixed with urban areas, Tangxia village became an urban village with little farmland. The development of the urban village has been greatly influenced by the development of the surrounding urban areas. First, the enlargement of Guangshen Railway, Zhongshan Road and Huangpu Road, as well as the construction of Guangyuan Highway, strengthened its connection with the new CBD. Second, numerous high-tech enterprises and exhibition centers were established in Tianhe Science Park. They not only generated commercial opportunities, but also caused the individual housing rental market in Tangxia village to flourish (Lin and De Meulder 2011). The development of the urban village in turn has contributed to urban development. For example, several large-scale specialized markets (such as steel products markets, decorating materials markets, and electrical equipment markets) have been established on the collective lands and provide services for the city. The construction of a Best Fresh Supermarket in 1997 has also greatly promoted the development of the surrounding areas (Guangzhou Tianhe District Tangxia Committee 2003).

With compensation from requisitioned land and improved accessibility, the collective organizations established two industrial zones on reserved land (Guangzhou Tianhe District Tangxia Committee 2003). In the early 1990s, these industrial zones contained more than 100 enterprises, including technology companies, papermaking factories, garment manufacturers, motor repair shops, etc. Through a site visit in September 2009, we observed that many collective projects were concentrated on collective lands that were adjacent to urban roads. These projects focused on the development of manufacturing businesses and small shops, based on collective–private partnerships. However, due to the decline of labor-intensive industries in the past few years, many buildings were vacant or in poor condition. With the development of the surrounding urban areas and the increasing land value of the collective lands, these areas could be easily occupied by new types of development in the near future. New integrated strategies are urgently needed for their redevelopment.

Mass rural migrants and new graduates have been attracted by the industrial sectors and moved to live in Tangxia village. Our survey showed that the majority of rural migrants worked in labor-intensive industries, while most new graduates were employed in the Tianhe Science Park. In order to accommodate the increasing population, villagers have extended their one- to three-story houses into four or five storeys. Over the past few years, we have observed that peasant houses

The symbiotic relationship between urban villages and the city 251

have gradually "grown up" to accommodate the increasing numbers of migrants and new graduates, who were attracted by the new development of the surrounding urban areas. Many new shops were also established along several village main roads that connected to urban roads. Furthermore, about 10 private schools for migrant children were dispersed through the ViC. Excluded from public schools in the city, migrants turn to private schools for their children, relying on reciprocity and market mechanisms (Lin *et al.* 2011a). However, poor access to state funding has caused many schools to fall into disrepair and be shut down by local government.

Discussion

These two cases studies show that there are multi-relationships between urban villages and urban areas. The proximity of urban roads, industrial areas, commercial activities and amenities greatly contributes to the development of urban villages. The inferior quality developments on collective land in turn provide services for the city. They play an important role in urban development. However, it should be noted that cheap collective lands and peasant houses are crucial for these developments. Redevelopment strategies for urban villages should take account of these. The residential areas of urban villages provide available housing and services for both migrants and new graduates, who contribute to urban development but are largely excluded from the formal urban system. They also provide cheap land or buildings for private schools for migrants' children. In this sense, urban villages not only function as low-income neighborhoods in the city but also provide public goods for migrants. Nevertheless, the development of urban villages results in poor infrastructure and living conditions. Migrants are also largely excluded from public facilities in urban villages. There is an urgent need to improve the existing living environment and create more public facilities which are accessible to migrants. Although the spatial layouts of urban villages are different from urban areas, there are some specific connections, such as the village main roads.

As mentioned above, these two urban villages have many common aspects. However, they are different in terms of location, industrial development, spatial structure and redevelopment opportunity. Generally speaking, Shipai village is a typical case of the mature ViC, while Tangxia village is representative of the growing ViC. Located in the new city center, Shipai village is intensively involved in the development of the tertiary industry that mainly provides services to urban territory. In close proximity to urban industrial areas and traffic lines, Tangxia village has well-developed labor-intensive industries. There are few new constructions in the residential areas of Shipai village, while houses are gradually "growing up" in the residential areas of Tangxia village. There are more opportunities for spatial and economic restructuring in Tangxia village, as it contains a larger amount of collective projects at the periphery and has better infrastructure, newer houses and more open space in the residential areas. Integrated strategies are urgently needed for the (re)development of urban villages at the urban fringe.

Redevelopment strategies

Although urban villages provide affordable accommodation for rural migrants in many Chinese cities, the majority of existing planning approaches to urban villages are based on a "demolition–redevelopment" model, which is dominated by market mechanisms and does not provide homes for low-income rural migrants (Zhang 2005). However, many redevelopment projects for urban villages, which aim to replace the existing spatial layout with modern towers and a large infrastructure, have in fact not gone beyond the initial study state, with lack of realization caused by conflicts of interest among various stakeholders (Lin *et al*. 2011a,b). On the one hand, municipal governments are incapable of investing in the reconstruction of urban villages, proposing that developers and the collective organizations can self-finance redevelopment projects. On the other hand, villagers are worried that they might not acquire enough compensation and would be in conflict with city governments. Only a few urban villages (such as Liede village and Linhe village) with very high land value are under market-oriented redevelopment. Since 2010, the redevelopment of urban villages in Guangzhou has been embedded in another redevelopment strategy called "three olds redevelopment (*san jiu gaizao*)." This redevelopment strategy focuses on the regeneration of old urban areas (*jiu cheng*), old villages (*jiu cun*), and old urban factories (*jiu chang*). As "old villages," 52 urban villages are planned to be demolished and redeveloped. Apparently, this strategy did not consider the important role of urban villages in the functioning of regular urban areas.

The market-oriented redevelopment of urban villages has been criticized by many scholars in recent years. These projects not only demolish the existing spatial layouts of urban villages, which contain the survival strategies of migrants, but also destroy the proximity of urban services, jobs and amenities, which have a redistributive income for low-income migrants and are crucial for the urban system (Lin *et al*. 2011a). Without a policy that would lead to the provision of affordable housing for migrants, a possible adverse consequence is the reproduction of shanty settlements in other parts of the city, when low-income migrants are forced to move out from urban villages to search for alternative places to live (Zhang 2005). Large scale redevelopment also could conceivably lead to large scale intra-city migration of displaced tenants, promoting new development pressure in the outer districts and the decline of their environmental conditions (Hao *et al*. 2011a). Therefore, many scholars suggest that, instead of demolition and redevelopment, upgrading the existing spatial structure could be an alternative approach for the sustainable redevelopment of urban villages.

Regarding the multi-relationships between urban villages and urban development, a vision at the city scale, which specifies the role of urban villages in the functioning of regular urban areas, is required for mixed development and coexistence (Lin and De Meulder 2012). The redevelopment of urban villages should integrate poverty reduction strategies (such as providing education programmes for migrants and upgrading low-income neighborhoods), economic restructuring, and urban road networks at the city level. Consensus building between multi-stakeholders

The symbiotic relationship between urban villages and the city 253

(including multi-level governments, the collective organizations, developers, etc.) is required for integrated development. A long-term perspective is also required for the integration of different actions in a specific urban village (Lin and De Meulder 2012). Effective regulations should be made for urban village planning and building (re)construction. The redevelopment of collective project sites seems a great opportunity for economic restructuring in both urban areas and urban villages (in particular those located at the urban fringe), replacing decayed labor-intensive industries with cultural and high-end industries as well as advanced services. Close collaboration of the central government, the provincial government, and the municipal government may well be required for the urban village redevelopment. Without redistributive resources (such as comprehensive financial support) from the state, urban village redevelopment that closely combines social projects and low-income neighborhood upgrading seems difficult.

Conclusion

The study shows that there are multi-relationships between urban areas and urban villages. Urban areas are primary areas which are rigid, inflexible, and regular, while urban villages are secondary areas which are loose, flexible, easily adapted, and not well organized (Lin and De Meulder 2012). Both of them together function as a whole. Urban villages are informal settlements in the formal city and specific areas in general areas. They respond quickly to new demands and socio-economic dynamics in the city and provide alternatives to the rigid and formal urban system. They not only function as low-income neighborhoods in the city, but also provide services for the surrounding urban areas. They allow the integration of flexible workers (such as temporary workers) into the urban system and provide resources for marginal social groups. They also facilitate substandard developments (such as small shops, specialized markets, and labor-intensive sectors) that serve the city. Although there are many problems, many opportunities also exist. Rather than "cancers" in the city, urban villages could be used as driving forces for the further development of the city (Lin and De Meulder 2012).

However, the current redevelopment strategies of urban villages neglect the positive role of urban villages in the functioning of urban areas. Market-oriented redevelopment projects destroy the proximity of jobs, living, and public facilities, which provide a redistribution income for migrants and is crucial for the urban system. They also demolish low-income neighborhoods in the city and wipe out substandard developments that are important for the urban economy. In order to achieve a balance between economic growth and social equity, the role of the state in redistribution (such as subsidizing the improvement of public facilities and housing for low-income migrants) should be emphasized. Regarding the complex spatial, social and economic relationships between urban areas and urban villages, a vision at the city level is required for coexisting and mixed development. Integrated strategies are urgently needed for the (re)development of urban villages.

254 Yanliu Lin, Bruno De Meulder and Shifu Wang

References

Guangzhou Tianhe District Shipai Committee (ed.) (2003) *Shipai Cunzhi (Annals of Shipai Village)*, Guangzhou: Guangdong People's Press.

Guangzhou Tianhe District Tangxia Committee (ed.) (2003) *Tangxia Cunzhi (Annals of Tangxia Village)*, Guangzhou: Guangdong People's Press.

Hao, P., Geertman, S., Hooimeijer, P. and Sliuzas, R. (2011) "The land use diversity of urban villages in Shenzhen." unpublished paper presented to 2nd International Conference on China's Urban Transition and City Planning, Cardiff.

Hao, P., Sliuzas, R. and Geertman, S. (2011) "The development and redevelopment of urban villages in Shenzhen," *Habitat International* 35(2): 214–24.

Huang, Q. L. and Li, T. (2007) "In the shadow of the metropolis – case study on the urban village in Guangzhou, China," unpublished paper presented to 1st International Conference on China's Transition and City Planning, Cardiff.

Jie, F. and Taubmann, W. (2002) "Migrant enclaves in large Chinese cities," in J. R. Logan (ed.), *The New Chinese City: Globalization and Market Reform*, Oxford: Blackwell Publishers.

Lan, Y. Y. and Guo, Z. L. (2006) "The community security system of village in the city and its significance for urbanization: a case study of village in the city in Guangzhou" (chengzhongcun de shequ baozhang ji chengshihua yiyi: yi Guangzhou yi chengzhongcun wei li de yanjiu), *Social Science Front Bimonthly*, 2: 188–93.

Lan, Y. Y. (2005) *Village in the City: the Field Study on a 'New Village Community'* (*Dushi li de cunzhuang: guanyu yige 'xincunshe gongtongti' de shidi yanjiu*), Beijing: Three Unite Book Shop.

Li, J. F. (2004) *The Renewal of "Villages in the City" (Chengzhongcun de gaizao)*, Beijing: Science Press.

Lin, Y. L. and De Meulder, B. (2011) "The role of stakeholders in the bottom-up planning processes of Guangzhou, China," *Journal of Urbanism*, 4(2): 175–90.

Lin, Y. L. and De Meulder, B. (2012) "A conceptual framework on the urban project approach for the sustainable redevelopment of 'villages in the city' in Guangzhou," *Habitat International*, 36: 380–7.

Lin, Y. L., De Meulder, B. and Wang, S. F. (2011a) "Understanding the 'village in the city' in Guangzhou: economic integration and development issue and their implications for the urban migrant," *Urban Studies*, 48(16): 3575–90.

Lin, Y. L., De Meulder, B. and Wang, S. F. (2011b) "From village to metropolis: a case of morphological transformation in Guangzhou, China," *Urban Morphology*, 15(1): 5–20.

Ling, H. S. and Xing (2008) "Is the redevelopment of 'villages in the city' an opportunity or challenge?" *Information Daily*, 14 January.

Liu, Y. T., He, S., Wu, F. and Webster, C. (2010) 'Urban Villages under China's rapid urbanization: Unregulated assets and transitional neighborhoods', *Habitat International*, 34 (2): 135–44.

Lu, Y. D. and Yang, G. S. (eds) (2004) *Chinese Old Dwellings (Zhongguo mingju jianzhu)*, Guangzhou: South China University of Technology Press.

Xu, J. and Yeh, Anthony G. O. (2003) "City profile," *Cities*, 20(5): 361–74.

Zhang, L., Zhao, S. X. B. and Tian, J. P. (2003) "Self-help in housing and chengzhongcun in China's urbanization," *International Journal of Urban and Regional Research*, 27(4): 912–37.

The symbiotic relationship between urban villages and the city 255

Zhang, L. (2005) "Migrant enclaves and impact of redevelopment policy in Chinese cities," in L. J. C. Ma and F. L. Wu (eds), *Restructuring the Chinese City: Changing Society, Economy and Space*, New York: Routledge.

Zhao, G. M. (2004) "Urban Shopping Malls and the Transformation of the Urban Spatial Structure in Guangzhou," unpublished Master's thesis, Department of Architecture, Urban and Regional Planning, K. U. Leuven.

Zhou, X. (2005) *The Evolution of Urban Morphology in Guangzhou (Guangzhou chengshi xingtai yanjin)*, China Architecture & Building Press.

15 Planning for *chengzhongcun* in Guangzhou and Shenzhen

Redevelopment in the Chinese context

Him Chung

Introduction

Recently, the literature on 'urban villages' (*chengzhongcun*) has been growing. Urban villages are an interesting, yet complicated, feature of rapidly developing Chinese cities. Conventional discussions on urban villages generally focus on three issues: (1) migrants, (2) housing and (3) land use. Urban villages were initially considered to be migrant settlements but the presence of native villagers and their control over economic and social resources has reasserted their uniqueness (Chung 2010). Despite this, a significantly high proportion of migrants living in these settlements have made urban villages an eye-catching urban phenomenon. Zheng *et al.* (2009), in their Beijing survey, investigated the housing consumption behaviour of migrants and explored the rationale behind their agglomeration in urban villages. Lin *et al.* (2011) further suggest that, while migrants are excluded from accessing most of the social goods in the city, urban villages have provided them with accessible, informal resources to support their housing, education and employment needs. Focusing on the heterogeneous nature of migrants in urban villages, Liu (2000) revealed their differences with migrant communities derived from network migration.

Housing is another area that has received a lot of scholarly attention. Adopting a functional perspective, Zhang *et al.* (2003), Song *et al.* (2008) and Wang *et al.* (2009) emphasise the role of urban villages in providing affordable accommodation. They consider such a function as a spontaneous response to the increasing demand for low cost accommodation in cities as a result of a growing rural–urban migration. They also think urban villages have reduced the cost of urbanisation by maintaining social stability in the absence of government support for migrants. Unlike studies and reports which describe urban villages as hotbeds of unlawful activities (Zhang 2003; Wei 2000), these studies thus indicate a positive view of these settlements. The focus on housing has led to concerns about land and its development. For example, Tian (2008) focuses on property rights within urban villages and suggests that incomplete and unsecured property rights have led to an increase in the informal land and housing market.

While these studies have addressed the function of urban villages, very little attention has been given to planning and related issues or to their implications

Planning for chengzhongcun *in Guangzhou and Shenzhen* 257

for urban development and impacts on urban residents. Urban planning, in many cases, is highlighted as a background issue in discussions of urban villages. Chung (2009), however, has made an initial effort to investigate the planning system of urban villages. Through his investigation of the planning, administration and financing of urban village redevelopments in Shenzhen city, he shows how government authorities are seeking to institutionalise a 'space of disorder' into the governance system. Indeed, in a country where city planning is considered a form of central regulation (Xie and Costa 1993), an investigation of the planning system and practices should bring to light the government's intention for redevelopment and its underlying logic. In particular, in the context of China's economic reform and power decentralisation, an investigation of the local planning system enables a better understanding on how central power is translated into local power. This localization process implies that reasons for planning and redevelopment are apparently not the same across time and space. Although the role of local government in planning has received a lot of scholarly attention, the way that local agendas differ across various geographical contexts remains poorly discussed. By comparing the planning for redevelopment in Shenzhen and Guangzhou cities, this chapter explores the two cities' particular way of handling redevelopment, examines the underlying reasons for such differences and discusses the effectiveness of each approach. Through an investigation of these issues, this chapter attempts to explore redevelopment plans in the context of China's government-led and land-based economy. Information on Shenzhen's planning system is based on Chung (2009), while information on Guangzhou is drawn from government documents, news reports and interviews of planners and stakeholders.

Town planning in the Chinese context

Unlike in Western countries, where planning systems are embedded in democratic political systems, liberal economies and vibrant societies, China's planning system has developed in a completely different context – initially from a centrally planned economy and subsequently from a hybrid system characterised by both state planning and market mechanisms. This spatiality suggests that planning in China has its own distinctive operational logic. Yet, rather than seeing China as the exception, it is suggested by Friedmann (2005: xxv) that 'China must be understood on its own terms'. The implication of this perspective on any discussion of China's urban planning system is that any attempts to understand planning systems and practices should go beyond the preoccupation of mainstream, Western rationalities and consider multiple truths (Connelly and Richardson 2005; Watson 2006) and the conditions which give rise to them.

Concerns about the different settings that affect planning approaches suggest the importance of taking into account local situations and conditions when attempting to understand planning practice in China. This has also been highlighted by scholars who focus on Chinese issues. Reviewing the literature on China's urban planning approach, Tang (2000: 351) criticises its failure to link

258 *Him Chung*

analysis with the state's 'governmental reasoning and practice'. He highlights the traditions of the Chinese state and suggests that meaningful discussions on the country's urban planning system should consider political rationality. In other words, the role of the state, its governing techniques and discourses on China's urban planning system need to be taken seriously (Tang 2000). Further, examining land and housing reform in China, He and Wu (2009) also highlight the differences between the country's 'neoliberal urbanism' and the Western stereotype. Although these studies focus on different aspects of China's planning system, their arguments have provided useful insights into the country's specific conditions and the differences stemming from them. The spatiality of China's town planning system is thus demonstrated by the country's changing political and economic contexts and the planning framework embedded in it. It is to this subject that the discussion now turns.

When the People's Republic of China was established in 1949, the country followed the Soviet experience and established a command economy to regulate production and consumption, allocate resources and provide community facilities and infrastructure. This traditional, planned economy was regarded by Tang (1994) as a 'police state', characterised by 'total administration of the economy and society' (Ng and Tang 1999: 593). Lying behind such a system was a rigid, top-down mode of governance, with the central state at the top controlling the political, social and economic aspects of life through centrally imposed policies. Government policies and operations were guided by Chairman Mao's blueprint, which combined socialist ideologies, Chinese reality at the time and the Communist Party's war-time experience, which aimed to build a socialist and industrialised China.

The adoption of a command economy suggests that city planning was also 'a form of central planning' (Xie and Costa 1993: 104). According to Fisher (1962: 252), planning in socialist cities aims: '(1) to correct the ills inherited from the era of capitalism and (2) to develop a new pattern for the city which will indicate clearly the inherent unity of the people, the classlessness of the society'. Under Mao's desperate attempts to industrialise the country, these objectives were translated into the construction of 'producer cities' (*shengchan chengshi*) and the promotion of self-reliance, with a strong emphasis on the former (Ma 1979; Kwok 1981; Xie and Costa 1993). Studies on urban planning and development in the pre-reform period vividly demonstrate that urban planning was used to support the national development strategy of industrial construction – a duplication of the Soviet model of development (Yeh and Wu 1999). Its major task was to coordinate the physical design of industrial construction projects which were decided by the central state. Precisely, the focus of urban planning was to select new industrial locations and factory sites, design the layout of industrial towns and arrange infrastructure for industrial development (Kwok 1981). The central allocation of resources in a command economy suggested that wherever there were industrial projects approved by the central state's economic plan, land development followed. Thus, unlike planning in the West which aims to control undesirable development, planning in China aims to stimulate industrial development.

Planning for chengzhongcun *in Guangzhou and Shenzhen* 259

Economic reform since 1978 has shifted the state's governing logic from Mao's idealism to Deng Xiaoping's pragmatism, but it has not changed the nature of planning. Urban planning is still considered a government process. The traditional, top-down mode of planning has been retained, despite the fact that it has been heavily criticised (Ng and Wu 1995; Xu and Ng 1998; Ng and Tang 1999). If urban planning in the pre-reform period represented a single-handed approach to land development dominated by a unitary state, post-1978 has seen new ideologies, new players and multiple approaches, hence giving rise to diversified outcomes.

Under Deng's pragmatism, town planning came to be considered an 'instrument', echoing the argument that China's market reforms and grassroot elections are a governing technique aimed at solving economic problems resulting from a rigid command economy and improving the power of the state, respectively. A significant development in the reform era that has affected the instrumentalisation of town planning is the decentralisation of decision-making power. Land use decisions and planning rights have been devolved to the government at the city level, allowing local authorities to take local characteristics into consideration and hence produce plans and mechanisms that suit local needs. The impact of power decentralisation on urban planning and local development has been addressed by scholars such as Xu and Ng (1998), Zhang (2002) and Wu (2007). Planning has become a powerful tool for city governments to create economic drivers for local growth (Mertha 2005). Even though the increasing role of city governments in planning and development has been investigated, concerns about local authorities' discretionary power and its impact on the effectiveness of planning controls have also been raised (Ng and Tang 1999).

Town planning, therefore, has become an important avenue to translate decentralised administrative power into local, territorial power. Central to this process is the institutionalisation of the planning system at the city level, an attempt to consolidate what Mann (2003) calls the 'infrastructural power' of a state. At the same time, the pace of urban expansion has accelerated to include increasingly more space/land under the control of the planning system. These two developments form a vital part of the power consolidation process in which the local state 'develops its agenda and finds its own agency' (Hsing 2010: 8). This territorialisation of the local state (Hsing 2010) allows a city government to extend and strengthen its control over land and other resources, making it much more than an agent of the central state. Tang (1997, 2006) makes a similar, but broader, argument. He suggests that town planning in China is a governing technology which allows the state to regulate the spatial structure of a city.

The way in which local states attempt to dominate a territory is a highly contested process. Desperate attempts to promote land-based urbanisation (Lin 2007) and confrontations and resistance stemming from land (re)development provide good illustrations of how this process works (Ming 2010). In response to societal challenges, normative concepts like 'people centred' (*yiren weiben*) and 'harmonious society' (*hexie shehui*) have been introduced to soften the social impact. At the same time, territorialisation of the local state has to follow the general

260 *Him Chung*

framework of the central state, and is thus subject to central regulatory measures, including financial and credit measures, policies and hard targets. Therefore, it is within the context of the territorialisation of local states that this chapter seeks to investigate urban village redevelopments and their planning.

Urban redevelopment and urban villages

Urbanisation in China is a fragmented process which fails to integrate urban and rural areas. Lying behind this fragmentation is the country's prolonged sociospatial-institutional dualism between urban and rural (Tang and Chung 2000). This dualism suggests that urban and rural systems are operating independently and are incompatible with each other. Urban land use, for example, is managed by the city government, planning, land resources and construction authorities, while rural land use is regulated by the agricultural ministry. Urban land is owned by the state (*guo jia*), while rural collective units (*ji ti*), such as villagers' committees, village groups and village and township collective economic entities, claim full ownership of rural land, including farmland and residential land. The rights associated with land ownership are different: the land use rights of urban land are transferable but this does not apply to rural land. Further, the planning of urban and rural land is regulated by two incompatible sets of regulations – the *City Planning Act* and the *Village and Township Planning and Management Ordinance* respectively (Zou 2003). Urbanisation does not automatically reconcile this dual regulatory structure. As a result, when a village's farmland is being encroached upon and its residents physically designated to a city, its land use, planning and public administration are still regulated by the rural organisational network. The failure to integrate these aspects into the urban system gives rise to a fragmented urban space where urban planning and associated administrative requirements are not effectively implemented. Such a space is not just imagined, but physically exists as an urban village (*chengzhongcun*), and many of these are commonly found in rapidly urbanising Chinese cities, including in the cities of Shenzhen and Guangzhou.

Chinese scholars, such as Li (2004), Xie (2003), Zhang (2003), Jing (1999) and Fang *et al.* (1999), suggest that urban villages are an inevitable outcome of China's urbanisation. Jing (1999) argues that the introduction of the *Land Management Law* institutionalised urban–rural dualism in regard to land management and hindered the reconciliation of both when cities encroached on the countryside. Likewise, Tan and He (2002) argue that the dualism in China's social and economic systems, such as the household registration system, has also played a crucial role in the formation of urban villages. This institutional and spatial fragmentation has created what Chung (2009, 2010) considers to be 'a space of disorder' in Chinese cities. This is vividly illustrated by the chaotic situation in urban villages characterised by illegal construction, indiscriminate land use and other unlawful activities.

These spaces of disorder represent an obstacle for the territorialisation of the local state. The redevelopment of urban villages is thus an attempt to overcome

Planning for chengzhongcun *in Guangzhou and Shenzhen* 261

such obstruction which, as noted, was created by the country's fragmented urbanisation process. By doing this, redevelopment also completes the unfinished business of urbanisation by reconciling the incompatible urban and rural systems. Flaunting the banner of improving land use efficiency and city competitiveness, redevelopment of urban villages in both Guangzhou and Shenzhen cities is associated with an institutionalisation process which intends to convert rural land ownership into national ownership, include the planning and development of these spaces of disorder into the urban planning system and transform the rural collective unit into one that fits into an urban economy. Redevelopment, in this sense, is a political process which aims to spatially expand the governance and institutional network and hence consolidates state power at the city level. This process is concomitant with the territorialisation of local power.

Expanding the governance network allows the local government to have better control of, or monopolistic access to, economic and social resources and hence creates a controllable/predictable mechanism for capital accumulation. This argument echoes He and Wu's (2009) analysis of China's seemingly neoliberal urban redevelopment, in which the state maintains its control over valuable resources and 'creates conditions for market operation' (He and Wu 2009: 296). The control of urban land ownership and housing, for instance, has allowed city governments to capitalise on urban land, thus contributing to the country's rapid pace of urban development and subsequently forming a land-based urban economy (Lin 2007). While the huge amount of revenue generated from land development has become a major source of income for city governments (Lin and Yi 2011), the latter have further exaggerated the pace and scale of urban expansion, resulting in a growing number of land appropriations, forced evictions and dislocation. The Chinese government at the central level has responded to aggressive urbanisation and its associated problems by imposing land use controls (such as agricultural land protection) and land development quotas for cities and counties. In the context of a land-based urban economy, actions to control land development have challenged the vested interests of local governments. In a country where central orders and regulations are always resisted and distorted, city governments always have their counter-measures to respond to regulations imposed by authorities at a higher level. In this case, urban redevelopment bypasses the control of land use/development quota, as parcels for redevelopment are arguably not included in a city's annual land development quota. This weak link has encouraged cities to launch large scale redevelopments in urban areas, including in areas of old villages and factories and in rundown urban districts. In Guangzhou, an inception report suggests that there is an additional 318 km^2 of land available for redevelopment – 38 per cent from old factory sites, 9 per cent from rundown urban districts and 53 per cent from old villages (Yuexiu Government 2010). Based on an annual expansion of 20 km^2, it is estimated that this land stock will allow the Guangzhou government to keep pace with urban construction until 2020 (Yuexiu Government 2010).

Thus, redevelopment of urban villages is a vital process in the territorialisation of local power. It is neither a purely environmental upgrade project nor a rational response to 'urban problems' or 'corners of urbanisation'. At one level, it is a

262 *Him Chung*

powerful economic engine to drive growth and local revenue – territorialisation in an economic sense. In a broader context, it is a political process which aims to expand government control. Redevelopment as a territorialisation process is a contested one. City governments have initiated different ways to implement redevelopment to meet targets, or to bypass restrictions, set by governments at a higher level, on the one hand, and to achieve local agendas on the other. The discussion now turns to the particular way in which the cities of Shenzhen and Guangzhou have tackled the redevelopment of urban villages.

Urban villages in Shenzhen and Guangzhou

Both Guangzhou and Shenzhen were among the first cities to benefit from the country's economic reforms in general and the coastal development strategy in particular. Guangzhou is the provincial capital of Guangdong and has a history spanning thousands of years, whereas Shenzhen city is a product of China's economic reform. Despite the big difference in history, both cities have experienced rapid urbanisation, a massive influx of migrant workers, large scale urban redevelopment and inadequate housing. The similar development experience suggests both cities are facing similar planning problems.

Urban villages are a common feature found in the urban districts of Guangzhou and Shenzhen. According to Ding (2005), there were 241 urban villages in Shenzhen with 91 located in the Shenzhen Special Economic Zone. In Guangzhou city, the provincial capital located about 100 km northwest of Shenzhen, there were 139 urban villages with 45 found in the city proper (*Yangcheng Evening Post* 2000). These settlements were initially identified by academics and urban planners in the early 1990s (Zhou 1993). However, not until 2000 did the authorities begin to take action to tackle the problems found in these settlements. This development could perhaps be explained by the local state's desire to utilise precious yet limited land resources.

The country's economic reform since 1978, as well as globalisation more broadly, has resulted in keen competition between cities in the Pearl River Delta (Xu and Yeh 2005). In Shenzhen, preferential city policies successfully transformed the economy from an agricultural one to one dominated by export-oriented industries (Ng 2003). Since the 1990s, Shenzhen has adjusted its economy to maintain its pioneering position in economic reform, as well as in regional competition. The strong desire to develop the city into a world class metropolis has pushed the Shenzhen government to adopt comprehensive measures to find land to (re)develop. According to the *Shenzhen City Master Plan* (1996–2010), the city will be transformed into an international modern metropolis, concentrating on financial, communication and new commercial services industries. While the future of Shenzhen is portrayed as a garden city, with new industries, development is constrained by the shortage of land. The total area of Shenzhen city is 1,952.8 km^2 while the Shenzhen Special Economic Zone accounts for 327.5 km^2. During its transformation from a border town to one of the most prosperous cities in China, Shenzhen's population increased from 0.3 million to 8.6 million between

Planning for chengzhongcun *in Guangzhou and Shenzhen* 263

1979 and 2007 (Shenzhen Statistical Bureau 2008) and its economy evolved from one dominated by primary industries to one today dominated by secondary and tertiary industries. Increasing population growth and the economic restructuring process, as well as other development targets set forth by the Five Year Plan, have placed extra demands on space. This suggests that the existing land stock in Shenzhen city, in particular land in the Shenzhen Special Economic Zone, is insufficient to satisfy the growing land use demand. While land available for development is bounded by Shenzhen's administrative boundary, the dearth of available land for further development has thus given the authority a strong motivation to redevelop urban villages to improve land use efficiency.[1]

Unlike Shenzhen, Guangzhou does not have the imminent problem of land shortage. Land resources, which facilitate the city's plan to improve its competitive power and desire to become a modern metropolis 'leading the whole province, radiating Southern China and influencing South-east Asia' (Guangzhou Yearbook Editorial Committee 2001), have been provided by a series of territorial expansions in the past decade. In 2000, Guangzhou city had a substantial boundary adjustment, with two adjacent counties designated as urban districts. Another round of territorial expansion in 2005 further designated two rural counties as urban districts. These changes have led to the city's area expanding 2.5 times to 3,725.4 km^2, housing over 10 million people in 2007 (Guangzhou Statistical Bureau 2008). Territorial expansion has significantly increased Guangzhou's land resources, allowing the city to construct a new airport and deep water seaport and relocate its old, polluted industries from the city centre to the periphery (Chung 2008). As a result, the government's attitude to, and strategy for, the redevelopment of urban villages differs from that in Shenzhen even though both cities have launched measures at more or less the same time.

Although Guangzhou and Shenzhen have different concerns about land, both cities have adopted very similar tactics to deal with problems in urban villages. Both cities view urban villages as a source of urban problems. In Guangzhou city, the phenomenon and associated problems were extensively reported by major local newspapers such as the *Guangzhou Daily*, *Nanfang Daily*, *Yangcheng Evening Post* and *Nanfang Metropolis* (see for instance *Guangzhou Daily* 2007; *Yangcheng Evening Post* 2000). Urban villages were labelled as hotbeds of unlawful activities. In a detailed report in the *Nanfang Daily* (2000), these settlements were regarded as the 'malignant tumour (*duliu*)' and the 'shame' of the city, with their cluster of illegal buildings, disorderly conditions, poor hygiene, prostitution, gambling and drug trafficking. Statistics have also been released showing that about 40 per cent of criminal activities in Guangzhou are directly related to urban villages (Li 2004). An identical strategy is employed by the Shenzhen government, which launched propaganda campaigns to problematise urban villages. According to the *Shenzhen Special Economic Zone News* (2004, 2003), urban villages are regarded as an 'urban malignant tumour (*chengshi duliu*)' in a 'garden city', featuring a 'dirty, chaotic and inferior (*zang, luan, cha*)' living environment. Consequently, a series of campaigns have been launched to tackle the problems of sanitation, fire safety, illegal construction, migrant control

264 *Him Chung*

and public security in urban villages in both cities. Such actions are the prelude to the institutionalisation of the development of urban villages.

The availability of land resources has affected Guangzhou and Shenzhen's systems for redeveloping urban villages. Generally, Shenzhen city has adopted a proactive attitude while Guangzhou has a passive attitude towards redevelopment. These different attitudes have created different strategies and systems to handle the redevelopment of urban villages. These differences are examined in the following section.

Centralised administration vs fragmentary management

Shenzhen's proactive attitude has been translated into an institutionalised approach to formalise and standardise the redevelopment of urban villages. Such an approach is in-line with a recentralisation process at the national level, demonstrating a consolidation of state power. Chung (2009) considers this practice to be a new state-led approach. It aims to develop standard procedures by designating the responsibility and scope for action to different actors in each urban village redevelopment. This approach comprises three components: (1) the creation of a comprehensive planning network, (2) the building of a centralised administration system and (3) providing incentives for redevelopment. Central to these developments is the *Master Plan of Urban villages Redevelopment (2005–2010)* introduced in 2005 (hereafter the 'Redevelopment Master Plan') (Shenzhen City Planning Bureau 2005). It was the Shenzhen government's first comprehensive attempt to regulate urban villages, and also the first redevelopment master plan amongst all Chinese cities. The Redevelopment Master Plan has incorporated urban village redevelopments into Shenzhen's existing statutory planning framework, creating a network of prescriptions from the strategic to operational levels (Figure 15.1). The Redevelopment Master Plan, together with the *Provisional Regulations of the Redevelopment Plan of Shenzhen Urban villages* (Shenzhen City Government 2005a) and the *Implementation Notes of the Provisional Regulations of the Redevelopment Plan of Shenzhen Urban villages* (Shenzhen City Government 2005b), has thus provided stipulated regulations, substantial development targets, detailed procedures and standard guidelines to regulate urban village redevelopment (Chung 2009).

Conversely, Guangzhou had not had a comprehensive policy network for urban village redevelopment before a more structured 'three olds' (*san jiu*) urban redevelopment scheme was introduced in 2009. Previously, piecemeal policies for problems found in urban villages had been applied. As early as 2000, Guangzhou city organised consultancy studies to investigate possible ways to tackle the (re)development of urban villages. Despite a position paper entitled *Suggestions for Institutional Reform of Urban villages* (Guangzhou City Government 2002), being produced and based on experimental sites selected for pilot tests, sensitive issues over compensation, replacement, arrangement of collective properties and villagers' livelihoods dissuaded the government from launching any redevelopments. While the government was searching for a thorough and

Planning for chengzhongcun *in Guangzhou and Shenzhen* 265

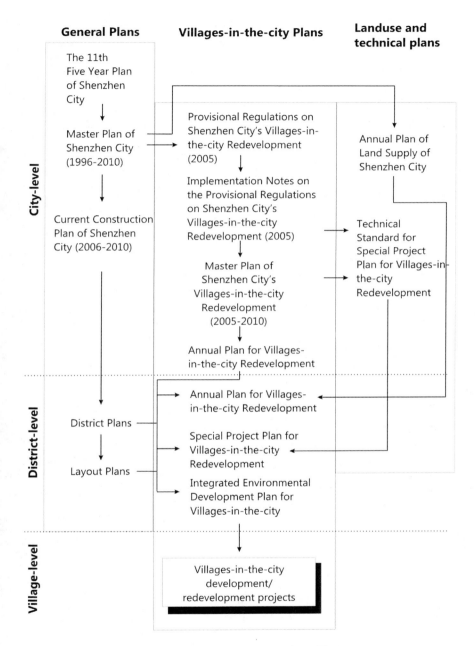

Figure 15.1 The planning framework of Shenzhen's urban villages.

long-term solution, various measures handled separately by different authorities were introduced to regulate land use, building and construction, management of 'outsiders', fire safety and rental activities in urban villages. Very little effort was spent on developing standard guidelines and transparent procedures. Therefore, in comparison to Shenzhen's approach, Guangzhou's approach provided more opportunities for the government to exercise its discretionary power. The lack of a comprehensive institution to organise control measures has led to an inefficient use of resources.

Administratively, a functionally specific system was established within Shenzhen's centralised system. The command body of this hierarchy is a special committee directly led by the Shenzhen government. The committee, known as the Leading Group for Shenzhen's Illegal Construction Investigation and Urban villages Redevelopment, comprises 20 members, including the mayor and leading cadres from the Planning Bureau, Construction Bureau and district-level government. Although a similar body (Leading Group for Urban villages Redevelopment) is found in Guangzhou, it is uncertain if it enjoys the same power as its Shenzhen counterpart. Official documents that guide the redevelopment of urban villages do not provide information about its scope of duty and power. Interviews with town planners reveal that the institution enjoys decision-making power, the right to initiate redevelopment projects and rights to examine, approve and modify redevelopment plans.[2] Therefore, when compared with the highly institutionalised system in Shenzhen, the administration in Guangzhou is a relatively loose one, with low levels of transparency.

If Shenzhen's highly institutionalised network represents a new state-led system, the Guangzhou government's strong intervention has demonstrated a persistence of the traditional form of a state-led system. Although the redevelopment of urban villages has been incorporated into the 'three olds' redevelopment framework with new guiding principles (Guangzhou City Government 2009), standard procedures to guide the formulation of plans, applications, reviews and approvals are still missing. Moreover, planning principles such as the 'one village one policy' and 'development starts when conditions are right' are ambiguous. In a country where communicative planning is rudimentary, it is the government which defines the development strategy and the time for development for a particular village. In this sense, 'state-led' in the development of urban villages in Guangzhou city has, to a great extent, retained the tradition of a command economy, facilitated by arbitrary power, commands and orders.

Master plan vs flexible plan

Shenzhen's Redevelopment Master Plan has established standard solutions, clear procedures and common criteria for redeveloping urban villages. For example, to tackle the problems stemming from property rights, the master plan promulgates state ownership, the opposite of collective land ownership. This suggests the collective unit of the redeveloped village will lose its control over residential land use while individual, native villagers give the ownership of their redeveloped residence to the state. Although this is not an entirely bad idea, the collective units, which represent the villagers during negotiations, do not automatically support it. Uncertainty, or disagreement, about property rights after redevelopment usually initiates other disputes over the redevelopment plan, the schedule and the relocation/compensation scheme imposed by the authorities. This has created resistance, as well as confrontation, and as a result the pace of urban village redevelopment has slowed.

Standard solutions and procedures do not exist in Guangzhou's redevelopment framework. Moreover, redevelopment principles are listed in administrative rather than in planning documents (Figure 15.2) (Guangzhou City Government 2008), demonstrating that urban villages redevelopment in Guangzhou is considered to be a public administration rather than a town planning matter. The two principles to guide the redevelopment are: (1) 'one village one policy' and (2) 'development commences when conditions are right'. Initially, property developers were not allowed to become involved (*Southern Metropolis Daily* 2002) but this restriction has been removed. Unlike in Shenzhen's master plan, which set a clear timetable and annual target for redevelopment, Guangzhou took a more cautious step, stressing that redevelopment should be tested at selected sites before it is promoted all over the city.

Instead of a master plan, the Guangzhou government introduced a unique framework for urban village redevelopment known as 'one village one policy' (*yi cun yi ce*). Unlike a master plan, it provides a flexible system for each redevelopment. Chung and Zhou's (2011) investigation suggests that the framework has provided a pragmatic way to deal with the various needs of different villages, and at the same time effectively addresses sensitive issues such as replacement and compensation. Investigating the redevelopment planning process of three urban villages, they demonstrate how different modes of redevelopment and compensation schemes have been formulated for different villages according to their specific conditions (Chung and Zhou 2011). While the flexibility of the 'one village one policy' takes local demands into consideration and minimises conflicts of

Figure 15.2 The planning framework of Guangzhou's urban villages.

268 *Him Chung*

interest between different stakeholders involved in the redevelopment, it also provides the Guangzhou government with a lot of opportunities to intervene in the planning process. Indeed, the village chosen for redevelopment, the timetable and redevelopment plan are steered by the government's political and economic agendas.

The emphasis on flexibility has overridden the efforts spent on developing standard guidelines and transparent procedures. For example, the meaning of the 'one village one policy' and 'development starts when conditions are right' principles as noted are ambiguous. Therefore, in comparison to Shenzhen's approach, Guangzhou's practice provides more space for the government to exercise its discretionary power. In this sense, being 'state-led' in the development of urban villages in Guangzhou city has to a great extent retained the tradition of a command economy, facilitated by arbitrary power, commands and orders.

Financing of redevelopment

Financing the redevelopment of urban villages differs between Shenzhen and Guangzhou. Initially, the Shenzhen government institutionalised the financing of urban villages redevelopment by providing direct funding from its budget through a Special Project Fund. Further to this, a Redevelopment Supporting Fund, fed by the government's Natural Resources Fund, was established to support infrastructure and utility improvement within urban villages in Shenzhen. These funds are managed and approved by the Leading Group, providing substantial incentives for individual villages to pursue (re)development. Apart from these funds, the Shenzhen government has adopted a liberal attitude towards property developers thus allowing involvement in any urban village (re)development projects if they reach agreement with the villagers.

In contrast, an early decision by the Guangzhou government clearly prohibited the involvement of property developers in any redevelopment (*Southern Metropolis Daily* 2002). According to local planners, this decision was driven by the desire to avoid speculation and to maintain social stability.[3] In addition to the lack of government funding in the early days, the exclusion of property developers implied that the funding for redevelopment was the sole responsibility of the villagers themselves. Financial constraints explain why the pace of urban village redevelopment was stagnant in Guangzhou city. Such a situation, in a wider context, could also demonstrate that Guangzhou city has no immediate need to redevelop urban villages.

In 2008, a relatively clear framework for the financing of urban village redevelopment was announced. The new framework suggests that governments at the city and district levels and the redeveloped village share equally in the redevelopment cost (Guangzhou City Government 2008). Government funding is allocated from its annual construction budget, and the redeveloped village is allowed to sell part of the collective land for a pooling development fund. The latter is considered as a policy change and can be viewed as a doorway for the involvement of property developers, albeit indirectly, in the redevelopment. Liede village was the first

Planning for chengzhongcun *in Guangzhou and Shenzhen* 269

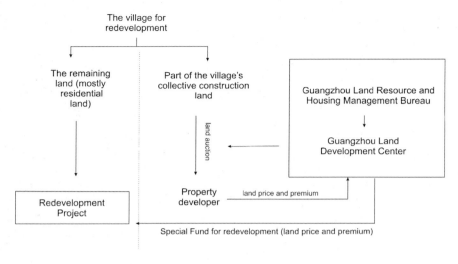

Figure 15.3 A new financial model for Guangzhou's urban villages.

village to initiate this idea. Figure 15.3 gives the details about its operation. A land parcel of 114,000 m² which was collectively owned by Liede was designated for sale in an open auction organised by Guangzhou Land Development Centre, a government agency subordinated to the Guangzhou Land Resource and Housing Management Bureau. In 2007, the land was sold to a private developer for 4.6 billion Yuan (*Nanfang Daily* 2007). The land premium paid to the Guangzhou government had fully rebated to Liede as a special fund for redevelopment. In addition to a number of preferential treatments, as a result of the flexible 'one village one policy', Liede village was able to finance its redevelopment with its own resources. This arrangement has created a win-win-win situation: Liede has raised sufficient funds for redevelopment; the property developer enjoys full development rights for their successful bid; for Guangzhou government, not only has its financial burden for the redevelopment project been eased, it also successfully transforms a space of disorder into part of a modern city landscape. Therefore, with the support of the Guangzhou government, this new arrangement has made Liede the first successful example of an urban village redevelopment. It also set a precedent for financing urban village redevelopments in Guangzhou and has been followed by other villages such as Yangji.

Conclusion

Urban village redevelopment is a process of multiple perspectives concomitant with the territorialisation of the local state. It reflects China's broken process of urbanisation. Given the prolonged sociospatial-institutional dualism between

270 *Him Chung*

urban and rural, redevelopment is an attempt to reconcile the two regions, particularly in the area of urban planning and management. This has led to an expansion of state control, which has significance for city governments, as they are major facilitators of local development. This expansion allows city governments to have better control of local resources, thereby enabling them to facilitate aggressive economic development projects. At the operational level, urban redevelopment provides a way of bypassing land development quotas imposed by authorities at a higher level, allowing the city to keep a certain pace of economic growth in a land-based economy. All these developments suggest that urban redevelopment projects in China are not merely for environmental improvement, nor simply a way to increase land values and land use efficiency. They fulfil multiple agendas in the unique political economy of China.

Shenzhen and Guangzhou cities' different strategies and planning systems for urban villages redevelopment have demonstrated the various ways of local power territorialisation. Constrained by the city's limited land stock in the context of rapid economic growth, Shenzhen has adopted a proactive attitude and inaugurated an institutionalised system for urban villages redevelopment to accommodate growing land use demands. Under the guidance of the Shenzhen government, a centralised administration has produced a single model for urban village redevelopment. Conversely, the huge supply of land resulting from territorial expansion has generated a passive attitude towards the redevelopment of urban villages in Guangzhou city. Very little effort has been spent on developing a comprehensive system similar to that in Shenzhen. Although a relatively integrated system was introduced in 2009 in Guangzhou, general procedures and transparent guidelines are still missing. Further, redevelopment principles like 'one village one policy' and 'development happens when conditions are right' are not clearly defined. Ambiguity surrounding the principles and procedures for redevelopment has allowed the Guangzhou government to exercise its discretionary power and to interpret redevelopment according to its own agenda. If Shenzhen's institutional approach for urban villages redevelopment represents a step forward in China's planning system and practice, then Guangzhou's approach remains conservative, retaining most traditional urban governance practices.

Although the Shenzhen approach represents an improvement in terms of governance, such an approach may not be effective enough to solve the complicated and sensitive issues inherent in the redevelopment process of urban villages. Conversely, the flexibility provided by the 'one village one policy' in Guangzhou has allowed the various needs of different urban villages to be met and the vested interests of different stakeholders, and their possible confrontation during redevelopment, to be settled. In this sense, the Guangzhou approach is a more effective system, despite its lack of transparency and the strong presence of government power. In the light of China's state-led urban expansion, this development suggests that the top-down authority of the state is still the most effective way to deal with any possible conflicts of interest during redevelopment. It is also the most effective way to tackle any possible contests between the government and society during the territorialisation of local power.

Notes

1. In 2010, Shenzhen extended its Special Economic Zone to cover the entire city.
2. Interview with a town planner at Zhongshan University, Guangzhou, 27 September, 2010.
3. Interview conducted at the School of Architecture, South China University of Technology, 15 April, 2009.

References

Chung, H. (2008) 'State regulation and China's administrative system: a spatial perspective', *The China Review*, 8(2): 201–30.

Chung, H. (2009) 'The planning of "villages-in-the-city", in Shenzhen, China: the significance of the new state-led approach', *International Planning Studies*, 14(3): 253–73.

Chung, H. (2010) 'Building an image of villages-in-the-city: a clarification of China's distinct urban spaces', *International Journal of Urban and Regional Research*, 34(2): 421–37.

Chung, H. and Zhou, S. H. (2011) 'Planning for plural groups? Villages-in-the-city redevelopment in Guangzhou city, China', *International Planning Studies*, 16(4): 333–53.

Connelly, S. and Richardson, T. (2005) 'Value-driven SEA: time for an environmental justice perspective?', *Environmental Impact Assessment Review*, 25: 391–409.

Ding, S. (2005) 'The problem of villages-in-the-city in Shenzhen and resolutions' (Shenzhen de chengzhongcun wenti yu wenti de jiejue), *Kaifang Daobao (China Opening Herald)*, 3: 39–42.

Fang, Q., Ma, X. and Song, J. (1999) 'Villages in the city: Policy problems during China's urbanization process' (Cheng zhong cun: wuguo chengshihua jincheng zhong yudao de zhengci wenti), *Chengshi Fazhen Yinjiu (Urban Development Studies)*, 4: 19–21.

Fisher, J. C. (1962) 'Planning the city of socialist man', *Journal of the American Institute of Planners*, 28(4): 251–6.

Friedmann, J. (2005) *China's Urban Transition*, London: University of Minnesota Press.

Guangzhou City Government (2002) 'CCP Guangzhou Committee Office and Guangzhou City Government Office's Suggestions for Institutional Reform of Villages-in-the-City' (Zhonggong Guangzhou shiwei bangongting Guangzhou shi renmin zhengfu bangongting guanyu chengzhongcun gaizhi gongzou de yougan yijian), Guangzhou City Government, General Office, Document No. 17, *Guangzhou Zhengbao (Guangzhou Policy News)*, 11: 10–15.

Guangzhou City Government (2008) 'CCP Guangzhou Committee Office and Guangzhou City Government Office's opinion on the advancement of policies about "rural to urban" and "villages-in-the-city" reform' (Zhonggong Guangzhou shiwei bangongting Guangzhou shi renmin zhengfu bangongting guanyu wanshan "nong zhuan ju" he "cheng zhong cun" gaizao youguan zhence wenti de yijian)', Guangzhou City Government, General Office, Document No. 10, Published in *Guangzhou Zhengbao (Guangzhou Policy News)*, 13: 13–17.

Guangzhou City Government (2009) 'Opinions on accelerating the pace of redevelopment of the "three oldies"' (*Guanyu jiakuai tuijin sanjiu gaizao gongzou de yijian*), Guangzhou City Government, Document No. 56, Published in *Guangzhou Zhengbao (Guangzhou Policy News)*, 1: 9–27.

Guangzhou Daily (2007) 'Redevelopment of Liede village commence after brewing for eight years' (Guangzhou Leide cun gaizao yunniang banian zhongpoti), *Guangzhou Ribao (Guangzhou Daily)*, 13 October, p. A05.

272 Him Chung

Guangzhou Statistical Bureau (2008) *Guangzhou tongji nianjian 2008 (Guangzhou Statistical Yearbook 2008)*, Beijing: Zhongguo Tongji Chubanshe.

Guangzhou Yearbook Editorial Committee (2001) *Guangzhou nianjian 2001 (Guangzhou Yearbook 2001)*, Guangzhou: Guangzhou Nianjian She.

He, S. and Wu, F. (2009) 'China's emerging neoliberal urbanism: perspectives from urban redevelopment', *Antipode*, 41(2): 282–304.

Hsing, Y. T. (2010) *China's Great Urban Transformation*, New York: Oxford University Press.

Jing, D. (1999) 'A study report on villages in city' (Chengshi lide nongcun yanjiu baogao), *Chengshi Guihua (Urban Planning)*, 9: 8–16.

Kwok, R. Y. (1981) 'Trends of urban planning and development in China', in Ma, L. J. C. and Hanten, E. W. (eds), *Urban Development in Modern China*, Boulder, CO: Westview Press.

Li, J. (2004) *The Reform of Villages in the City (Chengzhongcun de Gaizou)*, Beijing: Kaxue Chubanshi.

Lin, Y., de Meulder, B. and Wang, S. (2011) 'Understanding the "village in the city" in Guangzhou: economic integration and development issue and their implication for the urban migrant', *Urban Studies*, 48(16): 1–16.

Lin, G. C. S. (2007) 'Reproducing spaces of Chinese urbanization: new city-based and land-centred urban transformation', *Urban Studies*, 44(9): 1827–55.

Lin, G. C. S. and Yi, F. (2011) 'Urbanization of capital or capitalization on urban land? Land development and local public finance in urbanizing China', *Urban Geography*, 32(1): 50–79.

Liu, M. (2000) 'Shipai liudongrenkou jujuqu yanjiu (A study of the floating population in Shipai)', *Shichang yu Renkou Fenxi (Market and Demographic Analysis)*, 6(5): 41–6.

Ma, L. J. C. (1979) 'The Chinese approach to city planning: policy, administration, and action', *Asian Survey*, XIX (9): 838–55.

Mann, M. (2003) 'The autonomous power of the state: its origins, mechanisms and results', in Brenner, N. Jessop, B. Jones, M. and Macleod, G. (eds), *State/Space: A Reader*, Malden, MA: Blackwell Publishing, pp. 53–64.

Mertha, A. C. (2005) 'China's "soft" centralization: shifting tiao/kuai authority relations', *The China Quarterly*, 184: 791–810.

Ming, Y. (2010) 'Defending rights in baihutou village', *China Rights Forum*, 4: 36–50.

Nanfang Daily (2000) 'Dang chengshi zaoyu nongcun (When city meets villages)', *Nanfang Ribao*, 1 August: D1.

Nanfang Daily (2007) '4.6 billion Yuan: the commercial land in Leide village has successfully sold' (46 yiyuan: Leide cun shangyoudi chenggong churang), *Nanfang Ribao*, September, 30: 4.

Ng, M. K. and Tang, W. S. (1999) 'Land use planning in "one country, two systems": Hong Kong, Guangzhou and Shenzhen', *International Planning Studies*, 4: 7–27.

Ng, M. K. (2003) 'City profile: Shenzhen', *Cities*, 20(6): 429–41.

Ng, M. K. and Wu, F. (1995) 'A critique of the City Planning Act of the People's Republic of China: a western perspective', *Third World Planning Review*, 17: 279–93.

Shenzhen City Government (2005a) *Provisional Regulations of the Redevelopment Plan of Shenzhen Villages-in-the-city (Shenzhen shi cheng-zhong-cun (jiu cun) gaizao zanxing guiding)*, Shenzhen City Planning Bureau. Online. Available: http://www.szplan.gov. cn/main/czcgz/zcfg/200509120665.shtml (Accessed 10 January 2008).

Shenzhen City Government (2005b) *Implementation Notes of the Provisional Regulations of the redevelopment of Shenzhen villages-in-the-city (Shenzhen shi renmin zhengfu*

Planning for chengzhongcun *in Guangzhou and Shenzhen* 273

guanyu cheng-zhong-cun (jiu cun) gaizao zanxing guiding de shishi yijian), Shenzhen City Planning Bureau, Online. Available: http://www.szplan.gov.cn/main/czcgz/zcfg/200509120666.shtml (Accessed 10 January 2008).

Shenzhen City Planning Bureau (2005) *Master Plan of Villages-in-the-city Redevelopment 2005–10 (Shenzhen shi cheng-zhong-cun (jiu cun) gaizao zongtiguihua gangyao (2005–2010))*, Shenzhen City Planning Bureau. Online. Available: http://www.szplan.gov.cn/main/czcgz/ztghgy/20051109011737.shtml (Accessed 10 January 2008).

Shenzhen Special Economic Zone News (*Shenzhen Tequ Bao*) (2003) 'Seeking effective prescriptions for dirty, chaotic and inferior' (Tansuo genzhi zang luan cha liangfang), *Shenzhen Special Economic Zone News*, 10 July: A6.

Shenzhen Special Economic Zone News (*Shenzhen Tequ Bao*) (2004) 'Is it impossible to redevelop village-in-the-city?' (Cheng-zhong-cun bugaizao xingbuxing), *Shenzhen Special Economic Zone News*, 6 December: A4.

Shenzhen Statistical Bureau (2008) *Shenzhen Statistical Yearbook 2008* (*Shenzhen Tongji Nianjian 2008*), Beijing: Zhongguo Tongji Chubanshe.

Song, Y., Zenou, Y. and Ding, C. (2008) 'Let's not throw the baby out with the bath water: the role of urban villages in housing rural migrants in China', *Urban Studies*, 45(2): 313–30.

Southern Metropolis Daily (2002) 'Guangzhou refuse developer to involve in villages-in-the-city redevelopment' (Guangzhou jujue kaifashang chashou chengzhongcun jiuchenggaizao de fangxiang shi gaoluhua, jianchengshi guangchang he jianshe gonggong shezhi)', *Nanfang Doushi Bao (Southern Metropolis Daily)*, 13: A13.

Tan, B. and He, Q. (2002) 'Villages in the city: the corner of urbanization' (Chengzhongcun: Chengzhenhua de sijiao)', *Jingji Gongzuo Daokan (Journal on Economic Works)*, 3: 12–13.

Tang, W. S. (1994) 'Urban land development under socialism: China between 1949 and 1977', *International Journal of Urban and Regional Research*, 18(3): 392–415.

Tang, W. S. (1997), 'The Foucauldian concept of governmentality and spatial practices: an introductory note', *Occasional Paper No. 139*, Department of Geography, The Chinese University of Hong Kong.

Tang, W. S. (2000) 'Chinese urban planning at fifty: an assessment of the planning theory literature', *Journal of Planning Literature*, 14: 347–66.

Tang, W. S. (2006), 'Planning Beijing strategically: "one world, one dream"', *The Town Planning Review*, 77(3): 257–82.

Tang, W. S. and Chung, H. (2000) 'Urban-rural transition in China: beyond the Desakota model', in Li, S. M. and Tang, W. S. (eds), *China's Regions, Politic and Economy: A Study of Spatial Transformation in the Post-reform Era*, Hong Kong: The Chinese University of Hong Kong Press, pp. 275–308.

Tian, L. (2008) 'The chengzhongcun land market in China: boon or bane? – a perspective on property rights', *International Journal of Urban and Regional Research*, 32(2): 282–304.

Wang, Y. P., Wang, Y. and Wu, J. (2009) 'Urbanization and informal development in China: urban villages in Shenzhen', *International Journal of Urban and Regional Research*, 33(4): 957–73.

Watson, V. (2006) 'Deep difference: diversity, planning and ethics', *Planning Theory*, 5: 31–50.

Wei, A. (2000) 'Jujiao chengzhongcun (Focusing on villages in the city)', *Wenming Daobao (Cultural Report)*, 10: 4–12.

Wu, F. (2007) 'Re-orientation of the city plan: strategic planning and design competition in China', *Geoforum*, 38: 379–92.

274 *Him Chung*

Xie, Y. and Costa, F. J. (1993) 'Urban planning in China: theory and practice', *Cities*, 10: 103–14.

Xie, Z. (2003) 'Resolve the problem of villages in city during China's urbanization process' (Huajie chengshihua jincheng zhong de chengzhongcun wenti)', *Tequ Lilun yu Shiqian (Special Zone Theories and Practices)*, 8: 35–9.

Xu, J. and Ng, M. K. (1998) 'Socialist urban planning in transition: the case study of Guangzhou', *Third World Planning Review*, 23(3): 229–48.

Xu, J. and Yeh, A. G. O. (2005) 'City positioning and competitiveness building in regional development: New development strategies in Guangzhou China', *International Journal of Urban and Regional Research*, 29(2): 283–308.

Yangcheng Evening Post (2000) 'There are 139 villages-in-the-city in Guangzhou' (Guangdong "chengzhongcun" gong 139 tiao), *Yangcheng Wanbao (Yangcheng Evening Post)*, 6 September: A5.

Yeh, A. G. O. and Wu, F. (1999) 'The transformation of the urban system in China from a centrally-planned to transitional economy', *Progress in Planning*, 51: 167–252.

Yuexiu Government (2010) *Fourteen urban villages completed redevelopment scheme, thirty-five old factories applied for redevelopment (Shisitiao chengzhongcun wancheng gaizaofangan sanwuge jiucan ti gaizaoshenqing)*. Online. Available: http://www.yuexiu. gov.cn/yxxxw/xxgk/pop_jsp_catid_8893_id_100125.html (Accessed 18 August 2010).

Zhang, J. (2003) *A study of Guangzhou's villages-in-the-city (Guangzhou Chengzhongcun Yinjiu)*, Guangdong: Renmin Chubanshe.

Zhang, L., Zhao, S. X. B. and Tian, J. P. (2003) 'Self-help in housing and chengzhongcun in China's urbanization', *International Journal of Urban and Regional Research*, 27(4): 912–37.

Zhang, T. (2002) 'Decentralization, localization, and the emergence of a quasi-participatory decision-making structure in urban development in Shanghai', *International Planning Studies*, 7: 303–23.

Zheng, S., Long, F., Fan, C. C. and Gu, Y. (2009) 'Urban villages in China: a 2008 survey of migrant settlement in Beijing', *Eurasian Geography and Economics*, 50(4): 425–46.

Zhou, D. (1993) 'Discussions on the urbanization of rural communities locating at urban fringe' (Lun doushibianyuan nongcunshequ de doushihua), *Shihuixue Yanjiu (Studies on Sociology)*, 6: 13–20.

Zou, B. (2003) 'Challenges and measures for the implementation of urban-rural integration management' (Zhishi chengxiang yitihua guanli mianlin de tiaozhen ji duice), *Guihua Guanli (Planning Management)*, 8: 64–7, 85.

16 Conclusion

Chris Webster

Introduction

In this book, we have compiled a fascinating collection of accounts about China's migrant workers and about the neighbourhoods in which they live – particularly the *chengzhongcun* – villages in the city, or urban villages for short. The accounts variously emphasise migrants' motivations, job search and other migration strategies, wages, standards of living, housing conditions, local service provision, social and economic integration, risk appetite; and the regeneration, urban planning, integrity, linkages and sustainability of migrants' neighbourhood and the city and regional economies into which they are embedded.

A detailed summary of each study is left to the authors in their individual chapter conclusions. In this, the concluding chapter of the book, I seek to do something a little different: to comment on each study's contribution to some of the 'grand themes' underlying a study of migrants, urbanisation and development in contemporary China.

I take the liberty of using a series of seminal and mostly classical ideas from the early twentieth century to frame these themes. Apart from a single initial citation, I leave the detail as read (or readable) and proceed to draw out lessons learned in respect of these ideas from our chapters, adding additional commentary in-keeping with, but not necessarily the same as, the commentary of the chapters' authors. Any misrepresentation is the fault of this author alone and readers are directed to the full details contained in the respective chapters to contextualise and verify comments made here.

The first idea is that attributed to three classical development economists and known as the 'Lewis-Fei-Ranis model' and giving rise to the term 'Ranisisation'. This model understands industrial-led urbanisation as being driven by an infinite supply of cheap rural labour, attracted to cities by some minimal rural–urban (R–U) wage gap kept constant by competition from new migrants (Ranis and Fei 1961). All economic rent from labour is retained by owners of capital and surplus is ploughed back into new production technologies and processes, which expand the capacity to absorb yet more labour at the same constant price.

The second idea is Michael Todaro's model of the rational migrant family betting on future income in making its migration decision (Todaro 1969). This was originally posed to explain evidence that seemed to contradict the idea of

276 *Chris Webster*

Ranisisation: that migrants are not always absorbed immediately into efficient urban production and are often unemployed or underemployed for a length of time at wages below the level of rural wages + migration costs.

The third is the classical political economics view of economic development as an outcome of many individuals searching for ways of developing their human capital in order to improve their terms of trade as they cooperate with other individuals for mutual benefit via exchange of resources (Becker and Murphy 1992). The result in the labour market is an ever smaller and fragmented division of labour. Cities grow as individuals and firms co-locate in order to reduce the costs of exchanging increasingly specialised units of knowledge (Webster and Lai 2003).

Whether or not readers, and chapter authors, agree with the specific assumptions behind these – and their many derivative – grand theories, it should be possible to start with broad agreement on a set of stylised facts that bear clear connections to those narratives:

1. Rural migrants continue to flow into Chinese cities – cumulatively anywhere between 130 and 200 million have done so since the opening up.
2. There is little evidence of unemployment among migrants in China but some evidence of static wages (but recently, the wage began to increase).
3. Many, if not most, migrants in China talk positively about their urban experience. Unlike in many other countries, many have landed property rights back home and could relatively easily reverse the decision if prospects in the city looked bad. That means that the 'revealed preference' of most migrants indicates that they are better off in cities.
4. There is ample evidence, however, of very poor standards of housing consumption among many migrants, indicating a housing sector equivalent to the wage depression effect of limitless competition from new migrants. Inelastic supply of low income workers means existing migrants tend to have to sell their labour at the going rate, which remains near to rural income and also have to accept housing conditions near to rural conditions (or worse – a housing equivalent to Todaro's inter-temporal evaluation theory of the migration decision).
5. China's strong government means that there is a lower limit on a migrant household's choice of how much housing to consume. Living on the streets is not an option and neither, generally, is living in tents or shelters built with temporary or scrap building materials. This makes China's rural migrant phenomenon quite distinct from the norm. In principle, it should raise the cost of urbanisation and reduce the quantity of migrants. Possibly it could be expected to reduce the numbers of speculative migrants.
6. China's dual land market, an anomalous legacy institution that in many ways is inefficient and unjust, has come to the rescue, however, and provided the equivalent to the informal settlements that house rural migrants in the cities of other developing countries.
7. The *chengzhongcun* provide important low cost, low quality private-sector dormitories for the migrants.

8. All cities have their residual spaces that over time, as land values rise, succumb to the inevitability of formal, legal and transferable property rights. Before that happens, they typically support informal activity (e.g. markets, car parks, illegal trade). But China's residual spaces are massive (20 per cent of the land area of Guangzhou, housing 28 per cent of the population) and provide space for thriving and substantial informal economies. One case study in this book found that over 40 per cent of the mainly migrant community living in one urban village also worked in that village. This is a very unique type of residual space.

9. As has been documented of informal economies since they were first intensely studied in the 1960s, spillovers between formal and informal sectors are everywhere in China and it is no longer true to say, if it ever was, that these less-formal migrant dormitories and work places are in any meaningful way, separate from the main economic infrastructure of China's cities.

10. China's rural migrants face one barrier not found elsewhere: the legacy household registration system that labels people by place of origin and allocates state entitlements. As some of the chapters in this book illustrate, this is weakening but is not yet extinct. It still influences the migrant experience and affects migrant choices.

11. As the chapters in this book demonstrate in many graphical ways, these experiences and choices are not homogeneous. Some migrants make it into the commodity housing sector; some purchase urban *hukou*; some rent ex-work unit housing; some find their way into state schools; others buy private education of varying quality; some become entrepreneurs and use the informality of urban villages as an incubator environment, growing business with limited regulations and plenty of low cost labour, suppliers and customers. Some integrate and disperse; others cluster. Some rely heavily on place-of-origin social networks for welfare support, credit and job information. Others gain benefits from diversifying their support networks.

In the remainder of this concluding chapter, I select highlights from the preceding chapters to build upon these propositions; illustrating them, challenging them; deepening them; adding to them; weaving something like a tentative theory of contemporary Chinese rural–urban migration; or at least laying down pointers to elements of such a theory. The choice of themes is in no way systematic. It is offered as just one reflection of the rich accounts found in this book. Others doing the same thing would come up with very different lists that would no doubt be equally if not more useful in pointing to profitable theoretical agenda for further research.

Elements of a theory of contemporary Chinese rural–urban migration

Gains over time in spite of relatively static wages

In Fan and Chen's analysis of the differences between new and old generation migrants in **Chapter 2**, we find something that looks like evidence in support of

278   *Chris Webster*

the idea of Ranisisation: new migrants (born after the 1980s) tend to earn the same as old migrants. Wage data presented in other chapters tends to support the idea of modest increase in wages with successive job changes, which is not consistent with a pure model of constant static wages.

Migrants have apparently had sufficient labour-market power to win back a modest portion of rent from capital owners: Fan and Chen show that housing for new migrants in dorms is significantly better than housing for old migrants, for example. This is likely to be a result of competition between employers as well as regulations. Migrants can more easily vote with their feet between construction sites or factories than between cities (the investment to travel to a city is high and irreversible).

Unsurprisingly, new migrants have higher expectations, go to the city earlier than their parents and show signs of being more urban in culture than their parents (due no doubt in part to the smart-phones that they use to find jobs and build social networks that transcend their origins). But faced with lack of opportunities to increase wealth or at least to move into an urban-class job, they are increasingly prone to vote with their voice rather than feet. This is a very significant phenomenon and one that is exercising politician's minds. So we have a plausible proposition: that wage-suppression through a Ranisisation process plus social and other empowering modern media leads to voting with voice and a challenge to embedded institutions like hukou, labour laws, trades union laws and practices. Another result is corporations returning more profit to workers, although some of the evidence in the Foxcomm chapter of this book challenges the real additionality of concessions made – which would be in keeping with a dominant Ranisisation dynamic. Factories have responded to protests and worker suicides. What does this mean? It may only be acquiescence to pressure from politicians and the press – not driven by labour market power. Labour market desperation + press and political power raises wages. How sustainable is this? It may not be structurally sustainable if the basic dynamics are Ranis-like.

A more promising trend is the 10 per cent of migrants who will be able to buy their own urban home; the 50 per cent who have a formal job contract; the rising standard of manufacturer worker dorms; the 15 per cent who have welfare insurance; the reduction by 20 per cent of income remitted to home towns (meaning that migrant consumption is important to the urban economy and will endogenously generate a growing low-income oriented service sector and foster political integration); a rising rate of job change (which implies greater willingness to invest personal time and effort in seeking out better-fit jobs, which in turn implies growing efficiency of the lower end of the urban labour market); the rising educational level of migrants – 30 per cent are likely to be able to find permanent jobs in the urban labour market; the increasing propensity to bring children to the city; and the higher proportion of migrants among the new, that have a signed contract with their employer (somewhere just below 50 per cent). All this shows that migrant workers can achieve an increase in standard of living, even in the face of an inelastic supply curve for cheap rural labour.

The finding that 70 per cent of new generation migrants want to return to their region of origin (slightly less than first wave migrants) fits rather nicely with the estimation that 30 per cent have the educational credentials to find a permanent place in the urban labour market – we need some analysis to see if these match up. The 70 per cent is good for the prospect of the much-needed growth of the domestic consumer market in China and for the diffusion of modern industrial-urban development from the coast and other big cities to the hinterlands and down the urban hierarchy.

The picture described by Fan and Chen is a dynamic one, albeit based on a binary comparison of two waves of migrants. It shows that there are processes at work, even in a country with an unlimited supply of low wage rural workers and institutionalised urban/rural discrimination, which enable migrants to derive benefits from the city and to work their way into the urban economy. In this regard, it is of interest that rural hukou is not so much felt to be an impediment to integration into city life by new wave migrants. The labour market is reassuringly able to overcome an impediment to free and fair labour mobility as strong as hukou.

Entrepreneur and investor first, migrant second

Zhang's **Chapter 3** tells a compelling story of a family of rural peasants from the North West whose small land holding and entrepreneurial drive led them to develop non-farm business first in a local town, then in successively further away places. Each step was informed, it appears, by a rational assessment of opportunities and risks. A tragic accident destroyed 16 years of successful enterprise when a transport and petrol station business went up in flames. There followed an unsuccessful gold-mining foray into the Wild West and then a move to Shanghai to set up a regionally-specialised beef noodle restaurant.

This chapter gives an insight into the attitude towards risk found among rural migrants. In particular, it demonstrates that the migrants are differentiated by many characteristics – including risk appetite and entrepreneurial drive and skills. Mr Ma took a calculated risk in moving to Shanghai: it was a locationally specific investment, using borrowed (family) funds. He did not haphazardly end-up in the business. The story, as told by the researcher, clearly shows that he was an entrepreneur and investor first and a migrant second. Even his catastrophic loss did not turn him into long distance R–U migrant flotsam. It turned him into a gold prospector, borrowing and hiring labour and organising a year's prospecting trip. Shanghai was his next business venture.

This challenges the idea of Ranisisation, since it adds the idea of niche markets and even monopolistic competition in the restaurant industry. Monopolistic competition is a form of market structure, in which businesses produce products or services that have a degree of monopoly by virtue of branding or distinctiveness or quantity but not so much that they can raise prices with impunity. Raise them too much and customers will switch to a competitor. But with just the right product, branding, pricing and location, a small-scale migrant entrepreneur can make

280   *Chris Webster*

it in the urban economy. Most of Mr Ma's friends from back home have also dispersed throughout the country selling Lanzhou beef noodles.

The story shows the tertiary sector migrant economy as something very much more colourful, diversified and culturally and economically rich than the picture in Chapter 2. Mr Ma left a waged urban job (driving) in his home region to become a specialist entrepreneur in a place where he could anticipate a higher labour productivity for his unique set of skills (switching from one such skill – driving, to another – regional cuisine). This is a story of China's deepening division of labour – and of the deepening of the spatial integration of the economy: someone moving from the far northwest to Shanghai to exchange his cooking skills for money earned in any number of ways by the customers who for whatever reason happen to like Lanzhou beef noodles. It would seem remarkable a few decades ago that such an exchange could ever take place. It is the essence of social and economic development.

The lack of insurance-cover that led to the bankruptcy of the Ma family is a sad story. But in another way, it shows how it is the very underdevelopment of financial market institutions in a transitional and developing economy that fuels growth and diversification. Mr Ma would probably not have moved to Shanghai had his fuel station been insured. And if he does well, his great-grandson might not have become a famous Shanghaiese poet, enriching the lives of millions (I speculate).

Uninsured risks that are, in principle, insurable but remain uninsured because of immature financial markets are a temporary phenomenon. The severity of the Ma family catastrophe ensures that this is the case. The Ma family are unlikely to invest in a transport industry again and more generally, lack of insurance is likely to act as an impediment to local business development. For that reason, it can be expected that insurance cover will spread more thoroughly throughout the country to meet demand, supported where necessary by national enabling legislation – as illustrated in this chapter by the enactment of compulsory car insurance in China in 2006. Institutional deepening relies on failure and catastrophe to make a necessity out of a virtuous idea.

The relationship between tenure, labour mobility and integration

Analysing the patterns of migrant settlements, Wu (**Chapter 4**) notes that 'Few migrants in urban China make the transition from 'bridgeheaders' to consolidators even after years of living in the city, unlike the case in many other developing countries. Therefore, the security offered by housing tenure (ownership) is less relevant as a motivation in making housing decisions'. This is an interesting proposition that needs exploring further. It could, of course, be that the lack of property tenure contributes to the lack of 'bridgehead' behaviour among Chinese migrants. In which case, Wu has put his finger on an important element of Chinese rural–urban migration theory. Compared with some other developing countries, gaining land tenure plays a lesser role in migrants' migration calculus. What significance does this hold for their subsequent life experience?

Conclusion 281

The main insight from this chapter is that the combined effect of institutional discrimination (hukou) and landed property rights in Chinese cities, encourages an unusual (compared with other developing countries) degree of impermanence and lack of integration. Migrant workers not only face institutional discrimination but a lack of squatter and self-build opportunities contributes to lack of incentive to put down roots and invest in urban property. A relatively large proportion of migrant income gets remitted (although this is lower in new-wave migrants).

One consequence of the lack of opportunity for squatting as a route to ownership is that migrants are highly mobile in the rental sector. This may well have a bearing on migrant job mobility, which should be good for the economy and for individual incomes. China's peculiar property rights arrangement may also mean that there is less likelihood of migrant urban political movements arising to contend access to citizenship rights, local public goods, etc. (compared with Latin America, for example). This might have the effect of making migrants more mobile; making the local labour markets more efficient; and improving the flow of urban wealth to home rural areas.

Job search and the pros and cons of informal social networks

In Chen and Pryce's **Chapter 5**, we find more evidence that the flow of R–U migrants in China is not homogeneous and that the processes and experiences of urban integration are systematically differentiated. In particular, migrants' modes of job search differ by education and rural/urban place of origin and modes of job search is correlated with income potential and speed and trajectory of urban labour market integration.

The chapter is important for testing and unpacking the common notion that informal social networks help migrants establish a bridge-head in the city. It finds that social networks are particularly important for the less educated and migrating farmers but that acquiring a job via personal contacts, other things being equal, tends to lead to lower paid jobs. This is a fascinating finding that says something profound about the efficiency of markets in the process of migrant integration and more generally, in urbanisation and economic deepening. Migrants who have the experience and confidence to use market institutions to find a job (be-it first or subsequent job) tend, *ceteris paribus*, to get jobs offering higher wages. It tends to be the more highly educated and those migrating from other towns of cities who seek jobs through advertising (job posters, newspapers, radio, etc.), but the analytical models used in the chapter cleverly control for these factors by two stage model specification when examining the effects of job search mechanism.

This tells us that the more decentralised the information provision and use (adverts posted by individual firms and sought out and read by individual labourers) the better the match between jobs and workers. Workers expend effort looking for adverts in places they think are likely to yield better fitted, higher paying jobs and employers place adverts in places where they expect to find appropriate workers.

282 *Chris Webster*

It is of interest to read that private employment agencies tend not to yield jobs with wages any higher than those found via informal social networks. With informal networks, the wage-limiting effect results from a variety of factors mostly related to clustering of migrants from common origins. A network of migrants from the same home village, county or province is likely to have a limited range of job contacts. The chapter cites other studies that show a sectoral clustering of migrants from a common origin (e.g. female migrants from Anhui Province tend to be over-concentrated in domestic maid service and migrants from Sichuan, in the construction sector). So what starts as a positive role for informal institutions becomes negative.

A local and sector-specific version of Ranisisation happens as those who have helped each other compete for low-wage jobs, depress each others' wages in localised areas in particular sectors. This no doubt helps thrust some migrants caught in such a trap out, to explore alternative locations and types of job.

The poor performance of private employment agencies warrants further comment. Although this is partly because they attract less educated migrants, it seems that the effect remains when controlling for education; in which case, we may conclude with Chen that these market institutions are immature and inefficient. They apparently exploit the asymmetry in local knowledge to earn rent from the migrants above costs instead of improving their service to find more bespoke job matches. This is confirmed by the rate of wage increase in successive jobs, which is the flattest for employment agencies. The rate is highest for individual job search, which becomes the exclusive mechanism of choice in Chen's sample after four job changes – no respondents used either social networks or employment agency for their fifth job change.

Thus, an important insight from this chapter is that migrants learn to negotiate the urban job market as independent actors – roughly a quarter of the sample, cumulatively over the survey period of five years. Although the employment agencies are exploitative, we should expect them to become less so over time, since entry barriers are not high and they will loose customers to individual job search if they don't offer genuine time-savings with wage benefits. They can also help break the wage-depressing lock-in into particular sectors experienced by migrants that initially relied on friends and relatives. So we see another example of economic deepening as individuals develop person skills in job search and exchange these first informally for quid pro quo favours, guanxi and so on and then for formal payment in an immature labour market. Interestingly, the most mature market in job search seems to be at an individual labourer level. In principle, job agencies should be able to improve on the efficiency of individual job search but this is probably sector specific, for example, for jobs in more remote locations or in less familiar sectors. What we should expect is a growth in the job advertising industry, providing opportunities for migrant entrepreneurs to develop specialist skills in bringing individual employers and labourers together via individual search mechanisms rather than the less efficient mechanisms of the current style of job agencies.

Conclusion 283

Entry-cities and informal spaces

In **Chapter 6**, Andersson considers the role of urban villages as 'entry cities'. In principle, such places can work well or can become poverty traps. Physical institutional structure can make a difference, it is noted: flexible spaces, room to expand houses, transport connections with the rest of the city, all help determine a positive or negative outcome for this kind of settlement.

A nice example of a positive outcome is the specialisation in different urban villages in Guangzhou: women from Kunming collecting garbage came to Xian Cun, a village half an hour's walk away from the village where they live because there was less competition and more opportunity – the migrants in Xian Cun mostly working in service sector employment, not as self-employed workers as the Kunming women did. This shows how the migrant economies of non-contiguous urban villages intertwine and support each other in spontaneous ways.

Xian Cun also provides a good illustration of the importance of physical design to economic integration. Until Xian Cun became surrounded by a green buffer and fence (in preparation for the Asian games), the liveliest parts and the highest rents were on the edges, where the village connected to the city's grid. After the fencing, activities shifted to the centre of the village, which is likely to affect the performance of the village as an entry-point to the city.

Migrants in this study reported not having a close affinity to the villages who they share urban space with. This is due in part to the constant and long-lived threat of demolition. Their view was that they could easily find another low cost place to live in the city. This is an interesting finding in the light of the limited alternatives for migrant living. It can probably be accounted for by the large numbers of urban villages still in Guangzhou: Lin *et al.* reported in 2011 that 70 per cent of migrants lived in urban villages in the city and that migrants comprised 40 per cent of Guangzhou and urban villages 20 per cent of the city's urban land area.

The chapter starts and ends with stories of migrants carefully going about their illegal (unregulated) informal businesses in a way that calculates gains against risks of fines and confiscations – such as the deliverymen using banned tricycles to link the urban village economy with the wider economy. They operate at night when the fewer policemen around are also likely to be more lenient because of the lower chance of the tricycles causing congestion and nuisance on the urban grid. A story is also told of greater tolerance to unregulated street traders in the run-up to village demolition projects. The traders become temporary land users and are less of a threat to the orderly reconstruction of the harmonious modern cityscape and economy.

The account of the final and temporary stages of urban villages is much more like many accounts of informal sector spaces in other developing countries. In fact, there is resonance in these stories of the urban dynamics of cities the world over. All cities have temporary spaces, as I have already noted, and temporary less formal sectors of the land market, where land use rights are less clear and more

284   *Chris Webster*

subject to negotiation and invasion because of uncertainties and the high costs of policing clearer spatial and temporal rights compared to the benefits achieved by so doing. Even highly developed cities have such spaces – variously called 'terrain vague', 'in-between spaces', 'residual spaces' and similar (Mady 2010). It is highly likely that many urban villages will disappear before long (although Guangzhou's current experimental policy may change this – see below in commentary on another chapter). In which case, urban villages as we know them will have had a fixed life-time and played an important part in the historical development of Chinese cities. The part they play in their final months or years will have subtle differences to the part played in their early years – a story not yet told in the unfolding theory of Chinese rural–urban migrants.

Integration and housing market differentiation

A nice parallel to Chan's finding that migrants learn over time to become independent actors in the urban labour market is a figure from Gransow, quoted by Wissink and colleagues (**Chapter 7**), that between 1998 and 2008, the percentage of migrants renting on the private market (as opposed to living in dorms or private houses as maids) rose from 25 per cent to 50 per cent. This demonstrates that over time, migrants learn how to search for more bespoke housing solutions. As they do, housing market institutions develop to make this search activity more efficient and more low cost housing gets supplied with greater differentiation.

Differentiation within the housing market is also reported in this chapter, which records migrants living in four types of neighbourhood (urban village, pre-1949, ex-danwei and commodity) and paying significantly different prices for each sub-market. The differences are reflected also in other characteristics: urban village migrant residents are more likely to be lower educated, lower income, younger and temporary. Interestingly, ex-danwei neighbourhoods are the location of choice for older and retired migrants. The chapter does not evidence the degree of migrant entry into the ex-danwei owner-occupier market, but other chapters in this book indicate that this is happening. If so, then migrant housing market activity will have a knock-on effect to local resident housing markets, especially danwei housing, which has been extremely static since property rights were transferred to sitting tenants in the late 1990s and early 2000s – partly because of a lack of buyers (also because of a lack of affordable alternatives).

More evidence of the role of physical space in social and economic organisation comes in this chapter with the finding that urban migrants in urban villages have less homogeneous social networks than those in pre-1949 or danwei or commodity neighbourhoods. Commodity estates and old neighbourhoods are places where migrants from the same home location tend to cluster more. This is likely to make urban villages better for job searches. However, migrants in commodity estates have more job-type heterogeneity in their social networks – although this is greater in urban villages than in old neighbourhoods.

Over 50 per cent of social contacts of interviewees in this study are outside the neighbourhood on average, with commodity estate dwellers having greater

Conclusion 285

dispersal. The authors statistically identify four types of migrants with respect to their integration behaviour. More than a quarter falls into the 'intergratee' category, who are less reliant on home province social contacts. Integratees are the largest group in urban villages and danwei, revealing that there seems to be a process of integration associated with housing market differentiation.

Hukou versus income and property rights as a determinant of integration

More evidence is found in Li and Wu's **Chapter 8** on integration in Beijing, Shanghai and Guangzhou, of significant levels of migrant integration. The chapter focuses on urban villages, which it portrays as places that lower the transaction costs of integration. For example, they cite the role of Hubei restaurateurs and middlemen in the labour and housing markets and in Datang village, Guangzhou. They also cite the extraordinary levels of differences within urban villages, with landlord families and tenants having vastly different standards of living and opportunity within the same neighbourhood and with micro-spatial patterns of segregation emerging. The integration picture is a complex one, with a high degree of spatial integration between relatively wealthy landlords and migrant tenants on one count; but micro-level social segregation between these groups on another; and with widespread economic integration on another.

The chapter reports the interesting finding that hukou status is not significantly related to self-reported level of integration of migrants in the sample as a whole (although it is for Shanghai, see below). This absence of a hukou effect suggests a declining importance of institutional factors and a rising importance of market factors. The comparison between Beijing, Guangzhou and Shanghai is interesting: Shanghai, the city with the strongest legacy of central planning and the least influence of markets in its recent development, has a distinctly different set of correlates with migrant integration. Local hukou is a dominant determinant in Shanghai, while in Beijing and more so in Gaungzhou, income is dominant and hukou is insignificant. Income is particularly important in new-generation migrants (born <1980), showing the diminishing effects of legacy state allocation institutions and the rising importance of market institutions, particularly income and property rights, in providing opportunities for migrants to integrate.

Urban unrest and the possibility of real gains in the rate of labour exchange

You-Ren Yang tells the sad case of the Foxconn factory village in Shenzhen, in **Chapter 9**. This chapter provides a sober microscopic view of migrant living that shows just how powerful corporations can be in determining the effective rate of exchange for migrant labour. The totalising effect of living and working and socialising within the factory are vividly portrayed. This is the micro-mechanism of Ranisisation at its worst. The desperate protests, we can note, were only (thankfully) by a handful. But they no doubt represented the voice of hundreds of thousands.

286 *Chris Webster*

It is probably a sad fact that the history of urbanisation in every country has to include its own Foxconn story. As noted earlier, the institutional reforms needed to correct imbalances in labour, land and capital power are rarely smooth and tend to involve tragedy and crisis. A century after the equivalent period in Britain's urban-industrial development period, it was the institutions protecting labour power that needed breaking and it took the social suffering of the 1970s recession in the UK to break the monopoly power of the unions that were originally set up to give labour a fair share of the gains from production. Power shifts over time and it seems likely that some gains will be made for labour power in China in the coming decade. But as noted earlier, such gains have the current demographics of the country's labour market against them.

Are urban villages really that necessary for low cost housing supply?

The conclusion of Wang *et al.*'s **Chapter 10** is that urban villages in Shanghai are temporary dormitories. There are only a few left and the remaining ones are scheduled for demolition. Partly because of the city's aggressive redevelopment approach, migrants live dispersed through the city, renting from commodity property owners and in danwei estates as well as employers' dorms. It should be noted that the lack of urban village accommodation does not seem to have weakened the Shanghai economy. As in other cities, the survey shows that urban villages provide their residents with much smaller homes of a poorer condition. One might expect that the absence of this type of cheap accommodation would impact on wages since the costs of living in Shanghai should be higher as a result. It would be interesting to examine this effect with appropriate controls. The survey in this and other chapters show, however, that migrants have the capacity to both save and remit to relatives back home. In this situation, a rise in the cost of living through shrinkage in the stock of cheap informal housing need not necessarily convert into higher wage demand. The ready supply of replacement migrant labour means that the first thing likely to happen is that savings and/or remittances will be squeezed.

It is of interest in this study to find that 45 per cent of tenants in Shanghai urban villages (most of which are migrants) say that they will look for alternative accommodation in a similar or the same location after the village is demolished, accepting that their rent will rise. Fifty five per cent, on the other hand, say they will move to a less accessible location to keep rent expenditure low. This shows that for almost half of the migrant families living in Shanghai's urban villages, if pushed, they have capacity to absorb higher rent. It also shows that a significant proportion is prepared to trade-up, spending more on housing (and by implication, less on savings and remittances). Some might say that this vindicates the dominant 'demolish and redevelop' approach to urban villages. It forces migrants to greater urban integration by consuming more housing and to disperse. The 55 per cent not willing to pay higher rents can, however, apparently absorb extra travel time and cost. The upper limit on higher rent among Shanghai's urban village tenants is said to be 266 Yuan. Beyond this, they will leave the city. Presumably this can also be taken roughly as the upper limit in the value of increased travel time/cost. That being so, it should be possible to model the likely loss of migrants consequent upon the completion of the urban village demolition programme.

The knowledge that urban villagers can absorb higher rent and travel costs is of great significance for planners of other cities preparing to redevelop their own urban villages. Shanghai possibly shows that the urban economy can work without these informal private-market low cost dormitories and economic and social incubators; and the stated preference information in this chapter helps calibrate the impact of those redevelopments. However, evidence from elsewhere in this book indicates that the economy will be less well-embedded at all income levels in their absence. The full impact of urban villages as economic incubators has not been researched or told. It may be that the economic function of the *chengzhongcun* migrant enclaves is as important as or more important than the housing function.

In fact, the housing function could be seen as a by-product of urban village co-owner opportunism. *Chengzhongcun* could be said to be socially inefficient because (a) they do not allow land to gravitate to its 'highest and best' use and (b) the gains from urbanisation captured in rental values within the urban villages fall almost entirely to a small number of lucky villagers. That money might be recycled into the wider economy but greater social value could be obtained by formalising the land and raising tax from it and the activities undertaken on it. This line or argument parallels the idea developed in Zhao and Webster (2011) that unearned urban land value uplift probably belongs to the state rather than urban villagers. It is not necessarily a palatable view but it is one that needs to be factored into a theory of Chinese rural–urban migration.

Collective ownership and regeneration of industrial clusters

What Altrock and Schoon describe in **Chapter 11** is a fascinating case of *in-situ* regeneration of a spontaneous industrial cluster in Guangzhou, based in and around several urban villages. The cluster of textile traders emerged in the 1980s after mobile street traders were banned from the CBD and relocated to an area just south of Sun Yat Sen University. The cluster grew rapidly to include specialist support services as well as manufacturers up and down stream of the woolen yarn that was its original focus. The urban village location provides one of the chapter's most significant points although it is not one emphasised by the authors: the collective ownership of this part of the city – in the hands of joint stock companies co-owned by former villagers – made it possible to undertake a major multi-phase regeneration of the informal industrial cluster without wholesale redevelopment, relocation or organisational or financial restructuring. This is a remarkable feat and it is unlikely to have been achieved in the absence of collective land ownership. The collective system of property rights effectively turned the cluster into a multi-tenant organisation with strong unitary ownership of the land and buildings that constitute not only the collection of textile businesses but also the housing for the (mostly) migrants who work in them. This arrangement made it possible for

288 *Chris Webster*

business tenants, local government and villagers to come together in a typically Chinese public-private-partnership to affect the regeneration project without losing the small traders or the local low-income workers so crucial to its success.

Phase changes in property cycles as capacity constraints force property rights reform

In **Chapter 12**, Hao *et al.* provide a very comprehensive analysis of the spatial and functional morphology of urban villages in Shenzhen and of the determinants of this morphology. The overarching finding is a profound one: the development and evolution of urban villages, home to the bulk of Shenzhen's low paid manual workers, follows the normal logic of urban economics, albeit within a dual land economy. In response to migrant worker demand for accommodation near to job opportunities, urban villages first expand in land area, then densify and intensify. They do so in clusters, showing that the collective and individual village landlords are highly responsive to subtleties in the spatial patterns of migrant housing demand. Clusters of villages located favourably in relation to various combinations of attractors, develop and densify towards maximum capacity. The attractors are systematically related to urban village growth and densification, with the strongest influence being proximity to a metro station, closely followed by other accessibility measures, which vary by location. So for example, in the more peripheral areas, access to a major highway is the best predictor of urban village growth.

All this reveals a highly responsive and sophisticated informal housing production sector in which individual and collective small scale developers of village land are able to find both land and capital to respond to migrant worker demand in a timely fashion. This is true up to the point at which the land resources in the informal part of the dual land market become exhausted. The chapter provides the best account I have read of the process that unfolds as that point is approached, documenting the slowing of development as the capacity for lateral and vertical expansion and infill is reached.

At this saturation point, the interests of village landlords and migrant workers start to diverge. The only way forward to greater wealth for the villagers is to redevelop and a new growth coalition emerges: between villagers, local government and formal sector developers and investors. This is not the chapter's focus, but the study does provide some evidence of this stage of the story in its discussion of the earlier and more central urban villages within the SEZ, which have lost land to redevelopment schemes. Those schemes have tended to replace migrant worker housing with new high intensity urban uses such as high-end apartments and commercial towers.

The shift in growth coalition and change in mode, style and density of development that comes with a 'filling up' of the urban village 3D envelope is a special version of a local property cycle. Only in this case, it is not a repeating cycle. The capacity constraint is a permanent one given existing property rights. When villages reach this point, they are propelled, in search of higher returns, to accept property rights reform. Because there are two systems of property rights operating side by side, and to some extent with respect to villager choice, in competition, the property trends and cycles described in this chapter experience a phase change as one system is replaced by another. The discontinuities of development trends and step-changes associated with property rights reform are an important part of a theory of rural urban migration in China.

A future for urban villages by piecemeal redevelopment?

Details of Guangzhou's trail-blazing new policies for urban villages are discussed in **Chapter 13** by Schoon and Altrock. One policy is dubbed the 'three olds' (old village, old town and old factory) and another, for the 'old villages': '1 village 1 policy'. Some 138 villages are listed for this approach, with priority given to central villages and those near important development projects. An interesting and significant finding is that only 10 per cent of these villages have a preference for comprehensive redevelopment. The land values in the other 90 per cent are too low to fund comprehensive land optimisation for both villagers and developers/financiers. These therefore (at the moment) opt for piecemeal regeneration. This signals the possibility of gradual evolutionary improvement of China's urban villages and an evolutionary change in structure of migrant worker housing.

Where comprehensive redevelopment has occurred or will occur, gentrification is inevitable, even if the government has its way and regulates for 70 per cent subsidised housing in all residential parts of the redeveloped areas (unlikely since it is expressly making concession in order to secure the private sector partnership in these projects). Even in the piecemeal regeneration projects, rents are likely to go up. The result, therefore, will be further differentiation in the low- to mid-income rental housing market. This is extremely important for migrant integration into the urban economy and if it has to come at the expense of squeezing the very lowest end of the housing market, this may have to be a price the city has to pay in upgrading its land and housing markets and overcoming the constraining legacies of history. It would be consistent both with (a) upgrading the industrial base of the city to higher value-adding production and (b) increasing the opportunities for migrant workers to step up the housing ladder towards fuller integration into the urban economy and society.

Urban villages as motors of regional growth

Chapter 14 (Yanliu Lin *et al.*) is another examining the integration of migrant worker villages with the surrounding urban economy. Like the previous clustering chapter, we find that villages have specialised, providing high density concentrations of specialised workers, inputs and services, for example, for the ICT industry in Shipai village. Over 40 per cent of residents in Shipai work in the electronics sector. The authors do not attempt to separate out informal and formal in this context as this would be difficult given the mix of villager, migrant and external resources that have gone into creating this economic phenomenon. The local

290 *Chris Webster*

clustering linkages are found to extend beyond the village boundary, emphasising just how integrated have the urban village economies become with the surrounding city and how risky wholesale redevelopment would be for local and city economy. Shipai village, with its 70–80,000 migrant workers and 10,000 villagers living in less than one square kilometres, has become one of the most important computer distribution centres in Guangzhou and in South China.

Using migrant housing demolition to upgrade the urban economy

Chung provides a detailed comparison in **Chapter 15**, of the urban village redevelopment policies of Shenzhen and Guangzhou, with Shenzhen's being portrayed as more top-down, regulative, rigid and formulaic and Guangzhou's being more flexible and discretionary. The latter allows more private finance to flow into the schemes and distributes the costs and benefits more widely to interested parties. The difference is said to be due to Shenzhen's greater urgency in village redevelopment because it has run out of green field sites. Guangzhou also has a constraint – a nearly used-up land development quota imposed by higher tier government, but not quite such a pressing one. In any event, Guangzhou sees its relaxation of control in order to produce private finance solutions as a means of speeding up urban village redevelopment. The trade off is between speed and leakage of land betterment value from governments who by and large created it.

It will be interesting to see which of the two approaches is more successful and what the attendant risks are. Institutional competition is likely to be a feature of this ongoing saga as the two cities compete for similar footloose investors, employers and workers. It may be that in retaining its urban villages and regenerating them by selective infrastructural upgrade, land reform and organisational reform, Guangzhou may continue to keep the costs of urbanisation down compared to Shenzhen, where if all goes according to plan, urban villages will be very much fewer in the near future.

Of course, this might indeed all be according to plan in a bigger sense: during an interview with a high ranking housing department official in Shenzhen in 2005, the official announced with pride that he had just secured the removal of over 1 million square metres low cost homes. I asked him if securing low cost homes was not part of his ministry's responsibilities and he replied that his principal objective at the moment came from industrial policy not housing welfare policy: the city needed to remove urban villages in order to restructure its industry. If the city reduced its capacity to accommodate low-income migrant workers, its industrial base would more quickly shift into higher value-added sectors.

Final word

The authors of this book present these multiple and contrasting stories told about China's urban migrants, their *villages in the city* and other habitats in order to enrich academic, public and professional debates. The writing project emerged

Conclusion 291

from two projects funded by the UK's Department for International Development and Economic and Social Research Council looking respectively at urban poverty and urban villages.

We have documented, through these projects, some of the intricate internal mechanisms of the engine that has driven China's economic express train. The previous two books from the project (Wu and Webster 2010; Wu *et al.* 2010) focused, respectively, on poverty and marginalisation. The current book, by focusing on migrants and the spaces they inhabit, has given greater emphasis to the upside of the migration phenomenon. In this sense, the stories told and the regression models estimated are not that much different from those coming from studies of other rapidly developing countries.

The one big difference, however, that comes through in each of the chapters in this book: is the dual system of both landed property rights and rights to the city. Predictably, this has a fundamental influence on the profile and dynamics of poverty and marginalisation and on the process of spatial labour market adjustment from a rural-agricultural to an urban-industrial economy.

The ambiguous property rights that created China's unique urban villages have (a) given migrants a foothold into the city, (b) become hives of economic activity of local, urban and regional significance and (c) probably reduced the costs of urbanisation. On the other hand, the strict control of the formal part of the dual land market and the dual system of citizen rights has hindered the integration of migrants into the city and limited the space available for low cost homes and informal economic incubator clusters.

But the chapters in this book show that Chinese cities are indeed in transition, with the negative effects of hukou reducing; a responsive informal housing supply sector; migrants finding accommodation in a more diversified housing market; and many indicators of progressive social, economic and even political integration of migrant workers. The oddities of the legacy institutions and the transition period will leave their imprint; and tracking these is an important research agenda as Chinese cities 'normalise'. Because it involves major institutional changes, that normalisation process is necessarily lumpy. The current intense scrutiny given to urban villages and the new political will to experiment radically with their governance and future means that this particular part of the China's urban transition story is not complete. What happens in the Guangzhou experiment may have huge repercussions for millions of migrant workers and their families and hometowns and villages across the country. The success or otherwise of the city's new liberalism towards collective land ownership will determine whether one of the lasting legacies of the transition period for the future of Chinese cities is a modern form of corporate neighbourhood. Theoretically, multi-tenant property is the most efficient form of urban land ownership in terms of urban management and re-investment. It is not the most popular for all sorts of good reasons. If, for the sake of argument, 20 per cent of Guangzhou remains in the hands of collectively owned private corporations who are able to make corporate decisions about investing in neighbourhood infrastructure and other forms of public goods, then Guangzhou will be a very different kind of city to most the world has known in

292 *Chris Webster*

the history of modern civilisation. So the spaces initially created in cities by China's massive waves of rural-urban migration may lay the foundation for the organisation of urban life well into the future just as the migrants who first inhabited them laid the foundations for the country's economic future.

Of course, the last urban village may disappear within a decade (apart from a handful preserved as artist villages perhaps). Migrants will continue to arrive but be dispersed more uniformly across the city. The theory of Chinese urbanisation will prove to be less unique and we will all have been documenting and reflecting upon a time-limited transition period. The great challenge to urban thinkers in such a moment in history is to see if the accidental experiments of history have thrown up any innovations that might improve upon the way things have typically been done hitherto.

References

Becker, G. S. and Murphy, K. M. (1992) 'The division of labor, coordination costs, and knowledge', *The Quarterly Journal of Economics* 107(4): 1137–60.

Ranis, G. and Fei, J. C. H. (1961) 'A theory of economic development', *The American Economic Review* 51(4): 533–65.

Mady, C. (2010) Informal Spaces, Unpublished PhD thesis, School of City and Regional Planning, Cardiff University, Cardiff, UK.

Todaro, M. P. (1969) 'A model of labor migration and urban unemployment in less developed countries', *The American Economic Review* 59(1): 138–48.

Webster, C. and Lai, L. W. C. (2003) *Property Rights, Planning and Markets: Managing Spontaneous Cities*. Cheltenham: Edward Elgar.

Wu, F. and Webster, C. (eds) (2010) *Marginalisation in Urban China*. London: Palgrave McMillan.

Wu, F. Webster, C. He, S. and Li, Y. (2010) *China's Urban Poverty*. Cheltenham: Edward Elgar.

Zhao, Y. and Webster, C. J. (2011) 'Land dispossession and the enrichment of Chinese urban villagers', *Urban Studies* 48(3): 529–51.

Index

Note: Page numbers in *italics* refer to figures and page numbers in **bold** indicate tables.

adverts, 74, 75, 79, 281
African-Americans, integration of, 102
African immigrants, in New York and
Los Angeles, 124
age; as a criterion for defining
migrant workers, 18; of migrant
workers, 20–22
agencies *see* employment agencies
agricultural work *see* farming work
agriculture *see* farming
air conditioners, 173, 174
alienated urbanism, 147, 148–151, 161
All China Federation of Trade Unions
(ACFTU), 24
All-China Women's Federation (ACWF)
2011 survey, 23, 25
Altai (Aertai) Mountains, 45
Asian Games (2010), 9, 87, 95, 190, 197,
226
Asian migrants, 123
assimilation of migrants, 122; *see also*
integration of migrants
ASTER Digital Elevation Model (DEM)
data, 205
automobile insurance, 43

Baiyun District, Guangzhou, 226
Baiyun New Town, Guangzhou, 226
bathrooms, 173
Beijing, 7, 73, 101, 121, 165, 285; annual
mobility rates of migrants and duration
of residence in, *56*; development model,
128, 135; housing consumption
behaviour of migrants in, 256; housing
status and integration of migrants in, 6,
135, 142; income of migrants in, 135;
integration of migrants in, **131**, 135,

136–137, 142; living conditions of
migrants in, 129; migrant villages in,
101–102; number of migrants in, 128;
private cloth making workshops, 8;
redevelopment policies, 1; social
integration of migrants in, 6; spatial
mobility of migrants between first and
current residence by entry cohort, *57*;
tenure mobility of migrants in, *59*;
underground spaces as private rental
housing for migrants, 128; urban
villages in, 1, 129, *130*; variations
between Shanghai, Guangzhou and,
134–135; Zhejiang Village
(Zhejiangcun), 1, 8, 62
Beijing Bicycle, 89
bicycles, 8, 89, 90, 92, 175
billboard workshops, 94–95
blue-stamp household registration, 52–53,
101, 118; *see also* household
registration (*hukou*) system
bonding capital, 150
Bourdieu, Pierre, 150
bridging capital, 150

Canada, 122
Cantonese, 31
car insurance, 43
central planning era, 69
chain migration, 73
Chang Jiang (China) Textile City
(CJCTC), 8, 193–195
Chengdu, 17
chengzhongcun see urban villages
children; schooling for, 156; survey of
children of migrants, 25
China, population in, 164

294 *Index*

China Textile City, Keqiao, Yantze River Delta, 8, 189, 190
China Youth and Children Research Centre, 29
Chinese General Social Survey, 24
Chinese household surveys, 129
choice theory, 124
Circular of the State Council on Promoting the Economical and Intensive Land Use, 236
cities; migrant housing and settlement patterns in, 53–60; and mobile livelihoods, 36–50; proximity of urban villages to city centres, 215; spatial expansion of, 61; symbiotic relationship between urban villages and, 240–255; temporary spaces in, 283–284
citizenship, urban, 52, 126
city governments, and redevelopment of urban villages, 270
city planning, 258
City Planning Act, 260
civilisation (*shiminghua*), 125
classical social assimilation theory, 5, 102, 103
clean up campaigns, 92
clothing industry, 8, 73, 182–201
cluster theory, 185
collective ownership, and regeneration of industrial clusters, 287–288
commercial insurance, 43
commodity housing, 53, 55, 101, 106, 108, 110, 118, 202, 284
Communist Party, 258
comprehensive commercial facility clusters, 197
Construction Committee, 231
construction workers, 101, 210
contingency, 42
couple migration, 23, 25, 126
Craftsman, The (Sennett), 92

danwei housing, 100, 104, 284, 285, 286
Datang Village, Guangzhou, 127, 285
delivery men, 90, 94, 283
demolition–redevelopment model, 252
Deng Xiaoping, 185, 259
'development happens/starts when conditions are right' policy, 268, 270
'Development of Migrant Villages under China's Rapid Urbanization, The', 166
dormitories *see* factory dormitories
dormitory labour regime, 151

Douglas, Mary, 92
dual land market, 276

ecological protection zoning, 211
economic activities, 244–246
Economic and Comfortable Housing, 53
economic cluster(s); upgrading of, 185; Zhongda cloth market (ZDCM) as, 185–188
economic development, 276
economic reforms, 19, 259, 262
economic viability, 61
education, 79, 156; average number of years of schooling for Foxconn *pugong* and *non-pugong*, 152; and finding jobs, 80
educational attainment, **107**, 110; of new-generation and old-generation migrant workers, 23–24
employment agencies, 74, 75, 80, 282
employment contracts, 170
entertainment, 197
entrepreneurship, 279–280; and risk, 39–42
ESRC/DFID project, 'The Development of Migrant Villages under China's Rapid Urbanization', 166
ethnic disadvantage model, 102, 103
Europe, 102, 103, 122; literature on migrant integration in, 104
ex-danwei neighbourhoods, 284

facility conditions, in urban villages, 134
factory dormitories, 2, 7, 12, 30, 55, 101, 154
'factory labour regime', 7
family migration, 126
farmers, 13
farming, 21, 27
farming experience, 19, 26
farming work, 21
Fifth Migrant Sampling Survey 1993, 73
financing of redevelopment, 268–269
first generation migrants, 2; definition of, 18; timing of first migrant work, 19
Five Year Plan, 263
floating population, 237, 238
Floating Population Monitoring Survey 2010, 25, 28
formal labour market, 4
Foxconn, 7, 147–163, 278, 285–286; average years of schooling for *pugong* and *non-pugong*, 152; basic socioeconomic conditions of employees

in, 151–153; daily routine of a Foxconn *pugong* (ordinary worker), **149**; employees' choices for working and marriage in Shenzhen for the future, **155**; Guanlan campus, 151; income of *pugong* and *non-pugong* at, 152, **153**; job mobility of *pugong* and *non-pugong* at, 152; labour control strategy, 158–160; Longhua campus, 151, 152, 157, 158; management policies at, 159; overtime at, 160; promotion within, 153, 159; suicide of workers at, 17, 147; work shifts, 160; workers' resistance, 159; working life of migrant workers in, 157; workload at, 160; *see also* Shenzhen

France, integration of migrants in, 103
friendship relations, 104

Gangxia, Shenzhen, *206*
Gansu Province, 39
garbage recycling, 73
GDP, 238
Germany, integration of migrants in, 103
global financial crisis, impact on the unemployment situation of migrants, 1
globalisation, 262
gold-digging, 45, 279
Golmud, 42, 44, 45
Gou Tai-Ming, Terry, 151
government funding, 268
Guangdong province; land regulations, 223; redevelopment policies, 1, 11–12; three olds redevelopment policy, 9, 223–239
Guangdong Youth and Juvenile Research Centre, 29
Guangzhou, 6, 7, 11, 91, 121, 128, 285, 291; advances in urban upgrading in, 223–239; annual mobility rates of migrants and duration of residence in, *56*; attitudes towards redevelopment of urban villages, 264; Central Department of Urban and Rural Construction, 224; clothing market in urban villages in, 8, 182–201; collective land ownership in urban villages in, 125; commercial areas/public constructions, *245*; Commercial Belt of South Guangzhou road, 190; Datang Village, 127, 285; demolition of urban villages in, *10*; 'development happens when conditions are right' policy, 268, 270; development model, 135; development plan for a

commodity network in, 190; external traffic lines, *246*; financing of redevelopment of urban villages in, 268–269; Haizhu district, 190; high-rise buildings in, 128; history of, 241–242, 262; housing conditions in, 1; housing status of migrants in, 135; income of migrants in, 6, 135, 142; industrial areas in, 242, *247*; integration of migrants in, 99–120, 131, 135, **140–141**, 142; international trade in, 189; land resources in, 263; living conditions of migrants in, 129; market-oriented development model, 128, 135; mixed-use wholesale city, 195–196; Municipal Government, 224; neighbourhood types in, 104, *105*, **107**, **117**; 'one village one policy', 267, 270; planning for urban villages in, 256–274; planning projects in, *225*; policies for urban villages in, 289; problems in urban villages in, 263; proximity of urban villages to urban facilities and economic activities, 244–246; regeneration of an industrial cluster in, 287–288; research neighbourhoods in, *105*; social integration of migrants in, 6; social networks of migrants in, 5, 99; specialisation of different urban villages in, 283; specialized business center, 193–195; tertiary industry in, 244; Tianhe district, 91; urban development and urban villages in, *243*; urban village redevelopment in, 226, 261, 264–266, 267, 270, 290; urban villages in, 129, *130*, *225*, 228, 240, *245*, *246*, *247*, *248*, 262–269, 283; variations between Beijing, Shanghai and, 134–135; warehouses in, *248*; Zhongda cloth market at, 182–201
Guangzhou East Railway Station, 242
Guangzhou International Textile City (GITC), 8, 191–192
Guangzhou Land Development Centre, 269
Guangzhou Land Resource and Housing Management Bureau, 269
guanxi, 4, 72

Han-Chinese background, 104
harmonious society concept, 259
health insurance, 44
healthcare services, 44
Henan, 73

296 *Index*

Hispanic immigrants, in New York and Los Angeles, 124
home ownership, 54
home-towners, 115, 116, **117**, 118
Hon Hai Precision Industry Co. Ltd., 151, 152
Hong Kong, 185
house rent project, 86
household expenditure, 111, 116
household registration (*hukou*) system, 7, 52, 86, 89, 100–101, 147, 203, 277; agricultural *hukou*, 22; and barriers to integration of migrants, 104; blue-stamp, 52–53, 101, 118; control of self-initiated migration by, 69; as determinant of integration, 285; effect of, 281, 291; effect on migrant integration, 6, 99; and formation of urban villages, 260; as a hurdle for migrants to become permanent urban residents, 13; impact on migrant neighbourhood integration, 134; impacts of, 131, 134; versus income and property rights, 285; reform of, 53; rural *hukou*, 18, 54, 135, 279; and the rural-urban landscape, 84, 90–92; and separation of local residents from migrants, 64; transfer of, 155; urban *hukou*, 26, 126, 127, 135
household surveys, 99, 129
housing, 3–4, 52, 256; of new-generation migrant workers, 30, 278; of old-generation migrant workers, 30, 278; sources of assistance in search for, *60*
housing conditions, 1, 54, 55, 276
housing market; differentiation within the, 284–285; secondary housing market, 53
housing reforms, 53
housing tenure systems, 91
Hu Jintao, 53
Huangpu village, Guangzhou, 226
Hubei migrants, in Datang Village, Guangzhou, 127, 285
Hui Muslim national minority, 36, 45
hukou see household registration (*hukou*) system
human capital, 276

illiteracy, 24
Implementation Notes of the Provisional Regulations of the Redevelopment Plan of Shenzhen Urban Villages, 264
income, 61; average monthly income, 29, 152; as determinant of integration, 285

Index of Integration, 129, 135
Indian slums, 80
industrial clusters, collective ownership and regeneration of, 287–288
industrial development, 258
industrial-led urbanisation, 275
industrial parks, proximity of urban villages to, 210–211, 215
informal settlements, 154–155, 240; and integration of migrants, 125–128
infrastructural power, 259
infrastructure, 11, 13, 197, 211
insurance, 43, 280
Insurance Law, 43
integrated temporary registration migrants, 115, 116, **117**, 118
integration of migrants; in China, 99–120; choice theory, 124; and demographic variables, 131; determinants of, 131–134; dimensions impacting on, 126; factors that determine integration in Guangzhou, 118; and housing market differentiation, 284–285; and *hukou* status, 131; informal settlements and, 125–128; linear regressions for the determinants of, **132–133**; link to demographic features, 127, 128; measurement of, 129–131; multidimensional formulations of, 122; place stratification theory, 124; and socioeconomic variables, 131; spatial assimilation model, 123; theories on, 102–104, 122–124; in urban villages in China, 121–144
interim residence permit, 52
internal labour markets, 151
international migration, literature on, 106
Internet, 173
interprovincial migration, 28

Jacka, Tamara, 86
Jiang Zemin, 238
job adverts, 74, 75, 79, 281
job agencies *see* employment agencies
job referrals, 70
job search methods, 74; empirical results, 78–79; and human capital factors, 77; and informal social networks, 281–282; model of, 77; and wages, 70–71, 75, **76**; years of education and work experience, 77
joint-stock companies, 192

kitchens, private, 173
Kochan, Dror, study of migrant discourses in Chinese contemporary film, 88
Kunming, 95, 283

labour allocation system, 72
labour control strategies, 151, 158–160, 161
Labour Force Survey Data, 72
labour suicides, 17, 161
land; economic and intensive use of, 228; marginal land, 227; sandwich land, 227; wedged land, 227
Land Bureau, 231
land development quotas, 261
land management, in rural areas, 11
Land Management Law, 260
land ownership, rights associated with, 260
land prices, 232
land rent gradients, 61
land use(s); controls, 261; diversity, 214, 217; efficiency, 217; evolution, 212–216; land-use-related problems, 227; of urban villages, 8, 11
landed property rights, 281, 291
Lanzhou-style beef noodle restaurant, 36, 46, 280
'Lewis-Fei-Ranis model', 275
Liede village, Guangzhou, 91, 226, 268, 269
Lijiao village, Guangzhou, 241
literature, on international migration, 106
livelihoods, of migrants, 2–4, 7–8, 12, 36–50
living conditions, 7–8, 197
local dialects, 31
local hukou migrants, 111, 116, **117**, 118
local indicators of spatial association (LISA), 207
long-term residence, and integration, 134
Longhua campus, Foxconn city, Shenzhen, 151, 152, 157, 158

Ma family, 36–50; entrepreneurship and risk, 39–42; livelihood trajectory of, 47; risks and formal institutions, 42–44; social networks as an informal social safety net, 44–47
Mandarin, 31
Mao Zedong, Chairman, 41, 258, 259
Marcus, Georg, 87
marital status; of Foxconn *pugong* and *non-pugong*, 154; and integration, 134
market forces, 61

market-oriented redevelopment projects, 253
market stalls, 192
married people, job search methods of, 79
Master Plan of Urban villages Redevelopment (2005–2010), 264
membranes, 93
metro stops, 210
Mexican migrants, 123
Mexico-US migrants, 72
migrant enclaves *see* urban villages
migrant integration *see* integration of migrants
migrant labour regime, 161
migrant networks *see* social networks
migrant population, 236–238
migrant settlements; impact on the sociospatial transformation of Chinese cities, 61–64; patterns of, 280
migrant social networks *see* social networks
migrant villages, 147
migrant work; familiarity with, 19; first generation in family to do, 19; timing of first, 19
Migrant Worker Monitoring Survey 2009, 20, 24, 25
migrant workers *see* migrants
Migrant Workers Survey 2011, 25
migrants; attitudes towards, 100–102; barriers for migrants to settle permanently, 51; characteristics by neighbourhood type, 106, **107**; characteristics of migrant residents in urban villages, 284; in commodity housing estates, 106, 118; comparison to local residents, 108; decline in number and proportion with increasing age, 21; definitions of, 18–19, 106; food expenses of, 172; groups of, 111–116; habitats in urban China, 7–9; housing, 3–4, 53–60; incomes and expenditures, **172**; insecurity in urban China, 3; integration of, 6, 13, 104–106, 121–144, 289–290; job search data, 74–77; job searches in urban China, 69–83; livelihoods of, 2–4, 7–8; living conditions of, 7–8, 127; living expenses, 172; monthly household expenses per capita, 106, **107**; in old-street neighbourhoods, 118; probability of having contacts from one's own province, 110; province of origin, 106; relationship between occupations and

298 *Index*

origins of, 73; residential location of, 116; rural identity of, 126; separation from local residents, 64; settlement patterns in cities, 53–60; social lives in urban China, 4–7; and social networks, 5–6, 71–72; socioeconomic integration of, 123; spatial distribution of, 62; spatial mobility between first and current residence by entry cohort, *57*; standard of living of, 278; study of migrant discourses in Chinese contemporary film, 88; temporary migrants, 106; tenure mobility of, *58–59*; trans-locality, 5, 84–98; transient urbanism in urban China, 1–14; urban experiences of, 276; and urban village redevelopment, 9–12; and urban villages in Guangzhou, 84–98; in work-unit estates, 118

migration; chain migration, 73; couple migration, 23, 25, 126; family migration, 126; impact on cities, 65; rural–urban, 100; self-initiated migration, 69, 73; and socialist institutions, 52–53; sole migration, 23, 126

migration networks, 73
Minhang District, Shanghai, 74
minimum living allowance, 69
Ministry of Land and Resources, 12
mobility of migrants, 3, 55, *56*, *57*, *58–59*, 64
monopolistic competition, 279
moonlight group (*yueguangzu*), 29
Moran's *I* coefficient, 207
multiculturalism, in urban villages, 92
multinomial logit model, 78, 79, 80
municipal building survey, 218

National Bureau of Statistics, 20, 23
National Games, 190
National Population and Family Planning Commission (NPFPC), 22
Natural Resources Fund, 268
natural will, 148
neighbourhood integration, 134
neighbourhood types in Guangzhou, 104, *105*, **107**, **117**
neighbourhood workers, 115, 118
Netherlands, the, 103, 122
New Cooperative Medical Scheme (NCMS), 44
New Generation Migrant Worker Special Investigation 2010, 25

new-generation migrant workers, 2, 3, 17–35; age of first migration of, 26, 32; assimilation and integration of, 31; average number of years of education of, **24**; characteristics of, 19; choice of work among, 21, *22*; criteria for, **18**; definition of, 18; demographic characteristics of, 22–26; desire to return to their region of origin, 279; desire to stay permanently in the city, 31–32; destinations of, 28; determinants of neighbourhood integration of, 134; differences between old-generation migrant workers and, 32–33; educational attainment of, 23–24; and factory dormitories, 7; family and income, 135; farming experience of, 26; gender balance of, 22–23, 32; household structure of, 25–26; housing, 30; income, 32; industry and occupation, 27; integration in Beijing of, **136–137**; integration in Guangzhou of, **140–141**; integration in Shanghai of, **138–139**; integration of, 129, **132–133**, **136–141**, 142; job searches, 27–28; marital status of, 25–26; migration characteristics of, 26–30; motivation for migrant work, 26–27, 33; remittance and consumption, 29–30; sample studies on, **20**; size by age of, 20–22; social protection, 30–31; tendency to bring spouse and children to cities, 25; timing of first migrant work, 19; women as, 26; working hours and pay, 28–29

New Generation Migrant Workers Report 2008, 27
non-pugong (non-basic workers), 152; employees' choices for working and marriage in Shenzhen for the future, **155**; housing expenses, **155**; marital status of, 154; proportion living in rental peasant housing, 154; wages, expenses, work-hours, days off and wages sent home, **153**
nong min gong (peasant workers), 147

old-generation migrant workers; age of first migration of, 26; average number of years of education of, **24**; definition of, 18; destinations of, 28; determinants of neighbourhood integration of, 134; farming experience of, 26; housing, 30; industry and occupation of, 27; integration in Beijing of, **136–137**;

integration in Guangzhou of, **140–141**;
integration in Shanghai of, **138–139**;
integration of, 129, **132–133**, **136–141**,
142; job changes, 28; men as majority,
26; motivation for migrant work, 27;
working hours and pay, 28–29
old-street neighbourhoods, 118
'old village' redevelopment, 233–234
One-Percent Population Sample
Survey, 23
'one village one policy', 235, 268, 269,
270, 289
open labour market, 80

Pazhou Exhibition Centre,
Guangzhou, 226
Pazhou village, Guangzhou, 226
Pearl River Delta, 165, 182, 262; dual
communities in, 80; labour
market in, 152
Pearl River Textile City (PRTC), 8,
195–196
peasant workers, 147
peer review, 158
people centred concept, 259
People's Republic of China, establishment
of, 258
peri-urbanism, 147
personal computers, 173
Photo Documentation Project, 86, 88
pipeline gas, 173
place stratification theory, 124
planning principles, 266
Policy Research Office of the State
Council, 20
pollution, 92
Porter, Michael, 185
post-80s migrants, 18
poverty traps, 90
private cloth making workshops, 8
private employment agencies *see*
employment agencies
private households, accommodation for
domestic workers in, 101
producer cities, 258
property cycles, 288–289
property development, 216, 217
Property Ownership Certificate, 156
property rights, 134, 280, 291; as
determinant of integration, 285; reform
of, 288–289; in urban villages, 256
*Provisional Regulations of the
Redevelopment Plan of Shenzchen
Urban Villages*, 264

public facilities, 13
public health system, 44
pugong (basic workers), 152, 160;
employees' choices for working and
marriage in Shenzhen for the future,
155; housing expenses, **155**; job
mobility of, 152; marital status of, 154;
opportunities for promotion at Foxconn,
153; proportion living in rental peasant
housing, 154; wages, expenses,
work-hours, days off and wages sent
home, **153**
Purity and Danger (Douglas), 92
'putting people first' approach, 236
Putuo District, Shanghai, 74

Qinghai Hui minority, 39
Qinghai-Tibet Plateau, north-western
China, 36, 39

racial disadvantage model *see* ethnic
disadvantage model
Ranisisation, 275, 276, 278, 279, 282, 285
rational migrant family, 275
rational will, 148
Reconstruction Bureau, 231
recreation, 197
Redevelopment Master Plan *see Master
Plan of Urban villages Redevelopment
(2005–2010)*
Redevelopment Supporting Fund, 268
registration, as temporary residents, 101
rent, 278, 286
rental house management service
centre, 88
rental income, 127, 175
rental markets, 54
rental units, 53
Reserved Land Policy, 242
resident groups; composition of, **114**;
dispersion of, **114**; distribution over
neighbourhoods, **115**; dominant source
of, **114**
residential location, and household
expenditure, 116
residential mobility, 4, 55
resistance, 92, 93, 94
rights to the city, 291
risks, 47; attitudes towards, 279; and
formal institutions, 42–44
road networks, 211
rural citizenship, 52
rural labor force; age structure of, *21*;
choice of work among, *22*

300 Index

rural land uses, regulation of, 260
rural migrant workers, age structure of, *21*
rural migrants; attitudes towards risk among, 279; lack of access to benefits, 127; livelihoods of, 12; mobile livelihoods of, 3; number flowing into Chinese cities, 276; ways of finding jobs, 77
rural population, 121; age structure of, *21*
rural-to-urban migration surveys, 2
rural-urban divide, 84–85
rural villages, 205, 212; evolution to urban villages, **213**
Russian Jew migrants, 123

salaries *see* income
Sanyuanli Village, Guangzhou, 121, 226, 245
Saunders, Doug, 90
schooling *see* education
schoolmates, as good friends, 111
second generation migrants, 2; characteristics of, 19; criteria for, **18**; definition of, 18
segmented assimilation model, 103, 104, 106
self-employed migrants, mobility of, 55
self-help housing, 64
settlement patterns, housing and, 51–66
SEZ *see* Shenzhen Special Economic Zone (SEZ)
Shandong Province, 23, 73
Shanghai, 6, 7, 46, 62, 101, 121, 126, 142, 285; absence of slums in, 126; age of migrants in, 169; apartments in, 128; centrally planned economy, 128; comparison of migrants' incomes and expenditures with those of Shanghai's permanent population, **172**; development model, 135; dilapidated housing in urban villages in, 174–175; distribution of local and migrant population in, *63*; Fifth Migrant Sampling Survey 1993, 73; house owners' perspective on redevelopment, 177; housing facilities in urban villages in, 173–174; impacts of village redevelopment in, 176–177; income and expenditure of urban village residents in, 170–173; informal employment in, 170; institutional and market factors for migrant integration in, 142; integration of local residents in, 129; integration of migrants in, 6, **131**, **138–139**, 142;

living conditions in urban villages, 173–175; living conditions of migrants in, 129; living space of residents in urban villages in, 173; location of urban villages in, 167; migrants' work experience in, 69; number of migrants in, 128; population in, 165; reasons for living in urban villages in, 175–176; residents of urban villages in, 168–173; rural migrants in urban villages in, 168–169; self-built housing in, 8; spatial mobility of migrants between first and current residence by entry cohort, *57*; survey of migrants' jobs in, 74; survey of residents in urban villages in, 166; tenants' perspective on redevelopment of housing, 177; tenure mobility of migrants in, *58*; urban regeneration in, 1; urban spatial structure, 167; urban villages in, 7, 129, *130*, 164–181, 286–287; variations between Beijing, Guangzhou and, 134–135
Shanghai Labor and Social Security Bureau, 27
Shanghai Pudong Oriental Pearl Tower, 147
Shannon entropy measurement, 214
Shenzhen, 262; attitudes towards redevelopment of urban villages in, 264; barriers to settling in, 155–157; coldspots of expansion of urban villages in, 207; densification coldspots in, 207–208; densification hotspots in, 207; development phases of urban villages in, 206; distribution of urban villages and the city landscape in, *204*; financing of redevelopment of urban villages in, 268–269; floating population of, 203; Gangxia urban village in, *206*; history of, 262; hotspots of expansion of urban villages in, 207; industrial sector of, 210; intensification coldspots in, 208; intensification hotspots in, 208; land use diversity between SEZ and non-SEZ in, 214; land use diversity of urban villages in, 240; Leading Group for Shenzhen's Illegal Construction Investigation and Urban villages Redevelopment, 266; LISA cluster maps of urban village development in terms of expansion, densification and intensification, *208*; Longhua, 151, 152, 157, 158; morphology of urban villages in, 202–219, 288–289; planning for urban

villages in, 256–274; planning network for urban villages in, *265*; planning of urban redevelopments in, 257; population of, 203; problems in urban villages in, 263; Redevelopment Master Plan, 266; redevelopment of urban villages in, 261, 264; spatial evolution of urban villages in, 8, 202–219; spatial variation in urban villages in, 209–212; urban village redevelopment in, 270, 290; urban villages in, 203–205, 262–269; *see also* Foxconn

Shenzhen City Master Plan, 262

Shenzhen Municipal Building Survey 2009, 203

Shenzhen Special Economic Zone News, 263

Shenzhen Special Economic Zone (SEZ), 203, 209, 262, 263, 288; built intensity, 211, 216; ecological protection zoning, 211; intensification hotspots and coldspots, 208; jobs generated by mid- and large-scale manufacturers, 210; land use diversity in urban villages in, 215; proximity to metro stops, 210; road networks, 211

Shenzhen Trade and Industrial Development Bureau (STIDB), 205

Shenzhen Urban Planning and Design Institute (UPDIS), 203

Shenzhen Urban Planning and Research Centre (SUPRC), 205

Shipai village, Guangzhou, 11, 240, 245, 247–249, 251, 289–290

Sichuan, 25

single child privilege card, 156

single model for urban village redevelopment, 270

skills, 92–96

slums, absence of slums in Shanghai, 126

small businesses, 64

Smith, Michael, 87

social activities, 5

social alienation, 147–148

social assimilation theory, 5, 102, 103

social capital, 90, 150

social control, 86

social insurance, 170, *172*

social integration, 125; of migrants, 6, 13; spatial dimension of, 123; *see also* integration of migrants

social interactions, and the job search process, 70

social networks, 3, 12, 27, 31, 61, 70, 75, 80, 104, 150; among neighbours, 111; characteristics of, 71, 99, 108–111, 118; composition of, 109–111, **112–113**; dispersion of, 109–111, **112–113**; dominant source of, 109–111, **112–113**; heterogeneous social networks, 110, 118; homogeneous social networks, 110, 284; and housing-related information, 60, 64; as an informal social safety net, 44–47; job search and, 2, 6–7, 281–282; and migrants' access to job information in urban China, 72–73; migrants and, 5–6, 71–72; role in migrants' job finding, 4–5; sociospatial pattern of, 126; strengths of, 71

social problems, of migrant workers and the floating population, 238

social protection, 30–31

social relations, dominant source of, 111

social security, 31, 44

social support, 148

social welfare, 52, 134

socialist institutions, migration and, 52–53

socially non-mobile group, 115–116, **117**, 118

socioeconomic integration of migrants, 123

socioeconomic mobility, 55

socioeconomic variables, 142

sole migration, 23, 126

spatial assimilation model, 123

spatial error model, 214

spatial lag model, 214

spatial negotiations, 94

Special Project Fund, 268

Special Survey on the New Generation Migrant Workers, 23

spending power, **107**

squatter settlements, 54, 281

state control, 270

state socialism, 52

street traders, 283

Suggestions for Institutional Reform of Urban Villages, 264

suicides, of workers at Foxconn, 17, 161

Tang Renjian, 21

Tangxia village, Guangzhou, 11, 226, 247, 250–251

temporary migrants, 106

temporary registration, 111, 115, 118

territorialisation, 259, 261, 262

tertiary sector, 210

302 *Index*

textile clusters, 185
theory of contemporary Chinese rural–urban migration, 277–290
three olds redevelopment policy, 9, 10, 11, 182, 223–239, 252, 266, 289; agreements and concessions, 230; approval from villagers for, 228; challenges of, 228–229; compensation schemes and profit sharing, 230–231; concept of, 227–233; duty allocation on municipal and district levels, *232*; experimental urban governance, 234–236; external and unpredictable push factors, 233; government policy of supporting but not providing funds for, 229; government to balance economic and environmental interests, 229; incentive policies for the, 230; innovations in, 230–233; institutionalization of the process of the, 229; invitation of developers, 231–232; law tradition and lack of experience, 228; modes of redevelopment, 233–234; objective of, 227–228; professional support, 231; safeguarding and supervision, 232–233; transparency of, 231
Tianhe district, Guangzhou, 242, 247, 248
Tianhe Science Park, 11, 250
Tianhe Sports Center, 242
Tianjin, 36
Todaro, Michael, 275
toilets, private, 173
Tönnies, Ferdinand, 148
town planning in China, 257–260
transformation first and reconstruction second principle, 234
translocality, 84–98
tricycles run by migrants, 5, 86, 283

unemployment, among migrants, 276
unemployment benefits, 69
United Kingdom, immigrants job searches in the, 72
United States of America (USA), 122; literature on migrant integration in, 104
UPDIS, 205
urban areas, multi-relationships between urban villages and, 251, 253
urban citizenship, 52, 126
urban development; in Tianhe district, Guangzhou, 91; and urban villages, 260–262

urban facilities, and economic activities, 244–246
urban harmonious development, 92
urban *hukou*, 126, 135
urban jobs, educational requirements for, 24
urban land uses, 12; regulation of, 260
urban management, 238
urban migrants; job search methods of, 75; ways of finding jobs, *77*
urban planning, 11, 257, 258, 259
urban population, 121
Urban Regeneration Offices, 231
urban registration, 53
urban village redevelopment, 269–270, 290
urban villagers, 127
urban villages, 1, 2, 5, 7, 54, 101, 106, 125, 160, 275; ability to absorb higher rents and travel costs, 286, 287; areal size of, 215; as the arrival city, 90; average rental expense for *pugong* and *non-pugong* living in, 154; in Beijing, 62; characteristics of migrant residents in, 284; collective land ownership in, 125; and commercial areas/public constructions, *245*; demolition to upgrade the urban economy, 290; densification of, **207**; development of, 205–209, 211, 217, 218; as a dual community, 127; as economic clusters, 8; emergence of, 223–224; as 'entry cities', 283–284; evolution of, **213**, 217; expansion of, **207**; and external traffic lines, *246*; financing of redevelopment, 268–269; function as the habitat of rural migrants in urban China, 9; function of, 124; future for, 289; in Guangzhou, 262–269; heterogeneous nature of migrants in, 256; house rents in, 164; housing in, 156; identifying land ownership in, 227; as income source for owners, 178; as informal settlements, 154–155; integration of migrants in, 121–144; intensification of, **207**; isolation from the rest of the city, 5; land use in, 8, 11, 212, 215; living conditions of migrants in, 178; as local economic clusters, 182–201; location of, 8, 11, 215; low cost low quality dormitories for migrants, 276; as major settlements for low-income migrants, 165; market-oriented redevelopment of,

252; migrant population in, 236–238; and migrants in Guangzhou, 84–98; as migrants' transient habitat, 12; Moran's *I* coefficient of the expansion of, 206; multi-relationships between urban areas and, 251, 253; as multicultural sites, 92; necessary for low cost housing supply, 286–287; non-residential floor space in, 211; planning in Guangzhou and Shenzhen, 256–274; problems triggering redevelopment of, 227; prospect of settling in, 154–155; proximity to public services, 246; proximity to urban facilities and economic activities, 244–246; redevelopment of, 9, 11, 142, 178, 224–227, 260–261; redevelopment strategies, 252–253; and regional growth, 289–290; relationship between urban areas and, 241–251; research on, 165, 240; role of, 166; in Shanghai, 62, 164–181; in Shenzhen, 8, 202–219, 262–269; and social integration of migrants, 6; symbiotic relationship between cities and, 240–255; tactics to deal with problems in, 263; urban development and, 241–244, 260–262
urban welfare housing system, 52
urbanization theory, 182

Village and Township Planning and Management Ordinance, 260
villages in the city *see* urban villages

wage model, 78, 79, 80
Wageningen School, actor-oriented perspective, 36
wages, 282; job search methods and, 70–71; for new and old migrants, 278; *see also* income
wagon bikes, 84, 89, 94
walls, 93
Wang Xiaoshuai, 89

water heaters, 174
Wen Jiabao, 53
Wenzhou, 62, 73
West, aims of planning in the, 258
Wirth, Louis, 147
women, as new-generation migrant workers, 26, 32
work experience, 77, 78, 79, 80
work-unit compounds, 106, 108, 118
Wufeng village, *186*

Xian Cun, 85–86, 91, 92, 95, 283; average stay of migrant residents in, 88; food market in, *89*; photograph of, *94*
Xiang Ge, 156, 157, 159
Xiao Huang, 159
Xiao Wang, 158
Xiao Zhou, 160
Xiaogang, 226

Yangji village, 245
Yangtze River Delta area, 31

ZDCM *see* Zhongda cloth market (ZDCM) Guangzhou
Zengcheng Town, Guangzhou, 121
zhaijidi, 213, 214
Zhang Guangning (mayor of Guangzhou), 234
Zhejiang Province, 62, 189
Zhejiang Village (Zhejiangcun), Beijing, 1, 8, 62
Zhongda cloth market (ZDCM) Guangzhou, 182–201; in 2012, *197*; development of, 188; formation of ZDCM as economic cluster, 185–188; *in-situ* upgrading of, 191–196, **197**; location of, 185; Management Committee of, 189; before upgrading, **197**; upgrading of, 188–195
Zhujiang New Town, Guangzhou, 226